Coaching for Change

Coaching for Change introduces a model that shows why coaching is the intervention of choice for driving organizational change. The book helps you understand the principles and theories, practices and processes that are at play both in coaching and in change. A number of coaching and change models are explored with the goal of integrating them into a framework that can be applied to the individual, team, or organization.

The book explains the theories behind both coaching and change, and includes practical sections on developing coaching skills. A companion website supports this book as a learning tool, featuring a curriculum, instructor guides, PowerPoint presentations, and more.

Coaching for Change is a valuable book for students on coaching, change management, or organizational development courses, as well as professionals who want to develop their skills to drive successful change within their organizations.

John L. Bennett, PhD, has more than 30 years of progressively challenging and successful experience creating, leading, and being a part of change in various industries and teaching leadership, coaching, and organizational change management. Currently, he is Associate Professor of Business and Behavioral Science at the McColl School of Business at Queens University of Charlotte. In addition, he is founding Director of the Master of Science in Executive Coaching program and Director of the MS in Organization Development program. His coaching and consulting work has impacted for-profit, not-for-profit, and government-sector clients. John earned an MPA degree from the University of North Carolina at Greensboro and MA and PhD degrees in human and organizational systems from Fielding Graduate University. He is both a Professional Certified Coach and a Board Certified Coach.

Mary Wayne Bush, Ed.D. is a Board Certified Coach and Senior Manager of Organizational Effectiveness at a large Fortune 100 company in the Southwest US. She holds a doctorate from Pepperdine University in Organizational Change.

Mary Wayne is on the editorial board of Coaching: An International Journal of Theory, Research and Practice, and serves on the faculty of Colorado Technical University's Doctor of Management program. Mary Wayne is a member of the Association of Change Management Professionals, the Organization Development Network, the International Society for Organization Development, Academy of Management, and the American Psychological Society. She has published journal articles and contributed to several books on coaching as well as presenting at conferences, including the International Coach Federation (ICF), American Society of Training and Development (ASTD), Academy of Management (AOM), Association of Change Management Professionals (ACMP), The Conference Board, and the American Society for Quality (ASQ).

Coaching for Change

John L. Bennett & Mary Wayne Bush

NEW YORK AND LONDON

First published 2014
by Routledge
711 Third Avenue, New York, NY 10017

Simultaneously published in the UK
by Routledge
2 Park Square, Milton Park, Abingdon, Oxon OX14 4RN

Routledge is an imprint of the Taylor & Francis Group, an informa business

Library of Congress Cataloging-in-Publication Data

Bennett, John L. (John Lawton), 1958–
Coaching for change / John L. Bennett & Mary Wayne Bush.
pages cm
Includes bibliographical references and index.
1. Organizational change—Management. 2. Employees—Coaching of.
3. Organizational behavior. I. Bush, Mary Wayne. II. Title.
HD58.8.B46186 2013
658.4'06—dc23
2013005001

ISBN: 978-0-415-89781-5 (hbk)
ISBN: 978-0-415-89803-4 (pbk)
ISBN: 978-0-203-14097-0 (ebk)

Typeset in Adobe Caslon Pro
by Apex CoVantage, LLC

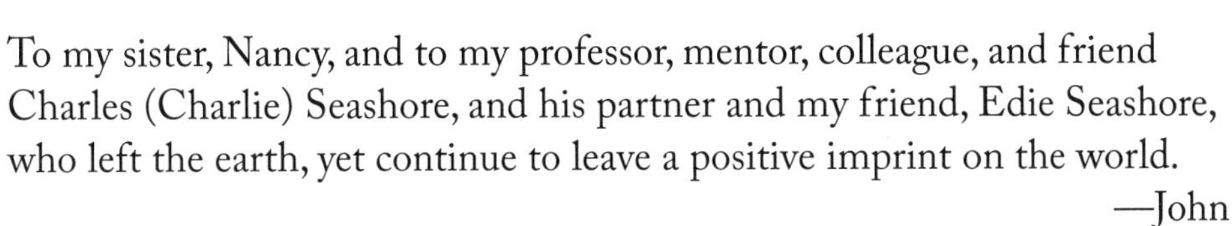

To my sister, Nancy, and to my professor, mentor, colleague, and friend Charles (Charlie) Seashore, and his partner and my friend, Edie Seashore, who left the earth, yet continue to leave a positive imprint on the world.

—John

To my parents, who taught me about change; to Julio, Vance, and Fredric, who taught me about coaching; and to Joel, Bev, Susan, and Gae, who exemplify the strategic and visionary change leadership that inspired this book.

—Mary Wayne

Acknowledgments

We were delighted when Sharon Golan, an editor from Routledge, invited us to write a book on this topic. Sharon has been an inspiration and guide. She believed in our ability to complete this project—and supported us every step of the way.

We are also grateful to the people that taught us about coaching, leadership, human development, psychology, organizational behavior, and much more. We appreciate what we have learned from our experiences as leaders, managers, participants, and students. Much of this learning through experience has occurred at times and in places we least expected it.

We want to acknowledge what we have learned about ourselves and these topics in our coaching and consulting work. We continue to marvel at the courageous leadership and immense responsibility that our clients demonstrate as they boldly steer their organizations through change. We also want to thank the students with whom we have had the privilege to facilitate learning. The science and art of teaching provide rich opportunities for learning—and the learning goes both ways! In sharing rich dialogue and discussion, we have learned from you.

In particular, we want to acknowledge the colleagues who reviewed the initial outlines and proposal for this book. Your feedback and suggestions helped shape the content and approach contained in this book. These reviewers include Francine Campone, Ruth Orenstein, Linda Page, and Will Sparks.

When writing a book of this type, we attempted to include references from many relevant sources. The thinking of these authors allowed us to build upon their work, theories, research, experiences, and ideas. We are grateful for the authors whose work we were able to include, as well as those who were not cited.

Students enrolled in an introductory coaching class at the McColl School of Business at Queens University of Charlotte helped with the research for Chapters 11 and 14. Melinda Harper provided research assistance to the development of the coaching readiness assessment and supported the validation analysis of the work completed by Demetria Henderson. Kelly Rogers provided valuable research related to coaching mastery.

We are thankful for the reviews of drafts by our colleagues Debrah Martin and Vic Settergren. Their feedback on our very first draft manuscript added significantly to the quality of content and helped us refine our message. We also thank our friends and colleagues for supporting our writing process: Sandra Clark, Sara Zeff-Geber, Joan Martin, Stacey Hartman, and Helen Miller. And, we are especially grateful for the editorial guidance provided by Peter Economy and Wanda B. Craig.

Mary Wayne would also like to acknowledge Brian Underhill of CoachSource, and her colleagues Rene Carew, Jeff Nally, Erica Desrosiers, Christine Williams, Winnie Lanoix, and Jennifer Habig, who have been wonderful thought-partners over the years through our association with the Conference Board Executive Coaching Conferences.

John is thankful for the support of Eric Johnson, who allowed him to devote a significant amount of time for the past year to researching and writing this book. Thank you for listening to me talk about the content, challenges, successes, and mundane details of this project. In addition, John wishes to acknowledge the learning about coaching that has been derived from working with clients and teaching graduate students. There is a great deal of truth in the concept of the teacher being the learner.

Contents

List of Figures

List of Tables

Preface

As professional coaches and consultants to a wide range of organizations over the past 20 years, as well as educators and researchers of coaching, we had noticed a pattern in our work with clients: It was all about change. While current literature verifies that change is occurring around the world with increasing frequency and intensity, our own experience confirmed that our clients were asking for help in dealing with change. The fact that our clients were asking for help was not surprising to us, since the current statistics about successful change are bleak.

Fortunately, we had a wide range of experience to offer, from our backgrounds in related fields, including communication, management consulting, project management, continuous improvement and Six Sigma, psychology, and business. Our interventions were often successful, and sometimes not, but when we reflected on them (and received feedback from our clients), we realized that coaching had consistently returned the most effective results in dealing with change. Assuredly, we also leveraged all of our combined skills and strategies in the service of clients, but time and time again, we found that the most efficient and helpful intervention was coaching. This discovery fascinated us, especially when we realized that, by coaching at the individual and/or group level, we could affect change in an entire organization or system!

What we realized in this process is that coaching—*all* coaching—is about change. Coaching is not about a discipline or application, such as psychology, business, or education. These disciplines inform and influence coaching and the coaching approach by nature of the experience and education of the coach, and the needs of the client. But they are not the fundamental focus of coaching. Coaching is about change. Good coaching facilitates an individual or group's movement from one state of understanding, behavior, and performance to the next.

We identified the key elements of effectiveness in coaching for change: coaching the right person at the right time for the right results. Recognizing and leveraging the key points of influence for change (people, process, and results), we were able to apply coaching to these "nodes" and impact a larger system, much as Euclidian geometry and social network analysis describe. When one accepts this premise, a clear strategy emerges: identify the desired change, recognize the people and actions that will support it, understand athe context in which the change will take place (the surroundings and the system), and apply a coaching model.

As we began to speak and write about this concept, we were able to clarify and ground it in the experiences, questions, and perceptions of others. We also researched the current academic literature to further expand what we were finding. The results of the sum total of our effort are presented in this book. It is our sincere hope that it informs and supports your own efforts at coaching change.

PART I
COACHING

1

INTRODUCTION TO COACHING FOR CHANGE

Our premise is simple: All **coaching** is coaching for **change**. Coaching is designed to change aspects of performance, development, and even transformation of individuals and groups, which can then impact changes in organizations and systems. Effective coaching facilitates an individual's or group's movement from one state to another, as the origin of the word suggests. The earliest meaning of "**coach**" derives from the 16th-century Hungarian word *for a wagon—a vehicle for getting from one place to another—built in the village of Kocs, Hungary* (Merriam-Webster Online Dictionary (2013); Underhill, McAnally, & Koriath, 2007). Whether coaching a leader to be more strategic, or coaching a team to be more productive, every coaching engagement holds the promise of moving the **client** in a better direction or to a more desired state.

Coaching is designed to elicit the motivation, vision, action, and integration to effect successful, sustainable change. Coaching is an optimal strategy for individuals and groups who desire some kind of change, whether focused on performance, development, or complete transformation. Successful coaching with individuals and groups can positively impact change for an entire organization or system by addressing key issues and engaging **stakeholders** at every level. Coaching a corporate merger steering team to honor and include the **cultures** of both companies can improve the **effectiveness** and sustainability of the merger. Coaching a leader about envisioning the positive future for the organization can lead to a transformation in the culture or even the brand of the company. And coaching a manager to consider the results of a stakeholder analysis can make a difference between compliance and collaboration in employees adopting a change.

While the authors claim that coaching is an optimal **intervention** for change at all levels, it is not the *only* support that is helpful in managing change successfully. Most changes can benefit from the additional **skills** and support of other

professionals. Change consultants, continuous improvement experts, communications specialists, and project managers are a few of the other professionals typically found in large-scale organizational change, while therapists, personal trainers, and nutritionists often facilitate changes for individuals. In the world of change, more support is better. While the authors advocate for the importance of the change-coaching role, it would be a mistake not to acknowledge the valuable contributions of others' perspectives.

Coaching as a skill and a process transcends any specific discipline, although it is informed and influenced by many. The theoretical foundations of coaching are derived from many disciplines: communications, **consulting**, management, psychology, **learning**, and systems theory, to name a few. However, the effectiveness of coaching for change is not dependent on any particular discipline. While coaches often claim that their "brand" of coaching is specific to a particular discipline, the authors' experiences are the opposite. Coaching is an overarching skillset that helps individuals and groups learn how to change, and helps them develop the capacity to change. In today's global environment of constant change, both coaching and increased capacity for change are tremendous assets.

Coaching for change is about coaching the *right* person at the *right* time using the *right* approach to achieve the desired results for the client. In accepting this premise, a clear strategy emerges: identify the desired change, focus on the people and actions that will support it, understand the context in which the change will take place (the surroundings and the system), and apply a coaching process that will address all of the above. Change coaching leverages key inflection points in the change process, providing just-in-time learning and support to individuals and groups in order to facilitate successful change. In addition, change coaching increases the clients' understanding of change and prepares them to address future changes more successfully. Coaching for change is an optimal intervention for change at any level.

Why This Book Is Important

Organizational change is increasing, enabled by many factors, including globalization, new technologies, mergers and acquisitions, and the proliferation of complex multinational companies. In a recent study by IBM Corporation on "making change work," the authors claim that "change is the new normal" (Thompson et al., 2008, p. 6). Companies no longer have the luxury of expecting day-to-day operations to maintain a static or predictable pattern that is occasionally interrupted by short bursts of change. "To prosper, leaders will need to abandon such outdated notions of change. In reality, the new normal is continuous change—not the absence of change" (Thompson et al., 2008, p. 6). According to the Corporate Leadership Council (2003), most organizations now acknowledge change as a continuous process that impacts the way companies manage change. "It is no longer appropriate to consider organizational change as a project or event, with a clearly defined beginning or end" (Corporate Leadership Council, 2003, p. 1). Change is now constant in all sectors (for-profit, government, and not-for-profit).

At the same time, coaching continues to grow as a practice for leaders and managers, as well as those in helping **professions** such as consulting, teaching, and human resources (Bennett & Bush, 2009; Hunt & Weintraub, 2006; Joo, 2005; Kombarakaran, Yang, Baker, & Fernandes, 2008; Thompson et al., 2008; Underhill et al., 2007). According to a 2007 study commissioned by the International Coach Federation (ICF) and conducted by PricewaterhouseCoopers, coaching is a $1.5 billion industry and growing. In addition, 65 percent of coaches have an education beyond a bachelor's degree, more than half of coaches are between 46–55 years old, and the average full-time coach earns $82,671 per year (International Coach Federation, 2007). A more recent ICF survey estimates there are 47,500 coaches worldwide, with 15,800 of that number in North America (International Coach Federation, 2012).

Many corporations, government agencies, and not-for-profit organizations provide individual and/or group coaching for leaders at all levels. Examples of companies and other organizations that utilize coaches for strategy, change management, and leadership development include Bank of America, Blue Cross/Blue Shield, BMW, Boeing, Coca-Cola, Daimler, Deloitte, the Federal Reserve Bank, Freddie Mac, Humana, Lockheed Martin, Lowes, PepsiCo, Raytheon, Turner Broadcasting System, UBS, United Way Worldwide, the U.S. Government, and Wells Fargo.

Today, the ICF is the leading professional association for coaches, with more than 15,000 members worldwide. Other professional coaching associations include the World Association for Business Coaches (WABC) and the European Mentoring and Coaching Council (EMCC). The American Psychological Association (APA), British Psychological Society (BPS), and the Organization Development Network (ODN) have special interest groups devoted to coaching. Scholarly and practitioner articles, conferences, and research related to coaching are presented by the Academy of Management (AOM), APA, BPS, Society for Industrial and Organizational Psychology (SIOP), and the ODN. As an example, the 2010 AOM conference featured 30 sessions focused on coaching. A variety of peer-reviewed coaching-related journals are available, both in print and online, including *Coaching: An International Journal of Theory, Research and Practice*; the

International Journal of Evidence-Based Coaching and Mentoring; the *International Coaching Psychology Review*; and the *International Journal of Mentoring and Coaching*. In addition, journals from various disciplines, including education, psychology, and management, often feature articles related to coaching.

As coaching grows in popularity, this field cannot be confined to any one profession or discipline. Despite its popularity, the efficacy of coaching is still not well understood, and there is no single, universally accepted definition (Bush, 2005; Joo, 2005; Levenson, 2009; Sherman & Freas, 2004; Underhill et al., 2007). Coaching's multidisciplinary roots reveal theoretical foundations arising from many separate sources. Nor is its effectiveness tied to a certain approach or set of beliefs or theories. Coaching is an effective skill for helping individuals and groups change, but a skilled practitioner will bring in practices, information, theories, and activities from one or more disciplines or perspectives to support the client's understanding of—and ability to make—the necessary change.

The danger is that, as specific disciplines and professions develop and claim "coaching" as their own, the field will proliferate into factions that become silos and subspecialties, such as coaching psychology, wellness coaching, life coaching, and career coaching. Attempting to distinguish "types" of coaching negates the simple truth that all coaching is about change. Coaching approaches may vary and may be enriched by many influences—such as the occupation or **training** of the coach, the client's needs, or constraints of the system in which the coaching takes place—but, the bottom line is that coaching is about change.

The authors would like all coaches to see themselves as change coaches, as coaching and change have much in common:

- Both are processes designed to move or alter an individual or group from one state to another, where success is neither easy nor guaranteed. There are many variables and aspects to address in order to be successful.
- Both are associated with a multitude of models, theories, guidelines, and approaches.
- Both deal with situations that are unique, while they often follow similar patterns, requiring knowledge and insight from the practitioner.
- Both require the practitioner to be self-aware and reflective of his or her own process and role in interacting with the individual or system to effect change.
- Both change and coaching are skills that can be mastered over time. The Mastery Model introduced in Chapter 6 applies to both coaching and change. With focus, **reflection**, and practice, change coaches can help individuals, groups, and organizations build change capacity and

develop the ability to adapt to change with increasing ease. In the same way, change coaches can build their own mastery of coaching for change, developing the skills, tools, and insight needed to create powerful and lasting interventions for successful change.

All the above suggests that change coaches need to be familiar with several basic approaches to change, as well as with a strong coaching model that integrates success factors for change into the process. Possessing these tools will enable the coach to tailor a strategy that will best meet the clients' needs and offer the greatest probability of successful change. Effective change coaches know about the dynamic processes of both coaching and change, and are able to identify the right strategy to use at the right time in the process with the right stakeholders, enabling the change to move forward effectively.

There are no easy answers or magic formulas in these complex, dynamic endeavors. An effective Change Coach™ will have a:

- Solid knowledge of how change works at the individual, group, and organization levels
- Familiar, trusted process for effective coaching
- Partnership with the client
- Clear, mutual agreement on the goals, boundaries, and strategy for the engagement.

Guided by the change coaching process outlined in Chapter 10, the Change Coach will be able to help clients effect changes needed to support improved performance, development, or transformation at the individual, group, or organization level.

It is important to note that coaching does not take place at the organization level, since coaching is an intervention for small groups and individuals. However, change coaching leverages the power of the individual (often a **leader**) or group to forward the organizational **goals**. Coaching for change is an effective process for focusing on the critical elements of a system to facilitate desired change with an individual leader, team, or steering committee. The process can have broader impact in the organization.

Using the process of change coaching also helps clarify the type of change needed for an individual, group, or organization. There are three basic focus areas for changes:

- **Performance.** Improving the way things are done, creating a higher level of excellence or efficiency (or both), becoming more closely aligned with a strategic target or goal (for example, better, cheaper, or faster). An example of this is increasing sales in a company department.

- **Development.** To learn, build, or grow a skill or capacity such as developing business acumen or public speaking skills, building a culture of respect and inclusion, or improving innovation in a group or organization. Development could also be supporting an executive in improving strategic thinking or presentation skills.
- **Transformation.** A complete shift from one state to another, such as a corporate acquisition or introduction of a new product line or brand. For example, think of an organization that must completely revamp its product line, or an individual who wants to make a job change to a different career path or discipline.

If change is indeed the "new normal" in life, then the challenge is to manage it, learn from it, and leverage it as an opportunity for continuous improvement. However, research indicates that approximately 70 percent of all organizational change initiatives fail (Beer & Nohria, 2000). Other scholars (Creasy & Hiatt, 2009; Kotter, 1996, 2007; Kotter & Cohen, 2002) agree that at least two-thirds of all change efforts fail, including mergers and acquisitions, introductions of new technologies, and changes in business processes. This statistic emphasizes the need to leverage any and all organizational resources to make change work. The premise of this book is that change coaching is an ideal way to ensure that change is supported at the individual and group levels for the benefit of the entire organization. Coaching is a unique intervention best suited to support change at all levels.

This book introduces a model of change coaching that effectively addresses change at the individual, group, and organization levels. The authors believe that coaching can support successful change by identifying who, what, and when to coach in order to create high-impact results during organizational change. Change coaching will be shown to be a valuable intervention for organizational change, which can range in scope from large scale (involving the entire company, or multiple companies or industries) to deployments that involve only one department or leader.

As an academic textbook, with potential appeal to broader audiences, this book's objectives are to lay a foundation for understanding the principles, practices, theories, and processes involved in both coaching and change, and to introduce an integrative framework for coaching as the intervention of choice for organizational change. The text provides tools and resources to support leaders, executive coaches, and human resource professionals in the application of coaching to produce measurable results and develop capacity in organizational change.

How This Book Is Organized

This book is meant to acquaint coaches with the basics of both coaching and change. It is not, however, meant to be an exhaustive reference for either. Coaches will be introduced to many topics about coaching and change, and urged to explore other resources to further their understanding of the topics. Each chapter follows a similar structure, including a brief introduction, learning objectives, explication of the content, a summary, suggested learning activities, and references. Throughout the book, three recurrent frameworks emphasize the basic constructs that tie together both coaching and change:

1. **Focus.** For both coaching and change, it is important to agree on a focus: performance, development, or transformation. Performance is about improving effectiveness in action or productivity, development is about increasing or adding new skills or knowledge, and transformation deals with creating something new or raising a standard to new heights.
2. **Level.** Both coaching and change can take place at individual and/or group levels. Change can have a positive impact on organizations or systems whether the coaching takes place with individuals or groups. While coaching does not take place at the organization level, individual and group coaching can positively impact change at this level and at any place in the hierarchy of an organization, from individual contributor to supervisor, manager or senior leadership.
3. **Mastery.** The Mastery Model outlined in Chapter 6 offers a depiction of the process through which individuals and groups move and become adept at change. This model serves as a gauge for coaches in working with individuals or groups, as well as a guide for developing and **mastering** the skills needed in coaching for change.

The first part of the book (Chapters 1–5) describes coaching and proposes a model to successfully support coaching in the three areas of focus: performance, development, and transformation. The coaching model also supports the three levels of change: individual, group, and organization. While coaching itself only takes place at the individual and group levels, coaching for change can also have an impact on the organization or system.

The second part of the book (Chapters 6–8) offers an introduction to change theories, models, and applications at the individual, group, and organization levels. This part shows how change addresses performance, development, and transformation. As individuals and groups change and develop, the goal of change coaching is to support the client in mastering the change process itself. The Mastery Model is introduced to outline the stages needed to master the change process, and it is equally applicable for coaches wishing to develop the skills needed to coach for change.

The third part of the book (Chapters 9–14) offers information and resources about coaching. Here, the coaching model and skills are integrated with change theory to produce a change-coaching process that is applicable at the individual, group, and organization levels. Additional chapters focus on roles of change coaching, ethical considerations, cross-cultural issues, the evaluation of coaching, and mastery of coaching. A final section of the book includes appendices associated with content in various chapters, as well as a glossary of terms.

Who Will Benefit From This Book

In this book, the authors provide overviews of current thinking in both coaching and change. This book is designed for specific audiences throughout the world. These audiences include educators, coaches, consultants, human resources and change practitioners, as well as leaders and managers:

- Educators. Including students enrolled in a variety of coaching courses, such as continuing education, academic courses, masters or doctoral degree programs in coaching, change management, **organization development**, leadership development, education, management/leadership, healthcare (nursing), and organizational psychology. In addition, this book will serve as a reference/resource for undergraduate students as well as researchers seeking to understand the application of coaching in the context of organizational change.
- Coaches, consultants, human resources, and change practitioners. Including individuals serving as internal and external coaches, internal and external management consultants, and internal and external learning and development professionals. In addition, there are thousands of small and large coaching and consulting networks and firms. All of these individuals and groups need resources to guide and hone their knowledge and skills as they support initiatives.
- Leaders and managers. Including leaders at all levels of organizations responsible for initiating and implementing change at the individual, group, and organization levels. This information is applicable in both for-profit and nonprofit organizations in the public and private sectors.

References

Beer, M., & Nohria, N. (2000). *Breaking the code of change.* Cambridge, MA: Harvard Business School Press.

Bennett, J., & Bush, M. W. (2009). Coaching in organizations: Current trends and future opportunities. *OD Practitioner, 40*(3), 12–17.

Bush, M. W. (2005). *Client perceptions of effectiveness in executive coaching.* Dissertation Abstracts International Section 66(4-A): 1417.

Corporate Leadership Council. (2003). *Literature key findings: Change management models. Washington,* DC: Corporate Leadership Council.

Creasey, T., & Hiatt, J. (2009). *Best practices in change management.* Loveland, CO: Prosci Research.

Hunt, J., & Weintraub, J. (2006). *The coaching organization: A strategy for developing leaders.* Thousand Oaks, CA: Sage.

International Coach Federation. (2007). *Module 1: Profile of coaching industry.* Lexington, KY: International Coach Federation.

International Coach Federation. (2012). Global Coaching Study, ICF, Kentucky.

Joo, B. K. (2005). Executive coaching: A conceptual framework from an integrated review of practices and research. *Human Resource Development Review, 4*(4), 462–488.

Kombarakaran, F. A., Yang, J. A., Baker, M. N., & Fernandes, P. E. (2008). Executive coaching: It works! *Consulting Psychology Journal: Practice and Research, 60*(1), 78–90.

Kotter, J. (1996). *Leading change.* Cambridge, MA: Harvard Business School Press.

Kotter, J. P. (2007, January). Leading change: Why transformation efforts fail. *Harvard Business Review*, 96–103.

Kotter, J. P., & Cohen, D. S. (2002). *The heart of change: Real-life stories of how people change their organizations.* Boston, MA: Harvard Business School Press.

Levenson, A. (2009). Measuring and maximizing the business impact of executive coaching. *Consulting Psychology Journal: Practice and Research, 61*(2), 103–121.

Merriam-Webster. (2013). Coach. Retrieved from www.merriam-webster.com/dictionary/coach

Sherman, S., & Freas, A. (2004). The wild west of executive coaching. *Harvard Business Review, 82*(11), 82–90.

Thompson, H. B., Bear, D. J., Dennis, D. J., Vickers, M., London, J., & Morrison, C. L. (2008). *Coaching: A global study of successful practices: Trends and future possibilities 2008.* New York, NY: AMACOM.

Underhill, B. O., McAnally, K., & Koriath, J. (2007). *Executive coaching for results: The definitive guide to developing organizational leaders.* San Francisco, CA: Berrett-Koehler.

2

What is Coaching?

This chapter will explore the background of coaching from a historical perspective, outlining the various definitions of coaching and types of coaching. It will show how coaching is distinct from other professional **helping relationships** and consider how coaching has evolved in the past, and continues to evolve today. The following questions will be addressed in this chapter:

- What is coaching?
- In what ways is coaching used as an intervention?
- How is coaching distinct from, yet related to, other professional helping relationships?
- How has coaching evolved as a discipline?
- How is coaching evolving as a profession?

Most of us have had, at one time or another, a coach in his or her life. Whether it was an athletic coach who guided a person through the particulars of properly hitting a baseball, or a teacher who helped a student unravel the secrets of quadratic equations, or a manager who led someone through a new procedure at work, or a minister who provided a family spiritual support as a parent suffered the debilitating effects of Alzheimer's disease, coaches play a vital role in many aspects of people's lives.

However, while many people believe they know what coaching is, no single definition has emerged on which everyone can agree.

What Is Coaching?

> People change. Recent research has established that people can change in desired ways, and the changes can be sustained over years. But the research has revealed an old axiom: we need others in order to develop. The coach can service this purpose. Enter the coaches. Professionals in these roles range from consultants who add a

> "consigliere" (i.e., trusted advisor) aspect to their practice, to social workers and therapists deciding to use their skills with people facing work challenges instead of anxiety attacks or eating disorders. The ranks of coaches are growing at a prodigious rate all over the world. The personal attention is both attractive and private. It does not require disclosing one's foibles or vulnerabilities in front of others. In many countries and cultures in which the "boss" is to be respected, feared, and not addressed with informality, executive coaches provide a convenient and safe way to explore development and change. (Boyatzis, Howard, Rapisarda, & Taylor, 2004, p. 30)

The root meaning of the verb "to coach" is to carry or convey a valued person from where she is to where she wants to be. Similarly, when people are *coached*, the coach helps them move from where they are to where they want to be in terms of the change options available to them. In a way, everyone is a coach whether or not he or she works in an organization. Someone might coach a friend in how to throw a great dinner party, or a spouse in the best ways to shop for a new car, or a child in how to hit a baseball.

The concept of helping people move to where they want to be also applies within an organization. People may coach others—formally or informally—in how to improve a skill, carry out certain work-related tasks, or navigate the subtleties of a company's culture. In addition, a person may be coached for a variety of reasons. In these situations, the service of coaching may be performed by a professional coach who has years of training under his or her belt, or by someone with little or no training or education in the practice of coaching. While coaching is currently not a profession, coaching may be considered a discipline continuum of skills and abilities applied in a variety of **relationships**, with the overarching intent of *helping* (Bennett, 2006; Lane, Rostron, & Stelter, 2010). These helping roles may include:

- Consultant
- Friend
- Manager
- Minister
- Parent
- Peer
- Professional coach.

Over the years, coaching has been defined by authors, educators, credentialing organizations, and training service providers—as well as **coaching service providers**—in a variety of different ways. Clearly, the notion of exactly what coaching is has evolved over time and is determined to some degree by its context.

In one of the first dissertations about coaching, Wilkins (2000) defined coaching as "an interaction between coach and client, where the coaching Purpose, Process, and Relationship interdependently function: seeking to develop the client to their fullest potential" (p. 153).

Witherspoon (2000) defined executive coaching as:

> an action-learning process to enhance effective action and learning agility. It involves a professional relationship and a deliberate, personalized process to provide an executive client with valid information, free and informed choices based on that information, and internal commitment to those choices. (p. 167)

Here are some other notable definitions of *coaching*:

British Psychological Society (BPS)

The BPS has adapted the following definition from Grant and Palmer (2003): "Coaching Psychology is for enhancing well-being and performance in personal life and work domains, underpinned by models of coaching grounded in established adult learning or psychological approaches" (British Psychological Society, 2009).

BlessingWhite

"Coaching is helping another person figure out the best way to achieve his or her goals, build skill sets or expertise, and produce the results the organization needs" (BlessingWhite, 2008).

Executive Coaching Forum

Coaching is a helping relationship built on trust that employs a discovery process intended to help the **person being coached** to discover his focus, identify actions to be taken, and assume responsibility for the outcomes. In other words, it is an action-oriented, results-focused conversation between a coach and a person or group being coached.

International Coach Federation (ICF)

Coaching is partnering with clients in a thought-provoking and creative process that inspires them to maximize their personal and professional potential (ICF, 2008).

Graduate School Alliance for Executive Coaching (GSAEC)

Coaching is "a development process that builds a leader's capabilities to achieve professional and organizational goals" (Graduate School Alliance for Executive Coaching, 2012).

No two definitions of coaching are quite the same. The lack of a unified definition of coaching creates challenges for a practitioner who hopes to settle on a particular definition within his or her organization. In partial response to this ongoing conundrum, Hamlin, Ellinger, & Beattie (2009) conducted a meta-analysis of 36 definitions of coaching found in the academic literature in an effort to identify common elements and evolve a unified definition. The results of this research led to the conclusion that coaching "is a helping and facilitative process that enables individuals, groups/teams and organizations to acquire new skills, to improve existing skills, **competence** and performance, and to enhance their personal effectiveness or personal development or personal growth" (Hamlin et al., 2009, p. 18). In addition, executive coaching "is a process that primarily (but not exclusively) takes place within a one-to-one helping and facilitative relationship between a coach and an executive (or a manager) that enables the executive (or a manager) to achieve personal-, job- or organizational-related goals with an intention to improve organizational performance" (p. 18). They also defined business coaching as "a collaborative process that helps businesses, owner/managers and employees achieve their personal and business related goals to ensure long-term success" (p. 18).

While there is no shortage of definitions for the practice of coaching, it is clear that coaching possesses the following key characteristics:

- Engaging in a discovery process
- Establishing an environment where individuals and groups can learn and develop
- Using a repeatable process
- Investing in **behavioral change** that is sustainable and can evolve
- Developing potential/growth.

Why should anyone be concerned with coaching? The simple fact is that coaching can be an effective way to help people give the very best of themselves while they work to achieve their goals and the organization's goals, whatever they may be.

According to a 2003 Corporate Leadership Council study, executive coaching helps improve management capabilities in experimenting with new approaches, shifting to an enabling style of managing, successfully dealing with difficult performance and team issues, and freeing up time for strategic thinking through more effective delegating. Coaches use a wide range of behavioral science techniques, theories, and methods to help clients achieve a mutually identified, job-related set of goals to improve the client's professional and personal performance (DeMeuse, Dai, & Lee, 2009). In addition, coaching has been shown to enhance performance and effectiveness through the elimination of unhelpful patterns of **behaviors** (Ozkan, 2007).

Furthermore, coaching also:

- Improves virtual team performance (Derosa & Lepsinger, 2010)
- Improves executive productivity, quality, organizational strength, customer service, and shareholder value; six times Return on Investment (ROI) (McGovern et al., 2001)
- Is a critical role managers/supervisors must play (80 percent ranked as extremely or very important) in times of change (Creasey & Hiatt, 2009).

While coaching may not be the right response for every organizational opportunity or challenge, when properly applied, it has the potential to be a significant net plus for the organizations that employ it—and for the people who receive it.

Coaching: A Growth Industry

Coaching has been around for centuries—perhaps millennia. While some might point to Socrates as the first coach, and there have been countless athletic coaches in the centuries since, the first academic article on the topic of organizational coaching did not appear until 1937.

Between 1950 and 1990, the idea of executive coaching took hold in the business world, with a distinct focus on performance improvement and corrective action emerging during the course of the 1970s. The question most often asked by coaches at that time was this: "How can we help somebody who is not doing well to do better at the work they are doing?" Psychologists and consultants were reported to be among the first to populate the field (Grant, 2003), and coaching soon became an integral part of the work strategies of organization development (OD) practitioners "in the context of effective OD interventions that dealt with the role of the leader in a change project" (Minahan, 2006, p. 5).

Coach training programs proliferated in the 1980s, with the first coach training program—Success Unlimited Network—emerging in London in 1981.

Hudson Institute in Santa Barbara, California, launched a coach-training program in 1987, closely followed by New Ventures West and Newfield Network in 1988. In 1992, Coach Training Institute (CTI) and Corporate Coach U were launched.

Human resources consulting firms offered organizational coaching in 1990 (Judge & Cowell, 1997), and by the mid-1990s, business magazines and the media popularized coaching in the mainstream press. Professional coaching organizations formed, including International Coach Federation (ICF) and Professional Coaches and Mentors Association (PCMA). *Newsweek* estimated that in 1996 there were 1,000 people who coached **professionally**, and *The Wall Street Journal* determined that by 2002 the number had mushroomed to 25,000.

At the same time, as the number of professional coaches rapidly expanded, so too did the number of journals devoted to organizational coaching. *Coaching: Theory, Research and Practice; International Journal of Coaching in Organizations* (IJCO); *International Journal of Evidence-based Coaching and Mentoring*; and *Coaching Psychologist* all commenced publication at the turn of the century. In addition, a variety of nonprofit, coaching-related organizations emerged. These organizations included the International Consortium of Coaching in Organizations and The Foundation of Coaching (a project of the Harnisch Foundation), which has since become the Harvard Institute of Coaching. Just as athletic coaches accelerated players' performance, leaders—in the for-profit, government, and not-for-profit sectors—understood that organizational coaches accelerate employees' performance, creativity, and commitment in the workplace.

What Is Coaching Used For?

Coaching serves many purposes. When reviewing the goals for coaching engagements, a coach might identify a variety of agenda topics. Often, the client will have more than one, and the goals will change or be modified as the coaching is conducted. Bax, Negrutiu, and Calota (2011) described executive coaching in this way:

> Executive, business or *performance* **coaching** can be simply described as helping someone to learn in order to improve his or her *performance.* It is usually, but not always, a one-on-one activity and is not about issuing instructions but is about helping, showing, giving feedback, explaining, and encouraging . . . Coaching recognizes that most *development* takes place on the job and that often real learning requires a demanding task or problem to be tackled. (p. 323) [italics added for emphasis]

Witherspoon and White (1998) identified four areas of executive coaching: learning, development, performance, and leadership agenda. The desired outcome for each is the same: behavioral change in terms of immediate or proximal outcomes (Joo, 2005).

At its highest level, coaching has three main purposes:

- Performing. Coaching focuses on refining skills and actions for performance in a particular context.
- Developing. Coaching focuses on changing thinking, feelings, and actions as well as learning (gaining knowledge in one or more contexts) to improve experience and success in a variety of contexts.
- Transforming. Coaching focuses on the whole person in a wide range of contexts.

According to Schlosser, Steinbrenner, Kumata, and Hunt (2007), the most commonly targeted capabilities/behaviors (the kinds of things worked on for development) identified by coaching clients, managers, and coaches sought through coaching are:

- Building relationships
- Communication skills
- Developing self
- Career advancement
- Executive presence
- Internal visibility/image
- **Listening** skills
- Self-awareness/self-reflection.

Often, coaching will focus on one or more of the following:

- Skill development
- Career development
- Job/career transition and onboarding
- Performance improvement
- Personal development
- Relationship improvement/enhancement
- Teambuilding
- Conflict resolution
- Executive presence
- Leadership development
- Innovation and creativity
- Employee morale and motivation

- Retention and job satisfaction
- Personal growth.

According to Bono, Purvanova, Towler, and Peterson (2009), the top 10 topics addressed in coaching by psychologists and non-psychologist coaches are:

1. Interpersonal skills
2. Stress management
3. Strategic thinking
4. Time management
6. Staffing
7. Management style
8. Leadership
9. Communication
10. Adaptability/versatility
11. Motivation

These areas of focus are generally pointed to one or more of the following: performing (refining and/or improving performance), developing (gaining knowledge, awareness, skills and behaviors), and transforming (going beyond current bounds or transmuting into a different state or stage) (see Table 2.1).

According to Coutu et al. (2009), the primary reasons for engaging executive coaches are "developing high potentials or facilitating transitions (48 percent), acting as a sounding board (26 percent) and addressing derailing behavior (12 percent)." Another key role of the executive coach is to provide **feedback** to the executive about the executive's behavior and its impact on others (within the organization and outside) (O'Neill, 2007; Witherspoon & White, 1996, 1998).

Table 2.1 Focus of Coaching

FOCUS	EXAMPLES
Performing	• Applying knowledge and skills to achieve a desired result (e.g., sales) • Acting on a plan; making decisions, and following through (accountability)
Developing	• Gaining self-awareness of strengths • Acquiring knowledge about a barrier to performance • Developing a skill • Creating an action plan and building supportive relationships required to implement a course of action • Moving to a new level of human development
Transforming	• Shifting professional and career focus • Transitioning from one level of responsibility to another (e.g., supervisor to manager, or senior leader to executive) • Focusing intentionally, creating a legacy and a desired future

Joo, Sushko, and McLean (2012) noted that coaching has rapidly become a significant part of many organizations' learning and development strategy. Lack of transfer in learning and sustained behavioral change point toward the need for more individualized, more engaged, more context-specific learning. "Learning, development, behavioral change, performance, leadership, career success, and organizational commitment are all concepts related to coaching" (p. 21). They found that the use of team organization structures, complex and challenging jobs, and talent management strategies provide a rationale for coaching.

According to Kombarakaran, Yang, Baker, and Fernandes (2008), there are five primary areas of executive change for which coaching can play a role and have an impact. These areas offer an understanding of the benefits of coaching.

1. **Effective people management**
   - Increased insights into how colleagues perceive one's actions and decisions
   - Better self-awareness and understanding of one's personal strengths
   - Better results managing one's direct reports and internal customers
2. **Better relationships with managers**
   - More productive relationships with better communication and feedback
3. **Improved goal setting and prioritization**
   - Ability to define performance goals
   - Ability to define business objectives with direct reports
   - Gained insights into the business drivers of decisions and their impact on others
4. **Increased engagement and productivity**
   - Better able to adapt to the work environment and more productive and more satisfied
5. **More effective dialogue and communication**
   - Increased partnership and open dialogue between managers and executives

According to a study commissioned by the American Management Association (Thompson et al., 2008), coaching is used in the following ways (in order of application):

- Improve individual performance/productivity
- Address leadership development/succession planning
- Increase individual worker skill levels
- Improve organizational performance

- Address specific workplace problems
- Boost employee engagement
- Improve retention rates
- Improve performance of employees whose supervisor is being coached
- Improve recruitment outcomes.

Most any organizational issue or opportunity can be addressed by coaching. Here are some specific results that organizations hope to achieve through their application of coaching:

- Increase productivity
- Improve quality
- Improve customer service
- Reduce customer complaints
- Retain leaders
- Reduce costs
- Increase bottom-line profitability
- Improve working relationships with direct reports, immediate supervisor and peers
- Improve teamwork
- Improve job satisfaction
- Develop to the next level of leadership
- Improve individual and/or team performance
- Improve working relationships
- Gain new and different perspectives on business issues
- Support learning and development efforts
- Address derailing behaviors
- Enhance career planning, decisions, and development.

Of course, not every coaching engagement is a successful one. In such cases, a decision has to made whether or not to continue the coaching effort or to terminate it. Here are a couple of frequently cited reasons why coaching engagements are terminated:

- Inability of certain employees to change
- Difficulty of measuring **return on investment** (ROI).

Survey results also indicated that the more survey respondents indicated that coaching was terminated due to difficulty in measuring ROI, the less likely they were to report overall success in coaching at their organization (Thompson et al., 2008).

Helping Relationships

Coaching can be identified as one of a range of "helping relationships." These helping relationships include coaching, consulting, **counseling**, teaching or training, and **mentoring** (Schein, 2009). Psychologist Carl Rogers (1989) wrote the following about helping relationships.

> If I can create a relationship characterized on my part:
>
> . . . by a genuineness and transparency, in which I am my real feelings;
> . . . by a warm acceptance of and prizing of the other person as a separate individual;
> . . . by a sensitive ability to see his world and himself as he sees them;
>
> Then the other individual in the relationship:
>
> . . . will experience and understand aspects of himself which previously he has repressed;
> . . . will find himself becoming better integrated, more able to function effectively;
> . . . will become more similar to the person he would like to be;
> . . . will be more self-directing and self-confident;
> . . . will be more of a person, more unique and more self-expressive;
> . . . will be more understanding, more acceptant of others;
> . . . will be able to cope with the problems of life more adequately and more comfortably. (pp. 37–38)

Coaching is often confused with other helping relationships, but it is in fact a distinct discipline with unique processes and practices. Coaching differs from mentoring in that the coach is often external to the organization and has not held the role that the coaching client performs.

While Rock (2006) noted, coaching tends to focus on solutions and asking, or evoking, rather than telling or problem solving. Wilkins (2000) describes mentoring as:

> a one-on-one relationship where an experienced member of an organization (mentor) offers advice, feedback, and support to a less experienced, usually younger member of an organization (protégé) for the purpose of aiding the mentee in learning about **organizational culture**, structure, and practice so that the mentee may advance in the organization and in their career. (p. 5)

Coaching differs from therapy, as well. Therapy usually seeks to heal emotional wounds from the past. Coaching is action-oriented and focused toward the future, while recognizing and being grounded in the past as context for the present and future. However, Kilburg (2000) recommended that coaches develop awareness of the psychological influences at work in any complex relationship, urging that coaches must have at least a rudimentary understanding of the nature and extent to which unconscious forces shape behavior at the individual, group, and organization levels. Coaches also must exercise judgment when a qualified therapist might be more beneficial to the client and should certainly avoid circumstances in which the client may harm himself or others. Another difference for executive coaching is that there are always three in the relationship: the coach, the client, and the organization.

> Unlike individual psychotherapy, in which the goal is exclusively increased personal effectiveness, the primary goal of executive coaching is for the business itself to become more successful. This is accomplished by increasing the client's personal effectiveness, but also by using interventions to help the organizational system become more effective. (Kiel, Rimmer, Williams, & Doyle, 1996, p. 69)

Counselors and therapists often focus on the reduction of symptoms and evaluating the pathology underlying the symptoms. Consultants often engage with the client (i.e., individual, group, or organization) for a specific area of expertise and are expected to deal with a task or situation that has not been resolved. As problem-solvers, consultants develop a sense of the problem, make a business diagnosis, and give feedback.

Effective coaching is located along a continuum between coaching and therapy, with the coach helping the client deal with personal issues in the context of the organization. The coach has a responsibility to identify and intervene with the factors and issues most likely to derail and enhance the client's effectiveness. Coaching tends to emphasize causes that are closer to the client's domain of control rather than distal causes (Nelson & Hogan, 2009). Armed with data that indicate a pattern of behavior or feedback from multiple sources, the coach may use directive interventions targeted to improving skills or behaviors or may help the client acquire new ones. Table 2.2 summarizes the distinctions between coaching and other helping relationships, including consulting, therapy, and mentoring.

In the context of coaching, helping requires a "helper" (the person doing the coaching) and a "receiver" (the person or group being coached) (Schein, 2009). It is important to keep in mind that when helping occurs, there is an imbalance in the relationship. Schein (2009) describes this imbalance as a "one up-ness" for the coach and a "one down-ness" for the person being coached. In other words, for helping to occur there must be a giver and receiver of help and the person or

Table 2.2 Helping Relationships

	CONSULTING	MENTORING	THERAPY	COACHING
Person Being Helped	Client: Individual, sponsor, and/or organization	Protégé (Individual)	Client: Individual, group, or family	Client: Individual, team
Helper	Consultant	Mentor	Therapist or counselor	Coach or person using coaching process and skills
Focus of Attention	Group, team, organizational system	Individual	Individual or group	Individual, group, or team
Expertise	Content and/or process	Organizational culture, resources, career progression, job, personal experience	Psychological framework, process	Process & sometimes content knowledge/ expertise
Formality	Formal, structured	Informal or formal; structured or unstructured	Formal, structured	Informal or formal; structured or unstructured
Remediation	Frequently	No	Usually	Infrequently
Assessment	Diagnostic	Current and future	Diagnostic; psycho-social history; pathology	Current & future
Frame of Reference	Past, present, and/or future	Past, present, and future	Past and/or present and future	Present & future
Terms	Contract	Agreement (formal or informal)	Treatment plan	Contract or agreement
Credential	Generally not required	Not required	Required	Not required
Remuneration	Sponsoring organization	Organization or voluntary	Individual or third party	Individual or organization

group seeking help is in a subordinated role in relation to the helper. This imbalance places the coach in a dominant role within the relationship and leads to potential traps for both parties.

For the helper/coach, traps may include:

- Dispensing wisdom prematurely
- Meeting defensiveness with more pressure
- Accepting the problem and overreacting to the dependence
- Giving support and reassurance
- Resisting taking on the helper role
- Attempting to rescue the person being helped
- Attempting to fix the person or the person's problem.

For the person being helped, traps may include:

- Initial mistrust
- Relief
- Looking for attention, reassurance, and/or validation instead of help
- Resentment and defensiveness
- Stereotyping, unrealistic expectations, and **transference** of perceptions.

The helper may assume one or more of the following roles, move back and forth between these roles, and in and out of them. The coach may assume the role of an "expert," having knowledge or wisdom that can serve to guide the person being coached toward achievement of the receiver's goals. Or, the coach may play the role of "physician" serving to diagnose the person's situation or needs and provide a prescriptive intervention in order to "heal" or fix the challenge or situation for the person being coached. Third, the coach may serve as a "process consultant," offering guidance on the side without imposing the coach's point of view or solution. A process consultant works with and not for the client and is generally contrasted with the role of expert consultant. It is important to note that while all of these roles may be played by the coach, the one that is preferred, and shown to be most effective, is that of process consultant. The **process consultant** and coach are most similar in the following ways: Each works with clients to effect change, the relationship is often formalized in terms of a contract, and the process orientation expertise of the coach or consultant serve to guide the client to developing solutions and implementing actions to achieve desired results (Schein, 2009).

According to Dattner (2005), the executive coach should avoid these three roles: evaluator, messenger, and **advocate**. The coach may be asked to provide a status report on a coaching client. It may come in the form of a question such as, "How is ______ doing?" or "Is ______ making progress?" Answering such questions places the coach in the role of evaluating the client's progress and likely violates the contracting terms of **confidentiality** with the client. The second role the coach should avoid is that of messenger. In the context of coaching in organizations, a manager may ask the coach to convey a message to the client related to her performance or goals. Coaches should avoid playing the role of messenger, since doing so would perpetuate, rather than eliminate, communication breakdowns. In addition, doing so will place the coach in the middle of a triangulated relationship for which the coach will likely be the "outsider" and will have the most to risk. Finally, the executive coach should avoid being an advocate. While the coach should keep the client's best interests in the forefront of the relationship, it is not the role of the coach to advocate on behalf of the client. Doing so places the coach in a role of evaluating and then advocating for the client. It may be perceived as a way for the coach to justify the value of his services.

To be an effective helper requires specific traits. Building on the work of Small (1981), such traits applied to coaching include being concrete; being willing and able to confront the person being coached; **empathy** for the situation and person; genuineness in care and concern; immediacy of availability, presence, and action; potency of the help provided; respect from the person being coached; a well-developed sense of oneself and ability to use oneself as an **instrument** in the coaching relationship; appropriate levels of self-disclosure in service of the person being coached; and a general sense of warmth.

The Nature of Coaching

Coaching draws from many disciplines, making it trans-disciplinary. In addition, it is informed by multiple professional and paraprofessional practices in the context of helping. Chapter 3 will explore the foundations of coaching. At this point, note that the practice of coaching is drawn from a variety of disciplines including the humanities (e.g., linguistics, philosophy) and social sciences (e.g., anthropology, cultural and ethnic studies, economics, political science, psychology, and sociology), as well as professional and applied sciences (e.g., business, divinity, education, health science, human physical performance, communication, public administration, and social work).

In addition, coaching is built on the foundation of numerous professional practices, such as therapy and counseling, leading, managing, facilitation, mediation, teaching, and pastoral care. These disciplines inform the professional practices that guide the manifestation of coaching through various roles such as peer, manager, professional coach, parent, and teacher. The focus of coaching is on helping the client gain knowledge in the form of self-awareness or cognition, developing skills and abilities, and/or performing a new skill or improving performance. Thus, coaching is a change process.

Coaching: A Competence and a Role

While there is no agreed-upon definition of coaching competence, various individuals and organizations have developed models or approaches. These include the International Coach Federation (ICF), Graduate School Alliance for Executive Coaching (GSAEC), European Mentoring and Coaching Council

(EMCC), Center for Credentialing and Education (CCE), and the Australian Psychological Society (APS).

Coaching Activity

According to a study by Anderson, Frankovelgia, and Hernez-Broome (2008), coaching in organizational contexts was most commonly provided to high-potential leaders who received individual coaching. The next most prevalent use was individual coaching for senior leaders, followed by individual coaching for leaders and managers who were derailing. Coaching mid-level managers appeared next in terms of frequency, followed by coaching for front-line supervisors, and team or group coaching.

Building on the work of Lippett and Lippett (1986) and Storjohann (2006), it is possible to derive a continuum of helping relationships that includes coaching (see Figure 2.1). The coaching role is on the left side of the continuum, with the coach serving as an objective observer and process counselor in a nondirective, client-centered, process-oriented manner. The focus of the coach is to listen and be present, as compared to the more directive, helper-centered, expert-oriented roles on the right side of the continuum.

Schein (2000) described coaching in this way:

> Coaching is a subset of consultation. Clearly, it can then be thought of as one kind of intervention that may be helpful to clients under certain circumstances. In this context

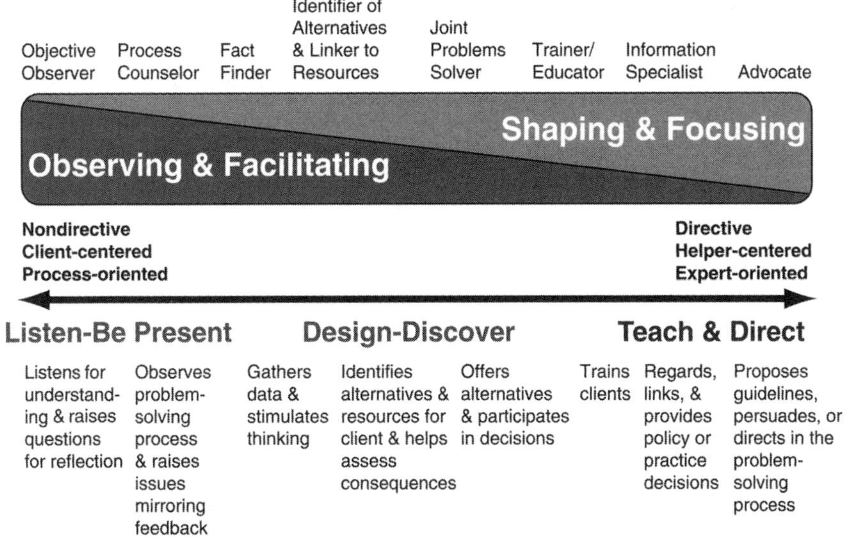

Figure 2.1 A Continuum of Helping Relationships

> I think of coaching as establishing a set of behaviors that helps the client to develop a new way of seeing, feeling about, and behaving in problematic situations. (p. 71)

In a study by Lore Institute International, coaching clients indicated they would prefer the coach to ask questions and help them explore the issues themselves. The challenge is that many coaches prefer to coach directly, while most clients prefer to receive help indirectly (Talkington, Wise, & Voss, 2002).

Winum (1995) catalogued executive coaching as one of nine types of consultation interventions. In 2001, Diedrich and Kilburg noted that executive coaching is a "largely ill-defined **competency** area of consultation" (p. 204). And Stern (2004) referred to executive coaching as "an important organizational intervention" (p. 154).

Coaching: Profession or Professional?

Individuals apply coaching skills in three difference ways. The first group comprises people who identify themselves as coaches, that is, professional coaches. This group is certainly the smallest of the three, and its members consider coaching to be a key part of their professional work and identity. A study by the International Coach Federation (ICF) estimated that there are about 47,500 "active coaches" (ICF, 2012). The second group comprises those people in helping relationships who use coaching as an instrument, tool, or intervention, for example, consultant or teacher. The third—the largest group by far—is made up of those people who apply coaching skills in their day-to-day interactions but are not identified or recognized as coaches—for example, parents, managers, peers.

While the debate about whether coaching is a profession or should be a profession continues, there is no doubt that the professionalization of coaching is important (Bennett, 2006; Campone & Awal, 2012; Cavanagh & Lane, 2012; Passmore & Fillery-Travis, 2012; Sperry, 1993, 2008). Professionalization enhances quality, provides regulation and control, recognizes and legitimizes the practice, and can attract practitioners.

Criteria for a Profession

The professionalization of coaching will help ensure that prospective coaches have attained a certain level of expertise. There are significant challenges, however, in shifting coaching from the territory of an informal economy to a field of professional practice and academic discipline. A review of the literature (Bennett,

2006) regarding required elements for a discipline, practice, or industry to be considered a profession indicated eleven criteria:

1. Identifiable and distinct skills
2. Education and training required to acquire proficiency
3. Recognition outside the community as a profession
4. A developed, monitored, and enforced code of **ethics** by a governing body to make the profession a self-disciplined group
5. Public service that is motivated by altruism rather than financial gain
6. Formalized organization
7. Evaluation of merit (**credentialing**) and self-regulation, encouraging diversity of thought, evaluation, and practice
8. An established community of practitioners
9. A status or state of recognition associated with membership in the profession
10. Public recognition from outside the practicing community that the profession is distinct and actually exists
11. Practice founded in theoretical and factual research and knowledge

While coaching meets several of these criteria, it does not meet them all. Bennett (2006) posited that coaching was not a profession, but rather an emerging profession for which having a defined body of knowledge and barriers to entry were among the key remaining requirements, and Jarvis, Lane, and Fillery-Travis (2006) confirmed this lack of status as a profession.

Several metaphors have been used to describe coaching's current state of affairs. One is to view coaching as a cube comprised of the focus of the coaching (the what), the approach to coaching (the how), and the coach (the who) (Segers, Vloeberghs, Henderickx, & Inceoglu, 2011). Another image of coaching is as a pyramid, with three sides representing the process and practice, form, and principals of coaching leading to transformation (Bresser, 2013). Fatien (2008) described coaching as "Play-Doh" to illustrate the evolving, malleable nature of the emerging discipline and profession. In all cases, the key message is that coaching lacks consistency and homogeneity in practice as well as in coach preparation.

Current State

Recent estimates of the number of coaches in the world vary. According to a report by the International Coach Federation (ICF, 2012), in 2012 there were approximately 47,500 people worldwide who identify themselves as coaches. A

2012 IBISWorld industry research report estimates 75,000 employees of more than 46,000 coaching businesses with annual revenues of $9 billion. These estimates do not include those who use coaching skills as part of their roles as a managers or consultants.

In a 2012 study conducted by the International Coach Federation (ICF), some 12,111 individuals from around the world responded, including both ICF members and non-members. Fifty-nine percent held a graduate degree (masters or doctorate) and 32 percent had earned an undergraduate degree (baccalaureate). This number is up from a 2007 study in which 53 percent reported having advanced degrees. Of those surveyed, 20 percent reported having 10 or more years of coaching experience. Coaches worldwide predominantly view coaching as a profession (69 percent). However, the only significant variance appears in Asia, where only 45 percent view coaching as profession. The remaining coaches from Asia view coaching as either a skillset (40 percent) or an industry (15 percent). A slight majority of coaches (53 percent) believed that coaching should become regulated, while nearly one in four (23 percent) coaches disagreed. The remaining coaches (24 percent) indicated that they were still unsure on the subject of regulation. Among those who believed coaching should be regulated, or who claimed to be unsure, the overwhelming majority (84 percent) felt that professional coaching associations were best placed to handle this responsibility.

What Is the Future?

According to the 2012 ICF study, "more than two in five (43 percent) respondents viewed untrained individuals who called themselves coaches as the main obstacle for coaching. That was followed closely by the feeling that there was still marketplace confusion about the benefits of coaching (39 percent). On the opposite end of the spectrum, the main opportunities were identified as an increased awareness of the benefits of coaching (36 percent) and the emergence of credible data on the ROI/ROE from coaching (28 percent)" (p. 12).

Chapter Summary

Coaching is a helping relationship distinct from consulting, counseling/therapy, facilitation, mentoring, and training. Grounded in numerous disciplines, coaching is an applied behavioral science, for example education/learning leadership, philosophy, psychology, sociology, and systems. It is an emerging and evolving discipline and profession that focuses on the individual and group levels and may impact organizational system changes. One can use the skills and tools of coaching whether in a formal, professional coaching role or in another role such as manager, peer, or parent. It involves cognitive, emotional, behavioral, and spiritual components.

Coaching can be used by leaders at all levels, with a focus on helping individuals, groups, and organizations prepare for, excel through, and improve from change. It can be taught and the core competencies developed. While there are varied approaches to the practice of coaching, all coaching is client centered, action oriented, results focused, and supportive of behavioral change. Self-awareness on the part of the client and the coach is required to achieve mastery.

Knowledge Check

1. What is coaching? Define coaching based on the information in this chapter.
2. What are the three focus areas of coaching?
3. How is coaching similar to and different from three other helping relationships?
4. What traps have you experienced as a helper? How have these traps impacted your work as a helper?
5. What are three of the hallmarks of a "helping" relationship?
6. What is the current state of coaching?
7. What are the factors that affect the designation of coaching as a profession?
8. What are the primary differences between coaching and therapy, mentoring, training, and consulting?
9. What are the characteristics of a good coach?

Learning Activities

Learning Activity 1: Helping Relationships

Consider and discuss the following:

- Identify a person who has provided "high-impact" help to you.
- What help was received?
- What did the other person ("helper") do?

- When did he or she do it?
- What made it particularly helpful?
- What characterized his or her behavior as a helper?
- Ask a friend or colleague to describe a specific event in which you were helpful. List your friend's or colleague's descriptive words and phrases. Identify the characteristics and behaviors that were exhibited as well as the **values** underlying the actions.
- Write a list of phrases or terms that come to mind when considering the following questions:
    - Why do I help people?
    - What is the motivation of my helping?
    - Whom do I want to help?
    - How am I, the helper, impacted by helping others?
    - How do I want to be perceived by those I help?
- Write a brief statement about your role as a helper.

Learning Activity 2: Coaching Distinctions

Watch one of the following films and consider these questions.

The King's Speech (2010)
Peaceful Warrior (2006)

- Where does coaching appear in the movie?
- Who are the coaches? Who are the clients?
- How does coaching in the movie you watched compare to the definitions of coaching described in this chapter?
- What examples of coaching were most effective? Why?
- What examples of coaching were least effective? Why?
- What can be learned from the applications of coaching that can be applied to your own development and practice as a coach?
- In the case of *Peaceful Warrior*, compare and contrast the two "coaches."
- In the case of *The King's Speech*, how is trust established, maintained, and challenged?

Learning Activity 3: Definition of Coaching

Develop a definition of coaching as it will be used in your life and professional work.

Learning Activity 4: Coaching Self-Assessment

Read each question carefully and circle the number that best describes one's actual, not ideal behavior. Use this to identify areas of potential strength and development.

		Almost Never	Rarely	Sometimes	Frequently	Nearly Always
1	I ask questions in order to draw out someone and more clearly understand their perspectives and desires.	1	2	3	4	5
2	I spend more time listening to get clarity about the "whole situation" than sharing my point of view or experiences.	1	2	3	4	5
3	I help other people move forward with their desired changes.	1	2	3	4	5
4	I encourage others to try new behaviors and approaches.	1	2	3	4	5
5	I encourage people to see different perspectives.	1	2	3	4	5
6	I assist people in seeing different perspectives.	1	2	3	4	5
7	I give honest, clear feedback about individual behaviors in a caring manner.	1	2	3	4	5
8	I focus on the desired outcomes of others than the specific details of problem.	1	2	3	4	5
9	I help people see the benefits of collaborating/partnering with others to achieve their desired outcomes.	1	2	3	4	5
10	I share observed behaviors with people in a timely manner.	1	2	3	4	5
11	I am OK with not knowing answers.	1	2	3	4	5
12	I honor the confidentiality of others.	1	2	3	4	5
Subtotal (total each column)						
Total						

Total Scores:

50–60: Continue to build on strengths

36–49: Focus development

12–35: Develop capabilities

Figure 2.2 Coaching Self-Assessment

References

Anderson, M. C., Frankovelgia, C., & Hernez-Broome, G. (2008). *Creating coaching cultures: What business leaders expect and strategies to get there.* Greensboro, NC: Center for Creative Leadership.

Bax, J., Negrutiu, M., & Calota, T. (2011). Coaching: A philosophy, concept, tool and skill. *Journal of Knowledge Management, Economics & Information Technology, 1*(7), 320–328.

Bennett, J. L. (2006). An agenda for coaching-related research: A challenge for researchers. *Consulting Psychology Journal: Practice and Research, 58*(4), 240–248.

BlessingWhite. (2008). *Coaching conundrum 2009: Building a coaching culture that drives organizational success—Global executive summary.* Princeton, NJ: BlessingWhite.

Bono, J. E., Purvanova, R. K., Towler, A. J., & Peterson, D. B. (2009). A survey of executive coaching practices. *Personnel Psychology, 62*(2), 361–404.

Boyatzis, R., Howard, A., Rapisarda, B., & Taylor, S. (2004, March 11). Coaching can work, but doesn't always. *People Management*, 26–32.

Bresser, F. (2013). *The global business guide for the successful use of coaching in organisations.* Stoughton, WI: Books on Demand.

British Psychological Society. (2009). Frequently asked questions. Retrieved from www.sgcp.org.uk/sgcp/about-us/frequently-asked-questions.cfm

Campone, F., & Awal, D. (2012). Life's thumbprint: The impact of significant life events on coaches and their coaching. *Coaching: An International Journal of Theory, Research and Practice, 5*(1), 22–36.

Cavanagh, M., & Lane, D. (2012). Coaching psychology coming of age: The challenges we face in the messy world of complexity. *International Coaching Psychology Review, 7*(1), 75–90.

Corporate Leadership Council. (2003). *Maximizing returns on professional executive coaching.* Washington, DC: Corporate Leadership Council.

Coutu, D., Kauffman, C., Charan, R., Peterson, D. B., Maccoby, M., Scoular, P. A., & Grant, A.M. (2009). What can coaches do for you? *Harvard Business Review, 87*(1), 91–97.

Creasey, T., & Hiatt, J. (2009). *Best practices in change management.* Loveland, CO: Prosci.

Dattner, B. (2005, June 20). *Three roles executive coaches should avoid.* HR.com.

DeMeuse, K. P., Dai, G., & Lee, R. J. (2009). Evaluating the effectiveness of executive coaching: Beyond ROI. *Coaching: An International Journal of Theory, Research and Practice, 2*(2), 117–134.

Derosa, D., & Lepsinger, R. (2010). *Virtual team success: A practical guide for working and leading from a distance.* San Francisco, CA: Jossey-Bass.

Diedrich, R. C., & Kilburg, R. R. (2001). Further consideration of executive coaching as an emerging competency. *Consulting Psychology Journal, 53,* 203–204.

Fatien, P. (2008). Des ambiguïtés de maux/mots du coaching. *Nouvelle Revue de Psychosociologie, Les ambiguïtés de la relation d'aide,* (6), 193–211.

Graduate School Alliance for Executive Coaching. (2012). Academic standards for graduate programs in executive and organizational coaching: Graduate School Alliance for Executive Coaching.

Grant, A. M. (2003). The impact of life coaching on goal attainment, metacognition and mental health. *Social Behavior and Personality, 31*(3), 253–264.

Hamlin, R. G., Ellinger, A. D., & Beattie, R. S. (2009). Toward a profession of coaching? A definitional examination of "coaching," "organization development," and "human resource development." *International Journal of Evidence Based Coaching and Mentoring, 7*(1), 13–38.

IBISWorld. (2012). Business coaching market research report. Retrieved from www.ibisworld.com/industry/default.aspx?indid = 1533

International Coach Federation. (2008). *ICF code of ethics*. Retrieved from www.coachfederation.org/ethics/

International Coach Federation. (2012). *ICF global coaching study: Executive summary*. Lexington, KY: International Coach Federation.

Jarvis, J., Lane, D. A., & Fillery-Travis, A. (2006). *The case for coaching: Making evidence-based decisions on coaching*. London: Chartered Institute for Personnel Development.

Joo, B.-K. (2005). Executive coaching: A conceptual framework from an integrative review of practice and research. *Human Resource Development Review, 4*(4), 462–488.

Joo, B. K., Sushko, J. S., & McLean, G. N. (2012). Multiple faces of coaching: Manager-as-coach, executive coaching, and formal mentoring. *Organization Development Journal, 30*(1), 19–38.

Judge, W. Q., & Cowell, J. (1997). The brave new world of executive coaching. *Business Horizons, 40*(4), 71–78.

Kiel, F., Rimmer, E., Williams, K., & Doyle, M. (1996). Coaching at the top. *Consulting Psychology Journal, 48*(2), 67–77.

Kilburg, R. R. (2000). *Executive coaching: Developing managerial wisdom in a world of chaos*. Washington, DC: American Psychological Association.

Kombarakaran, F. A., Yang, J. A., Baker, M. N., & Fernandes, P. E. (2008). Executive coaching: It works! *Consulting Psychology Journal: Practice and Research, 60*(1), 78–90.

Lane, D. A., Stetler, R., & Rostrom, S. S. (2010). The future of coaching as a profession. In E. Cox, T. Bachkirova, & D. Clutterbuck (Eds.), *The complete handbook of coaching* (pp. 357–368). Los Angeles, CA: Sage.

Lippitt, G., & Lippitt, R. (1986). *The consulting process in action* (2nd ed.). San Francisco, CA: Jossey-Bass/Pfeiffer.

McGovern, J., Linderman, M., Vergara, M., Murphy, S., Baker, L., & Warrenfeltz, R. (2001). Maximizing the impact of executive coaching: Behavior change, organizational outcomes, and return on investment. *Manchester Review, 6*, 1–9.

Minahan, M. (2006). The foundations of coaching: Roots in OD. *OD Practitioner, 38*(3), 4–7.

Nelson, E., & Hogan, R. (2009). Coaching on the dark side. *International Coaching Psychology Review, 4*(1), 9-21.

O'Neill, M. B. (2007). *Executive coaching with backbone and heart: A systems approach to engaging leaders with their challenges* (2nd ed.). San Francisco, CA: Jossey-Bass.

Ozkan, E. (2007). *Executive coaching: Creating a versatile self in corporate America*. Cambridge, MA: MIT Press.

Passmore, J., & Fillery-Travis, A. (2012). A critical review of executive coaching research: A decade of progress and what's to come. *Coaching: An International Journal of Theory, Research and Practice, 4*(2), 70–88.

Rock, D. (2006). *Quiet leadership: Six steps to transforming performance at work*. New York: HarperCollins.

Rogers, C. R. (1989). *On becoming a person: A therapist's view of psychotherapy*. Boston, MA: Houghton Mifflin Company.

Schein, E. H. (2000). Coaching and consultation: Are they the same? In M. Goldsmith, L. Lyons, & A. Freas (Eds.), *Coaching for leadership: How the world's greatest coaches help leaders learn* (pp. 65–73). San Francisco, CA: Jossey-Bass.

Schein, E. (2009). *Helping*. San Francisco, CA: Berrett-Koehler.

Schlosser, B., Steinbrenner, D., Kumata, E., & Hunt, J. (2007). The coaching impact study: Measuring the value of executive coaching with commentary. *International Journal of Coaching in Organizations, 5*(1), 140–161.

Segers, J., Vloeberghs, D., Henderickx, E., & Inceoglu, I. (2011). Structuring and understanding the coaching industry: The coaching cube. *Academy of Management Learning & Education, 10*(2), 204–221.

Small, J. (1981). *Becoming naturally therapeutic: A return to the true essence of helping.* New York: Bantam Books.

Sperry, L. (1993). Working with executives: Consulting, counseling, and coaching. *Individual Psychology: Journal of Adlerian Theory, Research & Practice, 49*(2), 257–266.

Sperry, L. (2008). Executive coaching: An intervention, role function, or profession? *Consulting Psychology Journal: Practice and Research, 60*(1), 33–37.

Stern, L. R. (2004). Executive coaching: A working definition. *Consulting Psychology Journal: Practice and Research, 56*(3), 154–162.

Storjohann, G. (2006). This thing called coaching: A consultant's story. *OD Practitioner, 38*(3), 12–16.

Talkington, A. W., Wise, L. S., & Voss, P. S. (2002). *The case for executive coaching: A research report.* Lore Research Institute.

Thompson, H. B., Bear, D. J., Dennis, D. J., Vickers, M., London, J., & Morrison, C. L. (2008). *Coaching: A global study of successful practices: Trends and future possibilities 2008.* New York, NY: AMACOM.

Wilkins, B. (2000). *A grounded theory study of personal coaching.* Retrieved from Dissertation Abstracts International. (UMI No. 9974232).

Winum, P. C. (1995). Anatomy of an executive consultation: Three perspectives. *Consulting Psychology Journal, 47,* 114–121.

Witherspoon, R. (2000). Starting smart: Clarifying coaching goals and roles. In M. Goldsmith, L. Lyons, & A. Freas (Eds.), *Coaching for leadership: How the world's greatest coaches help leaders learn* (pp. 165–188). San Francisco, CA: Jossey Bass.

Witherspoon, R. & White, R. P. (1996). Executive coaching: A continuum of roles. *Consulting Psychology Journal: Practice and Research, 48*(2), 124–133.

Witherspoon, R. & White, R. P. (1998). *Four essential ways that coaching can help executives.* Greensboro, NC: Center for Creative Leadership.

3

Foundational Frameworks of Coaching

In his 2011 book *Flourish*, psychologist Seligman states:

> Coaching is a practice in search of a backbone. *Two* backbones, actually: a scientific, evidence-based backbone as well as a theoretical backbone . . . As coaching stands now . . . its scope of practice is without limits . . . It also uses an almost limitless array of techniques . . . The right to call oneself a coach is unregulated, and this is why scientific and theoretical backbones are urgent . . . For this transformation of coaching, you first need the theory; next, the science; and then the applications. (p. 70)

Coaching is a trans-disciplinary field of practice influenced by a variety of professional practices and delivered in the context of providing help to a range of clients (Wilkins, 2000, 2003). This chapter will explore the trans-disciplinary nature of coaching and provide a theoretical framework for coaching for change at the individual, group, and organization levels. The focus of this chapter is to establish a framework for considering the disciplines and practices that inform coaching and the work of the Change Coach. For a thorough understanding of these topics, one would need to study them in depth. The following questions are addressed in this chapter:

- What is the trans-disciplinary nature of change coaching?
- What are the academic disciplines and professional practices that inform coaching for change?
- How do these academic disciplines and professional practices work together to inform and influence the practice of coaching?
- What are the applications of these frameworks to coaching for change?

First, there will be an exploration of the disciplines from which coaches may draw as sources of wisdom, followed by an examination of the professional practices in which coaches may have been trained or educated, and from which these coaching practices may have been drawn. Finally, applications to coaching will be addressed.

Frameworks for Coaching

There are various frameworks that define the ways in which coaching is applied as both a skillset and as a professional practice, for example:

Psychodynamic (Lee, 2010)

- Cognitive behavioral (Good, Yeganeh, & Yeganeh, 2010; Neenan & Palmer, 2012; Williams, Edgerton & Palmer, 2010)
- Person-centered (Rogers, 1980, 1989; Stephen, 2010)
- Gestalt (Bluckert, 2005; Nevis, 2005; Stevenson, 2010)
- Existential (Sartre, 1963, 1977; Spinelli, 2010)
- Transpersonal (Law, Lancaster, & DiGiovanni, 2010; Rowan, 2010)
- Transactional (Berne, 1964, 1976; Newton & Napper, 2010)

These are, however, approaches to coaching, not theoretical or academic disciplines and discrete approaches. Most of these approaches are rooted in the discipline of psychology and the practice of therapy or counseling. There are many genres or contexts of coaching, for example:

- Skills and performance coaching (McLeod, 2003; Wilson, 2007)
- Developmental coaching (Grant, Green & Rynsaardt, 2010; Laske, 1999; McLean, 2012; Palmer & Panchal, 2011)
- Transformational coaching (Cerni, Curtis & Colmar, 2010; Crane, 1998; Middelberg, 2012)
- Executive and leadership coaching (Altman, 2007; Augustijnen, Schnitzer, & Van Esbroecka, 2011; Bennett & Bush, 2013; Bluckert, 2005; Fitzgerald & Berger, 2002; Fontaine & Schmidt, 2009; Goldsmith, Lyons, & McArthur, 2012; Kampa-Kokesch & Anderson, 2001; Kilburg, 2000; McKenna & Davis, 2009a, 2009b; O'Neill, 2007; Orenstein, 2002; Ratiu & Baban, 2012)
- Team coaching (Clutterbuck, 2007; Goldberg, 2003; Hackman & Wageman, 2005; Kets de Vries, 2005; Tezania, 2008; Thornton, 2010)
- Life coaching (Biswas-Diener, 2009; Campone & Awal, 2012; O'Neill & Broadbent, 2003)

- Peer coaching (Hosmer, 2006; Showers & Joyce, 1996)
- Career coaching (Chung & Gfroerer, 2003; Hazen & Steckler, 2010; Hudson, 1999)

Some of these genres (e.g., skills and performance, development, and transformational) are oriented toward the client's coaching agenda, while others (e.g., executive and leadership coaching, peer coaching) are oriented toward the relationship between the coach and client in an organization or system. Still others (e.g., career coaching, life coaching) are oriented toward the context of the coaching agenda. As noted in Chapter 2, the authors define coaching as a process that supports change at the individual, group, and organization levels, with the agenda being focused on performance, development, and transformation. With this in mind, coaching is manifested in many forms. The ways in which coaching is practiced include the role a coach may play, whether as internal or external to an organization, as a peer, as a manager, or with a group. These are described and addressed more thoroughly in Chapter 12.

Coaching draws on many disciplines and practices. This rich cross-disciplinary heritage also makes it trans-disciplinary. Cross-disciplinary means the involvement of two or more academic disciplines, whereas trans-disciplinary adds the element of systematic coordination among disciplines to study and develop theory and practice.

Drawing on an analogy developed by Stein (2004), we will use the image of a large tree to illustrate this framework as the foundation and manifestation of change coaching (see Figure 3.1). The roots of the tree symbolize the academic disciplines that nurture and support the growth of coaching. These disciplines include communication, health, human development, leadership, learning, philosophy, psychology, and spirituality. Coaching is informed by many disciplines—no single discipline owns it.

The trunk of the tree provides strength to coaching. The professional practices that emerge from the roots, and which inform the practice of coaching, include consulting, management, mentoring, pastoral care, teaching, and therapy/counseling. Finally, the branches and leaves on the tree are the foliage, the new growth, which provides the seeds for further growth. This portion of the tree symbolizes the ways in which coaching is applied. Examples include peer coaching, managerial coaching, teachers coaching students, internal and external coaches providing coaching to leaders in organizational settings, and parents coaching children.

Knowing the frameworks and structures that inform coaching enables the coach to draw on his or her knowledge, skills, and abilities in an intentional manner.

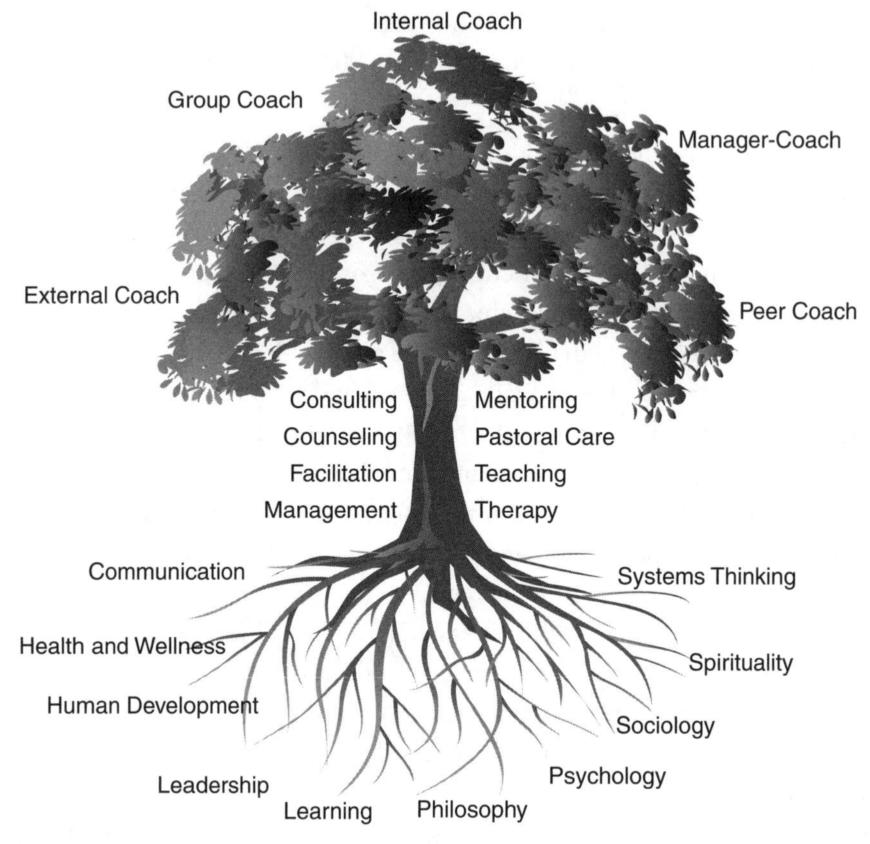

Figure 3.1 Foundational Framework of Change Coaching

Coaches are able to recognize and leverage strengths, to identify what support and information the client needs. The coach can then develop the needed capacity or refer to other sources, such as colleagues and professionals in other disciplines.

Disciplines That Inform Coaching

The academic disciplines are many and rich. They can be studied separately, or they can be studied from a post-modern perspective as interrelated. One example is educators studying learning, as well as human development and psychology. This combination of study offers a richer understanding of one's field and informs practice. It also results in the development of trans-disciplinary fields of study and practice, such as educational psychology and philosophy of learning.

In a 2003 study of the practices and approaches to coaching, Liljenstrand examined the differences in practices and approaches between coaches with an academic background in business, clinical psychology (and related fields), and industrial-organizational psychology (and related fields). She found that coaches with a background in industrial-organizational psychology use the title "consultant" more than any other groups or titles used. She believes this suggests that "these coaches view coaching as one of several services in their portfolio" (p. 4). The terms "executive coach" or "personal coach" are used more frequently by coaches with backgrounds in business. Sanson's 2006 study also found that "many executive coaches who are employees of consulting firms are engaged in providing a range of consulting services, with executive coaching being only a part of this mix" (p. 92).

Within the emerging field of study called "coaching psychology," "coaching is viewed as a method that is underpinned by models of coaching grounded in established adult and child learning theory or psychological approaches and aims to enhance well-being and performance in both personal life and work domains" (Jowett, O'Broin, & Palmer, 2010, p. 19).

As a relatively new professional practice, coaching draws from many other disciplines (e.g., communication, learning, leadership, and psychology) and engaged in other practices (management, therapy, teaching, and pastoral care). Sanson (2006) noted his study respondents as "having been involved in a wide variety of functional areas including human resources (HR) and training, sales & marketing, finance and administration. Several respondents also mention holding leadership roles such as 'President,' 'Director,' 'senior leadership roles,' [and] 'management'" (p. 92). As such, coaching is informed by, and informs, these disciplines and professional practices. A search of the contemporary academic publications will show that articles about coaching are appearing in management, education, nursing, psychology, and communication journals, to name a few.

The following sections identify some of the specific disciplines that inform coaching. In addition to a brief description of the discipline, key concepts related to coaching are listed, as are ideas for application to change coaching. These ideas serve as examples, since the linkages are as numerous and varied as the individual practitioner can imagine.

Communication

Communication is about giving and receiving messages. In the context of coaching, communication takes many forms, including verbal, written, visual, and mediated. Coaching is informed by communication as we consider that coaching is a conversation, a dialogue. The coach needs to be able to understand what is "said" and "not said" by the client and be able to share impactful messages that serve the client's agenda. Some key concepts related to communication that may be useful for the coach to understand and apply include:

- Dialogue
- Listening
- Narrative
- Nonverbal communication
- Persuasion.

Application to change coaching includes:

- Helping clients improve or enhance their communication skills
- Coaching a client to develop a communication strategy to support a change initiative at the individual, group, or organization levels
- Assessing the effectiveness of communication within the coaching relationship and making adjustments to the approach in order to improve the coach-client partnership.

Health and Wellness

Wellness is balance of the mind, body, and spirit that results in an overall feeling of well-being. Some key concepts related to health and wellness that may be useful for the coach to understand and apply include:

- Emotional well-being
- Mental illness
- Physical well-being
- Neuroscience.

Application to change coaching includes:

- Helping a client improve her health in order to be a more effective leader or participant in change at the individual, group, or organization levels
- Helping clients identify and understand how their work and relationships are impacted by their physical well-being, and developing strategies for improvement
- Using the principles of neuroscience to help clients understand and regulate their emotions.

Human Development

Some key concepts related to human development that may be useful for the coach to understand and apply include:

- Adult development
- Career development
- Cognitive development
- Ego development
- Emotional development
- Life course.

Application to change coaching includes:

- Understanding the developmental level of a client and helping her continue to grow
- Helping clients develop strategies for their career transitions
- Helping clients understand the people they are leading and managing in order to more effectively develop human and organizational potential.

Leadership

Some key concepts related to leadership that may be useful for the coach to understand and apply include:

- Decision making
- Ethical practices
- Executive presence
- Leader roles
- Management
- Motivation.

Application to change coaching includes:

- Helping a client develop a vision and strategies for change at the individual, group, or organization levels
- Supporting the client to develop stakeholder engagement
- Helping clients identify their roles as sponsors and influencers of desired change
- Helping a client function as a leader in the context of a change initiative.

Learning

Learning is acquiring new or modifying existing knowledge, skills, or behaviors contextually. This acquisition or modification usually occurs over time and is built on previous learning and experience. Learning is a process that produces changes that are relatively permanent. Some key concepts related to learning that may be useful for the coach to understand and apply include:

- Adult learning
- Experiential learning
- Organizational learning
- Reflective practice
- Somatic learning.

Application to change coaching includes:

- Assessing clients' learning styles and helping them leverage their learning style in growth and development as change leaders at the individual, group, and organization levels
- Understanding and applying appropriate learning approaches to support client growth and development as well as performance
- Using action-learning and continuous-improvement approaches to support change and development of change-related capacities
- Reflecting on change to identify and apply lessons learned.

Philosophy

This discipline is the study of general and fundamental problems connected, for example, with reality, existence, knowledge, and values in a critical, generally systemic, and rational approach. Philosophy is commonly used to refer to the beliefs held by a person. Some key concepts related to philosophy that may be useful for the coach to understand and apply include:

- Confucianism
- Cultural relativism
- Existentialism
- Humanism
- Materialism
- Marxism

- Phenomenology
- Postmodernism
- Rationalism.

Application to change coaching includes:

- Helping clients clarify values, beliefs, and assumptions as well as their impact on leading a change initiative at the individual, group, or organization levels
- Helping clients understand the philosophical foundations of their perspectives, decision making, and strategies
- Understanding one's own philosophical framework and the impact on one's interaction as a coach with the client.

Psychology

Psychology involves the study of mental functions and behaviors, with the goal of understanding individuals and groups. Psychology is focused on understanding the role of mental functions in individual and social behavior, while exploring the physiological and neurobiological processes that underlie cognitive functions and behaviors. Some key concepts related to psychology that may be useful for the coach to understand and apply include:

- Behavioral change
- Cognitive development
- Consulting psychology
- Developmental psychology
- Emotional and social intelligence
- Emotional development
- Organizational psychology
- Personality theories
- Social psychology.

Application to change coaching includes:

- Helping the client understand motivations and drivers by using **assessments**
- Helping the client make desired behavioral changes
- Understanding psychosocial issues that may require referral to a more skilled professional, such as a physician or psychologist.

Sociology

Sociology is the study of human social activity, such as social class and culture. Some key concepts related to sociology that may be useful for the coach to understand and apply include:

- Cultures
- Social norms, taboos, and interactions
- Groups and team development
- Values and mores
- Human relations.

Application to change coaching includes:

- Assessing existing group and/or organizational cultures to support change
- Assisting the client in understanding the existing culture in which a change is being directed in order to develop and implement change strategies in support of a change initiative
- Helping the client understand ways of working with dimensions of diversity such as class and power.

Spirituality

Spirituality is the concept of an ultimate or an alleged immaterial reality, or an inner path enabling a person to discover the essence of his or her **being**, or the deepest values and meanings by which people live. Spiritual practices, including meditation, prayer, and contemplation, are used to develop an individual's inner life. Spiritual experiences can include being connected to a larger reality, yielding a more comprehensive self, or joining with other individuals, nature, or the divine realm. Spirituality is often experienced as a source of inspiration or orientation in life. Some key concepts related to spirituality that may be useful for the coach to understand and apply include:

- Peak experience
- Meaning and identity
- Transpersonal psychology and the transcendent capacities of our consciousness
- Mindfulness and meditation.

Application to change coaching includes:

- Helping clients clarify personal mission, values, beliefs, and assumptions
- Helping clients understand the spiritual or transpersonal foundation of their perspectives, decision making, and strategy
- Gaining awareness and leverage of peak experience (for both coach and client)
- Understanding one's own spiritual framework as a coach and the impact of one's interaction with the client.

Systems Thinking

This discipline involves understanding how things (e.g., processes, reporting structures, resource allocation and utilization, interpersonal relations) influence one another within a whole. Some key concepts related to systems thinking that may be useful for the coach to understand and apply include:

- Complex adaptive systems
- Cybernetics
- General systems theory
- Social networks.

Application to change coaching includes:

- Assisting the client with developing and using a stakeholder network
- Helping the client leverage systems for successful change
- Helping clients become aware of the intended and unintended consequences of change on various systems.

Professional Practices That Inform Coaching

Returning to the tree metaphor (see Figure 3.1), the trunk of the tree represents the professional practices that inform the practice of coaching. These practices include consulting, facilitation, management, mentoring, pastoral care, teaching, therapy, and counseling. Each of these is introduced and examples of their application to change coaching are included. The competencies of these helping professions are compared to coaching in Chapter 2.

Consulting

"Executive coaching is a role management consultants can play and an intervention strategy that can be employed to manage change and leverage it at the individual and group levels for the benefit of the entire organization" (Bennett & Bush, 2013, p. 282). Like management consulting, coaching can be used to impact the organization or system levels while being most frequently focused at the individual or group levels. Some key concepts related to consulting that may be useful for the coach to understand and apply include:

- Action research
- Contracting
- Client relations
- Project management.

Application to change coaching includes:

- Understanding how the coaching engagement with an individual or group relates to consulting engagements occurring in the organizational context
- Applying coaching into their professional practices to empower leaders to take action on strategy and drive change
- Providing a trusted, safe, and personal relationship within which to give feedback and facilitate reflection and behavioral change with individual clients
- Using coaching as a "process step" in consulting to encourage integration and sustainment of actions that had been taken before moving on to other actions.

Facilitation

Facilitation is a process in which a person helps a group improve how it identifies and solves problems and makes decisions, to increase the group's effectiveness (Schwarz & Davidson, 2008). Some key concepts related to facilitation that may be useful for the coach to understand and apply include:

- Non-directive guidance and support for an individual or group
- Helping others discover answers
- Knowledge of processes for individual and group exploration, participation, and decision making.

Application to change coaching includes:

- Helping a group discover a shared agenda related to a challenge, and then helping the group develop a strategy for action

- Helping a client gain a new perspective about a change that is being implemented.
- Supporting a client (individual or group) in reflecting on underlying values or assumptions that may be presenting a challenge
- Guiding a structured decision-making process for an individual or group in support of moving a change action forward.

Management

Management is getting people (individually and collectively) to accomplish desired goals using available resources efficiently and effectively. Management involves planning, organizing, staffing, directing, and controlling one or more people, groups, or organizations in order to accomplish a goal. Some key concepts related to management that may be useful for the coach to understand and apply include:

- Budgeting
- Decision making
- Evaluating
- Monitoring
- Performance
- Planning.

Application to change coaching includes:

- Helping a client think through the development of milestones and measures for a change
- Supporting a client to effectively manage performance and budget with direct reports or **key stakeholders** involved in a change
- Addressing gaps in decision-making processes or practices
- Working with clients (individuals or groups) to support planning and monitoring of change actions
- Guiding clients through reflection on the change process, to evaluate success.

Mentoring

Mentoring is a one-on-one relationship between an experienced member of an organization (the mentor) who offers feedback, advice, and support to a less-experienced member of the organization (the protégé) for the purpose of aiding the protégé to learn about a role, the organizational culture, structure, and processes. Mentoring supports protégés in advancing through the organization and in their careers. Some key concepts related to mentoring that may be useful for the coach to understand and apply include:

- Advice giving
- Assessment strengths and areas for development
- Career planning
- Establishing goals
- Modeling behaviors
- Establishing relationships
- Providing feedback
- Understanding organizational cultures.

Application to change coaching includes:

- Helping a client identify and more effectively use strengths
- Helping a client establish a plan for internal or external networks
- Helping a client establish a career plan and strategies for action.

Note: Since mentoring is a one-on-one practice, there is no mention of group or organization applications to coaching.

Pastoral Care

This discipline is the ministry of care and counseling provided by pastors, chaplains, and other religious leaders to members of a congregation or to people of all faiths within the context of an institution such as the military, hospital, or company. Some key concepts related to pastoral care that may be useful for the coach to understand and apply include:

- Improving communication and resolving conflicts
- Connecting people with needed resources
- Supporting spiritual development and growth.

Application to change coaching includes:

- Identifying and developing personal resources to address change
- Supporting and encouraging individuals and groups to persist with change even during difficult times

- Providing a connection to a larger framework or vision (community or religious) to fortify an individual or group's determination and strength to change
- Reminding and **reframing** a current change challenge (or opportunity) to a larger, more transcendental context.

Teaching

Teaching is educating (formally or informally) through the application of pedagogical and andragogical principles. Some key concepts related to teaching that may be useful for the coach to understand and apply include:

- Facilitation
- Adult learning theory and principles
- Learning styles
- Adult development
- Knowledge transfer
- Motivation and engagement.

Application to change coaching includes:

- Helping a client understand how to develop the human capital within her group or team
- Understanding one's own and the client's learning style, to be more effective in communication and coaching
- Identifying activities that motivate and engage the client in all domains, including cognitive, affective, and behavioral
- Ensuring that the coaching is relevant to the change situation and can be quickly applied, so that it is used and retained
- Reflecting regularly on learning that has taken place, and how to engage others to transfer the knowledge within the group or system.

Therapy/Counseling

While there are many approaches to therapy and counseling, the following are often used to inform a coach's approach to working with coaching clients:

- Brief approach
- Cognitive behavioral approach

- Gestalt approach
- **Person-centered approach**
- Positive approach
- Psychodynamic approach
- **Transactional analysis** approach
- Transpersonal approach.

Application to change coaching includes:

- Using a specific approach(es) to inform the application of coaching
- Helping a client establish positive and productive boundaries in professional relations
- Contracting with a client for outcomes, roles, and engagement
- Understanding when and how to make referrals for other support such as therapy.

Note: The application of psychological concepts in coaching should not take the place of therapeutic intervention when warranted. Coaches should watch for therapeutic issues and be prepared to refer clients for psychological support when such issues arise.

Chapter Summary

Coaching arises from, and is informed by, many existing disciplines and practices. Each of these is a field of study in itself, and the exploration offered in this chapter is meant to inspire additional study. The metaphor of a tree has been used, its roots symbolizing the academic disciplines that inform our understanding of coaching, and its trunk representing the professional practices that shape the way we coach. Each has been linked to coaching application and supplemented with additional references for further study.

Knowledge Check

1. What are three professional practices that inform change coaching? Provide an example of each.
2. What are three disciplines that inform change coaching? Provide an example of each.
3. What are the applications of coaching skills identified in the tree metaphor?

Learning Activities

Learning Activity 1: Disciplines Influencing Coaching

Identify two to three disciplines of interest that might relate well to your work as a coach. Study them and determine how they can be used to inform your practice of coaching. Do the same with the professional practices. Focus on the type of coaching you conduct. Relate these and develop a plan for continuous professional development.

Learning Activity 2: Coaching Practice Identification

Use Table 3.1 to identify the focus of your professional coaching practice and to rate areas of strength and needs for development. Using three colors of pens or markers, highlight (for example) areas of current or desired practice (blue), areas of current strength (green), and areas for development (red). Then, create a development plan.

Table 3.1 Disciplines and Professional Practices

DISCIPLINES	PROFESSIONAL PRACTICES
Communication	Consulting
Health and Wellness	Facilitation
Leadership	Management
Learning	Mentoring
Philosophy	Pastoral Care
Psychology	Teaching
Sociology and Anthropology	Therapy/Counseling
Spirituality	
Systems Thinking	

Learning Activity 3: Influences

What are the key influences on your practice as a coach? Influences might include education, life experiences, professional focus, knowledge, skills, and relationships and connections. What impact do these influences have on your work as a coach?

Learning Activity 4: Coaching Approach

The purpose of this learning activity is to provide an opportunity to reflect on coaching experiences. What theoretical frameworks inform your coaching?

Develop a list of the top 10 activities and techniques that you use in coaching and identify their sources from the chapter's list of academic disciplines and professional practices. Analyze the list and reflect on whether there is a need to explore additional resources to broaden your coaching approach. If so, identify three to five coaching applications from the chapter and create an action plan to use them.

Learning Activity 5: Coaching for Change

Working with a partner, describe a familiar change (it can be from personal experience, movies, books, or other sources). Choose a character to coach in the change situation and identify the framework(s) and practice(s) to be used, as well as your rationale for choosing them. Then, explain the situation to the chosen partner and discuss the choices you would make and the rationale for these choices. Are your partner's choices different or similar to your own? Does the partner's answer stimulate different thoughts for approaching such a situation? If so, what action will you take to broaden your skills, knowledge, or awareness for applying a wider range of frameworks and practices in the future? Journal any reflections in writing or create an action plan to address these gaps.

References

Altman, W. (2007). Executive coaching comes of age. *Engineering Management, 17*(5), 26–29.

Augustijnen, M. T., Schnitzer, G., & Van Esbroecka, R. (2011). A model of executive coaching: A qualitative study. *International Coaching Psychology Review, 6*(2), 150–164.

Bennett, J. L., & Bush, M. W. (2013). Executive coaching: An emerging role for management consultants. In A. F. Buono, L. de Caluwe, & A. Stoppelenburg (Eds.), *Exploring the professional identity of management consultants* (pp. 281–299). Charlotte, NC: Information Age Publishing.

Berne, E. (1964). *Games people play.* New York, NY: Grove Press.

Berne, E. (1976). *Beyond games and scripts.* New York, NY: Grove Press.

Biswas-Diener, R. (2009). Personal coaching as a positive intervention. *Journal of Clinical Psychology, 65*(5), 544–553.

Bluckert, P. (2005). The foundations of a psychological approach to executive coaching. *Industrial and Commercial Training, 37*(4), 171–178.

Campone, F., & Awal, D. (2012). Life's thumbprint: The impact of significant life events on coaches and their coaching. *Coaching: An International Journal of Theory, Research and Practice, 5*(1), 22–36.

Cerni, T., Curtis, G. J., & Colmar, S. H. (2010). Executive coaching can enhance transformational leadership. *International Coaching Psychology Review, 5*(1), 81–85.

Chung, Y. B., & Gfroerer, M. C. A. (2003). Career coaching: practice, training, professional, and ethical issues. *The Career Development Quarterly, 52*(2), 141–152.

Clutterbuck, D. (2007). *Coaching the team at work.* Boston, MA: Nicholas Brealey International.

Crane, T. G. (1998). *The heart of coaching: Using transformational coaching to create a high-performance culture.* San Diego, CA: FTA Press.

Fitzgerald, C., & Berger, J. G. (Eds.). (2002). *Executive coaching: Practices & perspectives.* Palo Alto, CA: Davies-Black Publishing.

Fontaine, D., & Schmidt, G. F. (2009). The practice of executive coaching requires practice: A clarification and challenge to our field. *Industrial and Organizational Psychology: Perspectives on Science and Practice, 2*(3), 277–279.

Goldsmith, M., Lyons, L. S., & McArthur, S. (Eds.). (2012). *Coaching for leadership: Writings on leadership from the world's greatest coaches* (3rd ed.). San Francisco, CA: Pfeiffer.

Goldberg, S. (2003). Team effectiveness coaching: An innovative approach for supporting teams in complex systems. *Leadership and Management in Engineering, 3*(1), 15–17.

Good, D., Yeganeh, B., & Yeganeh, R. (2010). Cognitive behavioral executive coaching. *OD Practitioner, 42*(3), 18–23.

Grant, A. M., Green, L. S., & Rynsaardt, J. (2010). Developmental coaching for high school teachers: Executive coaching goes to school. *Consulting Psychology Journal: Practice and Research, 62*(3), 151–168.

Hackman, J. R., & Wageman, R. (2005). A theory of team coaching. *Academy of Management Review, 30*(2), 269–287.

Hazen, B., & Steckler, N. A. (2010). Career coaching. In E. Cox, D. Clutterbuck, & T. Bachkirova (Eds.), *The complete handbook of coaching* (pp. 311–323). Los Angeles, CA: Sage.

Hosmer, D. (2006). Cascading coaching: Building a culture of peer development. *OD Practitioner, 38*(3), 17–20.

Hudson, F. M. (1999). *The handbook of coaching.* San Francisco, CA: Jossey-Bass.

Jowett, S., O'Broin, A., & Palmer, S. (2010). On understanding the role and significance of a key two-person relationship in sport and executive coaching. *Sport & Exercise Psychology Review, 6*(2), 19–30.

Kampa-Kokesch, S., & Anderson, M. Z. (2001). Executive coaching: A comprehensive review of the literature. *Consulting Psychology Journal: Practice and Research, 53,* 205–226.

Kets de Vries, M. F. R. (2005). Leadership group coaching in action: The Zen of creating high-performance teams. *Academy of Management Executive, 19*(1), 61–76.

Kilburg, R. R. (2000). *Executive coaching: Developing managerial wisdom in a world of chaos.* Washington, DC: American Psychological Association.

Laske, O. E. (1999). An integrated approach to developmental coaching. *Consulting Psychology Journal: Practice and Research, 51*(3), 139–159.

Law, H., Lancaster, B. L., & DiGiovanni, N. (2010). A wider role for coaching psychology—applying transpersonal coaching psychology. *Coaching Psychologist, 6*(1), 24–32.

Lee, G. (2010). The pschodynamic approach to coaching. In E. Cox, T. Bachkirova, & D. Clutterbuck (Eds.), *The complete handbook of coaching* (pp. 23–36). Thousand Oaks, CA: Sage.

Liljenstrand, A. (2003). *Executive summary: A comparison of practices and approaches to coaching based on academic background.* Dissertation. California School of Organizational Studies, Alliant International University.

McKenna, D. D., & Davis, S. L. (2009a). Hidden in plain sight: The active ingredients of executive coaching. *Industrial and Organizational Psychology: Perspectives on Science and Practice, 2*(3), 244–260.

McKenna, D. D., & Davis, S. L. (2009b). What is the active ingredients equation for success in executive coaching? *Industrial & Organizational Psychology, 2*(3), 297–304.

McLean, P. (2012). *The completely revised handbook of coaching: A developmental approach.* San Francisco, CA: Jossey-Bass.

McLeod, A. I. (2003). *Performance coaching: The handbook for managers, H.R. professionals and coaches.* Bancyfelin, Carmarthen, Wales: Crown House Publishing.

Middleberg, T. (2012). *Transformational executive coaching: A relationship-based model for sustained change.* Austin, TX: River Grove Books.

Neenan, M., & Palmer, S. (Eds.). (2012). *Cognitive behavioural coaching in practice: An evidence based approach.* London: Routledge.

Nevis, E. C. (2005). *Organizational consulting: A gestalt approach.* Orleans, MA: Gestalt Press.

Newton, T., & Napper, R. (2010). Transactional analysis and coaching. In E. Cox, T. Bachkirova, & D. Clutterbuck (Eds.), *The complete handbook of coaching* (pp. 172–186). Thousand Oaks, CA: Sage.

O'Neill, M. B. (2007). *Executive coaching with backbone and heart: A systems approach to engaging leaders with their challenges* (2nd ed.). San Francisco, CA: Jossey-Bass.

O'Neill, T., & Broadbent, B. (2003, November). Personal coaching: This coach's for you! *Development,* 77–79.

Orenstein, R. L. (2002). Executive coaching: It's not just about the executive. *Journal of Applied Behavioral Science, 38*(3), 355–374.

Palmer, S., & Panchal, S. (Eds.). (2011). *Developmental coaching: Life transitions and generational perspectives.* London: Routledge.

Ratiu, L., & Baban, A. (2012). Executive coaching as a change process: An analysis of the readiness for coaching. *Cognition, Brain, Behavior: An Interdisciplinary Journal, 16*(1), 139–164.

Rogers, C. R. (1980). *A way of being.* Boston, MA: Houghton Mifflin Company.

Rogers, C. R. (1989). *On becoming a person: A therapist's view of psychotherapy.* Boston, MA: Houghton Mifflin Company.

Rowan, J. (2010). The transpersonal approach to coaching. In E. Cox, T. Bachkirova, & D. Clutterbuck (Eds.), *The complete handbook of coaching* (pp. 146–157). Thousand Oaks, CA: Sage.

Sanson, M. (2006). *Executive coaching: An international analysis of the supply of executive coaching services* (Doctoral dissertation). University of St. Gallen, Switzerland. (Dissertation no. 3106)

Sartre, J. P. (1963). *Search for a method* (H. E. Barnes, Trans.). New York: Alfred A. Knopf.

Sartre, J. P. (1977). *Existentialism and humanism* (P. Mairet, Trans.). Brooklyn: Haskell House.

Schwarz, D., & Davidson, A. (2008). *Facilitative coaching: A toolkit for expanding your repertoire and achieving lasting results.* San Francisco, CA: Pfeiffer.

Seligman, M. E. P. (2011). *Flourish: A visionary new understanding of happiness and well-being.* New York, NY: Free Press.

Showers, B., & Joyce, B. (1996). The evolution of peer coaching. *Educational Leadership, 53*(6), 12–16.

Spinelli, E. (2010). Existential coaching. In E. Cox, T. Bachkirova, & D. Clutterbuck (Eds.), *The complete handbook of coaching* (pp. 94–106). Thousand Oaks, CA: Sage.

Stein, I. F. (2004). Introduction. In I. F. Stein & L. A. Belsten (Eds.), *Proceedings of the first ICF Coaching Research Symposium.* Mooresville, NC: Paw Print Press.

Stephen, J. (2010). The person-centered approach to coaching. In E. Cox, T. Bachkirova, & D. Clutterbuck (Eds.), *The complete handbook of coaching* (pp. 68–79). Thousand Oaks, CA: Sage.

Stevenson, H. (2010). Paradox: A Gestalt theory of change for organizations. *Gestalt Review, 14*(2), 111–126.

Tezania, D. (2008). A framework for team coaching: Using self-discrepancy theory. *Development and Learning in Organizations, 22*(5).

Thornton, C. (2010). *Group and team coaching: The essential guide.* New York, NY: Routledge.

Wilkins, B. M. (2000). *A grounded theory study of personal coaching.* Dissertation. University of Montana, Missoula.

Wilkins, B. M. (2003, November 12). *Wilkins coaching theory: Applications, advances, & next questions.* Paper presented at the Coaching Research Symposium, Denver, CO.

Williams, H., Edgerton, N., & Palmer, S. (2010). Cognitive behavioural coaching. In E. Cox, T. Bachkirova, & D. Clutterbuck (Eds.), *The complete handbook of coaching* (pp. 37–67). Thousand Oaks, CA: Sage.

Wilson, C. (2007). *Best practice in performance coaching: A handbook for leaders, coaches, HR professionals and organizations.* London: Kogan.

4

The Essential Coaching Process

This chapter will present several coaching processes, or models, and compare and contrast them. An essential model of coaching is introduced that can be applied at the individual, group, and organization levels. In Chapter 6, the Mastery Model is introduced, integrating the stages of change with the essential coaching model shown in this chapter. In Chapter 9, the synergistic impact of integrating coaching and change will be discussed in greater detail.

The following questions will be addressed in this chapter:

- What are the essential coaching processes?
- How are they similar yet distinct?
- What is a framework for the practice of coaching?
- How does the coach determine if coaching is appropriate?
- What are the steps in a coaching engagement?
- How does the coach determine whether or not to move from one coaching step to the next?
- How does coaching build and maintain professional coaching relationships?

When considering how to introduce change coaching into an organization, the practitioner has a variety of possible options. At one end of the spectrum is an informal approach to coaching in which there are no formal coaching engagement process, no particular goals, and no ties to change within an organization. At the other end of the spectrum is a formal coaching engagement process that has specific goals tied to organizational change with clear milestones along the way.

In the authors' experiences, coaching is most effective when a formal coaching engagement process is applied that includes a number of distinct phases, including relationship building with key stakeholders, agreements, and honored commitments between coach and the client and stakeholders, assessment and data collection, and more. While accidental success is always possible, it is the exception. Coaching for change requires a planned and methodical approach—the kind of approach at the heart of this book.

Coaching Engagement Process

Coaching is a practice and process that can occur in diverse contexts, aimed at enhancing well-being and performance in both personal and professional domains. Coaching is also a practice and process that can bring about change in organizations. When applied as a formal process, coaching can be effective at achieving all of these outcomes. However, the authors do not claim that coaching is the only intervention that should be considered for change efforts. Especially in large-scale or transformational change, additional support can be indicated (e.g., project management, communications, and organizational development consulting).

The coaching process can be described by models that are outcome oriented, dynamic, are focused on the client's agenda/goals, and serve to guide the conversation. At the overall coaching engagement level, the process often looks much like a consulting-engagement process.

Here is an example of this consulting model applied to a coaching engagement:

- Entry phase. In this phase, the focus is on relationship building with key stakeholders (coaching client, client organization representative, human resources professional, client's manager, and possibly a coaching service provider). During this phase, the emphasis is on establishing the coaching relationship and identifying needs.
- Contracting phase. This phase includes establishing a contract for services as well as a contract with the client and key stakeholders about needs, expectations, success factors, exit criteria, processes, boundaries, confidentiality, and other ethical considerations.
- Assessment and data collection phase. Here the coach collects data about the client, which may include past performance as well as current and future challenges. Information may be obtained from interviews, direct observations, multi-rater assessments, personality and interest inventories and assessments, questionnaires, and surveys. The intent of this phase is to determine the area for development, underlying causes, potential areas for derailment, strengths, and impacts.

- Development planning phase. In this phase, the coach and the client mutually identify areas for focus within the engagement. Some of the goals that are agreed on may be shared with the stakeholders, and indeed, the coach should encourage the client to share goals as much as possible with stakeholders (especially his manager)—including peers and direct reports—and seek their ongoing feedback about behavioral changes. This process will increase the level of accountability for the goals, provide feedback, and increase the likelihood of support for the desired behavioral changes.
- Embedded coaching phases. This phase is when the coach and client work together using the coaching model. It may be necessary for the coach and client to seek additional information and to reassess priorities and goals while monitoring the process.
- Development and change phase. In this phase, the coach helps the client to be accountable for action plans and commitments, practices behavioral changes, and develops and uses support systems to foster continued learning and development as well as mastery.
- Concluding phase. This phase is the end of the coaching engagement, during which the coach works with the client and stakeholders to put closure on the engagement. Results and impact are assessed against initial goals as well as goals that have emerged during the coaching process. The coach should use this time as an opportunity to seek feedback about the effectiveness of her work with the client and the client system (Block, 2000; Riddle, Zan, & Kuzmycz, 2009).

Coaching follows the principles of experiential learning, reflection in learning, and problem solving. A coaching relationship is bidirectional: both the coach and client must be engaged and committed to creating the desired changes (Ratiu & Baban, 2012). A benefit of coaching is that both the client and the coach can learn and develop through the process. During the initial and contracting phases of the coaching process, the coach establishes **credibility** and models the behaviors of listening and asking questions that serve as cornerstones of the coaching engagement.

Coaching Readiness

Coaching clients have varying degrees of receptivity to coaching. While some are highly receptive, others are not, and the rest reside somewhere in between. Clients who are less receptive to coaching limit their development, performance, and transformation. In addition, they fail to own problems by following a single way of action. The terms "**coachability**" or "coaching readiness" are used to describe a person or group's willingness and openness to development, performance improvement, and transformation through the engagement with a coach (informal or formal). Coachable individuals are committed to change; have a strong motivation to improve their knowledge, skills, and abilities; and are willing to take responsibility for their outcomes. They are motivated. From a learning perspective, the coach should understand developmental readiness and learning goal orientation, including readiness for change and commitment. "Readiness for coaching refers specifically to clients' readiness for change and their needs for change and development" (Ratiu & Baban, 2012, p. 143).

A common, and sometimes incorrect, assumption regarding coaching is that individuals seek a coach's assistance when they are ready and willing to participate in the change process (Franklin, 2005). Laske (1999, 2003) claimed that for an individual to receive the change benefits of coaching, the client must be mentally, emotionally, and developmentally ready to change.

Bennett and Harper (2008) developed an assessment, the Executive Coaching Readiness Assessment Scale (ECRAS),

> to assess the psychometric properties of an individual's suitability for executive coaching using a "coachability scale" or "coaching readiness assessment" applied to middle and senior level executives engaged in a professional coaching relationship. (p. 1)

The Executive Coaching Readiness Assessment Scale is a 26-item instrument utilizing a Likert scale ranging from 1 (*Strongly Disagree*) to 5 (*Strongly Agree*). Higher scores are an indication of greater readiness for coaching. Three additional psychometric assessments are embedded in the precoaching assessment to help establish **validity** of ECRAS. Boyatzis, Smith, and Blaize (2006) conducted a study that included professionals who agreed to work with a professional executive coach for a minimum of five individual **coaching sessions** to occur over a three- to four-month timeframe. The study was voluntary and included a total number of 42 individuals. The **sample** comprised three different cohorts, each completing the **scale** at different times.

The assessment tests a client's readiness on four factors: (a) openness, (b) partnership, (c) engagement, and (d) agenda setting. These four factors are supported by research that embodies the key client characteristics required for a successful change (Boyatzis et al., 2006).

1. Openness. The **mindset** of a client is critical to success. Success hinges on a client being receptive to the change process, trying and testing new behaviors and perspectives, and willingness to learn from prior mistakes (Evered & Selman, 1989; Franklin, 2005).
2. Partnership. Trust between a coach and client allows the client to be open and honest, which is vital to the development of the client. According to Peterson (1996), "a partnership requires that coaches earn the trust of people they work with, so they can provide the right amounts of challenge and support throughout the process" (p. 79).
3. Engagement. When the level of trust increases between the coach and client, the level of engagement is increased. Engagement requires accountability. A critical factor for the success of a coaching engagement is that the client must be committed to investing the time and energy required in the change process. In addition, the client must possess the knowledge necessary to implement the targeted behavior and the personality traits necessary to complete the tasks required.
4. Agenda setting. It is very important that everyone engaged in the coaching process remember that during coaching it is the client's agenda that is worked on. In change coaching, the client's role and influence on the change becomes part of the coaching agenda.

Independent research findings suggest that the assessment has promise, and it is suggested that further research is warranted to strengthen it. An evaluation showed the ECRAS to be psychometrically sound and well validated (Henderson, 2012). Coaching readiness assessment factors of openness, partnership, engagement, and agenda setting map to the characteristics found by other researchers (see Table 4.1).

To perform a preliminary screening of coaching readiness, the coach can ask the prospective client the following questions:

- What is your understanding of the focus and process of coaching?
- What, if any, experiences have you had working with a coach?
- What change prompts you to seek a coach? What is the nature of the change for which you are seeking coaching?
- What goals do you have for our potential work together?
- What do you consider to be your strengths and area(s) for improvement?
- What would others (boss, peers, direct reports) say are your strengths and areas for improvement in relation to the change?

Table 4.1 Coaching Characteristics in Relation to the ECRAS Four Factors

EXECUTIVE COACHING READINESS ASSESSMENT SCALE (ECRAS) FACTORS	EVERED & SELMAN (1989) CHARACTERISTICS OF CHANGE	HICKS & MCCRACKEN (2011)	SCHMIDT (2003) COACHING FACTORS	HANNUM (2012) FACTORS CRITICAL TO CHANGE PROCESS	FRANKLIN (2005) COACHING CLIENT CHARACTERISTICS
Openness	Willingness to coach and to be coached	Recognition of the need to change		Hope that change is possible	Recognition and acceptance that there is an aspect of their life that must be worked on
	Willingness to go beyond what's already been achieved			Awareness of the existence and nature of a problem	A belief that change is possible
	Honoring the uniqueness of each person, relationship, and situation				Accurate insight into the real nature, cause, and maintenance of their difficulties
Partnership	Partnership, mutuality, relationship		Involvement of the coach	Social support, especially from a change agent	Ability to form a good working relationship with the coach
	Responsiveness of the individuals to the coach's interpretation		Trust and quality of the coaching relationship		
Engagement	Commitment to producing a result and enacting a vision	Capability of making the change	Cooperation	Readiness to experience anxiety and difficulty	Accepting primary responsibility for change
	Practice and preparation	Willingness to invest the necessary effort		Willingness to confront the problem	Willingness to examine and face up to the contributing problems in their life
	Speaking and listening for action			Willingness to expend the effort needed to change	Persistence when faced with setbacks or failures
					Preparedness to experience more discomfort in the process of change
Agenda Setting			Clarity of goals		Ability to set specific and realistic goals

- How important is it to you to achieve your goals through our potential work together? What happens if you do not achieve these goals?
- What are your expectations of me as your coach?
- How will I know when I have challenged you too much or too strongly?
- What is important to you in your life (personally and professionally)?
- How do you learn?
- What support do you have for the development work you are setting out to do?

Coach-Client Relationship

Coaches and clients work together to optimize performance by developing the client's professional, personal, and social capacity. The relationship developed between the coach and client "is central to coaching because this relationship can often become the principal process vehicle from which its members' needs are expressed and subsequently goals are fulfilled" (Jowett, O'Broin, & Palmer, 2010, p. 20).

The working alliance between the coach and client that emphasizes the quality and strength of the purposive, collaborative work of the dyad is that of Bordin (1979, 1994). Bordin identified three core features associated with purposive collaborative work: goals (a clear, shared understanding about the goals of the work and the desired outcome is required), tasks (mutual understanding of how the coaching will take place along with agreement on those tasks or roles which coach, client and key stakeholders will undertake), and bonds (mutual empathy and respect need to exist). The alliance is an interpersonal, interactive, dynamic, and collaborative relationship (Jowett et al., 2010). The coaching alliance reflects the quality of the client and coach's engagement in collaborative, purposive work within the coaching relationship, and is jointly negotiated, and renegotiated, throughout the coaching process (O'Broin & Palmer, 2007):

> There are five broad key aspects considered important in establishing, developing and maintaining a coaching alliance. These are: (1) active negotiation (and where necessary renegotiation) of the alliance; (2) the use of alliance-fostering strategies; (3) the recognition that there are different conceptual approaches to the relationship and implications for the interventions and activities of the coaching arising from these different approaches; (4) awareness and management of interpersonal dynamics of both coach and client; and (5) renegotiation of any disruptions in the alliance. (p. 24)

O'Broin and Palmer (2007) suggested that "coach self-awareness and awareness of the **coachee** are important to both coachees and coaches; adaptation of the coach to the individual coachee was important to some participants; that the bond and collaboration were perceived differently by participants, however not by coachees and coaches; and that trust was a key aspect of bond and engagement. The quality of interpersonal interactions between coachee and coach, and an emphasis on co-creation of the coaching relationship were highlighted as superordinate themes subsuming several of the study's findings" (p. 124). "Two broad observations are suggested across the results of this study: that the quality of the interpersonal communication between coachee and coach is highly salient to both members of the dyad, and that the coaching relationship is co-created" (p. 136).

The coaching intervention maximizes its efficiency by adjusting itself to the developmental needs of the client (Ely et al., 2010). Coaching needs represent a unique combination of individual and organizational needs. Coaching follows the principles of experiential learning, reflection in learning, and problem solving (Feldman & Lankau, 2005; Sherman & Freas, 2004; Stern, 2008). According to Jowett et al. (2010),

> The premises of organizational learning theory and those of socio-cultural learning provide a framework for shared problem solving in which the coach and the coachee develop an action plan. By considering this reflection context, the imperative for change is of frequent occurrence (Wise & Jacobo, 2010) . . . A coaching relationship is a bi-directional; both coach and coachee need to be engaged, and committed to creating the desired change. (p. 141)

Having a process or model for coaching serves to guide the coaching conversation; offers a proven process, thus enhancing credibility; is predictable for the client; provides a sense of direction and comfort to the client as well as the coach; and increases the likelihood that positive and productive outcomes will emerge.

Coaching Processes

There are a variety of coaching models and processes used by coaches. These include, for example, the GROW model, an acronym for the five steps in the process: **G**oal setting, **R**eality, **O**bstacles and Options, and **W**ay forward. While no one person can be clearly identified as the originator of this model, Graham Alexander, Alan Fine, and Sir John Whitmore are recognized for making significant contributions to it. GROW is well known in the business context and has applications in everyday life. The particular value of GROW is that it provides an effective, structured methodology that helps set goals effectively *and* is a problem-solving process.

- **G**oal setting (where the client wants to be or what she wants to achieve)
- **R**eality (how far away from the goal the client currently is)
- **O**bstacles (challenges or limitations that may prevent the client from achieving her goal) and Options (resources and means to overcome those barriers)
- **W**ay forward (a plan of action that will move the client toward achievement of desired goals).

The development pipeline model was developed from research conducted by Peterson (1993, 1996, 2006; Peterson & Hicks, 1995, 1996). Peterson suggests that there are five necessary and sufficient conditions for behavioral change. Under these conditions, people will make changes and improve their performance and results. Each stage in the pipeline responds to a fundamental question:

1. Insight. Does the client know what he wants to get better at and where improvement will make a difference?
2. Motivation. Is the client willing to invest time and energy to accomplish those results? Is the client aware of the personal payoff?
3. Capabilities. Does the client have the skills and knowledge to make the change?
4. Real-world practice. Does the client experiment with what he knows in a real setting to break down old habits and build new habits?
5. Accountability. Does the client stick with the change, and are there meaningful consequences for making the change? (Kauffman & Bachkirova, 2008)

Jowett et al. (2010) proposed that the relationship between a coach and the client is comprised of four key components. The first is closeness, which relates to the affective connection and includes interpersonal expressions of trust, respect, and appreciation. The second is commitment, which reflects the coach and client's cognitive ties. The third is complementarity, which reflects the acts of cooperative interactions. And the fourth is co-orientation, which is the perceptual interdependence and common ground of the coach and client relevant to how they view the quality of their relationship. These components form a working alliance with three key features: (1) goals (clearly and mutually agreed-on desired outcomes), (2) tasks (mutually agreed-on understanding of how the coaching will be performed along with agreement on the roles which each party will play), and (3) bonds (mutual empathy and respect between the parties). In the context of coaching, O'Broin and Palmer (2007) suggested that a "Coaching Alliance reflects the quality of the [client's] and coach's engagement in collaborative, purposive work within the coaching relationship, and is jointly negotiated, and renegotiated throughout the coaching process over time" (p. 305).

According to Duckworth and De Haan (2009), there is a positive correlation between the quality of the coaching alliance and the number of coaching outcomes. The alliance was found to mediate the link between the number of coaching sessions and the coachee's self-efficacy (Baron & Morin, 2009).

In a study of key aspects in the formation of coaching relationships, O'Broin and Palmer (2010) found that coach attitudes and characteristics (warmth, friendliness, openness, collaboration, coach's self-awareness and self-management), the bond and engagement (trust, listening, rapport, openness), and collaboration (two-way relationship, respect, support) were the key aspects identified by both coaching clients and coaches as being important on the formation of coaching relationships. Newsom and Dent (2011) said "coaches draw on specific competencies related to relationship building and behavioural interventions with the client, and competencies that allow for coaches to develop independent coaching practices/businesses" (p. 18).

The quality of the relationship between the coach and the client is critical for the ultimate success of the coaching engagement. The coach must create an atmosphere of trust so that the client can risk being honest about his concerns, perceptions of others in the organization in which the coaching is taking place, and expectations for the coaching itself.

> Second, the coach must be perceived as an expert in facilitating change and knowledgeable about business processes, the status of the client's organization, and the nature of effective leadership. Finally, the coach must be able to respond empathically to clients, allowing them "to feel respected and understood even as they develop new self-perceptions, understand how others perceive them, and learn how to lead more effectively. (Nelson & Hogan, 2009, p. 15)

The Essential Coaching Process

One of the main tools that a Change Coach uses to help the client move through change is conversation. All coaching involves conversation, although other skills including observation and assessment are often leveraged to support the process. The predictable and purposeful structure of a coaching conversation makes it distinct from, say, a chat with a friend. The coaching conversation has as its goal providing a vehicle for forward movement, while the chat can ramble wherever and have little purpose other than creating or sustaining rapport. The purpose of a chat with a friend is not necessarily or predictably action oriented. The Change Coaching Model illustrated in Figure 4.1 enables the coach to guide the coaching conversations within this context. The steps are:

1. Current Situation
2. Needs/Desired Goals
3. Information Gathering

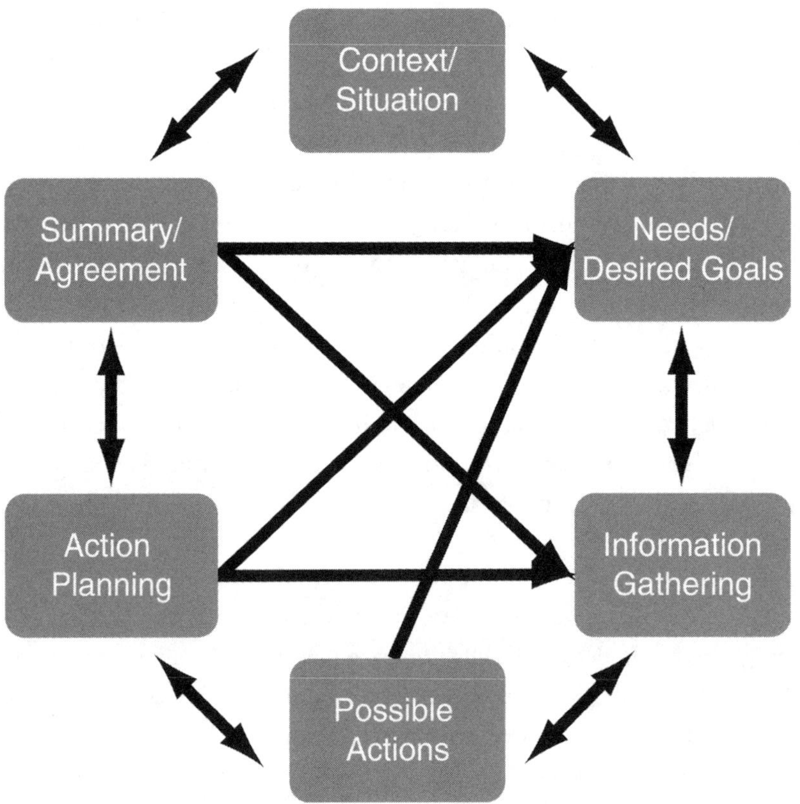

Figure 4.1 Change Coaching Model

4. Possible Actions
5. Action Planning
6. Summary/Agreement

Due to the dynamic nature of the coaching, the conversation may move from one step to the next in a linear fashion; however, it is more likely that the conversation will move back and forth and between steps in a nonlinear fashion. When the conversation moves back in the process, it will continue forward in a linear manner. When conducted properly, the conversation will always begin with Step 1 (Current Situation) and end with Step 6 (Summary/Agreement). The conversation most likely will not move through the steps in a linear fashion, but rather may move back and forth as the coach seeks to define, explore, and advance understanding of the client's issues. Here is an example of the potential flow of a hypothetical coaching session as well as an example of the coaching conversation (see Table 4.2).

Step 1 (Current Situation) to Step 2 (Needs/Desired Goals) to Step 3 (Information Gathering) to Step 2 (Needs/Desired Goals) to Step 3 (Information Gathering) to Step 4 (Possible Actions) to Step 5 (Action Planning) to Step 3 (Information Gathering) to Step 4 (Possible Actions) to Step 5 (Action Planning) to Step 6 (Summary/Agreement).

The following are descriptions for each of the steps in the change coaching model, along with sample questions or statements to support each step. The coach will want to find language that is natural and comfortable.

Step 1: Current Situation

The focus of this step is to establish or reestablish the coach-client relationship, obtain and update from the client recent occurrences in the context of the coaching goals, assess progress on previous action items, and acknowledge success and breakthroughs that may have occurred. If this is the first coaching session in a multi-session coaching engagement, the primary focus should be on establishing the relationship and defining the purpose, scope, and operating agreements for the engagement. If, on the other hand, this is a single coaching session engagement, the relationship development and contracting, as well as the coaching process described here, will all occur in the single session.

Sample questions:

- How are you today?
- What accomplishments (setbacks) have you had since our last coaching session?

Table 4.2 Analysis of a Change Coaching Conversation

COACH/CLIENT DIALOGUE (EXCERPTS)	ESSENTIAL COACHING PROCESS STEPS
Coach: How has your work been since our last coaching conversation?	Step 1 (Current Situation)
Client: The big project is going well. . . .	
Coach: As we focus our time together, what would you like us to focus on today?	Step 2 (Needs/Desired Goals)
Client: My challenge is getting everything completed on time.	
Coach: So, you would like to focus on time management.	
Client: Yes, . . .	
Coach: Tell me more about the time management challenges you are having.	Step 3 (Information Gathering)
Client: I have so many deadlines . . . I never seem to have the right material with me at meetings . . . And, I don't think we have the right priorities for the change project . . .	
Coach: As we focus on what is most important for you today, I am hearing at least three potential coaching topics: managing deadlines, having material for meetings, and project priorities. Which would you like to focus on first?	Step 2 (Needs/Desired Goals)
Client: Well, now that I hear those three played back to me, I think the one that is most important for me today is managing deadlines. That is the one that I have the most control over. The priorities for the change project, however, are critical. I have some influence, but not control, over those priorities.	
Coach: I want to make sure we meet your needs today. So, which do you want to focus on first?	
Client: Deadlines.	
Coach: OK . . . deadlines . . . tell me more about the challenge you are facing related to deadlines.	Step 3 (Information Gathering)
Client: I have so much to do. Sometimes I don't know what to do first. I always seem to have competing deadlines. And, since we lost a member of my team last month, I have not been able to reassign that work, so I've been trying to do it as well as my job.	
Coach: Let's start with the last item—the team member. Is there anything keeping you from reassigning that work?	
Client: No . . . just time to do it.	
Coach: OK. I wasn't sure if there was something else going on.	
Client: Actually, if I took time to reassign that work, I would probably reduce my stress, increase my productivity, and be able to do the things that are most important for me to do.	

Coach: It sounds like you believe taking time to reassign that work would be a wise step.	Step 4 (Possible Actions)
Client: Yes.	
Coach: Is there anything else you can think of to do?	
Client: Yes . . . block out the time on my calendar and do it.	
Coach: OK. So, you are already planning some action.	Step 5 (Action Planning)
Client: I need to schedule two hours to review the work I picked up when the team member left the team and to set priorities. Then, two hours more to consider who is best suited to do it.	
Coach: I'm curious, when you review the work that needs to be reassigned, what criteria will you use to make the decision about priority and reassignment?	Step 3 (Information Gathering)
Client: For priority, I will consider whether or not the work is "mission critical," impacts another project, or can wait until I hire a new team member. For reassignment, I will consider who has the knowledge and skills to do the work, who has time, and, you know, I will also use this as an opportunity to give some other team members "stretch assignments" to build their capacity.	
Coach: I'd like to recap . . . you have a focus, you have a plan of action, and you have your criteria for decision-making.	Step 4 (Possible Actions)
Client: What's next?	
Coach: When will you get this started?	Step 5 (Action Planning)
Client: I will find the time on my calendar today. My intent is to find time by the end of this week to review the work and by the middle of next week to determine who might receive the new assignments. One more step I'd like to add . . . after I draft the reassignments, I'd like to meet with each team member that will be impacted and discuss it with them. I think it is important for them to know why I'm asking them to take on more work and to assure them that I will support them. What do you think?	
Coach: I think you have a terrific plan. One more question. How soon do you expect you can meet with each of your team members?	
Client: I think it will take me two weeks from today to complete this. In the meantime, I'll keep trying to keep the priorities and deadlines in order.	
Coach: Great. Now, as we wrap up this session today, please summarize what you received from the coaching session and your next steps.	
Client: I gained clarity about the challenges I'm facing and the need to delegate. I developed a plan of action to reassign the work of the team member that left. And, I feel very good. There is a sense of relief in knowing that I have a plan of action. Thank you!	Step 6 (Summary/Agreement)
Coach: Good. . . . and, I believe we are scheduled to meet again in 3 weeks.	
Client: Yes. And, at that point, I will be able to report on the work I did to manage the deadlines, delegate work, and support the development of my team members.	

- What has impacted you since the last time we met?
- It sounds like you completed your assignments since we met.

Step 2: Needs/Desired Goals

The focus of this step is for the coach to gain an understanding of the client's current reality, understand and agree on the goals for the coaching session, align those goals with the overall goals of the coaching engagement, and, if necessary, adjust the goals of the engagement. Adjusting the goals may be necessary, because the coach will need to determine if the conversation should move to the Information Gathering step or continue the focus on Step 2 (Needs/Desired Goals). This determination will be based on whether or not clarity and mutual understanding exist between coach and client. The coach can align to the client's goals by a formal amendment to a contract or informally by a conversation with the client.

Sample questions:

- What would you like to focus on during our work together?
- What are your goals for our coaching session today?
- How will we know if our work together is successful?
- What are the gaps between where you are today and where you want to be in six months?
- What do you want?
- What is your goal?

Step 3: Information Gathering

The focus of this step is gathering information that serves the client's agenda, gaining a mutual understanding of that information, and identifying needs for additional data (which may become an action item for later consideration). As the process manager, the coach will need to determine if the conversation should progress to Step 4 (Possible Actions) or go back to Step 2 to refine Needs/Desired Goals. This determination will be based on whether there is sufficient information and shared understanding to begin exploring possible actions.

Sample questions:

- What does the feedback you have received tell you about your strengths (growth opportunities)?
- What expectations does your manager have of you?

- What expectations do you have of your direct report?
- Where can you find data that will help you make that decision?
- What does this feedback mean to you?
- What question would you like to ask them?
- What are your key development areas?
- How will you be able to recognize success?
- If you were sitting in their seat, how would you view the actions you are considering?
- What are your career goals?
- How is your behavior impacting others?
- How is your behavior supporting (or distracting) you from achieving your performance and/or relational goals?
- How important is it to you?

Step 4: Possible Actions

The focus of this step is to explore possibilities for action that will serve the client's needs and desired goals for the coaching session. In this step, the client generates ideas for possible action, establishes criteria to evaluate those options, considers barriers to implementing them, and establishes priorities for action.

Sample questions:

- What ideas do you have for addressing this?
- What will help you achieve your goals?
- What resources are available to support you in this quest?
- What will you do about that?
- How will you decide which step to take next?
- What action can you take in this moment to help you achieve this?
- What has worked for you in the past?
- If there were something else you could do, what would it be?
- What needs to happen to move you forward?

When helping the client develop and explore possible actions, apply the following:

- Do not evaluate. Evaluation slows or stops creativity. Suspend critical judgment.
- Allow the ideas to emerge, encourage ideas; clarify later.
- Help the client develop "wild" ideas.

- Encourage the client to expand on her own ideas and experiences as well as those of others.
- Track the ideas for the client; they can be repeated once the idea generation has slowed.
- Offer (sparingly) ideas or questions to "prime the pump."

The coach will need to determine whether or not to progress to Step 5 (Action Planning) or go back to a previous step (Information Gathering, Needs/Desired Goals) or continue developing possible actions. This determination will be based on whether or not there is a clear understanding of the information available, possible actions to support achievement of the desired goals, and a commitment to consider action steps for implementation.

Step 5: Action Planning

The focus of this step is to develop action steps (what the client will do, by when, with what outcome, and with what support), insure accountability and commitment for implementation, and determine resource and support needs as well as how those resources will be acquired. The coach will need to determine whether or not to progress to Step 6 (Summary/Agreement), go back to a previous step (Information Gathering, Needs/Desired Goals, Possible Actions), or continue developing possible actions. This determination will be based on whether there is clarity and commitment for the action steps developed, and agreement about what the client will do next—by when, and with what support (if appropriate).

Sample questions:

- What will you do by when?
- What barriers can you foresee that will need to be addressed as you implement your action plan?
- What are one or two things you can do to meet this challenge?
- What will you do about that?
- Who will you speak with?
- Where will you find that?
- What support will you need from your manager?
- What, if any, negative consequences are there for the course of action we discussed?
- Who else needs to be involved?

Step 6: Summary/Agreement

The focus of this step is to review insights and commitments gained from this coaching session, identify possible agenda items for future coaching sessions, and reinforce that ownership of the coaching agenda and actions are held by the client. The coach will need to determine whether or not to end the coaching session or return to a previous step in the coaching process (Information Gathering, Needs/Desired Goals, Possible Actions, Action Planning). This determination will be based on whether there is shared agreement about next steps, if the designated length of the coaching session has ended, or if a new area of focus has emerged.

Sample statements and questions:

- What have you gained from this coaching session?
- What are your next steps? Please summarize.
- What did you gain from this coaching session?
- Please remind me. What will you do as a result of this coaching session?
- What is the date/time of our next coaching session?

Tips for More Successful Change Coaching

There are certain things coaches can do to improve the effectiveness of their coaching efforts with individuals and groups. Here are some of the most significant:

- Build trust, respect, and credibility with clients.
- Let the client set the agenda.
- Help the client stay focused on her agenda for coaching.
- Help the client stay focused while helping her continually refine and redefine the focus.
- Master the art of asking high-impact questions (see Chapter 5).
- Help the client identify options and possibilities.
- Help the client determine action to be taken.
- Define action steps: Do what? By when? What outcomes/results?
- Help the client discover barriers to successful implementation and then develop strategies to overcome the barriers.
- Speak less than 20 percent of the time; don't be afraid of periods of silence; ask simple, focused questions and then wait at least seven seconds for a response.

- Actively listen for content, context, meaning, what is being said, what is not being said, congruence, and incongruence.
- Be willing to maintain silence while the client processes.
- Celebrate breakthroughs and achievements.
- Ask the client for feedback on the coaching: What is working well? What is not working well? What should be done differently?
- Allow clients to take full responsibility for their own discoveries, growth, ideas, and achievements. Avoid imposing solutions on clients.
- Help clients be responsible for their actions.
- Coaching is about helping clients discover their own answers, not about the coach's being a sage. A person does not need to be a content expert to be an excellent coach.
- Challenge any incongruence between what the client has said previously and what she says in the current coaching conversation.
- Challenge any discrepancies between the client's commitment to action and his lack of actual action.
- Respect the communication and thinking styles of the client, while keeping the conversation moving through the coaching process.

Chapter Summary

There are a variety of different ways to introduce coaching into an organization, from informal to formal. The most effective technique is based on a formal coaching engagement process, applying a planned and methodical approach. The formal coaching engagement process is comprised of seven phases: entry, contracting, assessment and data collection, development planning, embedded coaching, development and change, and disengagement. Each coaching session encompasses six essential steps: Current Situation, Needs/Desired Goals, Information Gathering, Possible Actions, Action Planning, and Summary/Agreement.

Many different coaching models and processes are used by coaches. Some of these models and processes include the GROW model (goal setting, reality, obstacles and options, and way forward), the development pipeline model, and others. The coachability—or coaching readiness—of individuals is an important consideration for coaches. Coachable individuals are committed to change, have a strong motivation to improve their knowledge, skills, and abilities, and they are willing to take responsibility for their outcomes.

Coaches can improve the effectiveness of their efforts in a variety of different ways, including building trust, respect, and credibility with clients, letting the client set the agenda, helping the client stay focused, mastering the art of asking high-impact questions, defining action steps, and helping the client identify and overcome barriers.

Knowledge Check

1. What are the six steps in the essential coaching process? What is one question that a coach could ask during each step?
2. In what ways is the coaching conversation process dynamic?
3. What is important to keep in mind when considering a client's readiness for coaching?
4. Describe the impact (importance) of the coach-client relationship on successful coaching.
5. List ten things that coaches can do to improve the effectiveness of their coaching efforts with individuals.

Learning Activities

Learning Activity 1: Developing Questions

Referring to the six-step Change Coaching Model shown in Figure 4.1, develop six additional questions and statements for each step that might be used in coaching engagements.

Learning Activity 2: Observation

Listening to or observing a coaching session, track the conversation by following the steps in the coaching process. Observe:

- Is the process being followed?
- What is the flow of the conversation?
- What decision points led the conversation to move forward or backward in the coaching process model?

Learning Activity 3: ECRAS

Think of specific current and potential (upcoming) coaching clients. Review the ECRAS and identify the ways in which the current/past client was ready for coaching and what challenges or barriers arose. Then, consider prospective clients and how you can work with these clients to help them increase their readiness for coaching.

Learning Activity 4: Interview a Coach

Interview a professional coach. Ask him/her to talk about his/her coaching process. Ask the coach to describe specific examples in which he/she made a decision to move forward and backward in the process. What led the coach to make those decisions? Reflect on the experience of the professional coach. Consider how his/her experience might influence your professional development and application of the coaching model.

References

Baron, L., & Morin, L. (2009). The coach-coachee relationship in executive coaching: A field study. *Human Resource Development Quarterly, 20*(1), 85–106.

Bennett, J. L., & Harper, M. (2008). *Executive coaching readiness assessment scale.* Presented at Academy of Management, Anaheim, CA.

Block, P. (2000). *Flawless consulting: A guide to getting your expertise used* (2nd ed.). New York, NY: Pfeiffer.

Bordin, E. S. (1979). The generalizability of the psychoanalytic concept of the working alliance. *Psychotherapy: Theory, Research & Practice, 16*(3), 252–260.

Bordin, E. S. (1994). Theory and research on the therapeutic working alliance: New directions. In A. O. Horvath & L. S. Greenberg (Eds.), *The working alliance: Theory, research, and practice* (pp. 13–37). New York, NY: Wiley.

Boyatzis, R. E., Smith, M., & Blaize, N. (2006). Developing sustainable leaders through coaching and compassion. *Academy of Management Learning & Education, 5*(1), 8–24.

Duckworth, A. & De Haan, E. (August 2009). What clients say about our coaching. *Training Journal Online,* 64–67.

Ely, K., Boyce, L., Nelson, J. K., Zaccaro, S. J., Hernez-Broome, G., & Whyman, W. (2010). Evaluating leadership coaching: A review and integrated framework. *Leadership Quarterly, 21,* 585–599.

Evered, R. D., & Selman, J. C. (1989). Coaching and the art of management. *Organizational Dynamics, 18*(2), 16–32.

Feldman, D. C., & Lankau, M. J. (2005). Executive coaching: A review and agenda for future research. *Journal of Management, 31,* 829–848.

Franklin, J. (2005). Change readiness in coaching: Potentiating client change. In M. Cavanagh, A. M. Grant, & T. Kemp (Eds.), *Evidence-based coaching (Vol. 1): Theory, research and practice from the behavioural sciences* (pp. 193–200). Bowen Hills: Australian Academic Press.

Hannum, M. (2012). 10 critical factors for a successful change initiative. Linkage. Retrieved from http://mylinkage.com/blog/10-critical-factors-for-a-successful-change-initiative-by-mark-hannum

Henderson, D. (2012). *An evaluation of a psychometric scale: Executive coaching readiness assessment scale.* Masters Thesis. McColl School of Business. Queens University of Charlotte. Charlotte, NC.

Hicks, R., & McCracken, J. (2011). Coaching as a leadership style. *Physician Executive, 37*(5), 82-84.

Jowett, S., O'Broin, A., & Palmer, S. (2010). On understanding the role and significance of a key two-person relationship in sport and executive coaching. *Sport & Exercise Psychology Review, 6*(2), 19–30.

Kauffman, C., & Bachkirova, T. (2008). Coaching is the ultimate customizable solution: An interview with David Peterson. *Coaching: An International Journal of Theory, Research & Practice, 1*(2), 114–119.

Laske, O. E. (1999). An integrated approach to developmental coaching. *Consulting Psychology Journal: Practice and Research, 51*(3), 139–159.

Laske, O. E. (2003, November 12). *An integrated model of developmental coaching (TM): Researching new ways of coaching and coach education.* Paper presented at the Coaching Research Symposium, Denver, CO.

Nelson, E., & Hogan, R. (2009). Coaching on the dark side. *International Coaching Psychology Review, 4*(1), 9–21.

Newsom, G., & Dent, E. B. (2011). A work behaviour analysis of executive coaches. *International Journal of Evidence Based Coaching & Mentoring, 9*(2), 1–22.

O'Broin, A., & Palmer, S. (2007). Reappraising the coach-client relationship: The unassuming change agent in coaching. In S. Palmer & A. Whybrow (Eds.), *Handbook of coaching psychology: A guide for practitioners* (pp. 295–324). London: Routledge.

O'Broin, A., & Palmer, S. (2010). Exploring the key aspects in the formation of coaching relationships: Initial indicators from the perspective of the coachee and the coach. *Coaching: An International Journal of Theory, Research & Practice, 3*(2), 124–143.

Peterson, D. B. (1993). *Skill learning and behavior change in an individually tailored management coaching and training program.* Dissertation. University of Minnesota, Minneapolis, MN.

Peterson, D. B. (1996). Executive coaching at work: The art of one-on-one change. *Consulting Psychology Journal: Practice and Research, 48*(2), 78–86.

Peterson, D. B. (2006). People are complex and the world is messy: A behavior-based approach to executive coaching. In D. Stober & A. M. Grant (Eds.), *Evidence based coaching handbook: Putting best practices to work for your clients* (pp. 51–76). Hoboken, NJ: John Wiley & Sons.

Peterson, D. B., & Hicks, M. D. (1995). *Development first: Strategies for self-development.* Minneapolis, MN: Personnel Decisions International.

Peterson, D. B., & Hicks, M. D. (1996). *Leader as coach: Strategies for coaching and developing others.* Minneapolis, MN: Personnel Decisions International.

Ratiu, L., & Baban, A. (2012). Executive coaching as a change process: An analysis of the readiness for coaching. *Cognition, Brain, Behavior: An Interdisciplinary Journal, 16*(1), 139–164.

Riddle, D., Zan, L., & Kuzmycz, D. (2009). Issues & observations: Five myths about executive coaching. *Leadership in Action, 29*(5), 19–21.

Schmidt, T. (2003): Coaching: Eine empirische Studie zu Erfolgsfaktoren bei Einzel-Coaching (Coaching: An empirical study of success factors in individual coaching). Technische Universität Berlin, Institut für Psychologie und Arbeitswissenschaft.

Sherman, S., & Freas, A. (2004). The Wild West of executive coaching. *Harvard Business Review, 82*(11), 82–90.

Stern, L. R. (2008). *Executive coaching: Building and managing your professional practice.* Hoboken, NJ: John Wiley & Sons.

5

Essential Coaching Skills

This chapter will provide the essential communication, interpersonal, and cross-cultural tools and knowledge required for coaching leaders at all levels. These tools and knowledge include listening, asking questions, providing insights and feedback, planning action, insuring accountability, and building support for achievement. In this chapter, the following questions will be addressed:

- What are the competencies of effective coaches?
- What are the essential skills/practices of coaches?
- How are these skills/practices applied?

Coaching is the practice of a science in the form of an art. The authors have found that there is both an art and a science to coaching. Learning the skills of coaching and the theories that inform coaching is one step toward becoming a coach and coaching in the most effective way possible. The other step is to integrate knowledge and practice in a way that is both comfortable and effective. Once this integration is accomplished, the next step is developing a level of mastery.

Mastery starts with the coach. While many can learn to coach and use the knowledge and skills employed by coaches, certain characteristics of those who do it well can be observed (Bergquist, Merritt, & Phillips, 1999; Bush, 2005; Crane, 2001; Flaherty, 1999; Guthrie, 1999; Hargrove, 1995; Hudson, 1999; Kilburg, 2000; O'Neill, 2007). There are a variety of coach competencies models available, including frameworks developed by the Center for Credentialing & Education (CCE), European Mentoring and Coaching Council (EMCC), Graduate School Alliance for Executive Coaching (GSAEC), and International Coach Federation (ICF). Successful coaches:

- Are educated in the art and science related to coaching
- Understand contemporary organizational issues, but not necessarily the detailed nature of the business

- Understand human motivation
- Understand the impact of emotions and interpersonal style on leadership
- Understand leadership and management issues from a multi-systems viewpoint
- Understand the political and economic realities within the organization
- Understand the competitive environment
- Are self-aware—they know their needs and do not depend on the coaching relationship to get those needs met
- Are able to maintain appropriate confidentiality
- Are able to maintain appropriate roles and behaviors between coach, executive, and stakeholders
- Are able to provide insights and assist executives learn new skills through modeling
- Have a passion for helping others grow and perform
- Are comfortable around top management
- Are able to notice and deal with paradoxes
- Are able to demonstrate interpersonal sensitivity
- Are able to detect hidden agendas
- Are able to flex and be creative
- Demonstrate approachability, compassion, and the ability to relate well with others
- Are able to actively listen and reflect accurately what is said
- Demonstrate high levels of integrity and personal honesty
- Build trust
- Ask powerful questions
- Provide emotional and motivational support
- Follow through
- Establish coaching goals with the client
- Monitor coaching results
- Develop themselves as human beings and in their roles as coaches (Kombarakaran, Yang, Baker, & Fernandes, 2008; Stern, 2008).

While there is a well-defined set of characteristics shared by successful coaches, potential clients may not be able to observe these characteristics until a coaching engagement is actually underway. There are, however, certain things clients look for when selecting a coach. These include:

- Industry experience
- Education

- Work experience
- Work at the appropriate level in the organization (leader and coach)
- Personal developmental level
- Coaching skills
- Chemistry/style
- Personality
- Demographics: gender, race, age, sexual orientation, etc.

Coaching works in many different environments, and supports a wide variety of differing intentions, frameworks, and assumptions. However, in the authors' experience, coaching works best when:

- Desired outcomes are defined
- Organizational support exists
- The organization embraces a culture of feedback, development, and support
- The coaching is developmental and not corrective
- The individual is ready for coaching—that is, she is open to feedback, has a desire to change/improve, and is able to devote the time and energy to self-discovery and behavior shifts.

Positive and productive coaching relationships do not often occur spontaneously. They require the right conditions in addition to skills and knowledge on the part of the coach. Here are some of the factors for coaches that are conducive to creating positive and productive coaching relationships:

- Helper empathy. When a coach possesses helper empathy, she attempts to see the world in the same way the client perceives it, by looking from the client's internal frame of reference. The coach does this preliminarily by thinking *with* rather than *for* or *about* the client. Empathy has two stages. Brammer and MacDonald (2003) referred to these as "feeling into" experiences of the client and being in a place of the client, that is, seeing the world as the client sees it. In the second stage, the coach becomes an alternative self for the client, an emotional mirror. Coaches enter this internal frame of reference by listening attentively and asking themselves questions such as: What is the client feeling right now? How does he view the situation he is facing? On the other hand, if the coach were to view the external frame of reference, he might ask question such as: Why is the client concerned? What is causing the situation? An effective coach tries to think and feel like the client.

- Helper warmth and caring. When a coach possesses warmth and caring, she conveys a closeness that extends beyond professional or clinical distance. Coaches demonstrate this through friendliness and consideration by smiling, maintaining a comfortable amount of eye contact, and other nonverbal behaviors. In addition, the coach demonstrates warmth and caring by showing compassion and sincere concern for the client.
- Helper positive regard and respect. When a coach possesses positive regard and respect, she has a deep concern for the client's well-being and respect for the client's individuality and worth. Rogers (1989) referred to this as "unconditional positive regard."
- Helper openness. When a coach possesses openness, she shares personal experiences in service of the client's agenda by disclosing thoughts and feelings. Coaches demonstrate this by disclosing thoughts and feelings as well as insights. This disclosure results in genuineness, authenticity, and congruence with the client.
- Helper concreteness and specificity. When the coach possesses concreteness and specificity, she communicates clearly, accurately, and concisely. Coaches demonstrate this by using language that is contextually appropriate and understood by the client. Coaches pay attention to the interpretation of their messages and seek opportunities to clarify when a client does not understand what was communicated.
- Intentionality. When the coach possesses intentionality, she selects responses to clients from a wide range of options. Coaches demonstrate this by selecting statements, questions, and nonverbal responses based on factors such as the client's cultural background, goals, personality, and learning style (Brammer & MacDonald, 2003).

In addition to establishing a trusting relationship with the client as well as other stakeholders (e.g., manager, human resources), the coach must be self-aware and personally and professionally evolving.

> A quality coaching interaction can't be pulled off with any amount of method expertise or dazzling command of theory. It's what culminates from deep personal work that the coach has done and continues to do to prepare for this kind of engagement. A heightened alertness to one's natural biases, tendencies, and their impact is necessary along with a nimble ability to choose. (Storjohann, 2006, p. 14)

Who Are Stakeholders? What Are Their Most Important Needs?

In any organization, there are numerous stakeholders—each with an interest in the coaching services being provided to employees and with the effectiveness of those services (see Figure 5.1). Some of the most common stakeholders—and their most important needs—include:

- Organizational purchaser of coaching services (may be HR or equivalent). Value, results, **reliability**, risk management
- Organizational provider of coaching services. Service, value delivered, margin, stronger relationship, future opportunities
- Organizational client (coachee). Enhanced capabilities, understanding of process, better alignment, more opportunity, greater self-confidence
- Coach: Service, value delivered, future opportunities
- Organizational client's manager. Improved and more reliable performance, fewer breakdowns and quicker resolution, better results
- Client's peers and direct reports. Fewer breakdowns, better collaboration and teamwork, better alignment, better results

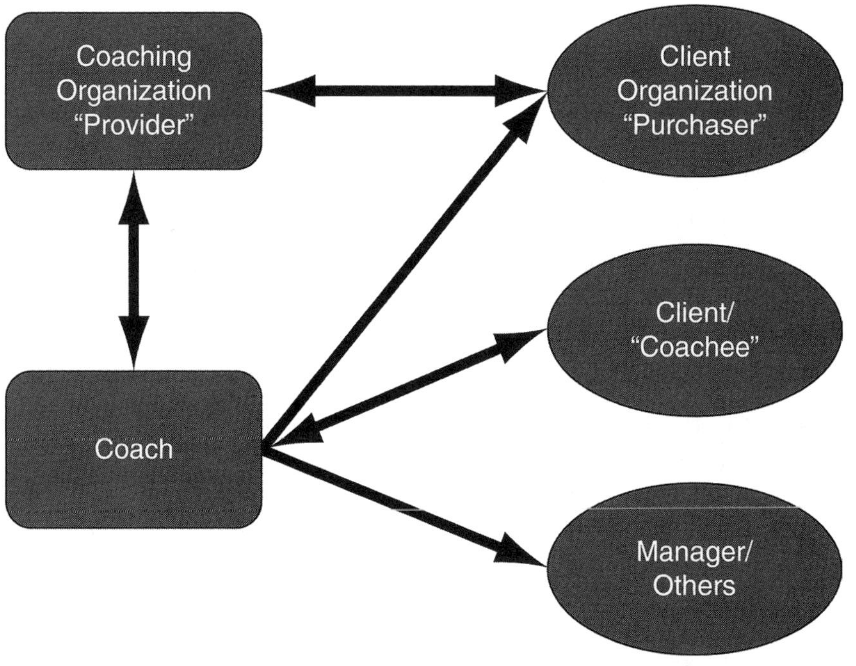

Figure 5.1 Change Coaching Stakeholders

- Client's customers. More satisfaction with value received, more trust in performer and process, better working relationships (Bennett & Lazar, 2011).

Coaching Competencies

Currently, there is no widely agreed upon competency model for coaching, or for coaching within any specialty group such as career coaching, personal coaching, or performance coaching. Instead, there are a variety of models. These have been developed by organizations such as the Center for Credentialing and Education, European Mentoring and Coaching Council, Graduate School Alliance for Executive Coaching, and the International Coach Federation. Considering that coaching is a helping relationship grounded in many professions and professional practices, it is important to note that the competencies that demonstrate proficiency may take many forms. Looking beyond coaching, the helping practices include consulting, facilitation, management, mediation, mentoring, pastoral care, teaching, and therapy and counseling.

Considering the range of professions and professional practices that inform the practice of coaching, it is possible to compare the various competency models and derive a set of competencies for coaching. A summary of some of the more widely used competency models (coaching, consulting, mediation, and pastoral care) can be compared to show that coaching is similar to and different from other helping professional services. Refer to Appendix A for an illustration of this comparison.

Newsom and Dent (2011) reported one of the most comprehensive studies on contemporary coaching competencies. They identified professional coach activities (i.e., assess practice needs, promote/market one's own coaching business, evaluate one's own coaching process, and engage in self-development activities), goal setting and attainment activities (i.e., directives aimed at behavioral change such as discussion of work-life balance issues, sharing an understanding of wellness, using knowledge of current business trends, and discussing obstacles for client progress development), and relationship activities (i.e., clarifying an understanding of client concerns and challenges; establishing trust, honesty, and respect in the coaching relationship; assessing client strengths and development needs; and using knowledge of theories and techniques).

A review of these models by the authors resulted in the finding that there are 11 common elements across the models that inform the practice of coaching. These 11 elements include:

1. ***Ethics***

    - Practice according to an established and recognized code of professional conduct (See Chapter 12)

2. ***Self-Awareness***

    - Demonstrate awareness of own values, beliefs, behaviors, competence, and experiences
    - Recognize how values, beliefs, behaviors, competence, and experiences impact the practice of coaching and client engagements
    - Use self-awareness to manage meeting the client's, and, where relevant, the stakeholders' objectives
    - Use self-awareness to inform self-development

3. ***Self-Development***

    - Building and maintaining professional knowledge
    - Understanding and appropriately applying theory and knowledge
    - Seeking and using feedback to improve as a coach
    - Obtaining and maintaining professional credentials
    - Engaging in professional associations and networks

4. ***Contracting***

    - Defining key stakeholders
    - Identifying the coaching client
    - Defining the work to be accomplished
    - Defining the process that will be used
    - Defining the scope of the work
    - Defining boundaries
    - Defining measures of success and processes for monitoring
    - Defining terms of remuneration, if any
    - Defining role and responsibilities
    - Defining the terms of informed consent and confidentiality

5. ***Relationship Building***

    - Establishing effective working relationships with the client and key stakeholders

- Establishing and maintaining credibility and trust while building a professional **reputation**

6. Basic Coaching Skills

- Communicating and listening for understanding
- Reflecting
- Asking powerful questions
- Providing insight and feedback
- Using assessments
- Exploring possible actions
- Action planning
- Gaining commitment
- Exploring and addressing obstacles for success
- Insuring accountability
- Developing networks of support

7. Coaching Process Skills

- Planning and goal setting
- Identifying courses of action and analyzing the consequences of each

8. Getting to Desired Results/Outcomes

- Managing progress and accountability
- Facilitating the client's desired goals during the coaching process, including monitoring client progress, decision making, and use of resources

9. Using Models and Tools

- Identifying and consciously applying models and tools appropriately to serve clients
- Using assessments to support client goal achievement

10. Organizational Acumen

- Understanding the organizational context and applying it to the coaching engagement

- Understanding and applying key terms and concepts associated with the organizational setting

11. Evaluating

- Personal performance as a coach
- Impact of the coaching
- Assessment of competence

Essential Coaching Skills

From the 11 common elements that inform the practice of coaching explored in the previous section, the authors propose that there are six essential coaching skills. These essential coaching skills can be split between foundational and applied skills. Foundational skills involve listening for understanding, identifying and asking powerful questions, and helping the client reframe or broaden the possibilities for awareness and action. These serve as a basis for the applied skills and are used more frequently during coaching conversations. Applied skills involve providing feedback and providing insight—both skills that help the client develop understanding and commitment for action. Another applied coaching skill is building partnerships for support in order to continue to sustain and evolve behavioral change.

Foundational Coaching Skills

- Listening for understanding
- Asking powerful questions
- Reframing

Applied Coaching Skills

- Providing feedback
- Providing insight
- Building support

In the sections that follow, the authors will explore and further develop each of these six essential coaching skills, considering how they help individuals coach in the most effective way possible.

Listening for Understanding

It has often been said that one of the best ways to demonstrate respect for others is to listen to them. In the context of coaching, listening is more than simply making sense of what the client says. Listening involves detecting what is *not* spoken and making sense of it by connecting data observed and gathered from other sources. These sources may be from assessment data (e.g., Myers-Briggs Type Indicator®, ViaEDGE™, Hogan Personality Inventory, WorkPlace **Big Five** Profile™, Benchmarks®, 360° Profiler) and from observations of the client or interviews with key stakeholders (peers, direct reports, customers, and managers). Coaches are constantly engaged in both sending and receiving messages in many different forms to and from their clients, and this process of sending and receiving messages is at the heart of communication in any context. Communication is a two-way street, and receiving the message is just as important as sending it. The key to receiving messages is listening for understanding.

One challenge associated with communication is that of accurately understanding the message being sent. When a client communicates during a coaching session, a message is sent. However, the client may have difficulty articulating the message, and it may not be perceived or understood by the coach in the same manner in which it was intended. When this situation occurs, the usual result is miscommunication or misunderstanding. Therefore, the coach's role is to help the client form that message and effectively send it to the coach (and clarify it for herself). This process of discovery is facilitated by the coach's asking powerful questions and providing feedback—two coaching skills that will be explored in detail later in this chapter.

Being aware of the filters the client may be using to communicate—as well as the filters the coach is using to interpret the message—may be useful as a means of reducing miscommunication and misunderstanding. Filters are the values, beliefs, and assumptions that influence, consciously or unconsciously, the message sending and the message receiving. In their book, *Effective Listening Skills,* Kratz and Kratz (1995) described five types or purposes of listening:

1. Listening to bond
2. Listening to appreciate
3. Listening to learn
4. Listening to decide
5. Listening to enable

The coach may use all five types of listening.

In the coaching conversation, the coach will typically spend 70–80 percent of the time listening to understand. The authors recommend that coaches strive to speak no more than 20 percent of the time during a coaching conversation, allowing the client to speak at least 80 percent of the time. Following this guideline will make statements and questions made by the coach more impactful.

Challenges to Listening Most people spend more time listening than they do any other communication activity, yet relatively few learn to listen well. One reason is that people develop poor listening habits that continue throughout their lifetimes. The following list contains some of the most common poor-listening habits:

- Not paying attention. Listeners may allow themselves to be distracted or to think of something else. In addition, not having the intention to listen often contributes to lack of attention.
- Pseudo-listening. Many times, people who are thinking about something else deliberately try to act as though they are listening. Such pretense may leave the speaker with the impression that the listener has heard some important information or instructions offered by the speaker, when the listener actually has not.
- Listening but not **hearing**. Sometimes a person listens only to facts or details—or to the way in which they are presented—missing the true meaning behind the words.
- Rehearsing. Some people listen until they want to say something—then they quit listening, start rehearsing what they will say, and shift their focus from listening to waiting for an opportunity to respond.
- Interrupting. The listener does not wait until the complete meaning can be determined but interrupts so forcefully that the speaker stops in mid-sentence.
- Hearing what is expected. People often hear, or think they hear, what they expect the speaker to say. Alternatively, they refuse to hear what they do not want to hear.
- Feeling defensive. Listeners assume they know the speaker's intention, or for various other reasons the listeners expect to be attacked.
- Listening for a point of disagreement. Some listeners wait for the chance to attack someone, listening intently for points on which they can disagree. (Marcic, Seltzer, & Vaill, 2000)

Techniques to Enhance Listening There are a variety of techniques available to help make practitioners better listeners. Here are some of the most effective:

Attending involves establishing and maintaining the culturally appropriate eye contact with the client while maintaining a natural, relaxed physical posture that demonstrates interest. This technique is supported by using natural gestures that emphasize the coach's intended message and by using verbal statements that relate to client statements without interruptions, questions, or new topics. It is important to convey that the coach understands the client's thoughts before responding.

Paraphrasing is a way to demonstrate to the client that his or her thoughts are heard and understood. It is a nonjudgmental way of validating that the coach believes the client's ideas are legitimate and respected. Paraphrasing provides the client an opportunity to hear how his ideas are being heard. Paraphrasing serves to clarify what is heard and encourages the client to think out loud in response. To paraphrase is to provide a concise response to the client that states the essence of the client's content in the coach's own words. Phrases that might be used to paraphrase include:

- It sounds like you are saying . . .
- Let me test my understanding of what I heard you say . . .

Once the client's thoughts have been paraphrased, pause and wait for the client to respond. The client's response may take one or more of the following forms: agree, seek to clarify, disagree, extend what has been paraphrased, or shift the focus of the conversation.

Drawing people out is another skill that can be applied to support clients in clarifying, developing, and refining their ideas. Drawing out demonstrates support and helps clients further explore what matters to them. It is particularly useful when someone is having difficulty clarifying an idea and when someone does not realize he is being vague and confusing to the listener. Drawing people out may also be used in coaching when the coach is not sure she understands what the client is trying to say. Phrases that might be used to draw people out include:

- Please say more about that.
- What do you mean by . . .?
- How is that working for you?
- What thoughts/feelings does that bring up for you?
- Tell me more.
- How does that appear?

Mirroring is a structured, more formal version of paraphrasing that demonstrates the coach's neutrality and builds trust. This technique is particularly useful in the early stages of a coaching relationship or during a particularly challenging conversation. Mirroring can speed up the flow of the coaching conversation and be used to facilitate idea generation. To mirror, repeat verbatim the client's words (substituting "I" for "you"). Restate the feelings and/or content of what the client communicated, while demonstrating understanding and acceptance. Try to mirror the words, pace, volume, tone, and gestures of the client. For example: The client says, "I feel am confused about the direction the company is taking with the change reorganization of responsibilities." The coach might say to the client—in a tone and pace similar to that used by the client—"I hear you saying, *I am confused about my responsibilities.*"

Tracking involves keeping track of various thoughts and feelings expressed by the client in a coaching session (or over a series of coaching conversations). Clients may express multiple ideas or pose several challenges within a short period, which can be confusing to the coach and the client. Tracking makes the thoughts and feelings visible to the client and asks the client to focus. The coach's task is to listen to those thoughts and feelings and help the client focus on the ones that are most important to be addressed or considered. Tracking comprises a four-step process: (1) the coach indicates she is going to summarize the conversation, (2) the coach names the topics or concepts that have been introduced, (3) the coach checks with the client for accuracy, and (4) the coach invites the client to determine how he or she would like to proceed. In the form of statements, the coach might say:

> It appears there are at least four topics involved in the conversation at this time. I want to make sure I am tracking with you and them. The points are A, B, C, and D. Am I hearing you correctly? (Pause for confirmation and/or clarification; do not defend what you said.) Now, how would you like to proceed with our conversation?

Acknowledging feelings is another skill that can be applied to listening for understanding. In this case, the coach identifies a feeling and then names it to assist the client in recognizing and accepting the feeling. This technique involves a three-step process: (1) the coach pays attention to the difficult elements of the coaching conversation and the experiences being shared (and not) by the client, with the coach looking for cues that might indicate the presence of feelings; (2) the coach asks a question that names the feelings she sees (examples include: "It sounds like you might be feeling worried/frustrated/angry etc.?" or "From the tone of your voice, I wonder if you are feeling . . .?" or "Is that what you are feeling . . .?"); and (3) the coach uses facilitative listening to support the client to respond to the feelings the coach named.

Validating is a practice that legitimizes the client's opinion or feeling without assuming a position of agreement or disagreement. Validating facilitates the client to open up and say more. Remember, the coach supports the client in expressing the client's truth. Validating involves a three-step process: (1) the coach paraphrases or draws out the client's opinion or feeling, (2) the coach considers whether the client needs additional support, and (3) the coach offers support by acknowledging the legitimacy of what the client said. Examples of this acknowledgment include:

I see what you are saying . . .
I accept that this is important to you.
Now I see your point of view.

Empathizing is the ability to understand and share the feelings of another. When empathizing, one puts oneself in another person's shoes and tries to view the world from the other person's point of view. The coach imagines what the person might be feeling and why, then forms any insights gained into a statement of acknowledgment and support. With empathizing, the coach attempts to identify with and share the actual feelings of the person being coached. There are many ways to empathize. The basic approach is to name what it is believed the client is experiencing (e.g., anger, disappointment, rage, sadness, happiness). The coach may name the factors that led to the client's experience (e.g., "With all the work you put into the project, I imagine that you were delighted with the outcome."). Another approach is to identify concerns about sharing feelings with others. The coach might say, "I can imagine it might be difficult to talk about this topic with your colleague." With each of these approaches, the coach should ask for confirmation by providing the client an opportunity to confirm or refine a shared understanding, as it is possible to misinterpret or misrepresent the client's experiences. Empathizing can also help the client reframe the experience in order to make an action plan.

Intentional silence involves remaining silent after a client or coach has spoken for an extended period of time. Remaining silent allows the client to formulate thoughts, process thoughts, and develop the next statement. Employing intentional silence also allows the coach to reflect on what is happening in the coaching conversation and formulate a question or statement. In addition, intentional silence can be used to slow the pace of the coaching conversation.

Listening with a point of view involves listening to what a client is saying or observing actions taken, then attempting to interpret them from the perspective of a manager, team member, regulator, customer, or other person.

Summarizing involves restating what the client has said, conclusions that have been formed, options that have been developed, or actions that will be taken. Summarizing is used to focus the coaching conversation, help the client form a new perspective, or commit to a perspective that has been formed. It is important that the coach use this technique sparingly in order to avoid doing the work of the client or inserting the coach's point of view. Asking a client to summarize a portion of a coaching session, possibilities being considered, insights gained, or commitments to action that were made can also be an effective way to use the technique (Bolton, 1979; Brammer & MacDonald, 2003; Kaner, 2007).

Coaches listen with their ears and eyes, as well as with the other senses. While a client's behaviors are most easily observed—they are the artifacts—a client's thoughts are not directly observable. Coaches do have clues to these thoughts, however, through the client's behaviors (words and actions). The client's emotions are often concealed and less visible.

Coaches can help clients by listening to the behaviors, exploring thoughts, and accessing feelings in a manner that is focused on self-discovery with the aim of serving the client's goals for coaching. Intent plus action yields impact; behavior plus feelings comprises effects. In other words, when the coach's intent to serve the client is combined with the coach's supportive behaviors, the intended impact occurs. The coach's behavior will evoke feelings from the client in response.

In consulting as well as in counseling, it is often said "the presenting problem is rarely the real problem." When coaching with an emphasis on solutions and less focus on problem solving, this axiom may best be restated as "the presenting issues are rarely the real opportunities." Helping the client develop understanding and acceptance of the deeper issues and a willingness to address them will result in greater and longer-lasting impact for the coaching. This approach requires listening and exploring.

There are a variety of things coaches can do to become better listeners, including applying the following tips for better listening:

- Remove distractions
- Listen for context
- Suspend assumptions and judgment
- Remain curious/interested

- Observe body language
- Ask for clarification
- Listen to others in the same way that the coach would prefer to be listened to.

In a study by Lore Institute International, coaching clients who were surveyed indicated that they would prefer the coach to ask questions and help them explore the issues themselves. The challenge is that most coaches prefer to coach directly, while most clients prefer to receive help indirectly (Talkington, Wise, & Voss, 2002).

Asking Powerful Questions

Asking powerful questions is arguably one of the most frequently used skills of a coach, second only to listening. Kilburg (2000) promoted the idea of "requesting permission to ask questions, explore issues, challenge or push the client" (p. 116). Coaches ask questions for many reasons including to explore, to understand, to put the focus back on the person being coached, to help the client verbalize, and to self-generate questions.

Using questions to *explore* is designed to help clients do many things, such as explore their thoughts, feelings, skills, interests, goals, and perceptions. Questions are used to *understand* what the client is saying and to help the client make sense of experiences. Coaches use questions to *put the focus back on the person being coached* in order to support the independence and interdependence of the client and to avoid dependence on the coach for answers or solutions. Questions may also be used to *help the client verbalize* thoughts, feelings, concerns, or understanding. In this way, the client is kinetically engaged in the process. And, finally, coaches use questions to help clients *self-generate* questions for themselves, which allows clients to process information and experiences for themselves.

In summary, questions allow coaches to gain deeper understanding and clarity, test gaps and perceptions, and engage the client—to draw them out.

There are five basic types of questions:

1. Closed. Seeking data, getting commitment ("How many apples do you have?")
2. Open. Seeking information, expanding and exploring possibilities ("What can you tell me about your apple trees?")

3. Leading. Seeking information and indirectly shaping the answer ("Why do you like apples best?")
4. Inquiry. Inviting active inquiry ("What are the criteria for judging the best apple?")
5. Transformational. Inviting active inquiry that assists with current "box" thinking and creates a shift ("What would it take for you to begin to like apples?")

Coaches are encouraged to use open-ended questions, because they tend to engage and draw out the client. Here are eight types of open-ended questions, along with examples of each:

- Exploratory ("Have you explored or thought of . . .?" "If time and money were no obstacle, what would you do?")
- Affective ("How do you feel about leaving this job?" "How do you feel about the new working relationship?")
- Reflective ("You said . . ." "What do you think causes these difficulties?")
- Probing ("What more can you say about . . .?" "Tell me more.")
- Fresh ("What requires it to be that way?" "What do you always (think, feel or do) . . .?")
- Connecting ("What are the consequences of these actions?")
- Analytical ("What prompted that to occur?")
- Clarifying ("How exactly would you do that?")

Asking questions can be challenging for many reasons. First, consider that, generally, in human social systems (home and work) people are expected to have answers, not questions. As a result, people tend to make statements. Also consider that behind every statement is a question. In other words, making a statement answers a question. For example, when a person says, "I am taking the following action," she is responding to the question, "What am I/are you going to do?" While the question may not be stated, it exists.

Of course, there are plenty of challenges to asking questions. Here are some of the most common:

- Time pressures
- Bias for action
- Having an answer
- Being an expert
- Wanting to help

- Seeking a specific answer
- Wanting to "save" the client
- Lack of interest in what the client is saying
- Unclear purpose/desired outcome
- Not having listened to the client.

Some questions have a higher impact than others. High-impact questions are related to the client's current situation, focused on the client's agenda, asked one question at a time (no "stacking" questions), brief (15 words or less is a good rule of thumb), focused on the topic, asked in language the client understands, and are facilitative (do not prompt defense). Leeds (1987) suggests avoiding questions that begin with "why" in order to minimize defensive responses. In addition, asking "why" questions may lead to more abstract, philosophical responses from clients than asking "what" questions, which prompt clients to generate concrete options (Isaksen, Dorval, & Treffinger, 1994).

Using the coaching model presented in Chapter 4, here are examples of questions for each step in the coaching process:

***Situation*:**

- What has happened since our last coaching session?
- What is going on in your world today?
- What is going on right now?

***Goals/Needs*:**

- What would you like to focus our coaching conversation on today?
- In five years, what would you like to be doing?
- Of the three things you've mentioned, which would you like to focus on first?
- What would you like to accomplish?
- How do you need to behave today in order to get better results in the future?

***Information Gathering*:**

- What do you know that will help you address that goal?
- What is keeping you from achieving your goal?

- How do your strengths align with your job?
- As you review the experiences/data, what patterns emerge?
- How do you interpret . . .?
- What are you afraid of?
- What is going on right now?
- What have you tried before?
- What resources do you have at your disposal in terms of time, people, skills, etc.?
- Please, share more about . . .
- What is working?
- If you say "yes" to this, what are you saying "no" to?
- . . . and what else?
- How does that make you feel?
- What are you thinking right now?
- How are you different today as a result of the experience?

Possible Actions:

- What are some possible actions you can take?
- Who could you consult?
- How could you modify your current actions/thoughts to reach a different conclusion?
- What would be possible if you combined two or more of the ideas you already have?
- What could you eliminate from the possible actions you have identified in order to create a new possible action?
- Say more.
- What is possible?
- What do you want to do next?
- What is needed here?
- What other options can we think of?
- What would happen if you do that?
- What is stopping you?
- Would you consider . . .?
- I invite you to (consider, try) . . .

***Action Planning*:**

- What action will you take? By when?
- What is next?
- What is the most important next step?
- What would be a good way to accomplish the immediate goal you have?

***Summary/Agreement*:**

- What have you gained from our coaching conversation today?
- Once again, what commitments for action are you making today?

Tips

This section explored how asking powerful questions is one of the most frequently used skill of a coach and explained the many different approaches to developing this vital skill. Here are some specific steps for using questions in coaching:

1. Listen to understand.
2. Pause to process what was "heard."
3. Tune in to one's own reactions (physical and emotional).
4. Craft a question with clear intention:
   - Inquire
   - Encourage dialogue
   - Draw out additional information
   - Provide direction, not the answers.
5. Deliver the question.
6. Embrace silence; wait for a response.
7. When stuck and it's not clear what to ask next, use (author of this book) John's Magic Question: "What should I ask you next?"

Reframing

As discussed in the previous section, a great deal of emphasis in coaching skills development is placed on asking powerful questions of the person being coached. In fact, asking questions frequently results in coaches developing a sense that their point of view, perspective, insights, knowledge, and experience about the issues faced by a person being coached are not important or should be withheld. In fact, a useful coaching tool is making statements to clients that enable the clients to see issues and solutions more clearly so they can take appropriate action. People hire professional coaches for many reasons, including their knowledge, experience, insights, and perspective. If these are not provided, the person being coached may not receive the help sought.

Reframing is another important coaching skill. It involves encouraging, guiding, and supporting the client to discover different or multiple perspectives. It is particularly useful when a client is trying to make sense of a circumstance or trying to develop strategies for action. Reframing may be used at any point in the coaching process; however, it will be most likely used during the Information Gathering and Action Planning phases. Reframing helps clients achieve their goals by discovering new information and developing new strategies.

Framing is naming an issue. By naming it, a coach focuses on how to address it. *Reframing* involves questioning the existing frame. The client may discard the frame and assume a new or different one. Reframing supports challenging assumptions and beliefs, discovering new perspectives, and envisioning a new future. When reframing, the coach helps the client develop and understand multiple perspectives, learn new perspectives, develop new insights, get "unstuck," challenge assumptions/beliefs, overcome fear, create a new vision of the future, and shift from tactical to strategic thinking.

The coach can help the client reframe perspectives, assumptions, beliefs, data, time frames, outcomes, and resources using a variety of tools including metaphors, analogies, role plays, envisioning the future, multiple perspectives, reflection, and time stretching (see Table 5.1).

The coach can reframe with a statement, question, or pause. Reframing works well when the coach is able to relate to the culture, experiences, and knowledge of the person being coached, and perhaps even share them in common. For example:

- Books read or movies seen
- Job changes
- Family experiences
- Hobbies or interests such as gardening or golf.

Tips When working with a client, keep in mind the following four steps to reframing. Help the client:

- Frame the current situation and his perspective
- Reframe the situation and her perspective to gain a new understanding

Table 5.1 Reframing Strategies

REFRAMING STRATEGY	STATEMENTS/QUESTIONS BY THE COACH
Metaphors	• What image comes to mind when you think about your experience? • If you considered a color or animal that might represent how you feel, what is it? • If you were to make a map of your journey, what would be your next stop along the way?
Analogies	• That sounds like. . . . I experienced a situation that may relate. • May I share it?. . . In what, if any, ways does that relate to what you are experiencing?
Role Plays	• I will play the role of the employee whose performance you are concerned about. You play yourself. • Let's have the conversation you need to have with the employee. • If ___ were sitting in front of you right now, what would you like to say to him/her?
Envisioning the Future	• What would you like to be doing in five years? • If you could achieve this goal for yourself, how would you imagine feeling?
Multiple Perspectives	• Who has gone before you and done well with this challenge? • How did they approach it? • What is another way you could look at the issue? • Put yourself in the other person's position on this issue. • What do you see?If you were hearing someone tell you what you want to say to this person, how would you feel?
Reflection	• Think of a time when you used that skill and it worked well.
Time Stretching	• What would it look like five years from now if you were accomplishing your dream? • If you fast-forward to six months from now, how will you have changed? • Imagine it is five hours (days, weeks, months, years) from now. What will have happened?

- Reclaim a position
- Proclaim this position through his words, thoughts, and actions.

The coach plays the role of helping the client see situations differently in order to gain new awareness and then process that new meaning to learn something, gain new meaning, or generate new possibilities. The coach then helps the client reclaim her new position or understanding and develop action steps.

Providing Feedback

It has been said "feedback is a gift." And, like all gifts, the receiver assesses feedback in terms of need and desire. Sometimes, gifts are accepted and not used. Other times, they are deflected (re-gifted), and sometimes they are rejected (not accepted). When applying these basic examples to feedback in the coaching relationship, it is important that the coach give the right feedback, in the right manner, at the right time.

Through the feedback process, coaching clients see themselves as others see them. Through feedback, they also learn how the coach sees them. Feedback gives information to a client through either verbal or nonverbal communication. The information the coach gives tells the client how the client's behavior affects the client and others, how the coach and others feel about the client's behavior, and what the coach and others perceive (feedback and self-disclosure). Feedback is also a reaction by others, usually in terms of their feelings and perceptions, telling the client how the client's behavior affects others.

What Makes Feedback Effective? Feedback may be used for many reasons, including to:

- Encourage certain thoughts, feelings, behaviors
- Increase awareness of thoughts, feelings, and behaviors ("blind spots")
- Discourage or change thoughts, feelings, and behaviors.

As part of a coaching engagement, observations that form the essence of feedback may be derived from one or more sources, including:

- The coach's observation of words and behaviors that are or are not in alignment with the client's goals for change
- Multi-rater (360-degree) feedback reports
- Assessment instruments such as Change Style Indicator, Hogan Personality Inventory, **Myers-Briggs Type Indicator**, ViaEDGE, WorkPlace Big Five Profile
- Comments (written and verbal) received by the client from peers, direct reports, managers, and customers.

Johari Window The Johari Window, developed by psychologists Joseph Luft and Harry Ingham (Luft, 1970), is a well-known and often-used framework for considering feedback. One can view the model (Figure 5.2) as a communication window through which coaches give and receive information about themselves and their clients. The four panes can be viewed in terms of columns and rows. The two columns represent the self, while the two rows represent the group. Column one contains "things that I know about myself," and column two contains "things

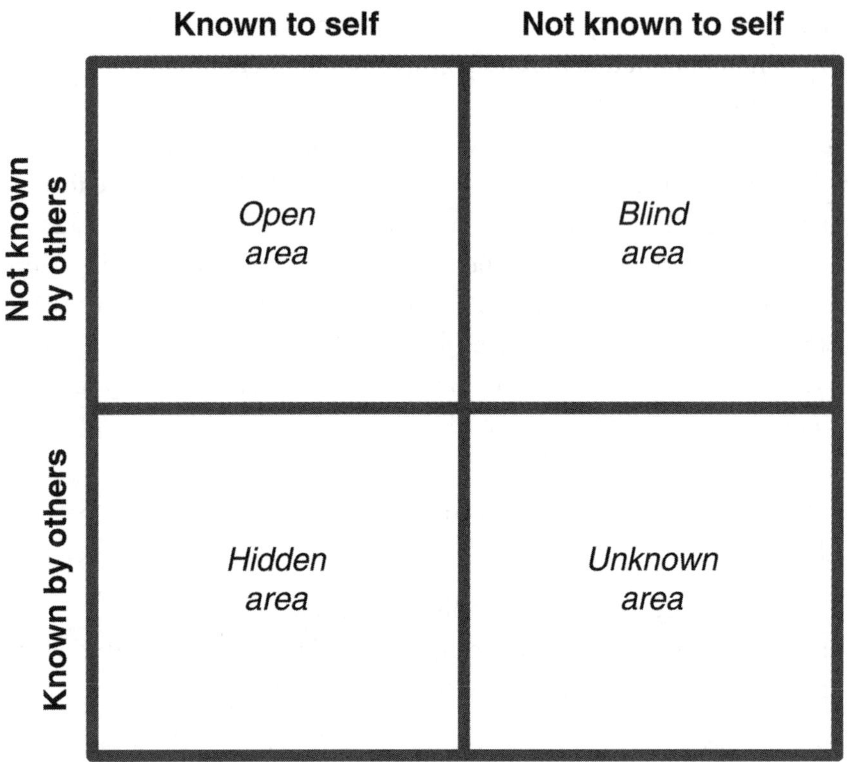

Figure 5.2 Johari Window

that I do not know about myself." The information in these rows and columns moves from one pane to another as the level of mutual trust and the exchange of feedback varies in the group. As a result of this movement, the size and shape of the panes within the window will vary.

The first pane—the Arena—contains things that I know about myself and about which others know. This pane is characterized by free-and-open exchanges of information between others (including the coach) and client; this behavior is public and available to everyone. The Arena increases in size as the level of trust increases between individuals or between an individual and others. Clients share more information, particularly personally relevant information.

The second pane—the Blind Spot—contains information that the client does not know about, but that others (including the coach) may know. As the client begins to participate in interactions with others (including the coach), the client may not be aware of the information being communicated to others. Others learn this information from verbal cues, mannerisms, the way things are said, or the style in which the client relates to others. For example, the client may be unaware of looking away from a person when speaking or of throat clearing before saying something.

Pane three—the "Facade" or "Hidden Area"—contains information that the client knows about, and others (including the coach) do not know. The client keeps these things hidden from others for a variety of reasons, including fear that if the others know these feelings, perceptions, and opinions, they might reject, attack, or hurt the client. As a consequence, the client withholds this information. Before taking the risk of telling others something, the client must know there are supportive elements with the coach or other support systems. The client may want others (including the coach) to judge positively feelings, thoughts, and reactions that are revealed.

The fourth and final pane—the "Unknown"—contains things that neither the client nor others (including the coach) know. The client may never become aware of material buried far below the surface in the unconscious. The client and others may learn other material, however, through a feedback exchange. This unknown area represents intrapersonal dynamics, early childhood memories, latent potentialities, and unrecognized resources. The internal boundaries of this pane change depending on the amount of feedback sought and received. The clients knowing all about themselves is extremely unlikely, and the unknown extension in the model represents the part of the client that will remain unknown: the unconscious.

The Johari Window panes are interdependent. Changing the size of one pane forces the size of corresponding panes to change. For example, when the size of the Blind Spot or Facade panes is reduced through giving and soliciting feedback, the Arena pane might increase in size.

Principles of Effective Feedback Not all feedback is effective feedback. To be effective in providing feedback to coaching clients, consider applying the following principles:

- Be descriptive rather than judgmental or evaluative. Tell the person being coached what behavior was noticed or what happened. Focus on behaviors and impacts.
- Be specific instead of general. Describe exactly what was observed, heard, or experienced so that facts, not impressions, form the basis for the feedback.
- Time it. Feedback should be given as soon as practical after the situation described.
- Use hypotheses. Offer hypotheses to test one's impressions and conclusions.
- Focus on what can be changed. Make suggestions for change that clients are capable of implementing and that are aligned with their goals.

- Check the feedback. Make sure one's understanding is accurate and fair. Check with the client to avoid misjudging the situation or behavior.
- Demonstrate care. Offer feedback with the positive intent of helping the other person.

Before offering feedback in a coaching situation, there are a variety of things to first consider. When offering feedback, coaches should first ask themselves the following questions:

- What about me is showing up in the feedback I want to offer?
- Is the recipient open to receiving the feedback at this time?
- Am I the best person to deliver the feedback?
- What is the best way to convey the message (tailoring the message) to this person?
- What evidence do I have to support the feedback I will offer?
- What are my expectations of the person to whom I am offering the feedback?
- How will I respond to a wide range of potential responses from the recipient?

Feedback Models

Satir A model attributed to family therapy expert Virginia Satir provides a framework for coaches to use when giving feedback (Seashore, Seashore, & Weinberg, 1997). Here is how the model flows:

- A *message is sent* (use of eyes, ears, skin, etc.) that *elicits*
- *Meaning* (here and now) that *triggers*
- *Feelings about the meaning* (past and present) that *activate*
- *Feelings about those feelings* (OK or not OK) that *evoke*
- *Defenses* (denying, ignoring, projecting, distorting) that *require*
- *Rules for commenting* (compulsion and choice) that *direct*
- *Responses* (congruent or incongruent).

CBIR One approach to delivering feedback is known by its acronym CBIR, which stands for:

- **C**ontext
- **B**ehavior
- **I**mpact
- **R**equest.

Here are two examples of how CBIR can be used as an effective framework for delivering feedback in a coaching context:

Example 1: "Yesterday, in the meeting about the new project (context), I noticed that you spoke up more than usual and offered several useful questions and suggestions for the team (behavior). This input helped us see the project in a different way and develop strategies that had not been considered (impact). Please continue to speak up and share your questions and ideas (request). Doing so will help all of us do a better job."

Example 2: "I've noticed over the past three weeks (context) that you have been making more mistakes on the reports you have been analyzing for the team (behavior). In particular, the reports have had both content and grammatical errors. In addition, the level of analysis has not been as thorough as you have performed in the past or that we expect (behavior). As a result, the reports have been returned to you for additional work, I have had to review them more often and more thoroughly than I would expect, and we have been late distributing our weekly reports (impact). Please tell me what can be done to correct this going forward (request).

SBI Another model—the SBI Model, used by the Center for Creative Leadership—is similar to CBIR. It is used to refer to the perception of performance in three areas: the **S**ituation in which the behavior occurred, the **B**ehavior, and the **I**mpact of that behavior on others (Kirkland and Manoogian, 2001). For purposes of coaching, it may also be used to refer to how the behavior was perceived to impact the client's espoused goals.

Feedback may enter the coaching engagement from one or more sources:

- Peer
- Manager
- Spouse or significant other
- Customer or client
- Vendor or supplier
- Team member.

The feedback provided in a coaching engagement may be offered in one or more of these forms:

- Informal comment
- Performance review
- Multi-rater feedback

- Customer feedback
- Email.

Feedback may be related to any one of a wide variety of possible organizational topics, for example:

- Performance
- Executive presence
- Interpersonal relationships
- Career advancement.

Reactions to Feedback

Feedback is offered to help the person being coached change. That change may range from continuing a behavior that is being developed, shifting to a new behavior, making sense of an event or feeling, or opening new possibilities for consideration. The responses may include denial/rejection, or anger related to the facts and perceptions associated with the feedback, or bargaining about the data. Certainly, the intent of the coach in offering the feedback is to help the client gain new awareness that can be used to develop skills and shift the client's mindset and behavior. The coach needs to be prepared for a wide range of responses and the possibility that the initial response will not be the longer-term response.

The client may take one of several approaches to dealing with the feedback that was offered. Consider that feedback may be disconcerting, empowering, or affirming. The client may have initial responses that change as the feedback is considered and a means of addressing it in a positive and constructive manner is developed. As the coach, it is important to provide the feedback and pause. Allow the client to receive the feedback and process it. Do not over explain the feedback and do not try to soften the message being delivered.

The client, upon hearing the coach's feedback, is faced with a number of choices as to how to react or respond. Clients may or may not be aware of the ways in which they attributed the choices they are making. Edie Seashore, a pioneer in the field of organization development and the use of "self," developed a theory of choice awareness that offers a framework for processing feedback and choices made. She refers to this as the Choice Awareness Matrix (Patwell & Seashore, 2006) (see Figure 5.3).

Individuals make choices about how they attribute decisions and actions. The attribution may be to themselves or others. These choices may be made

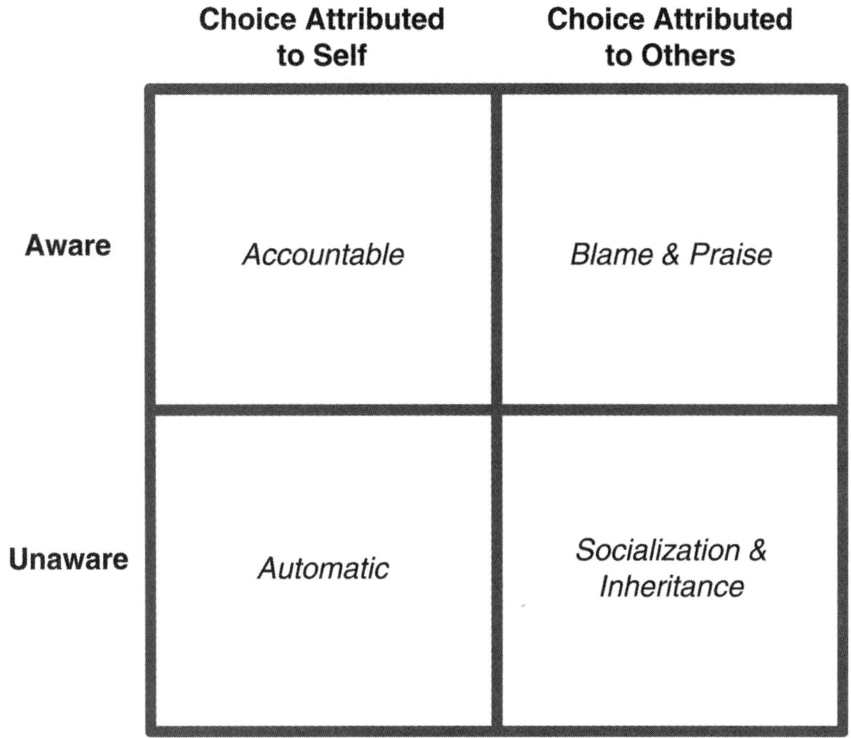

Figure 5.3 Choice Awareness Matrix

Used with permission.

consciously or unconsciously (aware or unaware). If the choice is attributed to others and is in the unaware category, it is called socialization, which may include following the norms of a group, organization, or social culture. Phrases that illustrate this approach include: "That's the way we do things around here" or "In America, we . . ." Automatic attributions of choices are in the lower-left quadrant. In this case, the choice is attributed to the person. However, the person is not aware of the choice—it is not an intentional choice. Automatic attributions may include doing something the same way it has been done for many years without consciously deciding to do it that way or considering other options. A person in this mode is not aware of his actions; reactions are automatic. Phrases used to illustrate this approach include "That's the way I do it" and "I've always done it that way."

In the upper-right quadrant is attribution to others and awareness of the choice. This quadrant is referred to as the blame quadrant. This choice can be illustrated by phrases such as, "I would have done it, but," "I've only been here a year," and "I'm new."

The fourth quadrant is where accountability for choices resides. The individual is responsible for the choices made and the impact of those choices. Phrases that illustrate this mode include "I made that decision" and "It was my choice to feel/act that way." The coach can use this framework to understand the level of understanding and commitment to feedback and choices made by clients, and to help clients take responsibility and be accountable for how they feel and behave, therefore, being accountable for results.

An overarching goal of coaching should be to help clients learn to seek and use feedback from various sources in an effort to continually learn and develop. The key point is that feedback is an opportunity to consider a different perspective and determine what, if any, adjustments are needed or desired. Receiving and applying feedback results in increased self-awareness and the opportunity to develop.

When a coach tends to avoid conflict or confrontations, or is challenged to process feedback from others, the coach will likely have a difficult time providing meaningful and timely feedback to clients. It is important for coaches to seek to understand their own responses to feedback as they develop the skill of providing feedback to others in the context of coaching relationships.

Language to Support Effective Feedback

When providing feedback to others in a coaching engagement, offering an opening for the feedback can help break the ice and prepare the client to receive what the coach is about to tell him. Here are examples of effective openings to feedback:

- I'd like to give you input about . . .
- I have an observation about . . .
- I have an insight that I think you might be interested in.
- I'd like to offer a suggestion, if you are interested.

Once past the opening, it can be helpful to draw from the kind of feedback language that has proven to be particularly effective over time. Here are examples of effective feedback language currently in use:

- When you . . . I sense that you are/not . . .
- I felt . . .
- I observed . . .

- You responded . . .
- You acted . . .
- You did . . .

Some feedback is better than others. Bens (2012) suggests the following principles of good feedback:

- Be descriptive rather than evaluative.
- Be specific instead of general with facts, not impressions.
- Solicit feedback rather than impose it.
- Time it to occur as soon as possible after a situation, observation, or experience.
- Focus the feedback on what can be changed—what the person is capable of implementing.
- Check the feedback to be sure it is accurate and fair.
- Demonstrate care by offering feedback with the positive intent of helping the other person.

When a coach is ready to provide feedback to a client, the authors suggest taking the following steps:

1. Notice one's behavior, thoughts, and feelings.
2. Analyze one's response.
3. Get the facts.
4. Make decisions about feedback:
   - Who is the most appropriate person to offer it?
   - When is the best time to provide it?
   - Where is the best location/setting to offer it?
   - How will the coach appropriate the person and present the feedback?
5. Prepare the delivery.
6. Deliver.

Tips

- Feedback is a gift, although it may not always be received the way in which it is intended.
- Develop a keen awareness of one's own responses to feedback (giving and receiving) in order to improve effectiveness and impact.
- Clients expect coaches to provide feedback—just do it.

- Once feedback is given, allow the recipient the opportunity and support to make meaning and take action related to the feedback.
- Own the feedback offered.
- Use facts to support claims about the client behavior observed; do not judge the person.
- Be specific.
- Always be aware of the intent for offering the feedback; make sure it is positive and constructive.

Providing Insight

"It is said that *the client holds the answers* and that the *coach helps uncovering* or discovering these answers through asking questions" (Askeland, 2009, p. 72). This approach is purely a non-directive one, and in reality, the powerful questions asked by a coach direct the client to look for answers by looking inside, gathering data, and making meaning of it. In addition to helping uncover the client's own answers, the coach is often called on to provide insights that the client might not be able to access by questioning alone.

Effective coaching is the use of "challenging." Challenging may involve seeking clarity, discovering blind spots, gaining understanding of meaning, or testing assumptions. In the therapy literature, a model of "supportive-challenge" is used. Where challenge is involved, the approach seeks to use intrinsic motivation (DiClemente & Prochaska, 1998; Miller & Rollnick, 2012). In coaching, these highlight the critical role of challenge in producing successful outcomes (Gonzalez, 2004; Hall, Otazo, & Hollenbeck, 1999; Jones & Spooner, 2006; Passmore, 2007). In general, the coach must be friendly without being a friend and balance high support with a high level of challenge—holding the client accountable—and to encourage deeper reflection and stimulate a change in circumstances that will enhance the drive to act. "Although such a level of challenge may be appropriate for individuals with high levels of resilience and who are highly functional, to provide such a level of challenge to vulnerable or dysfunctional counseling clients would be unethical" (Passmore, 2009, p. 275).

Hooijberg and Lane (2009) studied what clients of coaching engagements involving multi-rater feedback expected in terms of the role of the coaching in interpreting the data. They found that participants expected and wanted their coach to take an active role in interpreting and making action recommendations. When asked "What did your coach do that you found effective," 35 percent indicated that the coach interpreted results (gave straightforward explanation, analyzed strengths and weaknesses, analyzed gaps, and helped assimilate feedback), followed by inspired action (28 percent).

Providing insight may involve drawing on a coach's knowledge and experience base. In the context of coaching, this approach may be useful to identify areas for exploration. Providing insight may also lead to ways of helping clients discover for themselves solutions, insights, and resources. A word of caution: this skill should be used sparingly. Remember, the primary focus of coaching is to help clients discover for themselves the agenda, solutions, actions, and resources required to achieve their goals. Offering too many insights or offering them too frequently can lead to the client depending on the coach to "do the work." Coaches should help clients develop independence from the coach and an interdependency with the client's support network.

Insight should be offered as a non-judgmental description of behavior in clear and concise words and be grounded in observations of that behavior. The insight should be focused on the real issues versus some obscure or self-serving agenda. Stay focused on the client—not on others involved in the client's situations or issues.

The coach's voice can and should be heard in the coaching conversation. While using silence, asking powerful questions, and supporting the client to discover and take action are essential for effective coaching, offering the wisdom and insights of the coach is also valuable.

As stated above, providing insights to a coaching client is not a skill that is used in every coaching conversation. When it is used, here are steps to take:

1. Prepare.
2. Send the insightful message.
3. Wait in silence.
4. Listen to the defensive response.
5. Recycle the process, beginning with Step 2.
6. Focus the client on meaning-making, possible actions, and action planning.

Here are some important things to consider when providing insight:

- Listen for understanding.
- Consider how, if at all, what a coach observes and offers as insight to the client is actually a reflection of who the coach is.
- State the insight in as few of words as possible (target: 10–15 words or less).
- Be respectful and objective.
- Once the insight has been offered, stop talking; wait for a response.

Examples of Insights Consider the following example of how a coach can help a client develop insights into a work issue:

> Susan was a middle manager. She had an employee (Jane) who was new to a role that required building and maintaining effective relationships with peers across the organization. Susan had recently attended a workshop in which Situational Leadership® (Blanchard, Zigarmi, & Zigarmi, 1999; Hersey, 1984) was taught. As Susan described her situation with Jane, the coach was able to help Susan identify how she perceived Jane as an employee in the Situational Leadership framework. As the coach listened to Susan consider her options for action in helping Jane develop relationships, the coach observed that Susan could actually be treating Jane in a manner that was not in alignment with Jane's placement in the Situational Leadership model.
>
> After several attempts to get Susan to identify alternative approaches to working with Jane, the coach said, "Susan, based on your assessment of Jane, she is in a place where supporting her discovery of possible ways to develop these important relationships is possible. And, I noticed that solutions you identify are more directive in nature. Would you agree?" Susan said, "Yes. Perhaps Jane needs me to be more of a manger-coach than a supervisor in this situation. If I shift my behavior in the following ways . . . maybe it will allow me to improve the impact of my interaction with Jane."

Tips

- When possible, ground insights with data; make the observations based on low-inference data.
- Offer insights as opposed to declaring insights.
- Suggest insights or offer hypothesis, then ask the client to respond based on her observations and insights about herself.
- Be willing to be wrong or have an insight for which the client is not prepared to hear or act upon.
- Take ownership and responsibility for the insights offered.

Building Support

To reduce the client's dependency on the coach—and for the client to function effectively when the coach is not present—it is important for the client to develop, access, and use a support system. As the client is exploring possibilities, developing action plans, or establishing partners for accountability, it may be useful to help them identify individuals or groups with whom they can access information, role models, resources, and feedback.

The following questions can be used to foster partnership and build support independent of the coach:

- What is important to you in an accountability partner?
- From whom could you seek that information?
- Who in your network may have had a similar challenge and would be willing to provide you with information about their experiences?
- How might you ask someone to work with you?
- What are you doing right now that might be improved upon by developing a new partnership?

Tips:

- Help the client identify opportunities to develop partnerships for support and accountability.
- Help the client identify needs for role modeling and how to gain from the experiences of others.
- Remember that a goal of coaching is to help the client develop independence from the coach and interdependence with others.

Linking Skills to Change Coaching

While listening for understanding and asking powerful questions are used during each phase of the coaching process, other skills are more likely to be used for specific phases as illustrated in Table 5.2. This table illustrates which coaching skills are most likely to be used in each of the six steps in the essential coaching process (Chapter 4).

Table 5.2 Coaching Skills Linked to the Change Coaching Process

	SITUATION	GOALS/ NEED	GATHERING INFORMATION	POSSIBLE ACTIONS	ACTION PLANNING	SUMMARY/ AGREEMENT
Listening for Understanding	✔	✔	✔	✔	✔	✔
Asking Powerful Questions	✔	✔	✔	✔	✔	✔
Reframing			✔	✔		
Providing Feedback			✔	✔	✔	
Providing Insight			✔	✔	✔	
Building Support			✔	✔	✔	

Chapter Summary

Coaching is a competency that comprises a variety of different skills and practices that can be taught, learned, applied, and practiced. Among other things, successful coaches are educated in the art and science of coaching, they understand contemporary organizational issues and human motivation, they are self-aware, they are able to provide insights to their clients, and they have a passion for helping others grow and perform.

Coaching works best when desired outcomes are defined; organizational support exists; the organization embraces a culture of feedback, development, and support; the coaching is developmental and not corrective; and the individual is ready for coaching. Although there are many different coaching models, there are 11 common elements across all these models. These common elements include such things as ethics, self-awareness, self-development, contracting, relationship building, and organizational acumen.

Listening for understanding involves more than just processing a client's spoken words. It also requires making sense of what is not spoken by the client and of data observed and gathered from other sources: assessments, peers, direct reports, customers, and others. Coaches typically spend the majority of their time listening to understand, which allows the client to speak freely. Asking powerful questions brings information out of a client that might otherwise be unavailable, while providing effective feedback gives clients the information they need to make effective and long-lasting change.

Knowledge Check

1. List ten characteristics of an effective Change Coach.
2. What are five of the competencies of a Change Coach?
3. What are the foundational change coaching skills?
4. What are the applied change coaching skills?
5. What are two points to key in mind for each of the six coaching skills?
6. How could a coach use the Johari Window and the Choice Awareness Matrix as part of change coaching?

Learning Activities

Learning Activity 1: Listening

- Make a list of particular situations in which you use some of the poor listening habits discussed.

- Make a list of particular people with whom you use some of these poor habits.
- What about these situations and people (from the activities above) make it difficult to listen for understanding?
- How can listening practices be improved in those situations and with those people?

Learning Activity 2: Listening

- Think of a time when someone really listened to and understood you.
- Consider:
  - What was the situation?
  - Who was involved?
  - What did they do?
  - What did they not do?
  - How did it feel?
  - What impact did being heard have on your development? On your behavior?

Learning Activity 3: Listening Exercise

The purpose of this exercise is to provide practice in listening deeply, developing a helping relationship, observing the dynamics between the talker/speaker and the listener, focusing on accessing one's ignorance (lack of knowledge), and developing an ability to construct helpful questions. In completing the exercise, keep the following in mind:

- Try to be helpful—always.
- Stay in touch with the current reality.
- Access one's ignorance.
- Remember that everything one does is an intervention.
- Remember that the client owns the problem and is responsible for solving it.
- Go with the flow.

Instructions:
Think of a skill you successfully used to establish a "helping relationship" with a client, friend, or co-worker, and think of a skill to be improved. Share those skills with the group.

Think of a current unresolved challenge at work or home. Form triads (three-person teams) and spend 1–2 minutes each telling a story about the problem. Pick one of the stories to be told in depth over a period of about 10 minutes.

Choose one person to play the role of client. Have the "client" tell the challenge in detail. As the client tells the story, the two partners in the triad should write down questions that help them reduce their ignorance and increase their knowledge of all the facts, feelings, actions, and consequences of this problem. Make it a point not to ask questions or react to the story with advice, judgments, or emotional reactions—even if asked.

After about 10 minutes, discuss together the experience and feelings for both the listeners and the client. Share the questions that would have been asked if allowed. What types of questions were generated (open ended, closed ended, clarifying, probing, etc.)? Ask the client which questions would have been most helpful and which questions may have hindered the helping process.

Then, as a group, discuss the experience: what was observed about the experience, how did it feel, what was learned, and what will be done differently in the next helping role? Provide feedback to one another about the skills successfully used and skills they were trying to improve (Schein, 1999).

Learning Activity 4: Asking Questions

Using the coaching model described in Chapter 4, develop four questions for each step in the coaching process. Share the questions with a colleague and ask for feedback. Ask them to consider:

- Are the questions clear?
- Are the questions leading or have embedded information?
- Does the question support the step for which it was written?
- Is only one question being asked—no stacking?
- Do the questions invite a response?
- How many of the questions are closed-ended versus open-ended?

Learning Activity 5: Observing Oneself

During a conversation or meeting, pay attention to the statements that are made and the questions that are asked. How many of the statements are made under the assumption that a question was asked? Did the people hearing the statement actually have the question in their mind or was the statement based on the presenter's assumption of the listeners' need or desire to know? How many questions were asked? What made them effective, or not? How could the questions have been restated for higher impact?

Learning Activity 6: Reframing

Review a conversation you have had or heard that relates to a challenge or obstacle to performance. List as many of the claims and barriers named during the conversation. Identify two ways to reframe each claim and barrier using the information in this chapter.

Learning Activity 7: Providing Insight

Reword the following statements to make them clearer, more insightful, and more impactful. Try using 15 or fewer words.

Example A: I know you are busy and that developing the department budget is not one of your personal priorities, however, the boss is asking for it. Would it be possible for you to reassess your priorities in order to get the department budget ready in the next few days? What do you think? Is there anything I can do for you?

Example B: We have been working together for several months now, and I think I am beginning to understand you. It appears to me that you might, possibly, be having difficulty facing the poor performance issues related to Sam. I wonder if you are having difficulty, and if we need to talk about it.

Learning Activity 8: Coaching Case for Practice (A)

- **Gender:** Male
- **Race:** White
- **Age:** 53
- **Family:** 4 children, 2 grandchildren
- **Sexual Orientation**: Heterosexual
- **Marital/Partner Status**: Married
- **Education:** MA Marketing
- **Position:** Senior Vice President
- **Industry:** Healthcare
- **Business Transition:** Turning around a group or business

- **Role Transition:** Managing other managers
- **Personal Transition:** Managing strategic differences with a boss
- **Leadership Challenges:**
  - Balancing competition and cooperation among peers
  - Being right versus being effective—appreciating that peer conflicts taint all involved, regardless of who is "right"
  - Being overwhelmed (Benjamin & O'Reilly, 2011)
  - Dealing with poor performers and problem employees

Questions to Consider:

- What is known about the client that will help you prepare to coach him?
- What are the coach's strengths/limitations related to coaching this client?
- What will the approach be?

Learning Activity 9: Coaching Case for Practice (B)

- **Gender:** Female
- **Race:** African American
- **Age:** 45
- **Family:** 3 children
- **Sexual Orientation**: Heterosexual
- **Marital/Partner Status**: Married
- **Education**: MBA
- **Position:** Vice President/Managing Director
- **Industry:** Insurance
- **Business Transition**: Growth
- **Role Transition:** From taking responsibility for team performance to managing managers
- **Personal Transition:** Managing strategic differences with a boss
- **Leadership Challenges:**
  - Appreciating the importance of B and C players—not just A players
  - Listening to others rather than problem solving
  - Maintaining poise and composure under pressure
  - Dealing with poor performers and problem employees (Benjamin & O'Reilly, 2011)

Questions to Consider:

- What is known about the client that will help you prepare to coach her?
- What are the coach's strengths/limitations related to coaching this client?
- What will the approach be?

References

Askeland, M. K. (2009). A reflexive inquiry into the ideologies and theoretical assumptions of coaching. *Coaching: An International Journal of Theory, Research & Practice, 2*(1), 65–75.

Benjamin, B., & O'Reilly, C. (2011). Becoming a leader: Early career challenges faced by MBA graduates. *Academy of Management Learning & Education, 10*(3), 452–472.

Bennett, J. L., & Lazar, J. (2011). *Managing expectations, enabling results* (webinar series). International Consortium for Coaching in Organizations.

Bens, I. (2012). *Facilitating with ease! Core skills for facilitators, team leaders and members, managers, consultants, and trainers* (3rd ed.). San Francisco, CA: Jossey-Bass.

Bergquist, W., Merritt, K., & Phillips, S. (Eds.). (1999). *Executive coaching: An appreciative approach.* Sacramento, CA: Pacific Soundings Press.

Blanchard, K., Zigarmi, P., & Zigarmi, D. (1999). *Leadership and the one-minute manager: Increasing effectiveness through situational leadership.* New York: William Morrow.

Bolton, R. (1979). *People skills: How to assert yourself, listen to others, and resolve conflicts.* New York, NY: Simon & Schuster.

Brammer, L. M., & MacDonald, G. (2003). *The helping relationship: Process and skills* (8th ed.). Boston, MA: Allyn and Bacon.

Bush, M. W. (2005). *Client perceptions of effectiveness in executive coaching.* Dissertation. Pepperdine University.

Crane, T. G. (2001). *The heart of coaching: Using transformational coaching to create a high-performance culture.* San Diego, CA: FTA Press.

DiClemente, C., & Prochaska, J. (1998). Toward a comprehensive, transtheoretical model of change. In W. Miller & N. Heather (Eds.), *Treating addictive behaviours* (pp. 3-24). New York: Plenum Press.

Flaherty, J. (1999). *Coaching: Evoking excellence in others.* Boston, MA: Butterworth-Heinemann Publishers.

Gonzalez, A. L. (2004). Transforming conversations: Executive coaches and business leaders in dialogical collaboration for growth. *Dissertation Abstract International Section A: Humanities and Social Science,* Vol. 65 (3-A) 1023. Ann Arbor, MI: Proquest, International Microfilms International.

Guthrie, V. A. (1999). *Coaching for action: A report on long-term advising in a program context.* Greensboro, NC: Center for Creative Leadership.

Hall, D. T., Otazo, K. L., & Hollenbeck, G. P. (Winter, 1999). Behind closed doors: What really happens in executive coaching. *Organizational Dynamics, 27*(3), 39–54.

Hargrove, R. (1995). *Masterful coaching: Extraordinary results by impacting people and the way they think and work together.* San Francisco, CA: Jossey-Bass.

Hersey, P. (1984). *The situational leader.* Escondido, CA: Warner Books.

Hooijberg, R., & Lane, N. (2009). Using multisource feedback coaching effectively in executive education. *Academy of Management Learning & Education, 8*(4), 483–493.

Hudson, F. M. (1999). *The handbook of coaching.* San Francisco, CA: Jossey-Bass.

Jones, G., & Spooner, K. (2006). Coaching high achievers. *Consulting Psychology Journal: Practice and Research, 58*(1), 40–50.

Isaksen, S. G., Dorval, K. B., & Treffinger, D. J. (1994). *Creative approaches to problem solving.* Dubuque, IA: Kendall-Hunt.

Kaner, S. (2007). *Facilitator's guide to participatory decision-making* (2nd ed.). San Francisco, CA: Jossey-Bass.

Kilburg, R. R. (2000). *Executive coaching: Developing managerial wisdom in a world of chaos.* Washington, DC: American Psychological Association.

Kirkland, K., & Manoogian, S. (2001). *Ongoing feedback: How to get it, how to use it.* Greensboro, NC: Center for Creative Leadership.

Kombarakaran, F. A., Yang, J. A., Baker, M. N., & Fernandes, P. E. (2008). Executive coaching: It works! *Consulting Psychology Journal: Practice and Research, 60*(1), 78–90.

Kratz, D. M., & Kratz, A. R. (1995). *Effective listening skills.* Boston, MA: McGraw Hill.

Leeds, D. (1987). *Smart questions: The essential strategy for successful managers.* New York, NY: The Berkley Publishing Group.

Luft, J. (1970). *Group processes: An introduction to group dynamics* (2nd ed.). Palo Alto, CA: Mayfield Publishing Company.

Marcic, D., Seltzer, J., & Vaill, P. B. (2000). *Organizational behavior: Experiences & cases* (6th ed.). Cincinnati, OH: South-Western.

Miller, W. R., & Rollnick, S. (2012). *Motivational interviewing: Helping people change* (3rd ed.). New York, NY: The Guilford Press.

Newsom, G., & Dent, E. B. (2011). A work behaviour analysis of executive coaches. *International Journal of Evidence Based Coaching & Mentoring, 9*(2), 1–22.

O'Neill, M. B. (2007, Summer). *Executive coaching with backbone and heart: A systems approach to engaging leaders with their challenges* (2nd ed.). San Francisco, CA: Jossey-Bass.

Passmore, J. (2007, Summer). Coaching and mentoring—The role of experience and sector knowledge. *International Journal of Evidence Based Coaching and Mentoring*, 10–16.

Passmore, J. (2009). Seeing beyond the obvious: Executive coaching and I-O psychologists. *Industrial and Organizational Psychology: Perspectives on Science and Practice, 2*(3), 272–276.

Patwell, B., & Seashore, E. W. (2006). *Triple impact coaching: Use-of-self in the coaching process.* Columbia, MD: Bingham House Books.

Rogers, C. R. (1989). *On becoming a person: A therapist's view of psychotherapy.* Boston, MA: Houghton Mifflin Company.

Schein, E. H. (1999). *Process consultation revisited: Building the helping relationship.* Reading, PA: Addison-Wesley.

Seashore, C. N., Seashore, E. W., & Weinberg, G. M. (1997). *What did you say? The art of giving and receiving feedback.* Columbia, MD: Bingham House Books.

Stern, L. R. (2008). *Executive coaching: Building and managing your professional practice.* Hoboken, NJ: John Wiley & Sons.

Storjohann, G. (2006). This thing called coaching: A consultant's story. *OD Practitioner, 38*(3), 12–16.

Talkington, A. W., Wise, L. S., & Voss, P. S. (2002). The case for executive coaching: A research report: Lore Research Institute.

PART II
CHANGE

6
Organizational Change

This chapter will address organizational change—what it is, the different types of change, and why leading and managing change is a vital competency for organizations and the people who lead them. Key topics to be addressed are:

- What is organizational change?
- What are the causes and conditions for organizational change?
- What are the types of organizational change?
- What are the stages of organizational change?
- What promotes successful change, and why does change often fail?
- Why is leading and managing change a vital competency for organizations?

Change can be defined as making or becoming something different. It is a constant state for individuals, groups, and organizations alike. But for today's organizations, change is occurring at unprecedented rates. This fact is not a surprise, given the impact of dynamic environments, social and global systems, new technology, competition, and scientific discoveries. Entirely new industries are being created and expanded around the globe, while old industries are fading away. For example, who in 1969 would have anticipated the profound impact that the newly invented Internet would have on the world within just a few decades? Or the near-extinction of film cameras, superseded for the most part today by digital cameras and mobile phones? As an IBM study on global change declared, "Change is the new normal."

> Today's dynamic work environment is causing organizations to reframe the traditional view of what "normal" is. We are witnessing the effects of globalization, technology advances, complex multinational organizations, more frequent partnering across national borders and company boundaries—just to mention a few of the enablers and accelerators of change. No longer will companies have the luxury of expecting day-to-day operations to fall into a static or predictable pattern that is interrupted only occasionally by

Table 6.1 Types of Change

Individual	• New role or responsibility • New process or performance expectation • New location or culture
Group	• Performance review or audit • New or changing membership or team charter • Improvement of existing product or policy • New process or product
Organization	• New product development • New or adjacent market entry • New leader/strategy/direction • Organization redesign/restructuring • Merger/acquisition

> short bursts of change. To prosper, leaders will need to abandon such outdated notions of change. In reality, the new normal is continuous change—not the absence of change. (Jørgensen, Owens, & Neus, 2008, p. 6)

All of this means change is occurring within every level of organizations, including the for-profit, not-for-profit, and public sectors. In addition, changes within organizations often occur simultaneously—such as a change in technology systems at the same time two organizations undertake a merger concurrently with a new-product release. Harvard Business School's Professor John Kotter (1996) predicted more than a decade ago, "The rate of change in the business world is not going to slow down anytime soon. If anything, competition in most industries will probably speed up over the next few decades" (p. 161). Table 6.1 identifies examples of change at the individual, group, and organization levels.

By most every measure, Kotter's prediction has turned out to be true. As IBM's study on global change confirms, "Today's dynamic work environment is causing organizations to reframe the traditional view of what 'normal' is" (Jørgensen et al., 2008, p. 6). In effect, there is no "going back to the way things were." There is no more long-term stability in business, or in the ways that organizations do business. Companies no longer have the luxury of expecting day-to-day operations to maintain a static or predictable pattern, occasionally interrupted by short bursts of change. "It is no longer appropriate to consider organizational change as a project or event, with a clearly defined beginning or end" (Corporate Leadership Council, 2003, p. 1).

What Is Organizational Change?

(Hiatt & Creasey, 2002, n.p.) defined organizational change as "the process, tools and techniques to manage the people-side of business change to achieve the required business outcome, and to realize that business change effectively within the social infrastructure of the workplace" (Hiatt & Creasey, 2002). Because change is the new normal for organizations, the ability to adapt and prosper while changing is a key competitive advantage.

Conner emphasizes the focus on the human capital impacts of change in his 2013 definition: "Change Management: a set of principles, techniques and prescriptions applied to the human aspects of executing change initiatives in organizational settings. Its focus is not on 'what' is changing, but how' to prepare people to absorb the implications affecting them" (p. 13).

Cummings and Worley (2009) referred to "**planned change**" that is undertaken to improve an organization's effectiveness, typically "involving a series of activities for carrying out effective organization development" (p. 41):

> It [planned change] is generally initiated and implemented by managers, often with the help of an OD practitioner from inside or outside of the organization. Organizations can use planned change to solve problems, to learn from experience, to adapt to external environmental changes, to improve performance, and to influence future changes. (p. 23)

While random, unanticipated changes can occur in any setting, successful organizational change at any level is planned, led, or managed, with outcomes that are realized and sustained.

> With the force of constant change impacting leaders, organizations, and team members, change is indeed the "new normal" in organizational life. The challenge is to lead it, manage it, learn from it, and leverage it as an opportunity for continuous improvement. (Bennett & Bush, 2013, p. 282)

The bottom line for organizations, and individuals who work in them, is that change is here to stay. Whether change is planned, anticipated, sought after, or is an unexpected factor, change will occur. The best strategy for organizations—and people—is to proactively identify and address both internal and external factors that may introduce change.

What Causes Organizational Change?

There are two major sources of change in organizations. The first source of change is external (sometimes catastrophic or unexpected), such as when a hurricane destroys an offshore oil drilling platform, or when a change in tax laws causes an organization to modify its cash-management strategies, or when customer expectations shift. The second source of change is internal, such as the planned, strategic response to environmental changes or a transition in leadership.

There are three main reasons that organizations or groups choose to change: performance, development, and transformation:

Performance: accelerating or improving effectiveness and/or efficiency to meet or anticipate external environmental factors or gain a competitive advantage. In organizations, performance can center on operations or financials, meeting the challenge of a new technology that has been introduced to the market, new government regulations, an environmental or global imperative, or a perceived threat from a competitor. For example:

- The rapid proliferation of the Internet and its use by businesses beginning in the 1980s and extending through today.
- The enforcement of new clean air regulations in the United States, which cost businesses some $21 billion in lost productivity and necessitated changes in corporate equipment and performance (Greenstone, List, & Syverson, 2012).

Development: adding, improving, or strengthen ementing a new material requirements planning (MRP) system, or instigating a cost-savings strategy through lean manufacturing. For example:

- The adoption of lean manufacturing techniques by Duramax Marine, leading to efficiencies and cost savings as jobs are released to the floor and purchase orders issued more quickly.
- The rehiring by McDonald's of retired CEO James Cantalupo in 2001 to focus on reversing a two-year-plus decline in sales.

Transformation: growth or expansion through new corporate identity and branding, or introduction of a new product or competency, and in organizations, a new territory, merger and acquisition, or market expansion. For example:

- The introduction of Apple's iPhone, adding a smartphone to its computer product line, and growing the company from just over a million units sold worldwide in 2007 to more than 125 million units sold in 2012 (Apple iPhone Sales in Fiscal Years 2007–2012, n. d.).
- The transformation of Amazon.com from an online bookstore in 1994 to one of the world's largest online retail destinations for good of all types, including gourmet food, clothing, appliances, jewelry and lawn care items.

Success and Challenges in Organizational Change

What makes change succeed? With the proliferation of change, and the frequency and scope of its impact on organizations, this is a topic that interests most leaders today. And most authors agree that engaging leaders to drive change is imperative for success.

> Change has to start at the top because otherwise defensive senior managers are likely to disown any transformation in reasoning patterns coming from below. If professionals or middle managers begin to change the way they reason and act, such changes are likely to appear strange—if not actually dangerous—to those at the top. The result is an unstable situation where senior managers still believe that it is a sign of caring and sensitivity to bypass and cover up difficult issues, while their subordinates see the very same actions as defensive. (Argyris, 1991, p. 11)

Holman offers seven themes that were found in her research on change methods. These themes identify elements that support successful change:

- Envisioning a meaningful purpose—something larger than themselves—compels people into action.
- The power of individual contribution is unleashed.
- The whole person—head, heart, and spirit—is engaged.
- Knowledge and wisdom exist within the people in the organization or community.
- Information is co-created by members of the organization or community.
- The method creates a whole-systems view among members of the organization or community.
- Change is a process, not an event (Holman, 1999, pp. 4–5).

A 2012 study by Creasey & Hiatt suggests that the greatest contributors to change success are:

- Active and visible executive sponsorship
- Frequent and open communication about the change
- Structured change management approach
- Dedicated change management resources and funding
- Employee engagement and participation
- Engagement with and support from middle management (p. 9).

Their research found that that effective change management improved the ability to meet objectives and stay on schedule and budget, mirroring findings from the 2007 and 2009 studies. "Projects with excellent change management programs were nearly six times more likely to meet or exceed their objectives than those with poor change management programs" (Creasey & Hiatt, 2012, p. 9). Advice from practitioners included in this report listed the use of a change methodology, integration of project management with change, use of social media, training on change management, measurement, and establishing a change management functional group or Change Management Office (CMO) (Creasey & Hiatt, 2012).

However, despite a "virtual explosion of research and managerial attention devoted to conceptualizing and empirically testing a range of change management practices" (Kerber & Buono, 2010, p. 4), current rates of organizational change success are low. A worldwide survey of CEOs reported that the rate of those who had successfully managed change in the past increased just 4 percentage points, from 57 percent in 2006 to 61 percent in 2008 (Jørgensen et al., 2008). Maurer's research found that 70 percent of all changes fail (Maurer, 2010). A study by McKinsey found that only one-third of organizational change initiatives were viewed as successful by their leaders (Meaney & Pung, 2008), and a report by Right Management summarizes the current situation as:

> Although vital to organizational success, companies seldom plan, implement and execute effective change management processes as part of their workforce management strategy. Failure to do so can severely impair a company's performance and its very ability to compete. (Haid, Schroeder-Saulnier, Sims, Wang, & Urban, 2009, p. 4)

Prosci's research of more than 320 change projects showed the primary reason for failure in major change initiatives was an inability to manage the people side of a business's changes, taking into account culture and values changes in the organization. "Not managing the people side of change impacted their success and introduced risk into their projects" (Creasey & Hiatt, 2003, pp. 3–4). In any case, it is clear that an understanding of, and respect for, the complexity of organizational change is a prerequisite for its success. Higgs and Rowland (2011) have shown evidence that approaching change with an understanding of the complexity of the phenomenon plays a significant role in ensuring successful implementation.

Why is Leading and Managing Change a Vital Competency for Organizations?

The IBM study on global change (Jørgensen et al., 2008) concluded, "As organizations face increases in both the absolute volume of change and its level of complexity, widespread improvisation must yield to professional, formal change management methods—a priority most are beginning to recognize" (p. 24). This implication for leaders and employees alike is clear: as they face multiple layers of change occurring simultaneously, organizations must respond with agility, speed, and resilience to maintain or increase their levels of productivity and effectiveness in the wake of uncertainty and new ways of doing business.

However, Kotter (1996) notes that "The typical twentieth-century organization has not operated well in a rapidly changing environment. Structure, systems, practices, and culture have often been more of a drag on change than a facilitator" (p. 161). He warns that, for most of today's organizations, "We are talking about a great deal of rather fundamental change. That much change will not come quickly" (Kotter, 1996, p. 171). An IBM study suggested, that the "change gap" (i.e., the gap between an organization's expectation of change and its history of successfully managing it) has increased significantly over the past few years (see Jørgensen et al., 2008). The IBM study findings echo Kotter's concern:

> As the level of expected change continues to rise, many are struggling to keep up. Eight out of ten CEOs anticipate substantial or very substantial change over the next three years, yet they rate their ability to manage change 22 percent lower than their expected need for it—a "change gap" that has nearly tripled since 2006. (Jørgensen et al., 2008, p. 7)

The study confirms that the ability to manage change must be a core competence. Developing both people and systems to be flexible and agile can be a market differentiator. After even major changes, organizations that have mastered the art of change can be the first to capture opportunities that come from changing conditions and can maintain higher levels of productivity and effectiveness, due to their resilience and having increased their capacity to change. This change agility can become part of an organization's strategic advantage, and the change methodology can become a part of the culture. One study found that in continuously changing environments, organizations that adapted on an ongoing basis were more reliable (had lower variance in performance) than were organizations that remained stable over long periods of time. This study found that continuous change could affect an organization positively, dramatically improving long-term performance and reducing risk, compared to organizations that experienced change infrequently (Håkonsson, Klaas, & Carroll, 2009).

Once an organization recognizes that change competency is an advantage, leaders and **change agents** can ensure that people are trained and held accountable for agility, resilience, and the ability to learn and grow from past change experiences. Systems and processes can be streamlined and adapted for flexibility and resilience, enabling the enterprise to adapt more efficiently. Companies can even anticipate coming changes by paying close attention to change drivers, and then benefit from the increased capacity to change. Rather than an event to be tamed, change becomes a "key competency that must be built into the very fabric of the company; a structured methodology that incorporates training, communicating, listening, and process analysis and redesign. It is a way of thinking that becomes part of defining the organization" (La Marsh, 1995, p. 2).

Stages of Change

Organizations and groups are not capable of changing unless and until the people within them change. A building does not change by itself; neither does a team charter nor an organization strategy. Organizational change is, inherently about individual change at the behavioral level. When well-planned and deployed, these individual changes are aligned and directed toward a common, agreed-on goal. When they are not, the changes can appear to be random and diverse, and perhaps even undermine or limit the organization's goal attainment.

Stages of change are different than change processes. Stages offer a way to observe and understand when particular shifts in attitudes, intentions, and behaviors occur over time (Prochaska, Norcross, & DiClemente, 1995). *Change processes* are elements instituted by an organization's leaders and change agents to support the change and to ensure the maximum probability of success. Examples of change processes include effective communication, a strong business case, and solid project management. The goal of implementing effective change processes is to make the change successful. *Stages of change,* however, reflect individual and organizational reactions to change over time. These stages can be observed through individual behavior and language or evidenced by the organization's support—of lack of support—of the change efforts.

The Mastery Model

The pursuit of successful organizational change is a progressive process that predictably follows five stages: awareness, acceptance, adoption, integration, and mastery. These stages are outlined in the Mastery Model (see Figure 6.1) and they also describe the development of increased agility and resilience in change. The goal of moving through these stages of change is broader than successfully dealing with any one change—the goal is the development of the organization's (or individual's) capacity to change.

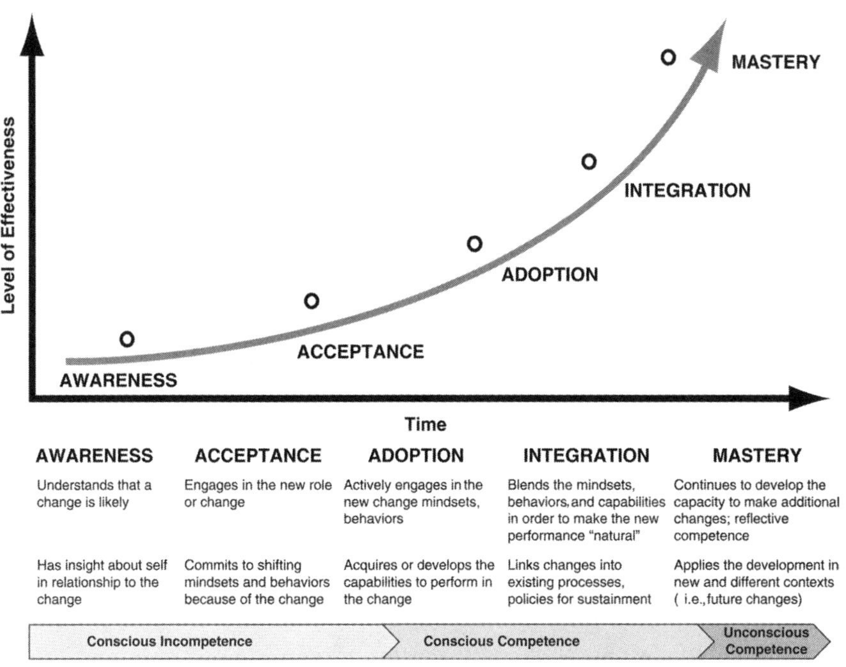

Figure 6.1 Mastery Model

This is a broader, more visionary and strategic concept than just "change management," and it requires an acceptance of change as the "new normal," employing interventions at multiple levels and requiring a longer timeframe. Such organizational capacity implies a focus on multiple, often iterative and overlapping, changes over time, which is different from the traditional view of organizational change as a series of isolated events. Building change capacity must become an ongoing, multifaceted development focus. Meyer and Stensaker (2006) define change capacity in terms of three inter-related capabilities: the capability to maintain daily operations, the capability to implement a single change, and the capability to implement subsequent changes. They argue that "the capability to effect strategic change is a core dynamic capability" and that building change-capable organizations should be a significant priority (p. 7). Developing this capacity can mean a competitive advantage and differentiation in the market for an organization.

Clients going through both coaching and change experience a similar process moving through these five stages. An individual will move through the stages of the Mastery Model during a successful coaching engagement, as self-awareness and other development occurs. And it is possible to see evidence of these stages during group and organizational change, as well. Lastly, this model is applicable to the change coach who strives to develop increasing mastery of the practice of coaching itself.

The five stages of change outlined in the Mastery Model are Awareness, Acceptance, Adoption, Integration, and Mastery (see Figure 6.1). They are described in more detail below:

Awareness. Individuals in the organization become aware that a change is imminent, planned, or needed. There is often shock, confusion, and concern at this time, especially if the change is perceived as a threat and/or is mandated without the individuals' choice. There is a reaction on at least three levels:

1. *Cognitive,* as individuals become aware of what the change will mean to them and the way they work or live.
2. *Affective,* as individuals realize the impact that the change will make to the structures, relationships, rewards, goals, and processes that have meaning for them.
3. *Behavioral,* as individuals understand what the change will mean in terms of the way they work and interact in the organization.

In the awareness stage, people seek more information or clarity about what the change involves. They need to understand what it will mean to them and how it will affect the way they work and interact with others. Prochaska et al. (1995) posit a prior stage of change for individuals, that of "pre-contemplation," where an individual is not yet aware of the need to change or is in denial of this need.

Acceptance. Individuals in the organization make peace with the change, and they explore or seek information to find out what the change will mean to them—including how to make the change successful and how to be successful with the change. There may still be concerns, confusion, and skepticism at this point, but the intention and attitude shifts from "Why should we do this?" to "How can we make this successful?" This stage can manifest on three levels:

1. *Cognitive,* as individuals learn more about what the change is about, what it will mean, and the impact it will have on the organization and themselves.
2. *Affective,* as individuals commit to shifting their mindsets and behaviors to support the change, perhaps while still having concerns or questions.
3. *Behavioral,* as individuals engage in the new way of working, try it out, make adjustments as needed to make the change work, ask questions and voice concerns, and offer feedback and suggestions for improvement.

Adoption. In this stage, individuals in the organization actively engage in the new mindsets, behaviors, and interactions that support the change. They acquire or develop the capabilities to perform in new ways, and they often help others understand and make the needed changes, as well. They act as advocates for the change and give feedback to help improve and develop the change, which can be manifest on three levels:

1. *Cognitive,* as individuals learn more about what the change is about, what it will mean, and the impact it will have on the way they work and interact with others.
2. *Affective,* as individuals commit to shifting their own mindsets and behaviors to support the change, perhaps while they still have concerns or apprehension.
3. *Behavioral,* as individuals engage in the new roles, new behaviors, vocabulary, interactions, ask questions, and offer feedback, concerns, and alternative suggestions for improvement to make the change successful.

Integration. Individuals in the organization have become used to working and interacting in the new way, and often there are results or accomplishments to show from the change that has been implemented. What was once the "new" change has by now been linked to organizational process and culture in a way that ensures it is not seen as new. The change has been embedded into existing structures, systems, and processes so that it is part of the way the organization operates and not dependent on current leadership to drive it. The change is now sustained by the organizational culture—it is now "the way we do things around here." This stage exists on three levels:

1. *Cognitive,* as individuals master the mindsets, behaviors, and capabilities to make the new change "natural"; they do not need to think about the change in order to perform or interact successfully in the new way.
2. *Affective,* believing that the change is a positive step forward, "part of the culture; the way things are done around here."
3. *Behavioral,* performing in the new way without needing to think about it; finding ways to link changes to existing processes and policies for sustainment.

Mastery. Individuals in the organization continue to integrate the change into other personal and organizational levels, perhaps with additional teams, external suppliers, or other business units. They also build increased agility and resilience, demonstrating improved capacity to make additional changes. Change management becomes an organizational differentiator and competitive advantage, which can manifest on three levels:

1. *Cognitive,* as individuals understand the benefits of being agile, flexible, and resilient, and identify ways to make change a personal and organizational differentiator.
2. *Affective*, as individuals embrace change positively as an ongoing, challenging part of organizational life, and demonstrate skills and knowledge to make change a personal and organizational competency.
3. *Behavioral*, as individuals develop skill in making and integrating changes, demonstrating increased agility, flexibility, and resilience, and applying this development to change in new and different contexts (i.e., future changes).

It is important to note that not everyone in an organization embraces change or moves through the stages of change simultaneously. There is often considerable resistance, and variance in the timing and behavior of groups or individuals, but when thinking of the organizational system as a whole, it is often possible for one to see the progress through the above stages.

The goal of change coaching is to help the client (individual or group) successfully implement the desired change and to develop increased capacity to make future changes, resulting in mastery or competency. The stages described in the Mastery Model apply to the experience of moving through change, and they also relate to the mastery of any skill or subject (such as coaching).

Types of Change

While it is important to know about the stages of change that an individual or group will experience, it is also crucial for a Change Coach to be able to identify the type of change that is planned (or occurring). There are many ways to categorize change: by frequency, strategy, scope or impact, source, etc. One way has already been presented in this book: focus. Looking at change through the lens of its intended focus (performance, development, or transformation) can help a Change Coach identify strategies that will facilitate the client's goals. Change can also be seen as either continuous (occurring constantly, simultaneously, or overlapping with other changes) or in discrete episodes (Tsoukas & Chia, 2000).

French, Bell, and Zawacki (1994) suggest that three strategies underlie organizational change. The first strategy is based on the assumption that all people are rational and that they will follow their own self-interest once they understand it. This "empirical-rational" strategy is founded on the idea that if a change is justified, people will accept it. The second strategy—which French and Bell label "normative-re-educative"—is based on helping people develop commitments to new behaviors and norms, and may involve values, attitudes, skills, and relationships—not just information. The third strategy relies on "power and compliance," the assumption being that those with less power in a system will be influenced to comply with the direction, policies, or practices of those with greater power (Waddell, Cummings, & Worley, 2007).

Another way to characterize change is to identify it along a spectrum from incremental (such as process changes, or small steps toward a goal) to transformational (such as reinventing oneself, rebranding an entire company, or expanding into a new market). Kerber and Buono (2009) describe three types of change along a continuum from "constrained" to "unconstrained," where "directed" change is more constrained, "emergent" change is less constrained, and "planned" change falls in between the two. While changes along any point in the spectrum can have a positive impact on the individual or organization, there are important distinctions in scale, timeframe, and the impact that must be recognized by the coach.

Jamieson and Sullivan (2011, pp. 14–18) categorized change into six types:

1. Revolutionary. A "jolt" to the larger system that is rapid and potentially deep, followed by a period of disruption
2. Evolutionary. More incremental, often improvement oriented and characterized by being continuous and cumulative
3. Transitional. Moving from a current state to a future state without changing some fundamental paradigms of the organization (for example: vision, mission, or culture)
4. Transformational. A significant, broad, and deep change that alters an organization's fundamental paradigms
5. Strategic. Change that realigns the organization's mission, environment, market, or strategy
6. Operational. Altering how the organization does work: processes, systems, workflow, design.

Jamieson and Sullivan (2011) also reminded coaches that change can be episodic, contained in periods of time—and limited to those periods—or continuous. The larger, more transformational the change is, the longer it will take to see results; the more of the organizational system will need to be involved; and the more the culture, systems, policies, and processes will need to be addressed in order to successfully implement and sustain the change.

Holman, Devane, and Cady (2007) offered a useful distinction for thinking about the type of system undergoing change.

- *Organizations* have discernible boundaries and clearly structured relationships that help determine which employees, functions, organizational levels, customers, and suppliers to include in a proposed change.
- *Communities* are more diffuse, often involving a range of possible participants—citizens, different levels of government, associations, agencies, media, and more. These systems are often emerging entities that exist around a common bond, sometimes based in purpose, sometimes in relationships. Alliances, cities, associations, cohousing groups, and activist rallies are examples of geographic communities, communities of interest, and communities of practice (Holman et al., 2007, pp. 17–18).

Holman et al. (2007) also offered a useful distinction about purpose: What is the focus of the change? What methods will best help achieve the change? They identified five overarching dimensions of purpose for changes involving groups or communities:

- *Adaptable* methods are used for a variety of purposes in organizations or communities, including planning, structuring, and improving. This group uses principles and practices that adjust to varying needs.
- *Planning* methods help people in communities and organizations shape their future together. These methods set strategic direction and core identity through activities such as self-analysis, exploration, visioning, value clarification, goal setting, and action development.
- *Structuring* methods organize the system to create the desired future. They rely on an effective plan and result in redefined relationships among people and redesigned work practices.
- *Improving* methods increase effectiveness and create operational efficiencies in such areas as cycle time, waste, productivity, and relationships. Basic assumptions of how the organization works often stay the same, while breakthroughs are achieved in processes, relationships, individual behaviors, knowledge, and distributive leadership.
- *Supportive* refers to practices that enhance the efficacy of other change methods, making them more robust and suitable to the circumstances and participants. They are like spices in a meal—enriching methods to

> satisfy the unique tastes of the client. They weave into and often become permanent elements of other methods (pp. 17–18).

Kotter (1996) identifies six types of large-scale changes in organizations, driven by the challenges and opportunities of globalization of markets and competition:

1. Reengineering
2. Restructuring
3. Quality programs
4. Mergers and acquisitions
5. Strategic change
6. Cultural change

The scope and scale of a change project also dictates the number of people and the amount of other resources that need to be dedicated to its success. For large-scale projects, such as those identified by Kotter (1996), an overarching change can spawn many subprojects, each requiring their own resources and management.

Another way scholars look at organizational change processes is the difference between *planned* (episodic) and *performative* (continuous) change models (Tsoukas & Chia, 2000). Planned change is often a replacement strategy whereby a new structure, strategy, or program replaces an old one. In this type of planned change, interventions are orchestrated interruptions intended to correct and/or remove a previous condition to restore balance (i.e., get things back to normal) (Ford & Ford, 1994). Planned change is goal oriented, rational, and intentional. Continuous change, on the other hand, consists of smaller, incremental changes that often emerge from experimentation and learning. Continuous change is processional, performative, and emergent (Ford, 2008).

Kerber and Buono (2005) describe types of change along a continuum, from constrained to unconstrained. They identify three types of change: directed change, planned change, and guided changing, using six distinguishing dimensions (see Table 6.2). Directed change is represented as a pyramid that starts with authority at the top, leading to persuasive communication in the middle, and on to acceptance at the bottom.

> [Directed change is] driven from the top of the organization and relies on authority, persuasion, and compliance. Leaders create and announce the change and seek to convince organizational members to accept it based on business necessity, logical arguments (rational persuasion), emotional appeals, and the leader's credibility. Directed change is a quick, decisive way to introduce change. (Kerber & Buono, 2010, p. 7)

Table 6.2 Approaches to Managing Change

	PRESCRIPTIVE OR DIRECTED APPROACH	PLANNED APPROACH	EMERGENT OR GUIDED APPROACH
Characteristics	Top down, hierarchical	Linear, "roadmap"	Iterative spiral
Change Goals (Ends)	Tightly defined, unchanging goal	Clear goal, with some modification as needed	Loosely defined direction
Change Process (Means)	Tightly constrained	Flexible, participative	Experimental, improvisational
Change Leadership (Role)	Tell, order, command	Devise a plan to accomplish the goal	Point the way, guide and watch over, instruct
Change Maker Dynamics	Persuasion	Influence, cooperation	Collaboration
Pace of Change	Urgent, fast, "just do it"	Go slow during planning to go fast during implementation	Act quickly, improvise, learn, react and continue to iterate

Adapted from Kerber & Buono (2010).

Kerber and Buono compare planned change to a road or path, noting that while it can originate from any level in the organization, it is ultimately sponsored by the top. "Instead of simply creating and announcing a change, planned change provides a 'roadmap.' It attempts to create the conditions for key stakeholders to become more involved in both the form and implementation of the change" (Kerber & Buono, 2010, p. 7). Underlying most planned change efforts is Lewin's model of unfreezing, changing, and refreezing. Change leaders strive to engage stakeholders in the process and outcomes of the plan, to mitigate resistance or loss of productivity (Beckhard & Pritchard, 1992; Beer and Nohria, 2000; Kotter, 1996; LaMarsh, 1995).

Guided changing is an emergent approach that can start at any level in the organization and leverages the organization members' commitment and contributions to the organization's purpose and "attempts to take full advantage of the expertise and creativity of organizational members, reconfiguring existing practices and models, and testing new ideas and perspectives" (Kerber & Buono, 2010, p. 8). This iterative process draws on **action learning** to implement change, discover the real-time impacts, and use the wisdom of the community to address them. "The resulting spiral of learning, innovation and development contributes to both continuous improvement of existing change efforts as well as the ability to generate novel changes and solutions" (Kerber & Buono, 2010, p. 8). They compare guided changing to an iterative spiral. Table 6.2 illustrates the key distinctions in these types of change.

Vaill (1996) introduced the term "permanent white water" to describe a continuous change state that never reverts back to "normal." As changes occur more frequently in organizations—and concurrently in multiple aspects of organizational life—this concept takes on more importance. Vaill (1996) says that this type of change "creates a felt lack of continuity, a felt lack of direction, absence of a sense of progress, absence of a feeling of cumulative achievement, a lack of coherence, a feeling of meaninglessness, and a lack of control" (pp. 176–177). The implications of **permanent white water change** strengthen the argument for organizations to address change as a competency rather than an event. As organizations become more adept at change, permanent white water can become an adventure, an exciting opportunity instead of a debilitating threat to productivity and growth.

One last aspect to consider in assessing types of change is the structural context in which the changes take place. Organizations that are part of relatively certain and stable environments are often bureaucratic and hierarchical, with highly defined lines of authority and roles, and well-documented policies, processes, and procedures. Other organizations, from more dynamic or uncertain environments, adopt an organizational form that is more open and informal, often with distributed decision making. In this case, the emphasis shifts to the interpersonal relationships within the organization rather than the formal structure. These relationships manifest as interdependent networks and nodes.

For example, individuals (agents) who connect to other individuals (agents) and interact represent a social network; these networks can act as agents, working with others to get information and accomplish tasks when the need arises. When there is no longer a need, these networks can dissipate and reform into other networks, or reconnect spontaneously when the situation requires it (Ford, 2008). This dynamic, improvisational organization is able to deal with change in ways that are far faster and more flexible than a more stable, bureaucratic organization would. Anyone coaching or consulting an organization must first assess what kind of organizational change is present, and also identify the kind of organizational structure or environment in which the change will manifest and mature. An example illustrates this difference:

> One of the things that attracted me to come here to begin with was that I was frustrated at my previous hospital by the fact that in order to get something changed or to do something you had to submit it to this committee. Then it went to this committee and that committee. Our CEO here told me if you need to change it, do it, if it works fine, if it doesn't that's okay too, you tried. If we need something for patient care that improves patient care, you don't have to justify it. (Wolf, 2011, p. 28)

Chapter Summary

This chapter introduced the topic of organizational change, providing a definition and description of the multiple influences leading to what is known and practiced in the field today. Causes for organizational change were identified, including changes on a globalization, new technologies, increasing competition in international markets, and changing workforce demographics, outsourcing, and virtual teaming. Different varieties of organizational change were described and discussed, as was the importance of understanding the complexity of change, and viewing change as an organizational competency. The Mastery Model outlined the five stages of change individuals, groups, and organizations experience in both coaching and change: awareness, acceptance, commitment, integration, and mastery. Finally, change coaching was identified as an optimal intervention for addressing successful and sustained change.

Knowledge Check

1. Define organizational change.
2. Why should an organization's ability to change so important today?
3. How can organizational change be an important competency for success?
4. What are the causes of organizational change?
5. Describe the stages that an individual, group, or organization experiences in the Mastery Model.

Learning Activities

Learning Activity 1: Change Awareness

Complete the questionnaire on change awareness in Vaill's (1996) *Learning as a Way of Being* (pp. 195–199). The purpose of this questionnaire is to identify areas of change specific to your own industry or company. What was learned about change in your organization (or client organization) as a result of completing the questionnaire?

Learning Activity 2: Current Changes

List all the changes currently going on in a familiar organization. What are the impacts of these changes happening concurrently? Are there any changes that could potentially conflict with others, or support others? What are the risks? If coaching the leader of this organization, how would you help him or her be successful?

Learning Activity 3: Change Experience

Think of an organizational change experienced at least a year ago. What was the actual change? What was the impetus or reason for the change? What was the impact of the change on the organization, the people in the organization, and the environment or system around the organization? Was the change successful in meeting the original outcome that was desired? Were there any unintended consequences of the change process? How was the organization's morale affected? Productivity? What was the leader's role in the change? Is the change still in place? Did it sustain itself? If not, why? In hindsight, was this change successful?

Learning Activity 4: Future Change

Think of a familiar organization or group. What change would be beneficial for this group? As a coach, what could you help the leader think about or do to make the change launch successful?

Learning Activity 5: Stages of Organizational Change

Using a familiar example of organizational change, trace the stages of organizational change and give examples of behaviors, ideas, language, or affect (mood, morale) that demonstrated each stage.

References

Apple iPhone sales in fiscal years 2007–2012. (n.d.) Retrieved from www.statista.com/statistics/203584/global-apple-iphone-sales-since-fiscal-year-2007/

Argyris, C. (1991). Teaching smart people how to learn. *Harvard Business Review. 4*(1), 4–15.

Beckhard, R., & Pritchard, W. (1992). *Changing the essence.* San Francisco: Jossey-Bass.

Beer, M., & Nohria, N. (2000). Cracking the code of change. *Harvard Business Review, 78*(7), 133–141.

Bennett, J. L., & Bush, M. W. (2013). Executive coaching: An emerging role for management consultants. In A. Buono, L. de Caluwé, & A. Stoppelenburg (Eds.), *Exploring the professional identity of management consultants* (pp. 281–299). Charlotte, NC: Information Age Publishing.

Corporate Leadership Council (2003). *Literature key findings: Change management models.* Washington, DC: Corporate Leadership Council.

Creasey, T., & Hiatt, J. (2003). *Change management.* Loveland, CO: Prosci.

Creasey, T., & Hiatt, J. (2012). *Best practices in change management.* Loveland, CO: Prosci.

Cummings, T. G., & Worley, C. G. (2009). *Organization development and change* (9th ed.). Cincinnati, OH: South-Western.

Ford, R. (2008). Complex adaptive systems and improvisation theory: Toward framing a model to enable continuous change. *Journal of Change Management, 8*(3–4), 173–198.

Ford, J. D., & Ford, L. W. (1994). Logics of identity, contradiction, and attraction in change. *Academy of Management Review, 19,* 756–785.

French, W. J., Bell, C.H., & Zawacki, R. A. (1994). *Organization development and transformation: Managing effective change.* Chicago, IL: Irwin.

Greenstone, M., List, J. A., & Syverson, C. (2012). The effects of environmental regulation on the competitiveness of U.S. manufacturing. Cambridge, MA: MIT Center for Energy and Environmental Policy Research.

Håkonsson, D. D., Klaas, P., & Carroll, T. A. (August 2009). *Organizational adaptation, continuous change, and the positive role of inertia.* Paper presented at Academy of Management Proceedings, Chicago, IL.

Haid, M. D., Schroeder-Saulnier, D., Sims, J., Wang, H., & Urban, M. (2009). *Ready, get set … Change! The impact of change on workforce productivity and engagement.* Philadelphia, PA: Right Management.

Hiatt, J., & Creasey, T. (2002). The definition and history of change management. Retrieved from www.change-management.com/tutorial-definition-history.htm

Hiatt, J., & Creasey, T. (2003). *Change management.* Loveland, CO: Prosci Research.

Higgs, M. & Rowland, D. (2011). Behaviors of successful change leaders: What does it take to implement change successfully? *Journal of Applied Behavioral Science, 47,* 309.

Holman, P. (1999, May/June). Unlocking the mystery of effective large-scale change, *At Work, 8*(3), 7–11.

Holman, P., Devane, T., & Cady, S. (Eds.). (2007). *The change handbook: The definitive resource on today's best methods for engaging whole systems* (2nd ed., rev. & expanded). San Francisco, CA: Berrett-Koehler.

Jamieson, D., & Sullivan, R. (May 2011). *Driving change to get new results.* Linkage Organization Development Summit. Chicago, IL.

Jørgensen, H., Owens, L., & Neus, A. (2008). *Making change work.* Somers, NY: IBM.

Kerber, K. W., & Buono, A. F. (2005). Rethinking organizational change: Reframing the challenge of change management. *Organization Development Journal, 2*(3), 23–38.

Kerber, K. W., & Buono, A. F. (2009). *Building organization change capacity.* Unpublished paper presented at 2009 Academy of Management, Management Consulting Division International Conference, Vienna, Austria.

Kerber, K. W., & Buono, A. F. (2010, Spring). Creating a sustainable approach to change: Building organizational change capacity. *SAM Advanced Management Journal,* 4–21.

Kotter, J. (1996). *Leading change.* Cambridge, MA: Harvard Business School Press.

LaMarsh, J. (1995). *Changing the way we change: Gaining control of major operational change.* Reading, MA: Addision-Wesley.

Maurer, R. (2010). *Beyond resistance: Why 70% of all changes still fail—and what you can do about it.* Austin, TX: Bard Press.

Meaney, M., & Pung, C. (August 2008). McKinsey global results: Creating organizational transformations. *McKinsey Quarterly,* 1–7.

Meyer, C. B., & Stensaker, I. G. (2006). Developing capacity for change. *Journal of Change Management, 6*(2), 217–231.

Prochaska, J. O., Norcross, J. C., & DiClemente, C. C. (1995). *Changing for good: A revolutionary six-stage program for overcoming bad habits and moving your life positively forward.* New York, NY: William Morrow.

Tsoukas, H., & Chia, R. (2000). On organizational becoming: Rethinking organizational change. *Organization Science, 13*(5), 567–582.

Vaill, P. B. (1996). *Learning as a way of being: Strategies for survival in a world of permanent white water.* San Francisco, CA: Jossey-Bass.

Waddell, D. M., Cummings, T. G., & Worley, C. (2007). *Organisation development & change.* South Melbourne, Australia: Cenage.

Wolf, J. (2011). Constructing rapid transformation. *International Journal of Training and Development, 15*(1), 20–38.

7

Change Theories and Models

This chapter offers an overview of organizational change models and theories, and describes the development of organizational change as both a cultural and process phenomenon in organizations today. Nine current models are described, and each is illustrated with examples. In addition, the authors identify strengths and limitations for each and provide a table that summarizes this information. In this chapter, the following questions will be addressed:

- What is the historical development of thought around organizational change?
- Why is it important for Change Coaches to know the theory of organizational change?
- What are at least nine different theories or models of change, including their main constructs, developers or major proponents, and historical timeframe?
- What are three categories of change theory, and who is a thought leader for each?
- What are the similarities and differences between change theories in terms of their strengths and limitations, and how each relates to, and builds upon, the other?
- Which models or theories could be used for individual, group, and organization (systems) change?

Change has long been acknowledged as a phenomenon. Heraclitus, the Greek philosopher, was said to have remarked, "No man can step into the same river twice," highlighting the fact that both people and their environment are changing at every moment. The French have a saying, "*Plus ça change, plus c'est la même chose,*" that translates to "the more things change, the more they stay the same." "The study of change and development is one of the great themes in the social sciences. Many of the social and natural science disciplines have developed theoretical literatures and empirical findings about the birth, development, transformation, decay, and decline of human and natural systems" (Pettigrew, Woodman, & Cameron, 2001, p. 697).

Chapter 6 addressed the nature of change in organizations—what it is, successes and challenges, and different types and stages of organizational change. This chapter takes a deeper look at change and examines many of the theories that seek to explain organizational change. That there are quite a number of theories is no surprise, given the fact that change in organizations is a complex construct both in theory and in practice.

The Development of Organizational Change Theory

From the 1950s into the 1980s, organizational change was considered to be a subset of organization development (OD), most often aimed at implementing changes as part of a long-range strategic plan (Cummings & Worley 2009; French, Bell, & Zawacki, 1994). The changes addressed often involved improvements for work teams, organizational structure, reward and recognition systems, cross-functional alignments, employee engagement, and organizational culture. However, as the nature of work began to evolve to more of a team or system focus—relying on more complex technologies—there was a call for leaders to take control over, and design, organization cultures and change rather than leave these aspects to chance (Sashkin & Burke, 1980; Schein, 2010). A study by Dunphy and Stace (1993) showed that universal models of change were inadequate to describe the diversity of approaches actually used by organizations. They found:

> In particular, the traditional organizational development (OD) model is unrepresentative of how change in many contemporary organizations is actually made. The OD model is also inadequate as a prescriptive model because very different change strategies, some dramatically different from OD, resulted in successful financial performance. (p. 905)

Later, in the 1980s, there was a movement toward organizational change programs becoming more radical, focusing on large-scale, fundamental changes in organizations (Burke, 2011; Waddell, Cummings, & Worley, 2007). Driven in part by new thinking and the rise of technology, these paradigm-shifting programs were referred to as "**organization transformation**" (OT):

> Also in the 1980s, the demands on organizations intensified: competition increased; customers demanded better products and services; the Total Quality movement

created winners and losers; information technology exploded; economic and political changes occurred. Organizations had to change—fast—to survive. The old ways of doing things were no longer good enough; the old belief systems were no longer adequate. Organizations had to be transformed, not just "tweaked." Paradigms had to be changed, not just adjusted. (French et al., 1994, p. 17)

By the late twentieth century, it became increasingly clear that change in organizations could be a response to external forces, such as market shifts, competitive pressures, and new product technologies, or could be internally motivated, such as the case of managers trying to improve existing methods and practices. Organization development was an emerging discipline concerned with improving organizational effectiveness, including leadership, employee engagement, and team collaboration (Waddell et al., 2007).

The 1980s also saw the rise of change management as a discipline outside of OD. Early experience with large-scale information technology (IT) and manufacturing systems implementations highlighted the importance of the addressing the "people side" of change, as well as the need for consulting and project management skillsets to successfully deploy such large and complex projects:

Change Management as a discipline began to emerge in the 1980s driven by leading consulting firms working with Fortune 50 companies. Early adopters, such as GE, Ford, and AT&T, were very large corporations that could derive significant savings through more efficiently implementing new programs and were accustomed to cutting edge thought leadership roles. This work resulted in early Change Management models such as GE's *Cha.nge Acceleration Process (CAP)* and John Kotter's Eight Step Process for Leading Change. At this time, Change Management offerings were mostly available through consulting services, with a limited number of books and textbooks available. During the 1990s, industries undergoing significant and rapid change in areas such as information technology and human resources began highlighting the benefits of Change Management programs on a broader scale. The experiences, consequences, and costs of implementing change without a structured approach has helped employees and organizations embrace Change Management tools. (*Change Management History*, n.d.)

Another approach to organizational change arose from the Total Quality Management movement, which emphasized continuous or incremental improvement and reliance on data-driven decision-making, utilizing feedback from systems as well as all levels of participants in an organization. It became "An umbrella methodology for continually improving the quality of all processes" (Westcott, 2006, p. 303). Early contributors to the total quality management approach included W. Edwards Deming, Joseph M. Juran, and Philip B. Crosby, who introduced concepts of statistical analysis

> of processes, quality control, and the elimination of defects as a way to improve quality in organizations.
>
> Total Quality Management (TQM) became an organizational change approach as well as a philosophy of managing organizational quality. By the early 1990's, quality standards such as the ISO 9000 series were introduced, and quality award programs such as the Deming Prize and the Malcolm Baldrige National Quality Award encouraged organizations to implement and measure system-wide changes in both processes and culture. As the Total Quality Management movement gained popularity, approaches to quality improvement proliferated (including Lean Manufacturing and Six Sigma) and were adopted by organizations to improve everything from profits to employee engagement and retention.

Early conceptions of organizational change focused on how "**planned change**" could be implemented in organizations (Bennis, 1966). OD was primarily concerned with how to build a system's capability to achieve goals, solve problems, and manage change. The focus was on planned change as an adaptive process for stabilizing and institutionalizing new activities within the organization (Waddell et al., 2007). Porras and Silvers (1991) label OD as a first-order change process. Second-order change refers to more radical change that takes on a transformational or revolutionary nature:

> Planned change interventions can be divided into two general types. The first comprises the more traditional approach, Organization Development (OD), which until recently was synonymous with the term *planned change.* The second, Organization Transformation (OT), is the cutting edge of planned change and may be called "second-generation OD." At present, OD is relatively well defined and circumscribed in terms of its technologies, theory, and research. OT, on the other hand, is emerging, ill defined, highly experimental, and itself rapidly changing. (p. 52)

Regardless of its origins, change can have significant social consequences, affecting people and their relationships. Since the time of Lewin, change theories have noted the impacts of change on people—as individuals and within systems (French et al., 1994; Kotter, 1996; Lewin, 1951; Waddell et al., 2007). Peter Drucker (1992), Lewin (1951), and others emphasized the importance of social change as a factor in making change successful. Drucker pointed to the rise of the knowledge worker, stating, "Every organization is in competition for its most essential resource: qualified, knowledgeable people" (1992, p. 8). For change to be successful, one must take into account that organizations are not made up of one type of employee, of the same gender, living in the same location. There are now multiple generations in the workplace, often working in virtual teams that span the globe and operate 24 hours a day, seven days a week, because they are in different time zones. For change to be successful, it must engage all constituents. Axelrod (2010) claims "Engagement is the new Change Management" (p. 23), and urges organizations to connect people with one another and create communities of action for successful, sustained change.

The influence of strategic, transformational change is a recent impact to OD. "As organizations and their technological, political and social environments became more complex and more uncertain, the scale and intricacies of organizational change increased" (Waddell et al., 2007, p. 15). From the 1980s onward, there were criticisms of planned change and OD, as Dunphy and Stace (1993) claim:

> turbulent times demand different responses in varied circumstances. So managers and consultants need a model of change that is essentially a "situational" or "contingency model," that is, one that indicates how to vary change strategies to achieve "optimum fit" with the changing environment. (p. 905)

Planned change seemed too slow, and too conservative. Proponents of transformational change sought to change the nature, structure, form, and/or function of an organization (and sometimes all four). Transformation was to be addressed on all levels: system or organization, group, and individual, to form a new culture and mindset with which to begin anew. It was to be rooted in performance, with strategic fit and culture change as reference points (Keung-Judge & Holbeche, 2011).

Cummings and Worley (2009) referred to transformation as paradigmatic modifications at both individual and organization levels. This process involves different ways of perceiving, thinking, and behaving. Transformative changes, such as downsizings, acquisitions, or mergers, require a formal change model and planned approach that addresses both the change process and the human aspects of change. In addition to planning and development of resources, it also requires that people adjust their values, beliefs, and assumptions to support appropriate patterns of behavior to implement strategy (Keung-Judge & Holbeche, 2011).

Kotter (1996) summed up the appeal of transformational change in today's challenging competitive environments by asking, "How long do you think it will take to move incrementally from the twentieth-century model to the twenty-first? And what do you think will be the consequences if you don't get there fast enough?" (p. 173). Kanter, Stein, and Jick (1992) offered two complementary change approaches: the "bold stroke" approach—rapid overall change—and the "long march" approach, which is incremental change leading to transformation over an extended period of time. Stace and Dunphy (2001) identified four approaches to change: consultative, collaborative, directive, and coercive. For Peters (1989), rapid, disruptive, and continuous change is the only appropriate form of change there is. Kotter (1996) noted the importance of leadership and documented his eight steps for effective change leadership.

Models of individual change were being developed concurrently, using research from psychology and social science as well. The intentional change theory is a good example. It involved longitudinal studies from Case Western Reserve that showed how adults could change their habits and develop competencies (both cognitive and emotional intelligence competencies) following a series of epiphanies or discoveries that Richard Boyatzis has called the intentional change model (Boyatzis, Howard, Rapisarda, & Taylor, 2004). This model suggests that people are more likely to achieve sustainable change when they actively seek to make five discoveries:

- the image of their Ideal Self and their desired future,
- a comparison of the Real Self (how you appear to others) and the Ideal Self,
- the creation of a plan to build on strengths and a few weaknesses to get closer to the Ideal Self,
- practicing the new behavior, and
- "the establishment a trusting relationship with someone who can help you through each of the steps in the process" (Boyatzis et al., 2005 p. 8).

With the increase in frequency and complexity of changes facing both individuals and organizations, there was equal interest in developing technologies and processes to address change at the individual, group, or organizational levels. This proliferation of change theories and models underscores the recognition of the importance of leveraging both individual and organizational change as a core competency in today's global environment. In the technology and systems implementation world:

> The 2000s marked widespread acceptance of Change Management as a business competency for leading change. This shift increased the credibility of Change Management in the business world and with project teams. The benchmarking data on "use of a methodology" shows a marked increase from 34% in 2003 to 72% in 2011. The value of Change Management was further validated through additional research on the impact of Change Management on business success by Prosci, IBM, and McKinsey.
>
> The market for Change Management tools and training grew rapidly through this period, with as many as 320 consulting firms having been identified as offering Change Management services by 2011. Some were established with their own Change Management methodologies while others previously offering only consulting services also began providing training and some level of product offering as well. The close of the decade saw the formation of the industry's first global association for Change Management practitioners, the Association of Change Management Professionals ("ACMP"). (*Change Management History*, n.d.)

As the understanding of change increases, new models of change emerge. Some are grounded in constructionist theory; they are generative, adaptive, and ultimately show the way toward transformational/revolutionary change. These change theories emphasize group and system processes, such as **appreciative inquiry** (Cooperrider, Sorenson, Whitney, & Yaeger, 2000; Whitney & Trosten-Bloom, 2003) and the generative capacity of social construction. They incorporate the dual transformational and transactional dimensions that have been shown to effect organizational change and address the transformational factors of change—environment, mission and strategy, leadership, and culture—to have broad systemic impact and create revolutionary change on an organization (Burke, 2011).

As the speed, complexity, and volume of change have increased, organization change has emerged as a specialty of OD (Conner, 1992; French et al., 1994). Organization change is a broad phenomenon that involves a diversity of applications and approaches, including economic, political, technical, and social perspectives. OD requires its practitioners to be fluent in the languages of business, organizational finance, and politics, strategy, metrics, and behavioral science. The emerging field of organization change is broadly focused and can apply to any kind of change (Waddell et al., 2007, p. 15). There are now academic programs, professional conferences, and associations dedicated to this growing field.

For the purposes of this book, key theories of change are organized into three categories according to their orientation: planned change, emergent change, and **prescriptive change**.

1. *Planned change* relies on a carefully thought out master plan to execute change, awareness of the steps or stages that occur, and using feedback to test the appropriateness of "next steps" before proceeding.
2. **Emergent change** theories are based on whole-systems approaches, often involving large-group interactions or meetings, and seek to explore all stakeholder perspectives, making decisions as much as possible with the whole group.
3. *Prescriptive change* approaches focus on results, action, and execution, are often "leader led," and applied to process improvement, IT systems migrations, and implementations of leadership strategy.

All of these theories can support a change focus on performance, development, or transformation. In the following pages, each of these categories is illustrated with example theories, which are identified with their major proponents, key concepts, strengths, limitations, and applications. Table 7.1 summarizes all of the presented theories and approaches for easy reference.

Table 7.1 Summary of Change Theories and Approaches

THEORY	PROPONENTS	TIMEFRAME INTRODUCED	KEY CONCEPTS
Planned Change Approaches			
Planned Change	Lewin	1940s	• Change is a process to be managed • It involves three steps, supported by action learning, group dynamics theory, and field theory
Transition model	Bridges	1980s	• Change involves individual psychological transition • Every change begins with ending (loss), involves a "wilderness" period of ambiguity, and culminates in a "new beginning"
Transtheoretical Model	Prochaska, Norcross & DiClemente	1990s	• Successful change involves six stages that must be sequentially accomplished • Individuals must identify the stage in which they reside in order to use tools and processes appropriate to that state
Emergent Approaches			
Appreciative inquiry	Cooperrider	1980s	• New paradigm for change, focusing on positive articulation rather than problem-solving processes • Utilizes groups' positive core and 4-D process to identify and implement change
Permanent white water change	Vaill	1980s	• Addresses change that is continuous, not a discrete event • Elements of white water change: surprising, novel, messy, costly, and unpreventable
Whole scale change/ Large Group Intervention	Alban & Bunker; Dannemiller-Tyson; Weisbord;	1980s	• Integrated intervention designed to foster change in multiple parts of the organization at the same time. • Enables the organization to work together to create and integrate the change
Prescriptive Change Approaches			
Eight-step change leadership model	Kotter	1990s	• Leadership is the engine that drives change, not management • There are eight steps to ensuring the best chance of successful change
Six Sigma	Various	1980s	• A project-driven management approach to process improvement and culture change • Change must be identified and managed through data and metrics
ADKAR	Hiatt	2000s	• Goal-oriented change-management system focused on results • Consists of five components: awareness, desire, knowledge, ability, and reinforcement (ADKAR)

Lewin developed action research as part of his planned change theory, emphasizing that change requires action, and that successful action is based on analyzing the situation correctly, identifying all the possible alternative solutions, and choosing the most appropriate one (Bennett, 1983). Lewin (1946) stated that action research "proceeds in a spiral of steps each of which is composed of a circle of planning, action, and fact-finding about the results of the action" (p. 206). Action research is an iterative process whereby the "research" (i.e., change) leads to action, and action leads to evaluation and further research (Burnes, 2004). Lewin's view was that this process produces both understanding and learning for the individuals and groups concerned, which then feed into changed behavior (Lewin, 1946). Action research stresses that for change to be effective, it must take place at the group level, and must be a participative and collaborative process, which involves all of those concerned (French, Bell, & Zawacki 1994; Lewin, 1947).

Strengths of this framework: Lewin was one of the first to place the individual at the heart of change, and to address the psychological and social impacts of change. He "provided an integrative frame for conceptualizing the processes behind how people and social systems change" (Mirvis, 2006, p. 49). His planned change theory was widely accepted and very popular, and the participative approach to behavioral change that he pioneered has proved remarkably applicable over time (Burnes, 2004). As Edgar Schein (1996) wrote:

> The key, of course, was to see that human change, whether at the individual or group level, was a profound psychological dynamic process that involved painful unlearning without loss of ego identity and difficult relearning as one cognitively attempted to restructure one's thoughts, perceptions, feelings, and attitudes. (p. 59)

Lewin's action research process offers a key advantage in applying the organization's (or the individual's) own experiences and insights into action that creates and sustains change.

Limitations of this framework: Despite the popularity and ubiquitous usefulness of Lewin's model, there was criticism about its simplicity. Its conception of organization-as-ice-cube was considered too linear and static, and "to the extent that there are stages, they overlap and interpenetrate one another in important ways" (Kanter et al., 1992, p. 10). Also, Lewin's approach leaned heavily on organizational or whole-systems participation, and depended on understanding and adopting his other theoretical frameworks (action research, field theory, and group dynamics) in order to make change successful and sustained. Due to the "project management" aspect of planned change, it can become cumbersome to manage in larger, more complex organizations.

Application of this framework: Lewin's three-step change process and related theories are applicable at all levels—individual, group, and system or organization—but are best suited for group or organizational change. While Lewin addressed the role of the individual in change, he believed that a holistic investigation of human behavior and learning must include the environment in which the learning is taking place, including the psychological environment of the learner and others with whom he interacts. His three-step change process will work well with an individual to help conceptualize the phased approach and the work or focus needed at each stage. However, the additional perspectives coming from a group or other organizational members add to the richness and depth of solutions and learning. As more people are involved in the action-learning process, there can be broader understanding and (potentially) shared commitment to making and sustaining the change in an organization or system.

Transitions Model

In the 1980s, Bridges proposed a new way of thinking about change. He suggested that it was not the change that was problematic for individuals and organizations, but rather the transition. He noted that the terms "change" and "transition" are often used interchangeably:

> Our society confuses them constantly, leading us to imagine that *transition* is just another word for *change*. But it isn't. *Change* is your move to a new city or your shift to a new job. It is the birth of your new baby or the death of your father. It is the switch from the old health plan at work to the new one, or the replacement of your manager by a new one, or it is the acquisition that your company just made.
>
> In other words, *change* is situational. *Transition,* on the other hand, is psychological. It is not those events, but rather the inner re-orientation and the self-redefinition that you have to go through in order to incorporate any of those changes into your life. Without a transition, change is just a rearrangement of the furniture. Unless transition happens, the change won't work, because it doesn't "take." (Bridges, 2004, p. xii)

Transition is a "three-part psychological process that extends over a long period of time and cannot be planned or managed by the same rational formulae that work with *change*" (Bridges, 1986, p. 25). The three phases are:

1. Letting go of the old situation or identity—every change starts with a loss of some kind.
2. Going through a "neutral zone" between the old way of doing or experiencing things and the new way that may be unclear.

3. Making a new beginning: "developing new competencies, establishing new relationships, becoming comfortable with new policies and procedures, constructing new plans for the future, and learning to think in accordance with new purposes and priorities" (1986, p. 26).

Bridges (1986) pointed out that, historically and in many cultures, there has been recognition of the importance of the transition process, with "rites of passage" and guidance to help deal with the adjustment to change. However, he claimed that in modern-day systems, this orientation process is overlooked or that individuals are unaware of the significance of this process. As a result, "difficulties with making new beginnings come not from a difficulty with beginnings per se, but from a difficulty with endings and neutral zones" (Bridges, 1986, p. 31). While both Lewin and Bridges proposed change models with three parts, they differed in a significant way: Bridges focused on psychological process and impact of transition through change, while Lewin addressed the process of change, emphasizing cross-collaboration and learning, whether at individual, group, or organization levels.

Bridges identified signs to look for in each of the phases. Disengagement, disenchantment, and dis-identification are symptomatic of the "letting-go" phase. Disorientation, disintegration, and discovery are hallmarks of the "neutral zone."

Strengths of this framework: Bridges's concept of "managing transition" as an important factor in successful change cannot be overstated. It is easily understandable and accessible, even at face value. It took Lewin's theory a step further, and incorporated the personal, psychological journey of change that parallels what Kubler-Ross identifies in the grief process (Kubler-Ross, 1997). And, recognizing that organizations are collections of individuals, Bridges's work pointed to specific actions that leaders can take to ease the transition process and achieve successful and sustainable change. Bridges's work is especially helpful in understanding the psychological dynamics of change and why change can be such an individualized process. His work also helps leaders understand the complexity of change, why it takes longer than they expect, and it helps them understand and reflect on the uniqueness of each team member going through the process (as well as their own processes). Acknowledging endings allows the feelings of loss to surface and be addressed. Leaders can use the former way as a path to the new.

Limitations of this framework: This theory is built on psychological concepts that many organizations and individuals neither appreciate nor believe they have time for. In command-and-control cultures, this model can be seen as too academic and not practical or action oriented enough. And, since the framework is specifically about the psychological process of transition, it does not address how to manage a change project in a structured manner.

Application of this framework: Bridges's theory can be applied at all levels in working with change: individual, group, and organization or system. While the psychological aspects of transition relate best to the individual, leaders can address the impacts and manifestations of transition even at group and organization levels. This framework can also be used with other frameworks to support the understanding of the change process.

Transtheoretical Change Model

Prochaska, Norcross, and DiClemente (1994) comprised a team of psychologists and researchers who devoted themselves to discovering how people intentionally change. They were looking for basic principles that would link to changes occurring both with and without psychotherapy, and they challenged the "action paradigm, wherein change was assumed to occur dramatically and discretely" (p. 14), which had been the dominant theoretical model for decades before their work challenged it. Their premise was that this model was inadequate to serve those wishing to change, and that "successful self-changing individuals follow a powerful and, perhaps most important, controllable and predictable course. Along this course are various stages, each calling for particular and different approaches to change" (Prochaska et al., 1994, p. 15).

Their process of change has been successfully applied to a variety of situations, including smoking cessation, weight loss, addiction, and anxiety disorders. "The key to success is the appropriately timed use of a variety of coping skills" (Prochaska et al., 1994, p. 15). The six stages of the transtheoretical change model are:

1. Pre-contemplation. People in this stage typically have no interest in changing and deny that they have anything to change. They resist change and may feel demoralized, acting as if the situation were hopeless and out of their control.
2. Contemplation. In this stage, people are aware that a problem exists and are seriously thinking about overcoming it, but have not yet made a commitment to take action. People can remain stuck in the contemplation stage for long periods (Prochaska, Norcross, & DiClemente, 1992, p. 1103).
3. Preparation. Most people in this stage are actively planning to make a change in the near term. An important step is to declare the change publicly, to resolve any ambivalence and plan carefully, and to develop a solid action plan.

4. Action. "The action stage is the one in which people most overtly modify their behavior" (Prochaska et al., 1994, p. 44). Action is the most-obviously busy stage, requiring the most commitment of time and energy.
5. Maintenance. This stage is where individuals consolidate the gains they have made in the prior phases and work consciously to prevent relapses. This stage can be a long, continuous process.
6. Termination. The ultimate goal is termination, and the authors admit to an ongoing debate about it. "Some experts believe that certain problems cannot be terminated but only kept at bay through a life of decreasingly wary maintenance" (Prochaska et al., 1994, p. 46). However, they address the matter by identifying which types of change can be successfully terminated and whisch will most likely require continued maintenance.

This theory requires that individuals know what stage of change they are in for the problem they want to overcome. "Our research has consistently shown that people who try to accomplish changes they are not ready for set themselves up for failure" (Prochaska et al., 1994, p. 39). They also note that one cannot skip stages and hope to be successful, and that, "Matching your challenges to your stage of change will help maximize your problem solving efforts" (Prochaska et al., 1994, p. 39).

While the stages must be accomplished in sequence, the overall process is more of a spiral, as the authors note that "most successful self-changers go through the stages three or four times before they make it to the topic and finally exit the cycle" (Prochaska et al., 1994, p. 48). For this reason, they recommend using the word "recycle" instead of "relapse," noting, "People who take action and fail in the next month are twice as likely to succeed over the next six months than those who don't take any action at all" (Prochaska et al., 1994, p. 50).

Strengths of this framework: This theory represents a breakthrough in thinking about change at the individual level, and has since been expanded to organizational change. By introducing discrete stages of change and focusing on encouraging people to identify and use appropriate tools for the stage they are in, this theory empowers people and encourages the reflection and self-motivation needed to make and sustain change. It is a model of intentionality, focusing on the individual or organization's decision making. It also serves well in explaining resistance to change.

Limitations of this framework: This theory addresses change at the individual level. While some of the concepts have proven to be useful in addressing group or organizational change (pre-contemplation, maintenance, termination), the applications, processes, and tools used to support this theory best support individual change.

Application of this framework: As noted above, this theory best addresses change at the individual level; however, the stages are useful in assessing and identifying change readiness in organizations. They can also be leveraged as indicators of progress toward successful completion of a change (in both individuals and groups), and can be used to provide metrics in larger change projects.

Emergent Change Approaches

Emergent change evolved from the field of organizational development (OD) and seeks to increase an organization or system's capacity to deal successfully with change. It features a "whole systems" orientation, often with large-scale conversations and decision making. Perhaps as a response to the increasing levels of complexity of changes needed in organizations and groups, emergent change is seen as a system-wide engagement (Axelrod, 2010, Burke, 2011, French et al., 1994; Waddell et al., 2007).

As the last century closed, it was the accepted view that emergent change was the more popular, dominant approach, as opposed to planned change (Burnes, 2004; By, 2005; Caldwell, 2006; Mintzberg & Westley, 1992; Pettigrew et al., 2001; Weick & Quinn, 1999). The emergent approach starts from the assumption that change is not a linear process or a one-off, isolated event, but is a continuous, open-ended, cumulative, and unpredictable process of aligning and realigning an organization to its changing environment (Falconer, 2002; Orlikowski, 1996). Weick (2000) had this to say about studies of emergent change:

> The recurring story is one of autonomous initiatives that bubble up internally; continuous emergent change; steady learning from both failure and success; strategy implementation that is replaced by strategy making; the appearance of innovations that are unplanned, unforeseen and unexpected; and small actions that have surprisingly large consequences. (p. 225)

Proponents of emergent change view organizations as power systems, and consequently, see change as a political process whereby different groups in an organization struggle to protect or enhance their own interests (By, 2005; Huczynski & Buchanan, 2001; Orlikowski & Yates, 2006). According to Keung-Judge and Holbeche (2011), this approach works best when there is an amorphous problem or a high level of uncertainty.

> It assumes that the environment is inherently unstable and change is a fluid movement, emerging from the people and their situation, making order out of chaos. In emergence, organizations are treated as a series of constructs, i.e. a series of relationships. (p. 263)

Emergent methods recognize that support for change comes about by connecting people to the organization's strategy, capturing their imaginations, respecting their contributions, and energizing the change process (Zolno, 2001):

> Recent research, particularly in the arena of social construction and system change, suggests that organizational change occurs as part of intentional collective action. Therefore, bringing about complex change in an organization is most likely to occur when people within that system are fully engaged in a cooperative process creating it (Zolno, 2009, p. 1).

Appreciative inquiry, **whole-scale change**, and permanent white water change theories illustrate the emergent approach to change. This approach has multiple proponents, each with their own process and methods. Other theories of emergent change are Weisbord (2012) and Weisbord and Janoff's (2010) future search, Lippett's (1998) preferred futuring, Owen's (2008) open space technology, and Jacobs's (1997) real-time strategic change.

Appreciative Inquiry

Developed by David Cooperrider and branded as a "new model of change management" (Cooperrider & Whitney, 2005, p. vii), appreciative inquiry (or AI) is a "coevolutionary search for the best in people, their organizations, and the relevant world around them" (Cooperrider & Whitney, 2005, p. 2). It has been described as "a radically affirmative approach to change which completely lets go of problem-based management" (White, 1996, p. 472).

AI seeks to approach change from a positive, or appreciative, position rather than from a problem-solving position. This theory rests on the foundational supposition of a "diverse set of assets, strengths, and resources that, when discussed, broadly constitute an organization or a community's positive core" (Cooperrider & Whitney, 2005, p. 9). AI "links the knowledge and energy of this core directly to an organization or community's change agenda, and changes never thought possible are suddenly and democratically mobilized" (Cooperrider & Whitney, 2005, p. 8). AI's claim is that a "shift from problem analysis to positive core analysis is at the heart of positive change" (Cooperrider & Whitney, 2005, p. 11).

AI is an appreciative, narrative approach that involves groups in identifying and describing aspects of the positive change core that will address issues currently facing the organization. The stakeholders are then moved through a series of activities designed to evoke visions or a positive future and propositions that will enable this future to be realized. Finally, teams are formed to actualize the proposals. According to Cooperrider and Whitney (2005), "Each AI process is homegrown, designed to meet the unique challenges of the organization and industry involved" (p. 15). In addition:

> The AI cycle can be as rapid and informal as a conversation with a friend or a colleague, or as formal as an organization-wide process involving every stakeholder group. Although AI has no formula, the change efforts of most organizations flow through the 4-D cycle. (p. 15)

There are four key phases that form the 4-D cycle. These phases are addressed sequentially, often in a large-group "AI Summit" meeting format that allows a day for each phase. The 4-D phases are described as:

- Discovery. Mobilizing the whole system by engaging all stakeholders in the articulation of strengths and best practices. Identifying "the best of what has been and what is."
- Dream. Creating a clear, results-oriented vision in relation to discovered potential and in relation to questions of higher purpose, such as, "What is the world calling us to become?"
- Design. Creating possibility propositions of the ideal organization, articulating an organization design that people feel is capable of drawing upon and magnifying the positive core to realize the newly expressed dream.
- Destiny. Strengthening the affirmative capability of the whole system, enabling it to build hope and sustain momentum for engaging positive change and high performance (Cooperrider & Whitney, 2005, p. 16).

Each AI process starts with an "affirmative topic choice" that sets the stage for the 4-D process. The topics get turned into questions to guide the discovery interviews, and, "They serve as seeds for the dreams phase and as arenas for crafting design propositions and taking action in the destiny phase" (Cooperrider & Whitney, 2005, p. 17).

Strengths of this framework: AI offers a new paradigm in the world of change, focusing on the positive potential in individuals, groups, or organizations, and evoking both motivation and ideas from identifying past successes. There is evidence of significant positive change in both organizations and individuals from the application of this theory (Cooperrider et al., 2000; Kelm, 2005; Orem, Binkert, & Clancy, 2007; Watkins, Mohr, & Kelly, 2011; White, 1996). It is a democratic, engagement-oriented process that gathers perspectives from all stakeholders in a change, and due to its appreciative, narrative methods, it does not require special ability or training to participate.

Limitations of this framework: This process can seem cumbersome and ambiguous to a very objective or scientific group, such as engineers. It requires engagement and the willingness to "let go of the problem" in order to focus on potential opportunities. In cultures entrenched with a "problem-solving" mentality, or where leaders are rewarded for "putting out fires," this approach may not be tolerated well.

Application of this framework: AI is universal in its appeal and usefulness as a change theory at all levels—individuals, groups, and organizations can benefit from exploring this approach. While most examples are of its implementation in large systems, AI has also been adapted for coaching (Orem et al., 2007) and other individual uses (Kelm, 2005).

Permanent White Water Change

In 1996, Vaill introduced the concept of "permanent white water" change: change that is "surprising, novel, messy, costly and unpreventable" (Vaill, 1996, p. 14). This kind of continuous change is like waves on the white water rapids of a constantly flowing river, not just a discrete event that occurs before things get back to "normal." White water change highlights the complex, unpredictable nature of organizational change, given that impacts are present both within and external to the system.

To Vaill (1996) the metaphor of permanent white water invalidates the model of a smooth-running, mechanistic organization. "The system is not a clock of mechanically engineered parts" (p. 8), since there is no way to take into account the complex interactions of the whole system, its external impacts, and the internal, operational changes that take place to keep the system functioning. His model emphasizes that organizations are *human* systems, and that each organizational member is a potential change agent—either for or against the change, knowingly or unknowingly. He likens this theory to chaos theory, in noting the power and potential of individuals' "on-the-spot wisdom, creativity and steadiness when things are going wrong at a particular moment, and white water is splashing in all directions" (p. 10).

Vaill (1996) points out that part of the reason for permanent white water is that, as organizations react to changes imposed by external forces (environments, governments, technology changes), they, in turn, make internal changes to adapt and innovate. "They are creating permanent white water for others by the changes they themselves introduce. Turbulence and instability are woven into the macrosystem; they are not just things that happen to it from the outside" (p. 7).

Vaill (1996) explains that all organizational change is individual change that must be aligned and directed; "our struggle to restore meaning to our immediate work environments leads us to take actions that may be experienced as white water by others" (p. 17). He emphasizes that the individual human aspects of will and judgment are what constantly impact the organizational system, and that it is futile to predict how these impacts will modify the system.

> Some of these changes are official, meaning that they go through a careful design review process and are incorporated at least somewhat planfully into the system (although designs and plans are no guarantee that changes will not create major disturbances). But just as many changes are informal—shortcuts, innovations, Band-Aids of one sort or another that individuals and groups apply to the system flow to solve the local problems they experience. These spontaneous innovations create a lot of unanticipated permanent white water for others upstream or downstream in the system. Valuable innovations are the positive result of this age of individual 'empowerment' that we live in, but the cost is likely to be continuing system disturbances owing to members' nonstop tinkering. (Vaill, 1996, pp. 8–9)

Vaill (1996) lists five characteristics of permanent white water: surprising, novel, messy, costly, and unpreventable:

- Permanent white water conditions are full of *surprises:* unexpected problems, unintended consequences, and things that are not "supposed to happen."
- Complex systems tend to produce *novel* problems—problems that haven't even been imagined or anticipated by the system.
- Permanent white water conditions are *messy* and often ill-structured (Ackoff, 1974). They do not come neatly packaged, are not simple, cause-and-effect chains, and often impact multiple levels and types of systems or structures simultaneously, demonstrating that "everything's connected to everything else" (p. 12).
- White water events are often *costly,* in terms of financial and other resources (time, talent, etc.). Vaill (1996) characterizes them as "extremely obtrusive." "In their messiness, costliness, and ramifications, they simply cannot be ignored" (p. 13).
- Permanent white water conditions are *unpreventable,* raising the problem of recurrence and often fostering additional red tape, bureaucracy, review levels, and processes. Vaill (1996) warns, "While such protections may be undoubtedly valuable in some circumstances, it is important to understand that no number of anticipatory mechanisms can forestall the next surprising, novel wave in the permanent white water" (p. 13).

Vaill (1996) notes that reactions to the confusion and turbulence of permanent white water change indicate that "experienced executives and others in organizations perceive that what they are trying to do is becoming more complex, problematic, and contingent as time goes on" and notes that "permanent white water means permanent life outside one's comfort zone" (p. 14). Permanent white water can also bring on "**change fatigue**," akin to burnout, in which individuals in a system get overwhelmed or disengaged due to constant change. Vaill (1996) cites study results of people feeling that permanent white water change is increasing, and feeling a lack of continuity, direction, coherence, meaning, and control. Vaill (1996) questions the "capacity to restore and sustain a sense of meaning in these new chaotic environments" (p. 17). Bridges (1980) supported Vaill's claims, adding:

> But it is not just the pace of change that disorients us. Many Americans have lost the old faith that all the transitions they are going through are really getting them anywhere. To be "up in the air," as one so often is in times of personal transition, is endurable if it *means something*—if it is part of a movement toward a desired end. But if it is not related to some larger and beneficial pattern, it becomes simply distressing. (p. 4)

Permanent white water change is a phenomenon that is increasing, not decreasing. Change coaches need to look for, and address, the signs of change fatigue and burnout that often accompany this particularly stressful type of change.

Strengths of this framework: The permanent white water model is especially helpful in cases of sudden change, disaster, or crisis. The model can be applied when unintended consequences or unforeseen impacts result from planned changes. Permanent white water encourages organizations to look internally as well as externally for change impacts and consequences. This concept is helpful to introduce change in large-scale systems where many concurrent impacts may need to be addressed, as well as in small, entrepreneurial enterprises (or groups and teams) that may be operating with little structure and few processes. The larger the vision, or broader the strategic intent of the change, the more this model will apply.

Limitations of this framework: This model is not directly applicable to single, small, incremental, or straightforward changes such as process changes or the introduction of a new system or new leader. The concept best addresses the complexities of multiple changes over time, or of disasters and crisis situations.

Applications of this framework: Vaill's (1996) model is best applied to groups or organizations/systems. While it is a useful concept for individuals to understand, the focus of the theory is on larger settings.

Whole-Scale Change

Building on the group approach of planned change, *whole-scale change* aims to include all of the stakeholders in the change process. Zolno (2009) described the approach:

> Taking a whole system perspective means creating an integrated intervention plan that is designed to foster change in multiple parts of the organization at the same time. Such a comprehensive intervention can bring about a profound shift in the organization's identity, view of its future and way of doing business. This approach to intervention design is more likely to support the organization in reaching its 'tipping point'—the point of critical mass—that moves the organization towards its desired new configuration (a 'whole field' change). (p. 2)

Holman (n.d.) elaborated, arguing that whole systems change utilizes:

> Processes that engage people from all aspects of a system, organization or community to:
>
> - Enable emergence of what is most important, individually and collectively; and
> - Increase the likelihood for achieving it by growing people's capacity to care for themselves, others, and the whole. (p. 2)

Dannemiller and Tyson developed this approach in the 1980s, evolving it from their work with real-time strategy change and real-time work design:

> It consists of a series of small and/or large group interactions that enable the organization to shift paradigms, working together to create and integrate all the needed changes. It applies action learning, using Whole-Scale events as accelerators. Through microcosms—groups representing the range of stakeholders, levels, functions, geography, and ideas in the organization—Whole Scale processes simultaneously work with the parts and whole of the system to create and sustain change. Whole Scale also enables a 'critical mass' of the organization to create a new culture in the moment. That critical mass then models what the organization can look like, becoming the vehicle for powerful change in the whole system. (James & Tolchinsky, 2007, p. 165)

Strengths of this framework: Whole-scale change can be used for a wide variety of strategic, complex organizational changes. It is easily scalable, and can work with small or large groups (up to thousands of participants). Whole-scale interventions engage everyone in a system or group and can support rapid system-wide change in a variety of settings, countries, and cultures. If a group or organization is experiencing several changes, or if new changes arise that need to be addressed during the period that the whole-scale change process is being implemented, these other issues are relatively easy to add to the scope. Whole-scale change processes can effectively integrate diverse changes or activities, often addressing such divergent issues as organization strategy at the same time as improving cycle time or improving other processes.

Limitations of this framework: Whole-scale change projects can be complex and logistically challenging for both leaders and facilitators. This approach requires attention to detail, strong sponsorship, intense planning at the outset, and a timeframe, schedule, and inclusive culture that allows for trust, accountability, and truth telling at multiple levels of group meetings. Whole-scale change can require a large amount of resources to implement. If the scope is large for the change effort, a dedicated change team is needed to implement this approach (these can be internal or external change agents, or a combination of both).

Application of this framework: By design, whole-scale change is focused on change at the group or systems, organization, or community level. This approach can be applied to any large systems change ,such as automating business processes across the organization, mergers and acquisitions, organization strategy or design, visioning, and rebranding, but it is also scalable for smaller projects or the group level. There are no examples of whole-scale change being used with individuals.

Prescriptive Change Approaches

Prescriptive change frameworks offer a set of processes or steps to be carried out by a leader or change agent (a person or group who drives change within the organization, by championing or promoting the change, and often by managing its implementation). The focus is on performance and a sense of urgency to drive action. This approach was influenced strongly by the increasing magnitude and immediacy of changes coming from environments, governments, economics, technology, and globalization.

In this paradigm, change is seen as something to drive, **sponsor**, and deploy—usually from the top down—while recognizing the importance of engaging the entire group or population for success and sustainment. As shown earlier in Table 6.2, the Kerber-Buono Differentiating Approaches to Managing Change, the description of Directed Change closely aligns to the Prescriptive Change approach. As examples, the authors offer Kotter's eight-step change leadership model, the **Six Sigma** continuous improvement methodology, and Prosci's **ADKAR** model to illustrate the prescriptive approach to change.

Change Leadership

Kotter (1996) developed this model after many years of teaching management at Harvard Business School and studying the ways that leaders dealt with their organizations. He was one of the first to emphasize the importance of leaders, claiming that leadership is the engine that drives change. He introduced a key distinction between leadership and management (Kotter, 2001), proposing that "managers promote stability while leaders press for change" (p. 3). "What leaders really do is prepare organizations for change and help them cope as they struggle through it" (p. 3).

Given this perspective, Kotter (1996) introduced an eight-step process that leaders can use to ensure the best possibility of successful change. He notes two important patterns:

> First, useful change tends to be associated with a multistep process that creates power and motivation sufficient to overwhelm all the sources of inertia. Second, this process is never employ effectively unless it is driven by a high quality leadership, not just excellent management—an important distinction that will come up repeatedly as we talk about instituting significant organizational change. (p. 20)

Kotter (1996) identifies eight fundamental errors that leaders make in dealing with change, and claims that his eight-step process for change leadership can "address all the barriers to change, and address them well" (p. 20). The eight steps are:

1. Establishing a sense of urgency. Examine market and competitive realities, and identify and discuss crises, potential crises, or major opportunities.
2. Creating the guiding coalition. Assemble a group with enough power to lead the change effort, and encourage the group to work as a team.
3. Developing a change vision. Create a vision to help direct the change effort, and develop strategies for achieving that vision.
4. Communicating the vision for buy-in. Use every vehicle possible to communicate the new vision and strategies and teach new behaviors by the example of the guiding coalition.
5. Empowering broad-based action. Remove obstacles to change, change systems, or structures that seriously undermine the vision, and encourage risk-taking and nontraditional ideas, activities, and actions.
6. Generating short-term wins. Plan for visible performance improvements, create those improvements, recognize and reward employees involved in the improvements

7. Never letting up. Use increased credibility to change systems, structures, and policies that don't fit the vision; also hire, promote, and develop employees who can implement the vision; and finally, reinvigorate the process with new projects, themes, and change agents.
8. Incorporating changes into the culture. Articulate the connections between the new behaviors and organizational success, and develop the means to ensure leadership development and succession.

Strengths of this framework: As with other examples of prescriptive change theories, Kotter's eight-step change leadership model focuses on tangible action: what must the leader *do* to drive and sustain change? This model offers a path forward for understanding and leading change at any level. Used in a large system, this model provides an action focus that can unify a whole organization or system with a common strategy. It is top-down change, appropriate for most types of change projects. It is based on Kotter's many years of research on what makes change work, and what makes leaders effective, and it addresses all of the success factors currently known about change. This framework offers a clear roadmap for even the most **novice** leaders, and a high probability of success for any that follow it.

Limitations of this framework: This change theory is dependent on the effectiveness of the leader that is driving the change. While there is supportive systems involvement built in through the creation of the guiding coalition, robust communicating strategies, and empowering, broad-based action, this framework relies on a strong, focused, engaged leader, and a clear, acknowledged organizational structure or chain of command. This model also works best when the leader is involved for the duration of the change project.

Application of this framework: This model is applicable at the individual, group, and organization levels as a set of steps that can be followed to ensure the maximum probability of change. It is scalable to large and small projects and can apply to any area of focus (performance, development, or transformational change). It is an excellent framework to use for new leaders or those who wish to develop their change leadership abilities. It is clear and easy to follow.

Six Sigma

Six Sigma method is a structured, data-driven, change management approach, often aimed at improving the quality of an organization's products, services, and processes by continually reducing defects in the organization. It can also be leveraged as a business strategy that focuses on improving service delivery, meeting customer requirements, and incrementally improving business systems, productivity, and financial performance. It is one of several types of continuous improvement approaches to change, including Lean Thinking, Kaizen, and the Theory of Constraints (Kwak & Anbari, 2006).

While Six Sigma is technically defined as a "statistical measure of quality" (Zornada, 2005, p. 2), the Six Sigma movement has become a respected change methodology in organizations around the world, both as a process for continuous improvement and as an enabler of culture change. Six Sigma offers tools and processes to address the smallest of changes, providing a structured methodology for improving any process in any type of business. This methodology can also be used to introduce paradigm shifts into the way organizations work and think (Zornada, 2005). The Six Sigma methodology was introduced at Motorola in 1987. Allied Signal adopted Six Sigma shortly afterward, as did GE (in 1995) and many other companies (Raytheon, Lockheed Martin, DuPont, 3M, Bank of America) followed suit (Zornada, 2005).

The main tenets of Six Sigma are to standardize process controls and use metrics to keep production and services within rigorous specification limits. As noted by Zornada (2005, p. 14), the approach is summarized in the acronym DMAIC:

"D-M-A-I-C":

- ***Define*** the problem or opportunity,
- ***Measure*** the current performance and capability,
- ***Analyze*** to identify root causes,
- ***Improve*** by implementing potential solutions, and
- ***Control*** by standardizing the solution and monitoring its performance.

While DMAIC works at the micro level for even the smallest of process improvements, it is also applicable at a systems or organization level. Companies have used the Six Sigma process to integrate multiple workforces from several major legacy organizations that brought with them deeply embedded work cultures, different ways of talking about similar concepts, and experience with various operating models and organizational structures.

One global aerospace company, Raytheon, used Six Sigma to create a common, customer-focused culture, improve productivity, integrate operations, reduce debt, and unite the company. The results were a significant drop in net debt, a 40 percent increase in stock price, and national awards recognizing the impact that its Six Sigma approach had on the organization's performance. In the years since Six Sigma's introduction to organizations as a quality process, it has been broadened to address systems and culture change issues, such as employee engagement, customer satisfaction, and vision development. Bill Swanson, Raytheon's CEO, noted that Six Sigma "has been indispensable in transforming the company, starting with a mindset that conveyed, 'Do what's right by our customers' " (Raytheon Case Study).

Strengths of this framework: Six Sigma and other process improvement change models offer practical, data-driven, step-by-step methods for identifying potential changes, defining change targets, developing a change plan, and implementing and sustaining the change once it is in place. "Some methods, such as Six Sigma, are wired from the start to identify potential benefits, tactically pursue them, and then audit the results" (Holman, Devane, & Cady, 2007, p. 11). It is a highly structured and data-dependent model that can pull a group or organization together quickly, creating a new, more effective culture. The standardized and efficient Six Sigma methods help companies streamline operations, increase value and reduce waste, and can be leveraged to change culture and increase employee engagement through participation on process improvement teams. Application of Six Sigma across an organization or team can help boost customer satisfaction, and cut cost at the organization level, and when adopted as a methodology throughout a culture, Six Sigma can significantly increase an organization's efficiency and effectiveness.

Limitations of this framework: One of the main criticisms of Six Sigma is that it is nothing new and simply repackages traditional principles and techniques related to quality (Catherwood, 2002). Other drawbacks are that these techniques can be complex and require a significant amount of training. Organizations must realize that Six Sigma is not the universal answer to all business issues and may not be the most important management strategy to employ at a given time. Also, Six Sigma may not address organizational culture or the human impacts of change.

Application of this framework: Six Sigma's main focus is on improving performance, adding value, and ensuring reliability for a process or customer. Due to its fundamental reliance on statistical tools and measures, Six Sigma is not often applied at the individual level, but is popular in corporate and small business environments around the world. The DMAIC process can be very helpful for individual change, especially if that person is experienced or trained in Six Sigma, and can adapt it to her personal change. For organizations and groups, it can be very powerful in enabling change mastery, becoming embedded in the culture with common goals, terminology, and processes enabled at every level.

ADKAR

Prosci introduced the ADKAR model in the early part of this century to address concern about the "absence of an end result" in current change theories and approaches. There are five components of ADKAR (Awareness, Desire, Knowledge, Ability, and Reinforcement). The model was first published in 1998, after research with more than 300 companies undergoing major change projects.

The five elements of the ADKAR model can be used as objectives or building blocks for successful change, specifically to be used as a deployment model after a change has been identified (as opposed to some of the other theory examples, such as Transtheoretical, Six Sigma, and Kotter's Change Leadership model, which include the creation of a vision or desired future state). Hiatt (2006) notes that ADKAR provides a framework and process for managing the people side of change, and that "All five elements must be in place for a change to be realized" (p. 1).

Addressing research that indicates the "people dimension" is the most commonly cited reason for project failures (Creasey & Hiatt, 2012), Hiatt (2006) offered the following representation of how the "people" side of change contributes to success as well as the "process" side:

> The elements of the ADKAR model fall into the natural order of how one person experiences change. *Desire* cannot come before *awareness* because it is the awareness of the need for change that stimulates our desire or triggers our resistance to that change. *Knowledge* cannot come before *desire* because we do not seek to know how to do something that we do not want to do. *Ability* cannot come before *knowledge* because we cannot implement what we do not know. *Reinforcement* cannot come before *ability* because we can only recognize and appreciate what has been achieved. (p. 3)

ADKAR can apply to organizations and to individuals. When deploying a major change in a group or organization, one of the first steps is to create awareness of the reasons for change. Next, it is important to ensure buy-in or commitment (desire to change) at the employee level and help them develop knowledge about the change and the ability to implement new skills and behaviors. Once the change has been implemented, it must be reinforced to avoid moving backwards to old behaviors.

ADKAR provides a model that supports change agents and leaders with specific guidance, tools, and actions for each of the five building blocks. The central premise is that executing certain tasks successfully (and in order) will produce the desired results. It is considered to be a prescriptive change theory, due to the focus on results and action, as well as the emphasis on leader or change agent as driver of the process.

Strengths of this framework: ADKAR is an easily understood model when taken at face value, and it offers a clear model for addressing the human side of change. It is scalable and can be helpful in situations where a clear change challenge, or mandate, has been issued to an individual, group, or organization, such as a new software program, a new government regulation to be adopted, or a new process or policy to implement. The model is easily understood, and is straightforward and comprehensive, providing guidance and a solid foundation for management activities that support change. Furthermore, utilizing ADKAR and its focus on individuals facilitates that acceptance of change more readily (Hiatt, 2006). There is a wide range of tools and training to support using ADKAR through Prosci.

Limitations of this framework: As Hiatt (2006) states, "The lifecycle for ADKAR begins after a change has been identified" and primarily addresses the "people side" of change (p. 3). For large implementations, additional project management and consulting support would be recommended.

Application of this framework: The ADKAR approach focuses on individual and group levels, but can also be applied to larger organizations and systems. It can be used as an implementation model to address the social aspects of change, and also in planning change processes. Further, when a change is not going well, ADKAR can be used to analyze the situation and provide a catalyst for identifying a missing step.

Chapter Summary

The focus of this chapter is the theories that inform an understanding of change in individuals, groups, and organizations or systems. The thinking behind what drives change in organizations has undergone a steady evolution, moving from a subset of organizational development to its own unique position of prominence. The development of thought about change theory can be summarized within four major categories of change, including planned change, emergent change, prescriptive change, and transformational change. The authors have presented key change theories for each category and proposed a new integrated theory of mastery that combines both coaching and change processes. By recognizing stages of change at the individual, group, and organization levels, coaches are able to observe the stages of change in their clients and the changes occurring at the context levels. This observation can be useful as coaches work with clients on behavioral shifts and change mastery.

Knowledge Check

1. What are the stages that an organization (or group or individual) goes through in successful change?
2. Describe the origins of organizational change as a discipline, and at least three of the major conceptual shifts that have occurred in the understanding of organizational change since 1950.
3. Identify at least six different theories or models of change, including their main constructs, developers or major proponents, and historical timeframe.
4. Decide which change framework would be helpful in the following situations, and give the rationale for this choice:

    a. A workgroup gets a new leader
    b. Two large Fortune 100 companies are contemplating a merger, even though their cultures and products are currently very different
    c. A small company's manufacturing process needs to be improved in order to maximize productivity
    d. A large manufacturing firm is outsourcing its call center offshore

---

Learning Activities

Learning Activity 1: Assessing Change Capacity

Think of a familiar group or organization. Using the Kerber-Buono Organizational Change Capacity Questionnaire (Appendix D), assess the change capacity of this organization or group. Compare the results to your own experience: Do they describe the reality as you know it? What theories of change would you recommend to the group or organization at this point?

Learning Activity 2: Applying Change Models (Individual)

Imagine coaching the leader of a large engineering organization that is entering a merger with another large multinational company. Which models should be used to help her understand and apply her role as a change leader, and which should be shared to help her communicate about change to the engineers? Why choose these particular models to help this leader?

Learning Activity 3: Applying Change Models (Group)

Imagine coaching a leadership team of five in a small high-tech startup company in Northern California. The company has been in business less than a year and has just introduced its first product, an innovative software system. This product may have applications beyond the ones that the company has thought of and may also provoke new government or intellectual property rights regulations internationally. The company is comprised of 17 people, all under age 30, and only the CEO and CFO have business backgrounds. They utilize a highly networked, distributed, and loosely structured operational model, and all important issues are resolved using a consensus-based decision-making process. Which models would help the team understand and apply its change leadership roles both internally and externally? What are your reasons for choosing these models to help this team?

Learning Activity 4: Using the ADKAR Framework

Identify a personal change that you have experienced and use the ADKAR Individual Change Exercise to identify each of the elements. Analyze your own process and how it differed from the ADKAR model. Write a reflection paper on the difference that might have occurred in the change if the ADKAR model had been utilized (see www.change-management.com/tutorial-adkar-overview.htm).

Learning Activity 5: Application

Think of a coaching client. Chart the client's progress through a change, based on the models/theories of change presented in this chapter. Then, consider: In what ways did the process experience follow the model? Which stages appeared easier? Which stages were more challenging? What supported and challenged the client through the change? How was coaching used, or how could it be used, to support the change?

References

Ackoff, R. (1974). *Redesigning the future: A systems approach to societal problems.* New York, NY: John Wiley & Sons.

Axelrod, R. (2010). *Terms of engagement: New ways of leading and changing organizations* (2nd ed.). San Francisco, CA: Berrett-Koehler.

Bennett, R. (1983). *Management research. Management Development Series, 20.* Geneva, Switzerland: International Labour Office.

Bennis, W. (1966). *Changing organizations.* New York, NY: McGraw-Hill Education.

Boyatzis, R., Howard, A., Rapisarda, B., & Taylor, S. (2004). Coaching can work, but doesn't always. *People Management,* March 11, 2004, 1–11.

Bridges, W. (1980). *Transitions: Making sense of life's changes.* Reading, MA: Addison-Wesley.

Bridges, W. (1986). Managing organizational transitions. *Organizational Dynamics, 15*(1), 24–33.

Bridges, W. (2004). *Transitions: Making sense of life's changes.* (25th anniv. ed.). Cambridge, MA: DaCapo Press.

Burke, W. (2011). *Organization change: Theory and practice* (3rd ed.). Thousand Oaks, CA: Sage.

Burnes, B. (2004). Kurt Lewin and the planned approach to change: A re-appraisal. *Journal of Management Studies, 41*(6), 977–1002.

Burnes, R. (2009). Reflections: Ethics and organizational change—time for a return to Lewinian values. *Journal of Change Management, 9*(4), 359–381.

By, R. (2005). Organisational change management: A critical review. *Journal of Change Management, 5*(4), 369–380.

Caldwell, R. (2006). *Agency and cha*nge. London: Routledge.

Catherwood, P. (2002). What's different about Six Sigma. *Manufacturing Engineer, 81*(8), 186–189.

Change Management History. (n.d.). Prosci. Retrieved from http://prosci.com/main/change_history.html

Conner, D. (1992). *Managing at the speed of change.* Toronto, ON: Villard Books.

Conner, D. (June, 2013). *Executing change: Achieving lasting business results.* Unpublished paper presented at Conference Board Change Management Conference, New York, NY.

Cooper, S. (2009). Theories of learning in educational psychology Kurt Lewin: Field theory of learning. Retrieved from www.lifecircles-inc.com/Learningtheories/gestalt/Lewin.html

Cooperrider, D., Sorensen, P., Whitney, D., & Yaeger, T. (2000). *Appreciative inquiry: Rethinking human organization toward a positive theory of change.* Champaign, IL: Stipes.

Cooperrider, D., & Whitney, D. (2005). *Appreciative inquiry: A positive revolution in change.* San Francisco, CA: Berrett-Koehler.

Creasy, T. & Hiatt, J. (2012). *Best practices in change management.* Loveland, CO: ProSci Research.

Cummings, T. & Worley, C. (2009). *Organization development and change.* Mason, OH: South-Western-Cengage Learning.

Drucker, P. (1992, September–October). The new society of organizations, *Harvard Business Review,* 95–104.

Dunphy, D., & Stace, D. (1993). The strategic management of corporate change. *Human Relations, 46*(8), 905–921.

Falconer, J. (2002). Emergence happens! Misguided paradigms regarding organizational change and the role of complexity and patterns in the change landscape. *Emergence, 4*(1–2), 117–130.

French, W., Bell, C., & Zawacki, R. (1994). *Organization development and transformation: Managing effective change.* Chicago, IL: Irwin.

Hiatt, J. (2006). *ADKAR: A model for change in business, government and our community.* Loveland, CO: Prosci Research.

Holman, P. (n.d.). *Whole systems change.* Retrieved from www.johnniemoore.com/Whole%20Systems%20Change.pdf

Holman, P., Devane, T., & Cady, S. (2007). Introduction. In P. Holman, T. Devane, & S. Cady (Eds.), *The change handbook: The definitive resource on today's best methods for engaging whole systems.* San Francisco, CA: Berrett-Koehler.

Huczynski, A., & Buchanan, D. (2001). *Organizational behaviour* (4th ed.). Harlow: Prentice Hall.

Jacobs, R. (1997). *Real-time strategic change: How to involve an entire organization in fast and far-reaching change.* San Francisco, CA: Berrett-Koehler.

James, S., & Tolchinsky, P. (2007). Whole-scale change. In P. Holman, T. Devane, & S. Cady (Eds.), *The change handbook: The definitive resource on today's best methods for engaging whole systems* (pp. 162–179). San Francisco, CA: Berrett-Koehler.

Kanter, R.M., Stein, B.A., & Jick, T.D. (1992). *The challenge of organizational change.* New York, NY: Free Press.

Kelm, J. (2005). *Appreciative living: The principles of appreciative inquiry in personal life.* Mt. Pleasant, SC: Venet.

Keung-Judge, M., & Holbeche, L. (2011). *Organization development: A practitioner's guide for OD and HR.* London: Kogan-Page.

Kotter, J. (1996). *Leading change.* Boston, MA: Harvard Business School Press.

Kotter, J. (2001, December). What leaders really do. *Harvard Business Review,* 3–11.

Kubler-Ross, E. (1997). *On death and dying.* New York, NY: Scribner.

Kwak, Y., & Anbari, F. (2006). Benefits, obstacles, and future of Six Sigma approach. *Technovation, 26*(5–6), 708–715.

Lewin, K. (1946). Action research and minority problems. In G. W. Levin (Ed.), *Resolving social conflict* (pp. 34–46). London: Harper & Row.

Lewin, K. (1947). Group decisions and social change. In T. M. Newcomb & E. L. Hartley (Eds.), *Readings in social psychology* (pp. 330–341). New York, NY: Henry Holt.

Lewin, K. (1951). *Field theory in social science.* New York, NY: Harper & Row.

Lippett, L. (1998). *Preferred futuring.* San Francisco, CA: Berrett-Koehler.

Mintzberg, H., & Westley, F. (1992). Cycles of organizational change. *Strategic Management Journal, 13,* 39–59.

Mirvis, P. (2006). Revolutions in OD: The new and the new, new, things. In J. Gallos (Ed.), *Organization development: A Jossey-Bass reader* (pp. 39–88). San Francisco, CA: Jossey-Bass.

Orem, S. L., Binkert, J., & Clancy, A. L. (2007). *Appreciative coaching: A positive process for change.* San Francisco, CA: Jossey-Bass.

Orlikowski, W. J. (1996). Improvising organizational transformation over time: A situated change perspective. *Information Systems Research, 7*(1), 63–92.

Orlikowski, W. J., & Yates, J. A. (2006). ICT and organizational change: A commentary. *Journal of Applied Behavioral Science, 42*(1), 127–134.

Owen, H. (2008). *Open space: A user's guide.* San Francisco, CA: Berrett-Koehler.

Peters, T. (1989). *Thriving on chaos.* New York, NY: Harper Paperbacks.

Pettigrew, A., Woodman, R., & Cameron, K. (2001). Studying organizational change and development: Challenges for future research. *Academy of Management Journal, 44*(4), 697–713.

Porras, J., & Silvers, R. (1991). Organization development and transformation. *Annual Review of Psychology,* 42, 51–78.

Prochaska, J., Norcross, J., & DiClemente, C. (1992). In search of how people change. *American Psychologist, 47*(9), 1102–1114.

Prochaska, J., Norcross, J., & DiClemente, C. (1994). *Changing for good: A revolutionary 6-stage program for overcoming bad habits and moving your life positively forward.* New York, NY: William Morrow.

Prochaska, J., Prochaska, J., Levesque, D., Deward, S., Hamby, L. S., & Weeks, W. (2001). Organizational stages and processes of change for continuous quality improvement in health care. *Consulting Psychology Journal: Practice and Research, 53*(3), 139–153.

Raytheon Case Study. Launching Six Sigma to drive a common culture and improve productivity for a global defense provider. Retrieved from www.raytheon.com/businesses/rtnwcm/groups/rps/documents/content/rtn_rps_cs_popup6.html

Sashkin, M., & Burke, W. (1980). An end-of-the-eighties retrospective: A commentary appended to organization development in the 1980s. *Advances in Organization Development,* 1, 347–349.

Schein, E. (1987). *Process consultation: Vol. 2. Its role in organization development* (2nd ed.). Reading, MA: Addison-Wesley.

Schein. E. (1996). Kurt Lewin's change theory in the field and in the classroom: Notes toward a model of managed learning. *Reflections, 1*(1), 59–74.

Schein, E. (2010). *Organizational culture and leadership* (4th ed.). San Francisco, CA: Jossey-Bass.

Stace, D., & Dunphy, D. (2001). *Beyond the boundaries: Leading and re-creating the successful enterprise* (2nd ed.). Sydney, Australia: McGraw-Hill.

Technology Today. (2011). 2010 Raytheon Six Sigma™ President's and CEO awards, Issue 2. Retrieved from www.raytheon.com/technology_today/2011_i2/r6.html

Vaill, P. B. (1996). *Learning as a way of being: Strategies for survival in a world of permanent white water.* San Francisco, CA: Jossey-Bass.

Waddell, D., Cummings, T., & Worley, C. (2007). Organisation development & change: Asia Pacific (3rd ed.). South Melbourne, Australia: Cengage.

Watkins, J. M., Mohr, B. J., & Kelly, R. (2011). *Appreciative inquiry: Change at the speed of imagination.* San Francisco, CA: John Wiley & Sons.

Weick, K.E. (2000). Emergent change as a universal in organisations. In M. Beer & N. Nohria (Eds.), *Breaking the code of change* (pp. 223–241). Boston, MA: Harvard Business School Press.

Weick, K.E., & Quinn, R.E. (1999). Organizational change and development. *Annual Review of Psychology, 50,* 361–386.

Weisbord, M. (1987). *Productive workplaces: Organizing and managing for dignity, meaning and community.* San Francisco, CA: Jossey-Bass.

Weisbord, M. (2012). Future Search: An action guide to finding common ground in organizations and communities. Sydney, Australia: ReadHowYouWant, LLC.

Weisbord, M., & Janoff, S. (2010). *Future search: Getting the whole system in the room for vision, commitment, and action.* San Francisco, CA: Berrett-Koehler.

Westcott, R. T. (2006). *The certified manager of quality/organizational excellence handbook.* Milwaukee, WI: ASQ Quality Press.

White, T. W. (1996). Working in interesting times. *Vital Speeches of the Day LXII*(15), 472–474.

Whitney, D., & Trosten-Bloom, A. (2003). *The power of appreciative inquiry: A practical guide to positive change.* San Francisco, CA: Berrett-Koehler.

Zolno, S. (2001). Appreciative inquiry: New thinking at work. In E. Biech (Ed.), *The 2002 annual: Developing human resources* (Vol. 1). San Francisco, CA: Jossey-Bass/Pfeiffer.

Zolno, S. (2009). Who's ready for whole system change?: Whole field assessment and the change readiness checklist. In E. Biech (Ed.), *The 2009 Pfeiffer annual: Training* (pp. 149–156). San Francisco, CA: Pfeiffer.

Zornada, M. (2005). Introduction to Six Sigma: Business process improvement through Six Sigma. Retrieved from www.slideshare.net/Sixsigmacentral/1-introduction-to-six-sigma-458-k-ppt

8

Essential Change Skills

Coaching for change is more than knowing about change history and theories. It involves a working knowledge of several frameworks, and tools used in change, and having the ability to choose among them, based on what the client or system needs. Successful change coaching is about coaching the right person, at the right time, in the right way. In this chapter, coaches will learn frameworks, skills, and tools to help address the challenges and maximize the opportunities of change in client organizations. In this chapter, the following questions will be addressed:

- What are seven essential change skills used in coaching for change?
- Which change support tools best support each of the skills?
- How are key change concepts, such as the "roles of change," "resistance," and "change fatigue" defined? What are examples of each?
- How can change concepts be leveraged at the individual, group, and organization levels?

Change Skills and Tools

The challenge of change is that it is now "the new normal" (Jørgensen, Owens, & Neus, 2008) in society, and requires skill and ability to manage change successfully. The goal of any individual in supporting others through change should be to succeed not only in the current change, but also to develop these skills and abilities to be more resilient and successfully manage future changes (Conner, 1995; Vaill, 1996). To truly help individuals and organizations change, the coach must also know something about change. Those who have experienced significant change themselves will likely be able to imagine what their clients are experiencing. It is useful to have personally experienced change at the level to which one is coaching (individual, group, or organization), and to have knowledge of change theories and tools. It is also helpful to know some change frameworks to support one's thinking about change. While the change literature in academic and practitioner sources offers both help and advice, it is important to remember that the study of change is relatively new and "far from mature in understanding the dynamics and effects of time, process, discontinuity, and context," as Pettigrew, Woodman, and Cameron (2001, p. 697) acknowledged.

Roles of Change

The premise of this book is that change coaching is an optimal support to facilitate effective change. However, the authors' do not claim that coaching is the *only* valid support. While individual change can be managed and accomplished by one person, larger change projects at the group and organization levels often require implementation of a change infrastructure (Cameron & Green, 2007; Cohen, 2005; Conner, 1995; Galpin, 1996; Kotter, 1996).

Examples of roles in a change infrastructure are a change sponsor, a change leader (or project leader), and a guiding team. For very large change deployments, multiple change teams may be chartered for specific aspects of the change (budget, communications, facilities, learning, etc.) (see Figure 8.1). Often, there are consultants and other specialists involved in supporting the change (e.g., project managers, change team leaders, communications or technology specialists, and continuous improvement experts). In some instances, the Change Coach may be part of a change team comprised of other specialists, or may be asked to take on one of these tasks in addition to coaching. Depending on the scope, size, outcomes, and duration of the intended change project, the addition of a specialist and a change infrastructure may be advantageous.

Conner (1995) wrote extensively about the roles of change, identifying four that he considered most important to be aware of:

1. Sponsors. An individual or group who has the power to sanction or legitimate change.
2. Agents. An individual or group who is responsible for actually making the change.
3. Targets. They focus the change and play a crucial role in making the change successful.
4. Advocates. An individual or group who wants to achieve a change but lacks the power to sanction it.

Change Coaches should note that these roles may be called different names in different settings, and one person can play multiple roles during a change. For example, a leader can be a change agent for the boss, as well as the sponsor to those who report to the leader. As a Change Coach, these roles are important for you to observe in the client or group: Who is acting in what role? Is that role formal or informal? How effective is the person in that role? How do others in the system respond to that person in that role? Is there adequate communication, cooperation, and coordination among the roles to ensure successful change? Are there roles that are missing or not being addressed appropriately for the desired result?

Conner (1995) explained, "The issue is not whether you are [coaching] a sponsor or whether you are [coaching] an agent, but in which type of situation you will be a sponsor and under what circumstances you will be an agent" (p. 107). Table 8.1 offers an adaptation of Conner's roles, with an explanation of key responsibilities, contributions, and items to be taken into consideration for each role. Even if a coach is not coaching the change leader or sponsor, the coach can support the client to understand the roles and address the responsibilities and actions that must take place.

With any change infrastructure come specific roles that facilitate the change, and it is important for Change Coaches to be aware of the roles that are present in the system, roles that are not present but needed, and which of the key

Table 8.1 Responsibilities and Considerations for Roles of Change

ROLE	RESPONSIBILITY OR CONTRIBUTION	NEED TO CONSIDER
Sponsor	• Decides which changes will happen. • Communicates new priorities to the organization. • Provides resources to enable the change.	• Potential changes, dangers, and opportunities. • Creating an environment where the change can flourish—on time and within budget.
Agent	• An individual or group that executes or implements the change. • Develops and/or deploys the plan for change.	• Potential problems, and tactics or strategies for dealing with them. • Who is in the other roles? • How well is the plan progressing?
Target	• Makes the change—the individual or group that is the focus of the change effort. • Those closest to the change can offer information and feedback about the change that is grounded in the work.	• The purpose of the change and the importance of their role in making it successful. • What is needed to implement the change: How must they change?
Advocate	• Individual or group who wants to achieve a change, but without power or position to sanction it. • Can offer influential communication or network, action, advice, and counsel.	• Where does the change need support, influence, and communication? • What relationships or resources are available to support the change?

stakeholders is in which role. Even in individual change, there may be supporting roles present or needed for success. As a Change Coach, one of the ways to help the client or group is to identify these supporting roles and ensure that each is being appropriately filled. This area is also good for Change Coaches to address, not only by coaching the client, but also by coaching each role holder—both individuals and groups regarding the interfaces and interactions among them—to ensure effective collaboration and coordination.

As a Change Coach, it is important to identify who the key stakeholders are in the system in relation to the desired change, and where the coaching client(s) fits among them. (This identification is important even when coaching an individual for change, since individual change takes place in a context. It is often very helpful to support the change client in identifying, leveraging, and relying on the support that others in the system can offer during individual change.)

In many cases, the Change Coach is not coaching the actual change leader or sponsor, but is instead coaching someone in another role. In this case, the coaching challenge is to help empower the client to be most effective in his or her role, to make the change successful, and to influence people in other roles to understand and perform their roles optimally. There are also circumstances in **matrix organizations** where a complex change initiative is being co-led by peers from different functions in the organization. This situation can lead to misunderstanding, political battles, and redundant action if the two leaders are not coordinating their efforts. It is critical for the Change Coach to learn about the context in which the change is taking place, and to identify the key stakeholders, how they currently interact, and how they may need to interact differently to make the change successful.

Conner (1995) and others (Cameron & Green, 2007; Cohen, 2005; Kotter, 1996) emphasized the importance of the sponsor role and change leadership for success:

> The fact that a person wants change to happen does not mean that he or she holds sanctioning power with the target population. Anyone can be an advocate: All it takes is what you consider a good idea and the ability to communicate it. Sponsorship takes far more than ideas and rhetoric; it requires the ability and willingness to apply the meaningful rewards and pressure that produce the desired results. (Conner, 1995, p. 112)

There are many ways that the sponsor must be engaged and knowledgeable about the change, such as understanding a project's implications; taking necessary action; committing energy, attention, action, and resources to the change;

and understanding the importance of follow-up for a successful change project. Conner (1995) identified the qualities of a good sponsor, including (at the top of the list):

- *Power*: the organizational power to legitimize the change with targets.
- *Pain*: a level of discomfort with the status quo that makes change attractive.
- *Vision*: a clear definition of what change must occur.
- *Resources*: a thorough understanding of the organizational resources (time, money, people) necessary for successful implementation and the ability and willingness to commit them.
- *Sensitivity*: the capacity to fully appreciate and empathize with the personal issues major change raises.
- *Persistence*: the capacity to demonstrate consistent support for the change and reject any short-term actions that are inconsistent with long-term change goals (pp. 111–115).

Conner noted that "the demands of being a successful sponsor mean that no one can sponsor more than a few major change projects at a time" (p. 117). "These options reflect the critical nature of the sponsorship—if it is weak, advocates must educate sponsors, replace them, or fail" (p. 115). For these reasons, Conner (1995) advocated a "cascading sponsorship" approach to change. This approach is a "network of sustaining sponsorship that constantly reinforces the importance of a change as it moves through the organization" (p. 123).

This cascading sponsorship enlists the commitment of managers at each succeeding level in the organization, and they, in turn, sponsor and sustain the change down to the target level. This commitment by managers provides oversight and support for the change at all necessary points in the system, and addresses incentives and course corrections needed at each level to make the change successful. Cascading sponsorship requires managed collaboration and coordination among the levels of sponsors, advocates, and agents, and underscores that "CEO, mid-level manager, or first-line supervisor—all must display a high level of resolve to actually achieve major change, nor merely announce it" (Conner, 1995, p. 124).

Coaches should try to identify who is playing each of the four roles of change in the group or organization, and assess how they communicate and interact in support of the change. (Even when coaching an individual on change, one should take the opportunity to identify and enroll other advocates in the client's change, for example, direct reports or family members.) In a group or organizational change, diagnose communication patterns and collaboration among the roles. Seek opportunities to coach the individuals who are in those roles. Support the client to influence other stakeholders for understanding and commitment to action in each role.

A coach working with only one client or group should identify and manage stakeholders—those who will be key in supporting and assessing the work. These stakeholders may be different than the clients' stakeholders identified for the change project. Also, coaches should closely manage their time and any "**scope creep**" that may occur. It is easy for change agents of any type (leaders, coaches, advocates) to become involved in an ever-expanding range of change activities and even additional projects. Often, this result is due to the growing interest and personal involvement of the agent, not necessarily at the request of the client. As part of the initial contracting with the client, the coach should be very clear about what amount, level, and degree of engagement is being offered, and stick to it (or renegotiate the contract).

Change Configurations

Conner (1995) asserted that there are three configurations that change roles take: linear, triangular, or square. In *linear* forms, the relationship is hierarchical, or chain-of-command:

> The target reports to the agent, and the agent reports to the sponsor. The sponsor delegates responsibility to the agent, who in turn deals directly with the target to ensure that the change occurs. (p. 107)

The *triangular* relationship occurs when two roles report to one another (for instance, the agent and target both report to the sponsor). This relationship is often an ineffective configuration, since it involves tasking the agent to make the targets comply with the change when they have no authority to do so. Conner (1995) added that the true culprit in such situations is the sponsors: "In effect, the mandate is to 'Tell people who don't report to you what they must do'" (p. 110), and when the change is unsuccessful, it is the agent who gets the blame. Sometimes this is the case in a matrix management structure, or when the role of sponsor is poorly understood or communicated.

Conner notes that he spends a great deal of time advising sponsors and agents on how to find success in these situations, recommending that the sponsors first endorse the change with the targets before asking agents to implement it. He warns agents to be wary of triangular relationships, and not to agree to a project where they must delegate or give orders to personnel that they do not directly supervise. He notes that agents can help facilitate change, but only after sponsors have presented the change goals and plan to the targets. He cautioned that, for effective change, "sponsors cannot pass on sanctioning power to people who do not hold that status with the targets" (1995, p. 109), and stated, "Having agents tell targets who don't report to them what to do almost always fails" (p. 109).

In a *square* formation, there are two sponsors: one who manages the agents and one who manages the targets.

> The problems occur when Sponsor One directs his agent to bypass Sponsor Two and go directly to the target to gain compliance for the change. Targets rarely respond to major change directives unless these directives come from their sponsor, who controls the consequences applicable to them. In such situations, Sponsor One and the agent are actually advocates because they have no power to sanction the change with the targets. We have found that unsuccessful advocates try to directly influence the targets usually failing because the targets' sponsor does not support the change. (Conner, 1995, pp. 110–111)

It is best for the two sponsors to publicly show support and agreement for the change before asking agents to implement it. Otherwise, Sponsor One and the agents are positioned as advocates, since they do not directly influence the targets. Imagine the vice president (VP) of engineering tasking one of his direct reports to go to the manufacturing organization and to make a change on the factory floor. This strategy would be neither effective nor wise without the engineering VP first obtaining agreement and advocacy from the VP of manufacturing. This situation would be an excellent opportunity for coaching either or both VPs as clients.

Change Coaches must be aware of the configuration that the client (individual or group) faces, in order to be able to support change within political and other structural constraints. In many organizations, a matrix structure predominates, which can resemble the triangular and square configurations. In a matrix organization, reporting relationships often cross product and functional lines. For instance, an engineer may report to a manager in the engineering department, while also reporting to the vice president of a certain product line. This structure resembles a lattice pattern, and is intended to combine the strengths of both a function-oriented organization structure and a product-orientation. In reality, it can be quite complex to navigate, especially when change is involved. Change Coaches need to help their clients be aware of the multiple roles that can exist in a matrix, how the client interacts in a change scenario, and how to engage for action and support among those in various roles. It is important to be clear about who is responsible for what (or whom) in a matrix and to leverage that responsibility in moving the change action forward.

Infrastructure for Large-Scale Change

Scale is also an important factor in managing change successfully. While many of the change frameworks are flexible enough to support change at the individual or large organization level, Kotter (1996) reminded us:

> Most major change initiatives are made up of a number of smaller projects that also tend to go through the multistep process [referring to his eight-step change process]. So, at any one time, you might be halfway through the overall effort, finished with a few of the smaller pieces, and just beginning other projects. The net effect is like wheels within wheels. (p. 24)

In most group or organization change projects, there are project managers or change leaders to support the levels of complexity and to drive action forward. However, it is important for Change Coaches to understand the dynamics of change at this scale, and to help their clients negotiate it successfully. Galpin (1996) advocated a team infrastructure to coordinate large-scale changes and suggested that the team structure and members be identified early in the change process. He also recommended that the size of the infrastructure be linked to the scope of the change project:

> For example, a change effort focused on one division or function—such as finance and administration—often needs only one or two teams with membership from that function. But change across an organization that involves several functions requires the establishment of teams from each area. (p. 19)

For this infrastructure, Galpin (1996) recommended a steering committee (which Cohen referred to as a guiding team). There can also be an integration team, and improvement teams if there are several work streams to be addressed in the change (see Figure 8.1 for an example of a large-scale change team infrastructure). Galpin (1996) suggested:

> The Steering Committee should have a designated leader, identified membership, and an established role of oversight, issue resolution, and allocation or approval of resources for improvement teams. Because a steering committee often includes senior members of an organization's management, it is usually not a full-time entity. Rather, the team members establish a meeting schedule to review project progress, resolve issues, and make key decisions as needed. (p. 20)

Both Galpin (1996) and Cohen (2005) offered recommendations for the steering committee/guiding coalition roles. In the change infrastructure, improvement

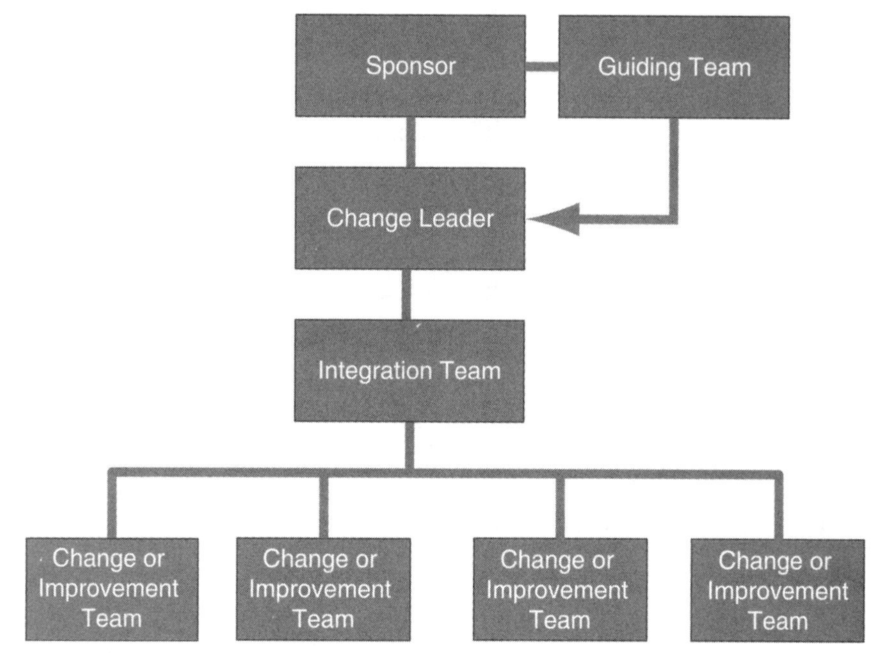

Figure 8.1 Change Team Infrastructure

teams "do the work of change" (Galpin, 1996, p. 21) and include a team leader. Being action oriented, these teams are convened to do the work of change and then dissolved. Galpin's (1996) point was that "teams create better results than individuals" (p. 22) and that group interaction and engagement stimulate creativity and commitment. He noted, "Participation does not guarantee success, but both management and employees find it far more difficult to criticize their own ideas than the ideas of others during testing and rollout [of the change]" (p. 23). Cohen (2005) offered an extensive guide to team elements for achieving change, team composition, transitions, and implementation challenges.

An additional role that Galpin (1996) recommended for large-scale change, in addition to the steering committee, is that of an integration team. The integration team coordinates across the improvement (or change) teams, identifying and resolving issues that are not addressed by individual teams. The integration team leader is a member of the steering committee, and the integration team members are the leaders of the improvement teams. The integration team provides a coordination function, offering a regular forum for communication and learning among all the teams. Galpin suggested a weekly exchange of information during major change efforts.

Gleicher Formula for Change

The Gleicher formula for change is another tool that is helpful in representing the factors promoting successful change. The formula was first introduced by Beckhard and Harris in 1977 (Burke, 2011) and attributed to David Gleicher. Gleicher's formula is similar to Lewin's force field analysis model in that it identifies both the forces that promote and inhibit change, so that they may be explored and leveraged. The formula can be used diagnostically to assess change readiness or to identify risk factors. It can be particularly helpful in explaining the dynamics of successful change to engineers and scientists who are used to working with formulas and equations.

The formula, as cited in Beckhard & Harris (1987) is:

$$C = (ABD) > X$$

"Where C = change, A = level of dissatisfaction with the status quo, B = clear desired state, D = practical first steps toward the desired state, and X = the cost of change" (Burke, 2011, p. 164).

Gleicher's formula suggests that successful change is possible only if the dissatisfaction with the current situation *and* the vision of what is possible *and* the proposed action steps enable the person or group to overcome their resistance to change. Since the formula involves multiplying the three variables, it suggests that if any one variable is completely missing or is too low (mathematically speaking, a zero), the end result will be negatively affected. This assertion implies that falling short on any one of these variables will make it difficult to get past the resistance.

The Change Curve

Another framework that is helpful in understanding individual approaches to change is the change curve (see Figure 8.2). The change curve maps the potential individual reactions to change along axes describing time and commitment to the change. Starting with satisfaction with the current situation, an individual's commitment to the change typically begins to decrease when the change is introduced. This decline continues over time, during a "Reaction" phase, until the reality of the change is accepted. After the point of acceptance initiates an "Action" phase, moving toward increasing commitment until there is full engagement in the new behavior or state.

The process often starts with a denial of the change ("This isn't going to happen to me. I won't be affected") and then resistance to the change, when the reality can no longer be denied ("I'm not having this. I'll find a way around it."). The bottom of the curve represents the milestone moment of acceptance, where a

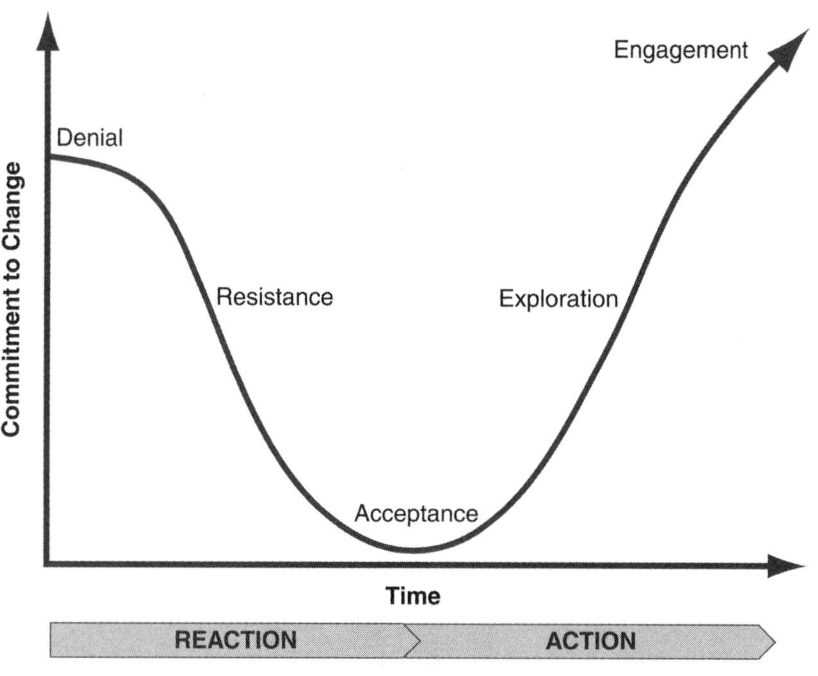

Figure 8.2 Change Curve

new attitude of curiosity creates positive momentum and a willingness to explore the change ("Could this work for me? Are there any benefits?"). Lastly, there is a commitment to the new way of working or being that is demonstrate by a positive future focus and engagement in the new behaviors ("I think I can make this work! It might be even better than before!"). At this stage, there is often a willingness to advocate for the change to others who are still in the acceptance process.

This graphic is helpful to use with individuals as well as groups in normalizing the feelings that they may be having about the change, and reassuring them that such feelings are (a) a natural part of the process of adjusting to change, and that (b) their feelings will evolve over time as that adjustment occurs. In addition, sometimes individuals experience setbacks that send them back to prior stages in the change curve.

The change curve is also a useful tool for helping leaders understand that each of their employees may be in a different step on the curve at any given time and that providing information about the change is a crucial, if complex, task. While the majority of people go through some form of this curve during the transition process, some may take longer than others. The change curve illustrates that change communications must address individuals at *all* levels (cognitive, affective, and behavioral), and in each stage of the curve in order to help them move forward.

For example, a person in the denial step needs to have solid information—facts and data—about the change: that it has been decided, that it is being implemented, and that there are expectations for each team member to ensure the success of the change. Someone in the resistance phase needs to have questions and concerns addressed so that he can personally understand the benefits of the change, know what the consequences may be if he does not accept the change, and make a reasoned decision about the future.

Learning about the change curve helps leaders be patient and recognize that a group goes through the change curve as individuals, each at a different pace, and not as a unit. Frequently, progress through the curve is not a linear process. People impacted by change move back and forth on the curve, often taking more time on one step than another—and perhaps even moving back to an earlier stage from time to time. As each individual learns more about the change and starts to see ways to embrace the new reality, group members are able to help one another adapt and progress is made.

Using this tool can help the client understand his or her own progress through the change curve, and to observe and assess where others may be. Used in a group setting, the curve can be a topic of discussion, promoting the realization that there is a normal process of accepting and adapting to change. This kind of discussion allows the opportunity for a leader or change agent to clarify any questions and concerns group members may have. This conversational approach also provides the leader an opportunity to reiterate the reasons, benefits, and vision for the change and to encourage group members to stay committed in support of the change.

The Change Adoption Lifecycle

Another helpful framework for reflecting on individual change is one by Moore (2002) in his book *Crossing the Chasm.* Originally labeled by Moore as a "technology adoption lifecycle," the model describes different degrees of willingness to embrace new technology and is easily adapted to the individual process of adopting change (Beal, Rogers, & Bohlen, 1957). Moore's (2002) framework suggests that there are some people who find change exciting and exhilarating and embrace it naturally, while others view change as a challenge. The five categories in the framework are described as:

1. Innovators. Approximately 2.5 percent of the population, they pursue new technology aggressively and sometimes seek it out or instigate it before a formal project has been launched.

2. Early adopters. Approximately 13.5 percent of the population, they adopt new technology and products soon after they are available, finding it easy to understand the change and imagine the potential benefits. Early adopters can often help others address concerns about change.
3. Early majority and late majority (two separate categories). Approximately 34 percent each of the population, they adopt the technology in stages, as products are proven and become more mainstream (the early majority adopt earlier than the late majority), and are influenced by observation and successes from the innovators and early adopters.
4. Laggards: Approximately 16 percent of the population, they take a long time to adopt the technology, or never do.

The five categories are described by Moore (2002) as a bell curve:

> The divisions in the curve are roughly equivalent to where standard deviations would fall. That is, the early majority and late majority fall within one standard deviation of the mean, the early adopters and the laggards within two, and way out there, at the very onset of a new technology, about three standard deviations from the norm, are the innovators. (p. 11)

Moore notes the importance of the innovators to success:

> There are not very many innovators in any given market segment, but winning them over at the outset of a marketing campaign is key nonetheless, because their endorsement reassures the other players in the marketplace that the product does, in fact, work. (p. 12)

When using this framework to consider individuals' or groups' reactions to change, it is helpful to realize that, over time, most of these positions can shift. In viewing their reactions in conjunction with the change curve (see Figure 8.2), it is evident that adoption or commitment levels can shift over time, given the right information and motivation—even for the laggards. Even so, it may take some time before everyone accepts the change.

Perceptive or experienced leaders may realize that threats and cajoling can only ensure compliance, not true commitment to the change. So it is best to give individuals time to come to terms with the changing situation. However, it is not wise to wait until everyone is "on board" before taking action, since it may take time for everyone to understand, accept, and commit to the change. Let the innovators and early adopters lead the way and influence others to join them.

For example, innovators may be eager to "jump in with both feet" and be the first to use the new product or process. In using it, they may prove its worth to the early adopters and even early majority pragmatists, who start deploying it more widely and even improving it. Over time, this group forms a critical mass that may be able to demonstrate enough solid evidence to win over the late-majority conservatives as well. Last, the laggards will need to make a choice about whether or not they will commit to the change. It is important to remember that even though the laggards can be slow to commit or accept the change (or may never do so), they may have legitimate, well-articulated concerns or questions about the change. These questions and concerns can be used as feedback and should be solicited regularly to improve the change process and results. At some point, when the decision has been made to proceed with the change, laggards must be clearly informed of their options, and some may choose to be left behind if they do not commit to making the change successful.

Essential Skills for the Change Coach

Assess Change Readiness

One of the first things that a Change Coach needs to understand about an individual, group, or organization is "What is the current situation?" (Cohen, 2005; Conner, 1995; Maurer, 2010a). A current-state analysis can be simple or complex but must answer the following questions:

- What is the nature of the change?
- Why is it necessary? Why now?
- What are the outcomes and benefits expected from making the change?
- Who will be impacted by this change?
- What is the level of urgency for the change?
- Are there other competing initiatives, commitments, or changes occurring simultaneously with this one?
- Who are the people involved in the change? What are their roles?
- Are they aware of and/or ready for this change? Do they embrace it or are they apprehensive, anxious, or resistant to it?
- Is there a change project infrastructure in place (i.e., a change leader, sponsor, change-guiding team, and/or project team)?
- Who is responsible for the outcomes of the change? Is he in a position to be influential? Is she committed to the change and the leadership role? What additional commitments and responsibilities does the change leader have?

A Change Coach can use several methods to discover this information: surveys, interviews, observations, and archived information (from reports, documents, and other analyses that may already exist). There are many change-readiness assessment tools available. One is the change readiness assessment from *The Heart of Change Field Guide* by Cohen (2005). It offers a comprehensive process with examples for performing and reporting on a change readiness assessment. Another is Maurer's "Support for Change Questionnaire" (2010b), a tool that offers a process for a series of guided conversations about change that can help coaches to assess the degree of support for the change. Each can be tailored for use with individuals or groups, or adapted as surveys or polls for larger organizations. In any case, it is helpful to get feedback in as many ways as possible about the change, to be able to plan ahead, and to coach clients on topics of risks and opportunities as the change unfolds.

These assessments can be valuable sources of metrics for the change project. Assessing individual and/or group or organizational readiness at the beginning of a change can also provide a baseline to measure against the same assessment used in the future. For a complex or long-term change project, repeating the same assessment every six months may reveal valuable trend information about the way the change is being viewed, and even about shifts in the organizational culture due to the change. Data from a readiness assessment can also highlight potential risks or opportunities that may arise.

Tools for Assessing Change Readiness

- Change Readiness Audit, pp. 12–17 from *The Change Management Pocket Guide* by Nelson and Aaron (2005)
- Change Readiness Assessment, pp. 207–222 from *The Heart of Change Field Guide* by Cohen (2005)
- Support for Change Questionnaire from *Change Toolkit* by Maurer (2010b)

Identify Current State Risks and Opportunities

After assessing the current situation for change, it is important to look at the current state of the individual or organization. At this point, using a Strengths-Weaknesses-Opportunities-Threats (SWOT) or Strengths-Limitations-Opportunities-Threats (SLOT) analysis is a good way to get a sense of the current environment. The basic four-block analysis is used to specify the objective of the change project and then to identify the internal and external factors that are favorable and unfavorable to achieving success.

The technique has also been adapted as SOAR (Strengths-Opportunities-Aspirations-Results) to focus on a more appreciative approach (Stavros, Hinrichs, & Hammond, 2009). A SWOT, SLOT, or SOAR analysis can be performed at the individual, group, or organization level, as a discussion, group or individual activity, survey, or interview. For best results, one should plan to engage others in this assessment, to get as many different viewpoints as possible. Make note of any additional changes or other efforts that are going on concurrently. The information from this analysis will help identify several important risks and opportunities to address:

- Readiness for change. Is the individual or organization in a position to take on this change now? Recall the importance of timing cited in the transtheoretical model of change (Prochaska, Norcross, & DiClemente, 1994). Is the change well understood? Do the individual or individuals involved know why the change is occurring and what will be expected of them? Is this a change that can be postponed or implemented in stages? Sometimes this approach is helpful to a client or group in managing the additional effort required of the change process.
- Appropriate choice of change approach. What model or theory underpins the individual or organization's approach to change? Is it congruent with the circumstances, time frame, desired outcomes, and urgency of the change needed? Has it been discussed and decided, or is it a default or unexamined choice? To explore this potential risk, use the Kerber-Buono Situational Change Mastery Questionnaire (Kerber & Buono, 2010a) (see Appendix C).
- Additional or concurrent commitments. Note the potential impact of multiple changes or other efforts occurring simultaneously. Each raises the level of complexity for the others and dilutes the time and attention available for change success—in both individuals and groups.

Look for signs of change fatigue or resistance that may slow the change momentum:

- Change fatigue. With the increasing rates of change impacting people both personally and professionally, it is no wonder that change fatigue is on the rise and becoming a threat to successful implementation and sustainment of change (Beaudan, 2006; Garside, 2004). "Any change initiative, whether one with a specific focus or comprehensive organizational change, will reach a point when it stalls" (Beaudan, 2006, p. 1).

This phenomenon is the natural tendency of an individual or group to tire of the effort, uncertainty, and ambiguity of making a significant change. Beaudan (2006) claimed that change fatigue typically sets in within 30 to 90 days of change being initiated, and he emphasized:

> Understanding this pattern and developing a clear strategy for getting through these traps is a must for leaders and managers who want to make change last, or who are looking for ways to revive or accelerate change efforts inside their organizations (p. 2).

Change Coaches must train themselves to recognize the symptoms of change fatigue and be ready to address them with clients. Beaudan (2006) offered six signs of change fatigue:

1. Those not leading the change increasingly question the value/objectives of the change effort.
2. Change effort leaders/coordinators are stressed out and/or leaving.
3. Those involved in the change are reluctant to share or comment on data about the effort.
4. Budget and resources are diverted to other strategic initiatives.
5. Customers become impatient with the duration of the change effort.
6. Key leaders do not attend progress reviews.

The question remains: Can something be done to avoid or diminish change fatigue? According to Garside (2004), "The answer is 'yes,' if we align the incentives such that there is congruence of aims, lead in the right way, avoid jargon, attach resources and time, and engender trust through delivery. Difficult—but worth it" (p. 90). The first thing is to recognize that the change initiative has derailed, gotten off track, or is about to fail. Change Coaches can facilitate an assessment of the current state of change readiness or deployment by gathering data to identify any concerns or misunderstandings among the key stakeholders. It is important to support clients in taking steps to address the issue of change fatigue, if it is found. The coach should start by reflecting and taking action on the following, as recommended by Beaudan (2006):

1. Rethink change goals and expectations.
    - Were the initial goals too ambitious, vague, or unrealistic?
    - Were the right success measures and metrics designed?

- Was the initial assessment of the change's impact on customers or employees off target?
- Have new developments blown a hole in the initial case for change?

2. Change speeds.
   - Has the coach been too slow in implementing change, or, conversely, was the pedal put to the metal—leaving people behind?
   - Has time been taken to learn and assess what is working and what is not working?
   - Are there clear milestones?
3. Change the mix of people.
   - Are the wrong people leading the way?
   - Is different expertise required on the change team?
   - Should outside voices be brought in?
4. Add excitement.
   - Go public. Reenergize the change and make it a priority.
   - Increase the stakes. Make the benefits for individuals or groups engaged in driving the change more immediate and visible.
   - Create a crisis. By insisting that failure is not an option, a constructive crisis is created that will stir people's sense of responsibility and lead to creative solutions.
   - Make it fun.

Resistance to Change As change is being considered or implemented, there is often resistance—the perception or reality that not all stakeholders wholeheartedly embrace the change. Despite strong initial motivation, vision, and robust planning, implementing change successfully can often fail due to resistance (Beaudan, 2006; Conner, 1992; Galpin, 1996; Kotter, 1996; Maurer, 2010a). After researching this question, Beaudan (2006) acknowledged that:

> The answer, confirmed by 10 years of research and interviews with leaders seeking to get their change efforts back on track, is simple but elusive: whereas initial planning for change is important to ensure a strong start, most change plans fail to adequately anticipate internal resistance and other unforeseen factors that cause change to derail over time. (p. 1)

According to Gestalt theory, resistance is a natural part of any system (Maurer, 2010a; Stevenson, 2004) and supports the reasoning process by which change is embraced. Cohen (2005) added that "resistance to change is natural and normal"

(p. 208), and Galpin (1996) noted that it can be found at any level in the organization. Both acceptance and resistance to change are part of the same psychological continuum, and it is pointless to try to focus on one end and avoid the other.

Resistance, or questions and differing points of view about the change, can serve to make the process and result stronger if they are honored and sought out. Leveraging the power of the opposite viewpoints and sharing information so that all can understand the nature and plans for change creates a partnership that makes the change more successful. The discussion is best held in the spirit of making the change work for all, with the understanding that when the decision is made, there will be a "point of no return" where each individual will make a decision to continue to be part of the change or not. After the time of discussion is past, there can be no holding back for any of the laggards that are still left undecided or unwilling to make the change.

To address resistance, it is important to identify and mitigate the resistance's potential causes. One cause can be the natural inertia of complacency in the current state. Unless there is a major threat or upheaval on the horizon, most people will opt for maintaining the status quo (even if it's known that one should be proactive about making changes). As shown in Gleicher's formula and Lewin's force field analysis, to overcome natural inertia the motivation toward the change must be more powerful than the satisfaction with the status quo (or anxiety about the change).

Overcoming inertia can be accomplished in a number of ways: developing and communicating a compelling case for the change and a motivating vision of the future, as well as a set of first steps that everyone can take. It is also helpful to engage all the key stakeholders in discussions about the change—their hopes, concerns, and suggestions—to involve them in the planned implementation, as part of the change infrastructure or in regular discussions or updates about the change progress. Another important aspect of dealing with resistance, or harnessing people's eagerness for change, is to leverage multiple strategies to engage people in the change. Strengthen change communications and stakeholder engagement by utilizing different approaches and motivators, for example:

- *Cognitive*: Relying on giving information, building understanding and ability to take action for the change;
- *Behavioral*: Translating the change vision and values into behaviors, offering rewards and incentives, training and coaching for the new behaviors, and giving feedback so that people know where they stand in terms of adopting the change satisfactorily;

- *Psychodynamic*: Helping people understand the change curve and addressing issues faced in the transition, surfacing hidden or emotional issues related to the change, being aware of and discussing the dynamics of groups and individuals going through change and transition; and
- *Humanistic*: Addressing emotions and the hierarchy of needs during change, fostering community and learning to support the change (Cameron & Green, 2007).

Another consideration for Change Coaches to be aware of is the source of potential resistance. Maurer (2010a) and Galpin (1996) offer different perspectives on the potential sources of resistance. Galpin (1996) identified three levels of resistance: not knowing, not being able to make the change, and not being willing to make the change. He noted that:

> Satisfaction at each level of resistance reduces resistance at the next level. For instance, when we respond to people's need to know, they become more open to learning the next skills and abilities involved in changing. And once they have the new skills, they will gain the confidence to overcome unwillingness to change. (p. 43)

Maurer (2010a) also offered a three-level view of resistance to change:

- Level 1: "I don't get it" can stem from lack of information, disagreement over the interpretation of the data, lack of exposure to critical information, and/or confusion over what it all means (p. 38).
- Level 2: "I don't like it" is an emotional reaction to the change. Blood pressure rises, adrenaline flows, pulse rate increases. It is based on fear. People are afraid that this change will cause them to lose face, status, control—maybe even their jobs (p. 39). Maurer warns that this emotional reaction is not mild, and can be deep. "When we experience Level 2 ourselves, it can feel as if our very survival is at stake" (p. 39). The "fight-or-flight" reaction that takes over can impair the ability to reason and listen effectively.
- Level 3: "I don't like *you*." Maurer claims that lack of attention to this possibility is a "major reason why resistance flourishes and changes fail" (p. 41).

In Level 3 resistance, people are not resisting the idea; they may even love the idea. They are resisting *you*. Perhaps their history with you makes them wary. Perhaps they are afraid that the coach won't see things through and this will be another "flavor-of-the-month" scenario (p. 41).

Maurer (2010a) pointed out that it might not be anything against the coach personally but what the coach represents, and Level 3 concerns do not have to be true in order to have negative consequences, on the coach or on the change effort (or both). Addressing these concerns takes "work and an amazing amount of persistence" (p. 42).

A thorough analysis of the individual or group's current state is a prerequisite for change coaches to be effective and to provide data-driven assessment of progress along the change journey.

Tools for Assessing Current State Risks and Opportunities

- Commitment Assessment, pp. 23–26 from the *Change Management Pocket Guide* by Nelson and Aaron (2005)
- SWOT Analysis, pp. 32–35 from the *Change Management Pocket Guide* by Nelson and Aaron (2005)
- SOAR Analysis from *The Thin Book of SOAR: Building Strengths-Based Strategy* by Stavros, Hinrichs, and Hammond (2009)
- Kerber-Buono Situational Change Mastery Questionnaire (see Appendix C)

Recognize and Support the Roles of Change

As mentioned above, Conner (1995) and others (Cameron & Green, 2007; Cohen, 2005; Galpin, 1996; Kotter, 1996) suggested supporting change projects with specific roles. Change Coaches should recognize that each role provides an opportunity for one's support. In addition, coaches should note the size and scope of the change and use data from the change readiness and SWOT analyses to make a recommendation about a potential change infrastructure. Assess commitment and engagement levels of the leader, sponsor, and guiding coalition (or steering committee), and validate that there is a team or other coordinating mechanism for communication and collaboration across the change infrastructure (groups or individuals).

Tools for Supporting the Roles of Change

- Key Skills and Attributes of Guiding Team Members, p. 28 from *Heart of Change Field Guide* by Cohen (2005)
- Sample Criteria Model: Selecting a Guiding Team Member, p. 29 from *Heart of Change Field Guide* by Cohen (2005)
- Guiding Team Self-Assessment and Assessment Diagnostics, pp. 51–55 from *Heart of Change Field Guide* by Cohen (2005)
- Key Team Elements for Achieving Change, pp. 42–43 from *Heart of Change Field Guide* by Cohen (2005)

Ensure the Right Vision and Change Communication

Ensure that the sponsor's vision for the change is robust, inspiring, and communicated to all levels. Cohen (2005) offered a wealth of suggestions for developing a powerful vision, as well as a suggested communication strategy:

1. Increase communication before developing the vision. Gather relevant information on key elements from multiple stakeholders before the vision is drafted;
2. Validate the vision with all stakeholders. Leaders, customers, management and employees from all parts of the organization, and consultants or outsiders who have solid knowledge of the situation;
3. Close the loop. Ensure that those who have contributed to the vision development know what input has been incorporated, what was not, and why;
4. Maintain constant communication with stakeholders. Communicate about the change process, key initiatives, the progress of the change, and its evolution; and
5. Make it clear that input is always welcome.

In addition, confirm that there is an adequate and appropriate communication plan to support the change. Change communication must differ from simple one-way transfer of information and must move participants to think and care about their role in the change success. Change communication must allow for two-way communication, providing feedback, ideas, and suggestions for improvement—for the change as well as for the change process. Quirke (1996, p. 18) offered a distinction between two aspects of change communication in organizations—information and relationship building:

> Information: What do I need to know, analyze, and interpret?
> Relationship building: How do I feel about the people around me, how am I valued, and what is the extent of my goodwill to put myself, my thinking, and my effort into going further?

Quirke noted that the aim of communication should be to "align attitudes, share knowledge, and manage information" (1996, p. 32). Quirke (1996) also added that additional objectives of change communication could include encouraging participation and stimulating thinking, networking, and learning across groups or functions, employee engagement, and process improvement. Change communication can help shape engagement, commitment, and understanding of the change project, resulting in increased probability of success.

Tools for Vision and Change Communication

- Leadership Alignment Assessment, pp. 27–31 from the *Change Management Pocket Guide* by Nelson and Aaron (2005)
- Characteristics of an Effective Vision, pp. 71–73 from *Heart of Change Field Guide* by Cohen (2005)
- The Vision Diagnostic, pp. 75–76 from *Heart of Change Field Guide* by Cohen (2005)
- Tactics to Guide Effective Communication of the Vision, p. 92 from *Heart of Change Field Guide* by Cohen (2005)
- Communication Plan, pp. 46–52 from *Change Management Pocket Guide* by Nelson and Aaron (2005)
- Communication Plan Template, p. 101 from *Heart of Change Field Guide* by Cohen (2005)
- Communication Diagnostic, pp. 108–110 from *Heart of Change Field Guide* by Cohen (2005)
- Audience Assessment Template, p. 97 from *Heart of Change Field Guide* by Cohen (2005)
- Communicating the Right Message at the Right Time, p. 100 from *Heart of Change Field Guide* by Cohen (2005)
- Feedback Form, pp. 78–81 from *Change Management Pocket Guide* by Nelson and Aaron (2005)
- Frequently Asked Questions (FAQ) Sheet, pp. 82–85 from *Change Management Pocket Guide* by Nelson and Aaron (2005)
- Key Messages Worksheet, pp. 53–58 from *Change Management Pocket Guide* by Nelson and Aaron (2005)
- Roles and Responsibilities of a Communication Network Owner, p. 74 from *Change Management Pocket Guide* by Nelson and Aaron (2005)
- Audience Assessment Template, p. 97 from *Heart of Change Field Guide* by Cohen (2005)
- Communicating the Right Message at the Right Time, p. 100 from *Heart of Change Field Guide* by Cohen (2005)
- Feedback Form, pp. 78–81 from *Change Management Pocket Guide* by Nelson and Aaron (2005)

- Frequently Asked Questions (FAQ) Sheet, pp. 82–85 from *Change Management Pocket Guide* by Nelson and Aaron (2005)

Facilitate Stakeholder Engagement

A Change Coach should understand who the key stakeholders are for the change project, whether the change involves one individual or an entire organization. Gather data to identify any resistance to the change, and leverage the ideas and suggestions of resistors to improve the change project. Know the roles involved in the change (especially for any clients being coached) and discuss where leaders may be on the change curve and in the change adoption lifecycle model. This discussion will help the coach and client(s) understand how their orientations may differ from the rest of the group or organization. Help find ways for all to play a role.

Tools for Ensuring Stakeholder Engagement

- Stakeholder Analysis, pp. 18–22 from *Change Management Pocket Guide* by Nelson and Aaron (2005)
- Stakeholder Enrollment Process and Plan Example, pp. 94–95 from *Heart of Change Field Guide* by Cohen (2005)
- Leadership Involvement Plan, pp. 59–63 from *Change Management Pocket Guide* by Nelson and Aaron (2005)
- Stakeholder Behavioral Map, p. 123 from *Heart of Change Field Guide* by Cohen (2005)
- Roles and Responsibilities Template, pp. 118–122 from *Change Management Pocket Guide* by Nelson and Aaron (2005)

Support Change Momentum

It can be challenging to start up a change project, get stakeholders engaged, deploy plans, and coordinate action. And it is imperative that the Change Coach monitor the pace, the intensity, and the direction of the project when it is underway. By observing and noticing risks and opportunities, and noticing if key stakeholders start to disengage or slow down the pace of change, a coach can be an "early warning system" to help clients prevent the change from derailing, or failing. By identifying and showcasing small "wins" and individual contributions, and celebrating key milestones along the change journey, leaders and sponsors can keep people enrolled in the change, and aware of positive outcomes. A robust communication plan is essential, as is coordination of key change activities, so that the entire community sees that progress is being made. Not only will these tactics support the successful conclusion of the change, but they will also aid in the transition to a sustainment plan after the change has been implemented.

Tools for Ensuring Change Momentum and Sustainment

- Implementation Checklist, pp. 88–91 from *Change Management Pocket Guide* by Nelson and Aaron (2005)
- The Enabling Action Diagnostic, pp. 132–134 from *Heart of Change Field Guide* by Cohen (2005)
- Systems and Structures Action Plan, pp. 108–112 from *Change Management Pocket Guide* by Nelson and Aaron (2005)
- Short Term Wins Planning Template, p. 145 from *Heart of Change Field Guide* by Cohen (2005)
- Short Term Wins Diagnostic, pp. 151–153 from *Heart of Change Field Guide* by Cohen (2005)
- Monitoring Key Organizational Areas, p. 167 from *Heart of Change Field Guide* by Cohen (2005)
- Rewards and Measures Alignment Template, pp. 113–117 from *Change Management Pocket Guide* by Nelson and Aaron (2005)
- The "Don't Let Up" Diagnostic, pp. 178–179 from *Heart of Change Field Guide* by Cohen (2005)
- Making It Stick Effectiveness Checklist and Diagnostic, pp. 197–199 from *Heart of Change Field Guide* by Cohen (2005)

Support the Development of Change Capacity in the Organization

The goal of successful change coaching is twofold: (1) to support success for the client's desired change, and (2) to build the capacity for the client (and the organization) to change in the future. The latter goal goes beyond establishing readiness for change, which is the client's desire and ability to implement the current change. Capacity involves supporting and building the client's ability (and agility) to successfully respond to future changes (whether internal or external). "In essence, building change capacity involves a systemic approach to developing the organization in ways that tap into people's natural capacity to change by supporting change and making it a basic part of organizational life" (Kerber & Buono, 2010a, p. 4).

Building organizational change capacity requires "interventions focused on organizational members (understanding and accepting different approaches to change, enhancing willingness and ability to change), structure (creating a change supportive infrastructure, ensuring appropriate resources), and culture (building a facilitative culture, ongoing strategizing)" (Kerber & Buono, 2010b, p. 6). Table 8.2 offers actions that address these three levels of intervention, and can be used as ideas for change coaching.

Remember "Self"

Change Coaches bring a valuable asset into an organization: *themselves.* Historically, there is agreement that the self can be an important instrument of diagnosis (Cameron & Green, 2007; Cheung-Judge, 2001; Hanson, 2000; Jamieson, Auron, & Shechtman, 2010; Seashore, Shawver, Thompson, & Mattare, 2004). Also, McCormick and White (2000) noted "many consultants and researchers regard it [self] as one of their best tools" (p. 58). Being an instrument of change involves everything from being intentional about one's personal demeanor with a group or client, to awareness of one's personal experience in interacting with a client or system, to how one addresses one's own issues, dilemmas, and challenges. It means leveraging "*self-awareness, perceptions, choices* and *actions* as the fundamental building blocks of our capacities to be effective agents of change" (Seashore et al., 2004, p. 55).

McCormick and White (2000) suggested using oneself as a diagnostic instrument—paying attention to one's emotional reactions as a reflection of the organization's (or client's) condition:

> When facilitating work groups and t-groups, when we become upset about something occurring in the group, we find it useful to see if it is not just our issue, but an issue for others. We mention our feelings to see if others agree. Sometimes our hunches are wrong, but more often than not they are correct. In this way, our feelings become a source of hypotheses to be tested. (p. 51)

McCormick and White (2000) also recommended paying close attention to one's initial perceptions, noting them and even writing them down when new to the system and before one has—even unconsciously—started adapting to the mindsets and beliefs of the client/system. Another skill they identify is the ability to understand one's own prejudices and bias, to be more objective in one's observations and assessment. While it is can be stated that no **participant-observer**

Table 8.2 Kerber-Buono Building Change Capacity

FOCUS	OBJECTIVE	POTENTIAL CHANGE COACHING AGENDAS
Organizational Members	Developing an understanding and acceptance of different change approaches *(Supports Awareness and Acceptance stages of the Mastery Model)*	• Adopt a common, enterprise-wide framework for thinking and talking about change • Develop widespread knowledge about different approaches to change and when each is appropriate • Develop deep expertise about change in the organization • Provide change coaching and consulting services • Establish change agent networks to share best practices, tools, and insights about changing • Debrief change initiatives with a focus on learning from experience
	Enhancing willingness and ability to change *(Supports Awareness, Acceptance, Adoption, and Integration stages of the Mastery Model)*	• Select, hire, evaluate, and reward people based on their ability to thrive on change • Form diverse teams to encourage innovation and creativity • Develop, reward, and promote supervisors and managers who enable change • Enhance the personal credibility of organizational leaders • Listen to, encourage, and reward mavericks and trailblazers • Create a climate of trust, honesty, and transparency
Structure	Building a change-supportive infrastructure *(Supports Acceptance, Adoption, Integration, and Mastery stages of the Mastery Model)*	• Frequent meetings to identify and critically assess opportunities • Encourage low-cost experiments with new ideas • Recognize and reward those who support, encourage, lead, and share learning about change • Creation of a fluid structure that allows the easy formation of new groups • Creation of systems to share knowledge, information and learning across boundaries • Responsive and proactive training and education
	Providing appropriate resources *(Supports Awareness, Acceptance, Adoption, and Integration stages of the Mastery Model)*	• Designate an owner of the goal to develop change capacity • Devote resources to continually scanning the environment for new ideas • Encourage external contact with stakeholders, especially with customers • Appoint committed change sponsors for specific initiatives • Target key change initiatives with enough resources to get public successes • Shelter breakthroughs with their own budgets and people

(*Continued*)

Table 8.2 *(Continued)*

FOCUS	OBJECTIVE	POTENTIAL CHANGE COACHING AGENDAS
Culture	Creating a change-facilitative culture *(Supports all stages of the Mastery Model)*	• Emphasize learning and information sharing • Encourage questions and experiments • Value alternative viewpoints • Tolerance for mistakes in the interest of learning • Stakeholder orientation • Shared purpose with a common language about change
	Ensuring ongoing strategizing *(Supports all stages of the Mastery Model)*	• Create a shared purpose • Think dynamically and systemically so that strategies can change quickly • Examine future markets, competitors, and opportunities • Factor future scenarios into today's decisions • String together a series of momentary advantages • Create and communicate a change-friendly identity, both internally and externally

is ever completely objective, being aware of one's own biases can lead to asking better questions when interpreting something from one's own reactions. Internal (as opposed to external) coaches are both participants and observers in the change initiative. One can also invoke "self as instrument" by postponing judgment to avoid coming to premature conclusions. Last, McCormick and White (2000) urged practitioners to pay attention to images and fantasies that come to mind when gathering information about a situation, as these are often more relevant and relatable to the client than academic models or examples.

It is important to remember, honor, and be aware of oneself in interactions with the client and the client system. The client(s) may be looking to the coach as an example of how to manage change. Be aware of how you are speaking and acting. Your behavior, along with its inherent biases, courage, and humor, will demonstrate to others the effective (and perhaps not-so-effective) ways of dealing with change, building understanding, and addressing challenges.

Change can challenge us in maintaining a positive perspective and recognizing progress. Take stock of any potential resistance you may have—both to the proposed change and to the client's ways of approaching it or engaging in it. This awareness of "self as instrument of change" can be powerful in the role of a Change Coach. Awareness of self in action requires vigilance, courage, openness to feedback, reflection, and carries with it a need for commitment to continual self-development.

Cheung-Judge (2001) noted, "If we aspire to both the labels and the roles of helper, counselor [sic], adviser and supporter, using ourselves as key instruments, we must undertake a process of life-long discovery and of owning and refining our instrumentality" (p. 11). She recommended "dedicating time to the on-going maintenance of both self-knowledge and technical expertise. Employing a shadow consultant, a mentor or even a therapeutic relationship to continually heighten our self-awareness" (p. 12). In addition, she suggested developing lifelong learning habits; working through personal issues around power, control and authority; building self-awareness; and committing to a regular schedule of self-care, optimally including both physical and spiritual practices (Cheung-Judge, 2001).

Other helpful practices include journaling, discussing change-coaching work with a peer who is not involved with the change, or working with a coaching supervisor while engaged in the change project. Monitor and reflect on your own behavior in order to be a positive influence for the client and the system.

Tools for Self as Instrument

- Choice Awareness Matrix (see Figure 5.3)
- Self-assessment tools such as the Hay Emotional-Social Competency Inventory (ESCI), Herrmann Brain Dominance Inventory (HBDI), Hogan Personality Inventory (HPI), Myers-Briggs Type Indicator (MBTI), and Motives, Values, Preferences Inventory (MVPI)
- Values identification and clarification processes, such as offered by Values in Action (VIA) at www.valuesinaction.net

---

Chapter Summary

This chapter introduced change frameworks, skills, and tools for addressing change at the individual and group levels. The frameworks are important foundations for understanding change at every level, and for being successful in coaching for change. Knowledge of change roles, configurations, and infrastructure is important in understanding success factors influencing change. Models such as Gleicher's formula, the change curve, and Moore's technology adoption lifecycle help explain the variation in the individual experience of change and transition.

Seven key skills are introduced for those working with change: (1) assess change readiness, (2) identify current state risks and opportunities, (3) recognize and support roles of change, (4) ensure the right vision and change communication,

(5) facilitate stakeholder engagement, (6) support the development of change capacity in the organization, and (7) remember self as instrument. The tools and resources offered in this chapter support the development of each of these skills.

Knowledge Check

1. Identify six of the eight change skills used in coaching for change.
2. Demonstrate an understanding of which change support tools best support each of the skills.
3. Describe Gleicher's formula for change and illustrate ways it could be useful to a Change Coach.
4. Describe Conner's roles of change, outlining responsibilities and things to consider for each.
5. Define and give an example of three change skill concepts and identify how they can be leveraged at the individual, group, or organization levels.

Learning Activities

Learning Activity 1: Change Skill Application

Think of a recent change situation and describe:

- How does Gleicher's formula applies to it? The change curve? Moore's technology adoption model?
- Who were the key stakeholders, and where were they on the change curve?
- Where was the individual or organization in the Change Mastery Model?
- Where/when did the change falter (if it did), and when did the momentum accelerate (if it did)? What caused either or both of these?
- Were there any indications of resistance and/or change fatigue? If so, how were they addressed?
- What role did you play in the change?
- What might you have done as a coach for the change?

Learning Activity 2: Kerber-Buono Situational Change Mastery Questionnaire

Think of a change situation and complete the Kerber-Buono Situational Change Mastery Questionnaire (see Appendix C).

- What change approach was in operation in the example: Directed, planned, or guided changing? Why was this approach selected?
- Plot the results of the questionnaire in Part 3. Did the initial diagnosis of the change approach match the results of the questionnaire? If there was a difference, explain why.
- How could you adapt the change coaching approach to accommodate and support the individual or organization in this change situation?
- How could you be of best service to the client in the situation described?

Learning Activity 3: Kerber-Buono Organizational Change Capacity Questionnaire

Think of a change situation and complete the Kerber-Buono Organizational Change Capacity Questionnaire (see Appendix D).

- In what ways could the approach be adapted to ensure that change capacity is being developed with this client?
- What ways would you need to develop your own capacity (regarding change coaching or change) to better support future clients to develop change capacity?

References

Beal, G. M., Rogers, E. M., & Bohlen, J. M. (1957). Validity of the concept of stages in the adoption process. *Rural Sociology, 22*(2), 166–168.

Beaudan, E. (2006, January/February). Making change last: How to get beyond change fatigue. *Ivey Business Journal*, pp. 1–7.

Beckhard, R., & Harris, R. (1987). *Organizational transitions: Managing complex change.* Reading, MA: Addison-Wesley.

Burke, W. (2011). *Organizational change: Theory and practice* (3rd ed.). Thousand Oaks, CA: Sage.

Cameron, E., & Green, M. (2007). *Making sense of change management.* London: Kogan-Page.

Cheung-Judge, M. (2001). The self as an instrument: A cornerstone for the future of OD. *OD Practitioner, 33*(3), 11–16.

Cohen, D. (2005). *The heart of change field guide.* Cambridge, MA: Harvard Business School Press.

Conner, D. (1992). *Managing at the speed of change: How resilient managers succeed and prosper where others fail.* New York, NY: Random House.

Galpin, T. (1996). *The human side of change.* San Francisco, CA: Jossey-Bass.

Garside, P. (2004). Commentary: Change management: Are we suffering from change fatigue? *Quality and Safety in Health Care, 13*(2), 89–90.

Hanson, P. G. (2000). The self as an instrument for change. *Organization Development Journal, 18*(1), 95–105.

Jamieson, D. W., Auron, M., & Shechtman, D. (2010). Managing use of self for masterful professional practice. *OD Practitioner, 22*(3), 4–11.

Jørgensen, H., Owens, L., & Neus, A. (2008). *Making change work.* Somers, NY: IBM.

Kerber, K., & Buono, A. F. (2010a). Intervention and organizational change: Building change capacity. In A. F. Buono & D. W. Jamieson (Eds.), *Consultation for organizational change* (pp. 81–112). Charlotte, NC: Information Age.

Kerber, K., & Buono, A. F. (2010b, Spring). Creating a sustainable approach to change: Building organizational change capacity. *SAM Advanced Management Journal,* 4–21.

Kotter, J. (1996). *Leading change.* Cambridge, MA: Harvard Business School Press.

Maurer, R. (2010a). *Beyond the wall of resistance* (rev. ed.). Austin, TX: Bard Press.

Maurer, R. (2010b). *Support for change questionnaire.* Retrieved from www.askaboutchange.com/wp/wp-content/uploads/2010/06/Toolkit-Page-118-SUPPORT-FOR-CHANGE_QUESTIONAIRE.pdf

McCormick, D. W., & White, J. (2000). Using one's self as an instrument for organizational diagnosis. *Organization Development Journal, 18*(3), 49–61.

Moore, G. (2002). *Crossing the chasm: Marketing and selling disruptive products to mainstream customers.* New York, NY: HarperBusiness.

Morgan, N. (2001, July). How to overcome "change fatigue." *Harvard Management Update.* Cambridge, MA: Harvard Business School Press.

Nelson, K. & Aaron, S. (2005). *The change management pocket guide: Tools for managing change.* Cincinnati, OH: ChangeGuides, LLC.

Pettigrew, A., Woodman, R., & Cameron, K. (2001). Studying organizational change and development: Challenges for future research. *Academy of Management Journal 44*(4), 697–713.

Prochaska, J., Norcross, J., & DiClemente, C. (1994). *Changing for good: A revolutionary 6-stage program for overcoming bad habits and moving your life positively forward.* New York, NY: William Morrow.

Quirke, B. (1996). *Communicating corporate change: A practical guide to communication and corporate strategy.* Berkshire, UK: McGraw-Hill.

Schein, E. (1987). *Process consultation: Vol. 2. Its role in organization development.* (2nd ed.). Reading, MA: Addison-Wesley.

Seashore, C., Shawver, M., Thompson, G., & Mattare, M. (2004). Doing good by knowing who you are: The instrumental self as an agent of change. *OD Practitioner, 36*(3), 55–60.

Stavros, J. M., Hinrichs, G., & Hammond, S. (2009). *The thin book of SOAR: Building strengths-based strategy.* Bend, OR: Thin Book.

Stevenson, H. (2004). Paradox: A gestalt theory of change. *Gestalt Review, 14*(2), 111–126.

Vaill, P. B. (1996). *Learning as a way of being: Strategies for survival in a world of permanent white water.* San Francisco, CA: Jossey-Bass.

PART III

Integration and Application

9

An Integrated Approach to Change Coaching

There are numerous professional practices at the individual, group, and organization levels for the purpose of supporting sustainable behavioral change that results in improved performance, development, and/or transformation. At its heart, all coaching is about change—for performance, development, or transformation at the individual, group, or organization levels. The goal is to coach the right person at the right time in the change process for the right results that will move the change forward toward success.

Skilled coaches are familiar with the coaching process first described in Chapter 5 and models and theories of change. Coaches are also informed by their professional disciplines and the approaches and practices learned in their coach training, which influence and inform how they will best support the client through change.

This chapter links the previous chapters related to coaching and change into an integrated model of coaching for change. The framework and considerations will be presented.

- What are the end-to-end processes used to in change coaching?
- What is the best-practice, research-related model for coaching for change?
- What key considerations must coaches take into account when working with organizations and clients in change initiatives?
- What tools and resources can be applied to each step in the coaching-for-change process?

Change Coaching Process

Coaching can be applied at several levels to support change for performance, development, and transformation. The following 10-step Change Coaching Process integrates important theories, models, and tools that are recommended for change

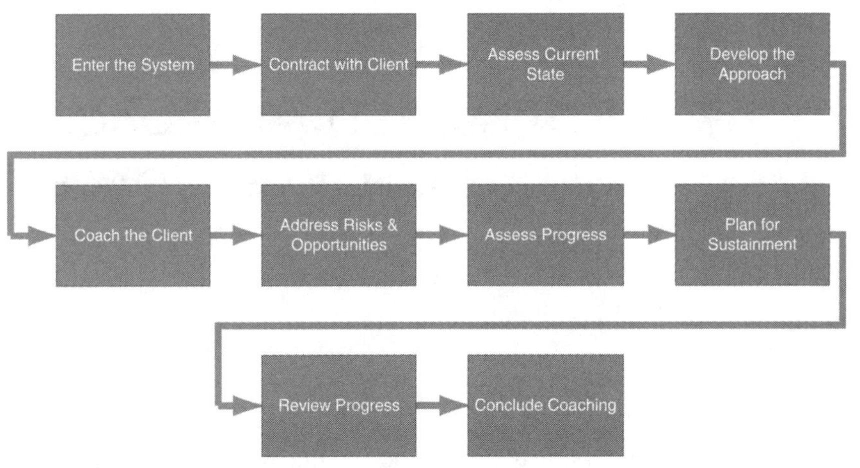

Figure 9.1 Change Coaching Process

coaching (Figure 9.1). Much like action research (Coghlan & Brannick, 2010; Lewin, 1946/1948; Lewin, Lippitt, & White, 1939; McNiff, 2000; Passmore & Friedlander, 1982; Reason & Bradbury, 2006; Sagor, 1992) and consulting models (Block, 2000, 2001; Schein, 1987, 1988), this approach provides a guide for supporting the transition of behavioral, cognitive, emotional, and spiritual change beginning with the initial entry into a system (individual, group, or organization) and concluding with reflection and learning for continuous learning and improvement.

Each step is presented along with examples to illustrate each. While the steps are presented in a linear form (see Figure 9.1), they are often more dynamic when applied. Practitioners may find themselves returning to prior steps and moving forward in the process to ensure that the needs of the client or system are adequately addressed. Also, the steps can be used as a diagnostic aid for the Change Coach's reflection about the work, which is often helpful to perform at regular intervals during the change coaching engagement. Reviewing the steps—either alone or in discussions with the client or change sponsor—can help identify areas for more work or aspects of the change that are going well and which can be celebrated. The regular practice of reflection and continuous improvement leads to mastery in change coaching, helping the coach learn and build change skills while helping the client or system develop capacity for future changes.

The 10 steps in the Change Coaching Process include:

Step 1: Enter the system. The focus of this step is to engage with a client or system to do the work. Entering can come about by being invited to help, for example, as a consultant, or by noticing a need and bringing up the option of change coaching. The latter situation is common for internal coaches, and it is important to remember that coaching takes place by request. Even if a need is observed, the impetus driving change coaching should be an offer, based on discussion and agreement. Once a client has requested change coaching, the objective is to become acquainted with the client's needs, the environment, key stakeholders, and constraints (e.g., budget, time, resources) to identify the most-effective means of working together and to explore the larger organizational/environmental context in which change is sought.

Examples of the outcomes of this step include:

- Relationships built with good faith to be able to work together
- Presenting needs identified
- Initial agreement to work together completed.

The desired product of this step is a mutual agreement that the coach will support the client with change coaching. This agreement involves an understanding of the client's need for change, an agreement to work together (an invitation), a preliminary investigation of the context and key players that will be involved, and a belief that this situation will benefit from change coaching and the coach will be able to work with the client effectively to address the change coaching needs.

Note: If the coach is not qualified, equipped, or able to do this work at the time, help the client procure another Change Coach.

Step 2: Contract for coaching. The focus of this step is refining the understanding of client needs, timing for the engagement, services to be provided, timeline for services, outcome expectations, costs, and communication for status checks.

Examples of the outcomes of this step include:

- Contract (formal or informal) agreed upon
- Identification of the scope of the coaching request (the change), the level of the request (individual or group coaching), and the focus of the change (performance, development, or transformation)
- Agreement on frequency, duration, and medium of change-coaching meetings (weekly for an hour over the phone, etc.)
- Understanding of any resources or constraints that will impact the change coaching (political, organizational, personal, financial, etc.)
- Clarity on how and how much the coach will be remunerated for change-coaching services (if the coach is to be paid), and agreement on how and when the contract can be terminated by either party.

The desired product of this step is an agreement of how the coach will work with the client, including an understanding of the client's desired outcome, the situation or context in which the change will take place, and the resources, timelines, and other tactical issues that will support the work.

Note: In the role of Change Coach, one primarily supports the client to be most effective in a specific change role. There are, however, additional aspects of change that may need to be observed, analyzed, or investigated. Be sure that these opportunities are discussed in contracting, so that there is enough flexibility built into the agreement to enable access to key stakeholders or others in the system as needed to track the change progress and validate that the change is being effectively managed. In some situations, the client may agree to the coach taking on other aspects of the change project, such as facilitating focus groups, or supporting communications or project management activities.

Step 3: Assess the current state of change mastery and change infrastructure. The focus of this step is to assess the change infrastructure and readiness, stakeholders, resistance to or appreciation of the change, organization culture, or context for change. This step may include readiness assessments, **psychometrics**, focus groups, and stakeholder interviews.

Examples of the outcomes of this step include:

- Identification of key stakeholders in the change. This outcome includes determining who they are, what roles they may be playing currently, and for the change, where they are on the change curve (see Figure 8.1) and Moore's technology adoption lifecycle.
- Assessment of change readiness. For an individual or group, this would involve a discussion to identify any current and competing commitments that could potentially impact the success of the change, and the development of a force-field analysis or change-readiness assessment for the change. For an organizational or large-scale change, this step might involve interviews of key stakeholders and/or surveys of the population to determine change readiness and agility.
- Investigation and analysis of environmental factors that may impact the change. This outcome includes multi-rater feedback or other assessments, interviews or focus groups with key stakeholders, and for organizations or groups, data about current and historical performance related to the change (stock prices, financials, staffing data, productivity trends, etc.).
- Presentation of a report to the client (formally or informally) about the current state of readiness and change agility.

The desired product of this step is data and analysis from multiple levels and perspectives that will give clients an understanding of where they are in the change process, their readiness to change, and potential barriers and enablers for their desired changes.

Step 4: Develop recommendations and approach. The focus of this step is to identify key elements to address in change coaching, to refine the approach for the engagement, and to create a recommended course of action.

Examples of the outcomes of this step include:

- Report with data analysis and proposed actions based on the data
- Recommendations about change infrastructure or other support needed (project management, sponsor, etc.) and scope of the change (i.e., address the entire change at once or separate it into increments to be executed over time and contracted for individually)
- Proposed change approach to use (directed, planned, or emergent)
- Identification of success measures (How will the coach and the client know that the change has been successful? How will the coach track the success of the coaching?)
- Refined contract for services, resources, and timetables
- Agreement upon the approach (who, what, when, how) for services.

The desired product of this step is a report or presentation (formal or informal) outlining the recommendations derived from the data analysis, and a project plan or set of actions for the client to consider and accept.

Step 5: Coach the client. The focus of this step is to provide coaching to individuals and groups to support change using the coaching process and six coaching skills presented in Chapters 4 and 5, while staying focused on the client's agenda and the Mastery Model framework.

Examples of the outcomes of this step include:

- Progression through the Mastery Model (see Figure 6.1)
- Improved performance, development, or transformation from the change
- Development of effective execution of the change, increased collaboration, and improved communications with key stakeholders.

The desired product of this step is an effective coaching engagement that facilitates the client's successful change, and development of skills and abilities that will build agility for approaching future changes successfully.

Note: In some situations, the support offered to the client may extend beyond change coaching, or may leverage change coaching with other groups or individuals involved in the change. This extension is especially likely with large-scale or long-term changes such as organization transformations. In these scenarios, the Change Coach is often a member of the change-management infrastructure, and he or she offers coaching and consulting or project management expertise to support the change. While these activities are value-added for the change project and also support the development of mastery for the client and/or system, it is important to differentiate these roles, both for the coach and the client.

Step 6: Recognize and address risks, opportunities, and successes. The focus of this step is on working with the client and system to observe and identify potential impacts to the change being implemented (both positive and negative), as well as the future development of change agility.

Examples of the outcomes of this step include:

- Two-way communication channels that allow for regular input and feedback about the progression of the change.
- Regular cadence of conversations with key stakeholders that foster engagement, openness, and improvement about all aspects of the change and its success.
- Identification and documentation of risks or concerns about the change, as well as actions taken to address them—and the same process for any opportunities that are discovered in the course of implementing the change. These risks or opportunities can be specifically about the success of the change or about other implications to the client or organization.
- Regular celebrations or recognition for "change champions" or stakeholders who have made exceptional or uniquely positive contributions to the change.

The desired product of this step is a document that identifies and tracks risks and opportunities, including actions to address each. Additional outcomes can include improved communication and stakeholder engagement, especially if contributions supporting the change are regularly acknowledged or rewarded, and if input or feedback about the change is sought and addressed.

Step 7: Assess progress. The focus of this step is to assess the effectiveness of the change implementation and the change coaching that supports it. Step 4 included a set of success factors, or metrics, as part of the coach's recommendations for change. If agreed on, the status of these factors must be monitored and communicated throughout the change process to ensure progress. In addition to regular change coaching meetings with the client, it is important to keep the channels of information open for input and feedback from all stakeholders about the change.

Examples of the outcomes of this step include:

- A regular cadence of communications between the client, key stakeholders, and any other change agents that may play a part in the infrastructure. (Communications can include surveys, interviews, focus groups, and other data gathering by the client or change project teams.)
- Regular reporting of status on the change project: Is it going according to plan regarding budget, milestones, actions, risk, stakeholder engagement, and accomplishment of key success factors?
- Continual awareness by the coach about how well the change approaches are working to involve stakeholders, identify and address resistance and change fatigue, and promote the success of the project. This information can be from the coach's observation or other data gathering and is important as an objective measure to facilitate effective action on the part of the client.

The desired product of this step is to ensure appropriate issues are addressed in coaching to support effective engagement of the client in the change process.

Step 8: Develop recommendations for future development and sustainment. The focus of this step is on ensuring the client's and/or system's ability to sustain the change accomplishment and build on it as needed. In addition, this step addresses the important aspect of mastery to improve the client's ability to prepare for, and manage, additional or future changes with improved skill and agility.

Examples of the outcomes of this step include:

- Development of recommendations for next steps following the change to ensure its sustainment and integration into the culture or lifestyle of the client, and to leverage the current achievements to support future change planning
- Reflection and discussion about what is going well and what could be done more effectively about any aspect of the change (including the Change Coach, key stakeholders, project planning and execution, and any of the steps in the Mastery Model)
- Reassessment of change readiness (formal or informal) to identify and address any unplanned issues that arose and areas of resistance or change fatigue
- Assessment of organizational change capacity and/or situational change mastery (using the Kerber-Buono questionnaires, Appendices C and D).

The desired product of this step is to recommend next steps for continued development of the client/system in planning, implementing, and responding to change. The recommendations should be based on current data from the client system and should incorporate the development of increased mastery and agility in change.

Step 9: Review lessons learned. The focus of this step is to reflect on the change achievement as well as the coaching engagement, develop further recommendations, acknowledge and celebrate successes, and identify what could be done more effectively in future change situations. It is a time to review what has happened, how success was achieved (or not), and how mastery was built. It can be a time to assess the impact of the change coaching and how well the coaching process worked as a methodology for facilitating change. The coach and client should also address any interpersonal issues or improvement feedback between them that will build the relationship for a future engagement.

Note: Lessons learned can be discussed at any time during a change project and should be a regular part of coaching conversations so that improvements can be addressed and implemented as they are observed and recognized. This process of action learning allows the change to be influenced by new ideas throughout the process, not just at the conclusion.

Examples of the outcomes of this step include:

- Holding an "after-action review" discussion (or event) to identify what went well and what did not concerning the change implementation, and what lessons learned are to be incorporated into any future change projects
- Formal or informal acknowledgment of the aspects of the change coaching that were most helpful and those that could have been done more effectively (This conversation is often a candid one between coach and client, reflecting together on the work and giving each other feedback about any opportunities for improvement.)
- A ceremony or celebration to recognize the achievement of the change and acknowledge key stakeholders and contributors
- Development of an updated project plan with agreement about action steps to address any further changes.

The desired product of this step is mutual agreement to close the change coaching, which includes documenting the change outcomes with a final report.

Step 10: Conclude change coaching. During this step, the change coaching engagement is concluded, allowing for the coach's and client's personal reflections on accomplishments and next steps for development.

Examples of the outcomes of this step include:

- A meeting with the client to close the change coaching engagement, involving an open and appreciative review of the engagement per the contract, as well as any acknowledgments the coach may have for the client or staff.
- A presentation of any metrics, assessment results, or success documentation that has been created. Typically, this presentation involves an assessment of the overall effectiveness of the change project in terms of the success measures that were identified in Step 4, along with quantitative (numbers, statistics) and qualitative (anecdotes, stories, or interview comments) data describing the change implementation and outcomes.
- A request for feedback or a follow-up survey about the change coaching.
- Creating a summary of lessons learned and documentation of an action plan to follow to further develop mastery.
- Personal reflection and a journal entry about one's experience with the client, the project, and one's role. This reflection is especially important after situations in which the coach may have taken on additional roles or responsibilities beyond change coaching in support of the client (for example, managing communications).

The desired product of this step is mutual agreement on the closure of the change coaching, which includes documenting the change outcomes with a final report, exchanging any final feedback, appreciating the work and relationships involved, and noting progress along the Mastery Model.

The goal of change coaching is to support the client through change and to develop the capacity to effectively anticipate, respond to, and manage future changes. Change coaching also develops relationships built on mutual experience and appreciation, and clients often turn to Change Coaches as trusted partners to help them navigate future changes. As coaches travel the path of change with their clients, they have the honor to support and witness their clients' growing mastery, while the coaches hone and develop their own.

Applying the Change Coaching Process

Change coaching is the art of integrating models and theories for both change and coaching to support the client's successful change and development of mastery towards future changes. Each of the aspects of change coaching—coaching and change—involve skilled selection and use of a variety of models, theories, and tools that have been documented elsewhere in this book. Table 9.1 outlines a selection of tools that are appropriate and helpful for each of the change coaching steps.

Table 9.1 Tools for Change Coaching

CHANGE COACHING STEPS	TOOLS AND RESOURCES
1. Enter the system	• Self as instrument • Mastery Model • Listening for understanding • Asking questions about other coaching skills • Observing • Contracting
2. Contract for coaching	• Change-readiness assessments • Surveys, interviews • Project and goal planning • Stakeholder identification and assessment • Coaching-readiness assessment • Organizational change capacity questionnaire • Focus and level of coaching
3. Assess the current state of change mastery and change infrastructure	• Focus of coaching (performance, development, transformation) • Mastery Model • Systems theory • Stakeholder analysis • Readiness assessments, psychometrics • Focus groups and stakeholder interviews
4. Develop recommendations and approach	• Contracting • Change approaches • Change frameworks and tools • Systems theory • Mastery Model • Project and action planning • Success factors and measures
5. Coach the client	• Coaching model • Coaching skills • Change Coaching Process • Change frameworks and tools • Practices from specific disciplines • Mastery Model • Stakeholder engagement
6. Recognize and address risks, opportunities, and successes	• Project management • Communication • Focus groups and stakeholder interviews • Reward and recognize contributions • Stakeholder engagement • Documentation of risks, opportunities, and actions to address

(*Continued*)

Table 9.1 *(Continued)*

CHANGE COACHING STEPS	TOOLS AND RESOURCES
7. Assess progress	• Feedback • Metrics • Communication
8. Develop recommendations for future development and sustainment	• Mastery Model • Project management • Communication • Focus groups and stakeholder interviews • Stakeholder engagement
9. Review lessons learned	• After-action review • Reflection • Journaling and reviewing personal observations and assessment with a coach or colleague
10. Conclude change coaching	• Mastery Model • Use of self • Reflection • Personal after-action review with action plan for integrating lessons learned into development

Chapter Summary

Change coaching is a transdisciplinary practice that is applied through numerous professional practices at the individual, group, and organization levels. Change coaching is based on sustainable behavioral and organizational change that can result in improved performance and broadened development and/or transformation. A 10-step Change Coaching Process provides a framework for change coaching that integrates coaching, contracting, change, and project management models.

Knowledge Check

1. What are the 10 steps in the integrated Change Coaching Process?
2. What is the purpose of each step?
3. What is a tool or resource that can be used to support each step in the model?

Learning Activities

Learning Activity 1: Review Experiences

Review recent coaching-for-change experiences. Using the 10-step Change Coaching Process, map your actions with clients to the steps. Were all of the steps included? Which actions worked well? Which could have been strengthened? What can be learned from this experience that will help you be a better coach for change?

Learning Activity 2: Assess Yourself as a Change Coach

Review the 10-steps in the Change Coaching Process. Which are your own strengths? Which are your areas for development and growth? Create a plan of action to leverage your strengths and develop the others.

Learning Activity 3: Plan for Application

Consider an upcoming opportunity to coach for change at either the individual, group, or organization levels. Once the level has been identified, identify the focus for the coaching: performance, development, and/or transformation. Next, outline a plan for the engagement by reviewing the 10-step Change Coaching Process.

References

Block, P. (2000). *Flawless consulting: A guide to getting your expertise used* (2nd ed.). New York: Pfeiffer.

Block, P. (Ed.). (2001). *The flawless consulting fieldbook & companion: A guide to understanding your expertise.* San Francisco, CA: Jossey-Bass/Pfeiffer.

Coghlan, D., & Brannick, T. (2010). *Doing action research in your own organization.* London: Sage.

Lewin, K. (1946/1948). Action research and minority problems. In G. W. Lewin (Ed.), *Resolving social conflicts* (pp. 34–46). New York, NY: Harper & Row.

Lewin, K., Lippitt, R., & White, R. K. (1939). Patterns of aggressive behavior in experimentally created "social climates." *Journal of Social Psychology, 10,* 271–299.

McNiff, J. (2000). *Action research in organisations.* London: Routledge.

Pasmore, W., & Friedlander, F. (1982). An action-research program for increasing employee involvement in problem solving. *Administrative Science Quarterly, 27,* 343–362.

Reason, P., & Bradbury, H. (Eds.). (2006). *Handbook of action research.* London: Sage.

Sagor, R. (1992). *How to conduct collaborative action research.* Alexandria, VA: Association for Supervision and Curriculum Development.

Schein, E. H. (1987). *Process consultation: Lessons for managers and consultants, Volume II.* Reading, MA: Addison-Wesley.

Schein, E. H. (1988). *Process consultation: Its role in organization development, Volume I* (rev. ed.). Reading, MA: Addison-Wesley.

10

Cross-Cultural Change Coaching

Many executive coaches today find themselves working with leaders from a variety of cultural backgrounds and coaching leaders who work with culturally diverse teams. It is, therefore, increasingly important that coaches understand the role of culture in their work (Peterson, 2007). In this chapter, the authors will explore organizational culture: how culture can impact coaching for change, identifying and dealing with cultural biases, and using an organization's culture to support coaching efforts. In this chapter, the following questions will be addressed:

- How is culture defined?
- What are some dimensions of culture that might be important in change coaching?
- What are ways to learn about and address cultural biases?
- Why is it important to leverage cultural differences and similarities to support change?
- What are the coach's own cultural biases?

Given the increase in globalization, immigration, and the diverse and global workforce, it is inevitable that coaches will find themselves dealing with cultural issues. The International Coach Federation (ICF, 2012) reports that coaching is currently well established in Western Europe and North America, but that coaches are increasingly coming from a variety of countries, including Latin America and the Caribbean (ICF, 2012). In addition, coaching is emerging in Brazil, China, and India (Passmore, 2009).

This chapter addresses culture as a phenomenon of ethnicity and nationality, and of social or organizational identity. Developing cultural competence and sensitivity is essential in coaching for change. It is important for coaches to look for and address the impacts of culture and cultural difference at the individual, group, and organization or system levels.

Culture Defined

Culture is an abstraction, a concept, and an observable product of thoughts, agreements, and feelings held by an individual and/or shared by a group. Culture "points to phenomena that are below the surface, that are powerful in their impact but invisible and to a considerable degree unconscious" (Schein, 2010, p. 14). While culture can function to guide behavior and facilitate group and individual behavior (Burke, 2011; Denison, Hooijberg, Lane, & Leif, 2012; Hofstede, Hofstede, & Minkov, 2010; Schein, 2010), it can also limit thinking and stand in the way of change (Argyris, 1977; Burke, 2011; Kotter, 1996; Marshak, 2006; Schein, 2010). An understanding and appreciation of culture as an enabler or inhibitor of change in individuals, groups, and organizations (as well as in oneself) is essential to successful coaching. Schein (2010) noted, "As we will see, whether or not a culture is 'good' or 'bad,' 'functionally effective' or not, depends not on the culture alone but on the relationship of the culture to the environment in which it exists" (p. 14).

The Merriam-Webster online dictionary defines culture as "the set of shared attitudes, values, goals, and practices that characterizes an institution or organization" and "the set of values, conventions, or social practices associated with a particular field, activity, or societal characteristic." Dictionary.com adds that culture comprises "the behaviors and beliefs characteristic of a particular social, ethnic, or age group," for example, the youth culture; the drug culture. It is interesting to note that other definitions of culture refer to "cultivating" or "educating," indicating that culture is a developed and shared phenomenon, rather than one that occurs randomly or by accident.

Hofstede et al. (2010) referred to culture as "the software of the mind" (p. 5), and asserted that culture is always a collective phenomenon shared with others who live or work in close proximity, and that it is learned, not innate. "*Learned* means modified by the collective influence of programming (culture) *as well as* by unique personal experiences" (p. 7). Hofstede et al. (2010) note that culture promotes group and individual identity ("in groups" and "out groups"), that people carry within them many layers of cultural messages, since everyone belongs to a different number of groups at the same time (racial, religious, gender, age, geographic, etc.), and that "these various levels are not necessarily in harmony" (p. 18). Schein (1994) also noted "it is quite possible for a group to hold conflicting values that manifest themselves in inconsistent behavior while having complete consensus on underlying assumptions" (p. 149).

Cultural bias is the tendency to perceive and interpret other cultures through the lens of one's own cultural preferences. This can lead to judging behaviors and preferences of others according to the standards of one's own culture. In many cases, individuals are not even aware of their own cultural biases, and do not realize that they are automatically assuming that their preferences are better than those of others.

Cultural Dimensions

Schein (2010) described four categories of culture and suggested "understanding culture at any level now requires some understanding of all of the levels" (p. 5). The four categories include:

- Macrocultures. Nations, ethnic and religious groups, and occupations that exist globally
- Organizational cultures. Private, public, nonprofit, government organizations
- Subcultures. Occupational groups within organizations
- Microcultures. Microsystems within or outside organizations (p. 2).

Within these categories, Hofstede et al. (2010) identified four basic manifestations of culture: symbols, rituals, heroes, and values (p. 7). They used the metaphor of an onion skin to suggest layers of increasing depth toward a center, "indicating that symbols represent the most superficial and values the deepest manifestation of culture, with rituals and heroes in between" (p. 7).

Schein (2010) offered, "In another sense, culture is to a group what personality or character is to an individual" (p. 14). He claimed that culture implies a level of structural stability in a group, is deeply embedded, and covers all of a group's functioning. Schein (2010) agreed with Weick's (1995) notion that culture derives from the human need to make the environment as sensible and orderly as possible, and added "any social unit that has some kind of shared history will have evolved a culture" (p. 17). The former chairman and CEO of IBM, Lou Gertsner, noted that, "You can quickly figure out, sometimes within hours of being in a place, what the culture encourages and discourages, rewards and punishes" (2003, p. 189).

The metaphor of an iceberg is often used in describing the levels of culture: The "tip of the iceberg" symbolizes the level of observable behavior and manifestations that reveal themselves in artifacts. At the next level, below awareness, behavior is linked to values and meaning shared by a group. This world of ideas and their emotional value is often unconscious, hidden as the "bottom of the iceberg."

Schein (2010) also identified observable phenomena that reflect culture in groups, including group norms, espoused values, and formal rituals and celebrations, but noted that it is a deep and often unconscious part of a group, "less tangible and less visible" (p. 16). He added, "Culture is something that survives even when some members of the organization depart. Culture is hard to change because group members value stability in that it provides meaning and predictability" (p. 16). He defined culture as "a pattern of shared basic assumptions learned by a group as it solved its problems of external adaptation and internal integration" (p. 18). He argues that this definition does not specify the size or location of groups or organization levels where cultures apply, and that culture can be associated with professions, religions, nations, ethnic groups, and other social units. He believes that the phenomenon of culture manifests in observable behavior, artifacts, and espoused values, and asserts that "culture change, in the sense of changing basic assumptions, is difficult, time-consuming, and highly anxiety-provoking" (p. 33).

Another way of looking at culture is offered by TMC/Berlitz (2010) as part of its Cultural Orientations Approach™ (COA) framework. It defines culture as "the complex pattern of ideas, emotions and observable/symbolic manifestations (including behaviors, practices, institutions and artifacts) that tends to be expected, reinforced and rewarded by and within a particular group" (TMC/ Berlitz, 2009, p. 3). Understanding these patterns of culture supports the development of "cultural competence" that will "reduce risk, enhance innovation, and maximize opportunities through both cultural differences and similarities" (TMC/Berlitz, 2009, p. 3).

One model of culture that focuses on groups or organizations is the Denison organizational culture model. Based on more than 20 years of research by Daniel Denison about culture transformations in global organizations, the model identifies four essential traits of organizational culture along two axes: flexibility and stability, and external and internal focus (Denison, n.d.).

- Adaptability. The ability to perceive and respond to the environment and customers.
- Mission. Employees know why they are doing the work that they do. They know how their work contributes to the whole. They are aware of the organization's strategic direction and intent, goals and objectives, and vision.
- Consistency. The organization provides a central source of integration, coordination, and control.
- Involvement. A sense of ownership that fosters a commitment to the organization and an increased capacity for autonomy, empowerment, and team orientation.

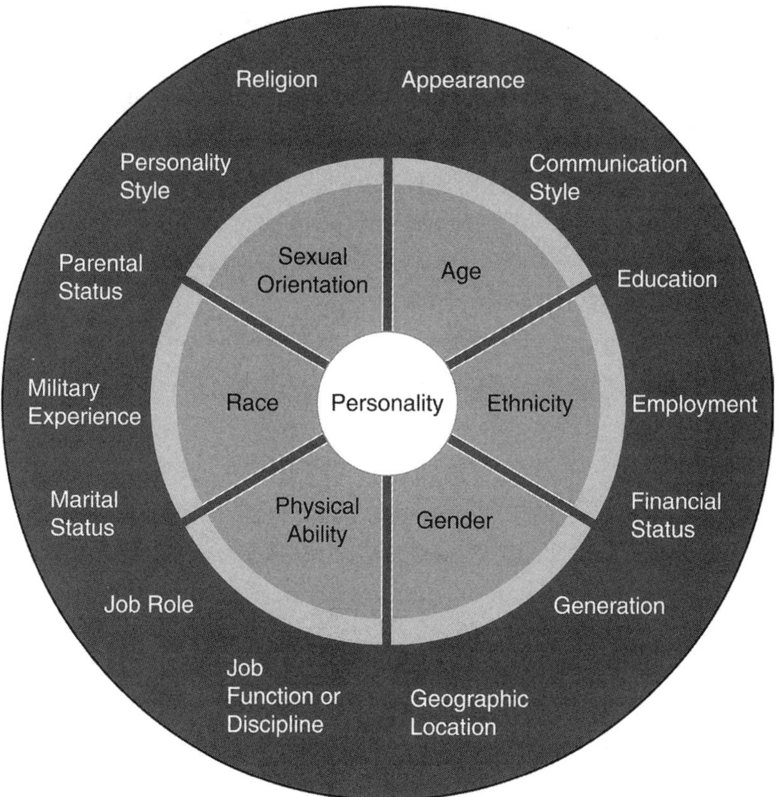

Figure 10.1 Dimensions of Diversity

Dimensions of diversity are often depicted as a wheel to acknowledge the unique attributes of all individuals and groups. Such a wheel introduces several different dimensions of diversity that need to be included in successful change coaching (see an example in Figure 10.1), and several authors suggest multiple levels of these dimensions (Gardenswartz & Rowe, 2003; Loden, 1995). Gardenswartz and Rowe (1994) identified four levels of diversity, including:

- personality, the "inner circle," which covers personal style;
- internal or core dimensions, which are not easily changed, for example, gender, age, mental, and physical capacity;
- external dimensions, which are more flexible (an exception is often made for religion or worldview, which can be argued to be a core dimension), for example, income, appearance, parental and marital status; and
- organizational dimensions, which relate to the context of employment and the work being done, for example, work location, type of employment, and duration of employment.

Primary dimensions of diversity can be described as those that are present at birth or that are difficult to change: ethnicity, heritage, age, and gender. Other aspects of diversity develop from personal choices later in life, for example, career, lifestyle, and education. Figure 10.1 is adapted from Loden (1995).

One important aspect of culture emerging in groups and organizations is generational diversity. "The workforce today is composed of three distinct generational cohorts . . . As a result, employees of different age groups do not share the same work ethic or expectations" (Weston, 2001, p. 11). The common life experiences among cohorts foster cohesiveness due to similar attitudes, beliefs, and values that frame the assumptions of that generation. While each human being is unique and cannot be stereotyped generationally, understanding generational differences and perspectives, and learning to coach individuals from different age groups, is essential for a Change Coach.

The Importance of Culture

Since culture has been identified as a major factor in facilitating or inhibiting organizational effectiveness and change (Argyris, 1977; Burke, 2011; Kotter, 1996; Marshak, 2006; Maurer, 2010; Schein, 1994), it becomes important to understand culture on many levels. "To perform effectively, business leaders need to know how to leverage cultural differences and avoid cultural misunderstandings" (Jenkins, 2006, p. 23). Schein (2010) noted that the concept of culture helps to explain and even "normalize" the coach and the client's reactions to change.

> If we understand the dynamics of culture, we will be less likely to be puzzled, irritated, and anxious when we encounter the unfamiliar and seemingly irrational behavior of people in organizations . . . Even more important, if we understand culture better we will understand ourselves better and recognize some of the forces acting within us that define who we are. We will then understand that our personality and character reflect the groups that socialized us and the groups with which we identify and to which we want to belong. Culture is not only all around us but within us as well. (Schein, 2010, p. 9)

Culture promotes a sense of group safety and cohesion and facilitates effective action and collaboration. It creates a set of boundaries, identifying what is "in" and "out" of consideration, and establishes processes, examples, guidelines, and norms of behavior for members. All of these influence a sense of individual belonging, smooth functioning, and well-being in the group. Schein (2010) claimed,

"If the growth and evolution of culture is a function of human interaction, and if human interaction is undergoing fundamental changes, then culture formation and evolution will itself change in unknown ways" (p. 4), and he cited several factors influencing change, underscoring the point that cultural awareness and competency are increasingly important to those in helping professions:

- The strong connection between culture and leadership, whether intentional or not. Schein calls leadership and culture "two sides of the same coin," noting that "In this sense, culture is ultimately created, embedded, evolved and ultimately manipulated by leaders" (p. 3).
- The increasing technological complexity and differentiation of occupational cultures, which can cause difficulty in coordination among these subcultures.
- The impact of the proliferation of global technology and networking, which is changing the way work is being defined and done, and how organizational boundaries are being identified.
- The rise of globalization and increased merger and acquisition activities mean that work is performed across microsystems and often in a multicultural setting.

Cultures are promoted and perpetuated in the background of organizational or group activity. The influence of a culture often inhibits change, but it can also promote change. Coaches who are aware of this can also be very powerful agents of change by bringing cultural influences to the surface. It is important to understand and respect a culture in order to bring about change. There is also danger of a coach embracing the culture too much ("going native") and colluding with the client by no longer being aware of differences. To fully support a cross-cultural client, the Change Coach needs to be aware of his own biases and preferences, as well as those of the client and the client system. With this awareness comes the best possibility of helping others be aware of how to successfully work in these dimensions.

Since cultural adaptation can be unconscious, clients are often not aware of how much competence they exhibit in a certain area. Having a trusted coach to observe and reflect with about this competence can boost the client's confidence and ability to be more powerful in cultural situations. Coaches who are culturally aware can help clients notice situations in which they are not being effective, and initiate a discussion about the possible reasons, consequences, and tradeoffs for the client in changing behavior. Finally, coaches themselves can be more successful with clients and client systems by identifying their own cultural competencies and biases, and developing more awareness, sensitivity and understanding in this important area. As Peterson (2007) noted:

> The broader a coach's understanding of culture, the better they are able to identify important dimensions of human behavior and explore their meaning. The deeper a coach's insights into how culture has shaped their own beliefs and values, the more sensitive they can be to how their assumptions shape their reactions and advice to the people they coach. (p. 262)

It is important to note that not everyone in a given cultural group will reflect all of the cultural distinctions of that group. Peterson (2007) explained that while culture is a group or organizational phenomenon, coaches primarily work with individuals. "Because coaches work one-on-one, they can discover and work with each person as a unique human being rather than forming opinions based on generalizations and stereotypes about the person's cultural background" (Peterson, 2007, p. 262). While the term "culture" is often interpreted as a phenomenon that exists at the group or organization level, it is important to remember that "all people (coaches and those who are coached) have their own individual cultural orientation" (Lennard, 2010, p. 4). According to Schein (2010), as people come to understand culture better:

> We will then understand that our personality and character reflect the groups that socialized us and the groups with which we identify and to which we want to belong. Culture is not only all around us but within us as well. (p. 9)

Some individuals will exhibit more or fewer characteristics typical of a given culture. This behavior is due to the influence of individual differences as well as other dimensions such as gender, ethnicity, age, sexual orientation, and so forth. When assessing a system or client in terms of culture, do not assume there will be an obvious pattern or stereotype:

> A good coach recognizes that people look at the world through different lenses. A good cross-cultural coach recognizes that sometimes they may not even know what that lens looks like, and so will scan for important dimensions that they may not fully understand or appreciate. (Peterson, 2007, p. 264)

A Change Coach should look for qualities, behaviors, and characteristics that may be indicative of culture, and invite additional inquiry or exploration. Also, as communications are issued from leaders, observe patterns of ownership or distancing at various levels or by subgroups within the organization. Keep an open mind to insights and information about a group or individual, and when discussing your perceptions, use neutral, non-judgmental language.

Developing Cultural Competence for Coaching Across Cultures

Effective coaching across cultures first requires the development of cultural competence. This section will focus on how to develop cultural competence—as the coach with individual clients, and for groups and organizations. Passmore and Law (2009) described cultural competence along four dimensions taken from the Universal Integrated Framework (UIF) as developed by Law, Ireland, and Hussein:

- personal competence: self-awareness, self-management;
- social competence: empathy and social skills;
- cultural competence: awareness and championing of other cultures; and
- professional competence: cultural knowledge and approaches that have a positive impact on coaching outcomes.

For the Coach and Individual Clients

"Effective coaching, even within a single culture, requires a high degree of interpersonal perceptiveness and sensitivity—emotional intelligence, if you will. Coaching across cultures magnifies the coach's challenge" (Peterson, 2007, p. 264). It is important for coaches to recognize that the questions they ask, and their ideas about the process and direction of the coaching, will contain their own cultural biases. Coaches need to be clear about their preferences and biases as they work with clients and be self-analytical about the way these forces may be operating (Abbott, 2010; Lennard, 2010). After the self-analysis, coaches then need to ensure their interactions with their clients are neutral and sanitized of their own cultural bias. That is, the self-analysis is the departure point for the important sanitizing step. For this reason, coaches should make it a priority to engage in their own processes of self-discovery to develop cultural competence.

Hicks and Peterson (1999) recommended some considerations for coaching across cultures, including looking for hidden layers, adapting the coaching approach to the person, and implementing the change in a way that best suits the individual or group. Peterson (2007) noted of a good cross-cultural coach: "Such a coach assumes there is always more going on than meets the eye" (p. 264) and advised coaches to study cultural distinctions in order to become familiar with the various ways people can differ. He concluded:

> As the coach gains insight into the individual's makeup, they can ask questions to identify the most effective methods and approaches for this particular person independent of their culture: What's the best way to foster the coaching relationship with this person? What's the best way for this person to learn? What skills, approaches, and style will be most useful for this person in their context? (p. 264)

Peterson's words are a reminder to step back and take an **inventory** of one's own skills in observing, assessing, and communicating non-judgmentally about culture. Start by asking these questions:

- Do I demonstrate an open attitude by avoiding quick judgments, tolerating ambiguity and complexity, and exhibiting patience and inquiry?
- Do I behave in a way that reflects my own values, beliefs, and attitudes as reflected in your behavior?
- What situations make me uncomfortable, and how well do I tolerate ambiguity and difference?
- Do I demonstrate a global mindset by challenging assumptions and recognizing the cultural values, attitudes, beliefs, and behaviors of others?
- Do I realize that others may have needs and expectations that are unexpressed or expressed indirectly? Peterson notes instances where the typical Western approach of directness is not productive in the coaching relationship and recommends ways coaches can develop a more indirect means of gathering information from the client or group (Peterson, 2007).
- Do I know enough about other cultures that I am engaged with to understand their social and business interactions? Do I have resources to get this information?

For Groups or Organizations

In order to better understand a culture, Schein recommended studying and reflecting on it "taking a 'cultural perspective,' learning to see the world through 'culture lenses,' becoming competent in 'cultural analysis' by which I mean being able to perceive and decipher the cultural forces that operate in groups, organizations and occupations" (Schein, 2010, pp. 12–13). Schein made the further point, "we need to find out what is actually going on in organizations before we rush in to tell managers what to do about their culture" (Schein, 1994, p. 147). Burke (2011) echoed Schein, saying, "In order to change culture, you must first understand it" (p. 244).

To increase effectiveness in working with cultural issues in groups, start by observing some of the major dimensions of culture. If the coach has access to individuals from the culture, engage in conversations or interviews to ask questions. Or simply observe behavior at meetings, in public spaces, and in other locations and situations. Schein (1994) offered the following distinctions to start with and notes that, "Of most value in this process will be noting *anomalies* and things that seem different, upsetting or difficult to understand" (pp. 150).

A Change Coach should observe and take note of:

- The organization's relationship to its environment. Is it dominant? Submissive? Harmonizing? Searching for a "niche"?
- The nature of activity. Is there a "correct" way to behave?
- The nature of reality and truth. How is "truth" determined? By pragmatic test? Social consensus?
- The nature of time. Is the focus on past, present, or future? Are time standards (such as meeting times) held strictly or more loosely (for example, is there a "culture" of consistently being 10 minutes late to meetings)?
- Relationships. What is the "correct" way for people to relate to each other? Is it more autocratic/paternalistic or collegial/participative?
- Homogeneity vs. diversity. Are individuals encouraged to innovate or conform?

Identify what is known or understood about the culture of the group or organization that the client is in. How does the client fit (or not fit) into that culture? In what ways is the culture inhibiting the client from changing in the way(s) he or she needs to in order to succeed? What are the coach's own biases about the culture and/or the way the client interacts with it?

> A cross-cultural coach needs to walk into every coaching engagement prepared to learn about new ways to be helpful to the person, and even prepared to learn new ways of going about their own learning, so they can readily adapt to new cultures and styles. (Peterson, 2007, p. 265)

Peterson (2007) referred to coaches who coach people from other cultures, as is often done. However, it can be assumed that coaches are always working cross-culturally, because they are always coaching from their own personal set of beliefs, values, and assumptions. And the client is working from his own set. Even a slight amount of difference in personal preferences can be a barrier to effective communication and rapport in coaching, not to mention other, perhaps more obvious cultural, religious, or lifestyle differences.

As Lennard (2010) concluded, the practice of coaching is strengthened when coaches develop and work with a coaching model that takes into account their individual cultural orientation and the cultural context of the choices they make. While the coach cannot be completely free from cultural conditioning, the coach can practice flexibility and openness to adapting when communicating with a culturally different person.

By acknowledging and appreciating differences, a coach can partner more effectively with clients and not impose the coach's beliefs and values. The coach can use each coaching engagement as an opportunity to further cultural awareness and develop competence—whether or not the client is an individual or group from a different nationality. Taking this approach can hone a coach's awareness of differences and the coach's skills for noticing and adapting to even subtle individual style, personal preferences, and more-evident differences due to geography, age, or ethnicity.

Tools for Coaching Across Cultures

There are a variety of tools that support coaching across cultures. The selection of tools will vary depending on whether the work is with individuals, groups, or entire organizations. This section will highlight some of the most commonly available—and effective—tools for coaching across cultures.

Tools for Working With Individuals

Coaches are increasingly faced with clients from a variety of cultural backgrounds and need to be aware of the role that culture plays in both individual and organizational effectiveness (Jenkins, 2006; Peterson, 2007). A grounded awareness and understanding of clients' cultural perspectives will add value to a multicultural coaching context (Abbott & Rosinski, 2007). Using assessments like the ones listed below can be useful for exploring one's own awareness and skill building, as well as identifying areas of potential focus for coaching with clients about cultural differences. Coaches should consider trying each of them to get a sense of which will be the most helpful in their own development and potential use with clients.

Individual assessment instruments such as the VIA Inventory of Strengths Survey, the DiSC Style Assessment, the Hogan Personality Inventory, the Herrmann Brain Dominance Inventory, the WorkPlace Big Five, Bolman-Deal Leadership Orientations Assessment, Wilson Social Styles Assessment, or the Myers-Briggs Type Indicator can help identify values, style, personality, or behavioral preferences that may contribute to differences in work interactions. These assessments can be used with individuals or groups and are effective in surfacing behaviors and assumptions that impact effectiveness at work. The Communication Effectiveness Assessment from *The Art of Connecting* (Raines & Ewing, 2006) offers ten statements that will help coaches identify the "current level of effectiveness at bridging the gap between you and people who differ from you" (p. 211).

Just as one's cultural orientations, preferences, and personalities inform one's view of the world, they also block, inhibit, or disallow other views. A helpful model for looking at the impacts and influences of cultural orientation is the Johari Window (see Figure 5.2). This model depicts areas where things are known to one and others, and where things are hidden from one and others. This model is useful in change coaching to promote discussion and awareness of what is known and what is hidden, and how to gradually develop a larger arena of shared information. This model can be especially helpful for a leader or Change Coach in facilitating a discussion with a team or group about their culture and how to be most successful in it.

Rosinski's (2003) Cultural Orientations Framework (COF) assessment is one of these tools, specifically oriented toward supporting cross-cultural coaching and offering a way to "understand and further explore culture as part of a coaching process" (Rojon & MacDowell, 2010, p. 2). The online assessment is accessible at no charge and can be used to promote discussion on differences around the 17 cultural orientations or dimensions that are defined as an "inclination to think, feel, or act in a way that is culturally determined" (Rosinski, 2003, p. 49). The COF can be helpful for coaches to use in self-reflection about their own cultural awareness, and to use with both individuals and groups to explore the cultural issues that may be impacting successful change, both positively and negatively.

The Cultural Orientations Indicator™ (COI), derived from the TMC/Berlitz cultural orientations model, is a validated self-assessment tool for identifying an individual's cultural preferences in the workplace. Results are organized into three dimensions: interaction style, thinking style, and sense of self. An added feature of the COI is the ability for users to compare their profiles to those of others in their group, as well as to compare it to an extensive number of country cultures that have been documented as part of the TMC/Berlitz Cultural Navigator® tool. This comparison allows an individual to assess her potential fit with a different country, group, or culture. The tool is excellent for helping clients understand the impact they may have on others, and in predicting how much adaptation will be necessary to be successful in a new country or culture.

Tools for Working With Groups or Organizations

In addition to focusing on individual cultural awareness and preferences, it is useful to understand the group or organization's culture. The surveys listed below help groups identify and explore their cultures and surface assumptions and beliefs. These instruments are very useful in working with groups or entire organizations as they go through change: to help them identify cultural elements or assumptions that promote or hinder change success, or to help the group proactively identify new culture norms and assumptions that will serve them best in the future. These surveys can be used with small teams, leadership groups, or entire organizations.

The Denison Organizational Culture Survey (n.d.) measures the specific aspects of an organization's culture and compares them to a database of other higher- and lower-performing organizations. The survey is designed to assess an organization's strengths and weaknesses as they apply to organizational performance. The 60 items included measure specific aspects of an organization's culture in each of the four traits and 12 management practices outlined in the Denison organizational culture model. The organizational culture survey is designed to:

- Assess the strengths and weaknesses that are impacting the organization's performance
- Identify areas of focus for improvement
- Align the organization's culture change and leadership development initiatives when leveraging both surveys
- Create action plans, often utilizing the Denison solutions

The Leadership Culture Survey™ developed by The Leadership Circle (TLC) organization, offers an "MRI" of a group's or organization's leadership culture, showing how group members view the current leadership style in comparison to the optimal leadership culture that is desired. The gap reveals opportunities for leadership development and identifies issues that are currently hindering change and success in the domains of creative competencies versus reactive tendencies. The survey will:

- Establish a compelling rationale for change
- Focus leadership development efforts
- Delineate cultural challenges associated with acquisitions, mergers, and restructuring plans
- Correlate leadership to productivity, profits, turnover, and other bottom-line metrics.

The Organizational Culture Assessment Instrument (OCAI) is based on the competing values framework of Cameron and Quinn (2009). This validated tool identifies competing values and their corresponding cultures in groups and organizations: clan culture, adhocracy culture, market culture, and hierarchy culture. The results offer:

- Insight into the dominant culture of the organization
- Insight into how market focused, hierarchic, personal, and/or innovative the organization works
- A measure of contentment by assessing the difference between current and preferred culture
- A quick-and-easy point of comparison before and after reengineering, change, or merger
- A clear image of the preferred culture as a starting point for a strategy of change
- An awareness of culture as an important factor in success
- An objective and validated measure of how culture is perceived, which is a starting point for change.

Challenges for Coaching Across Cultures at the Individual, Group, and Organization Levels

To be useful, a perspective on culture must be of practical value in helping individuals (1) navigate a broad spectrum of differences, (2) understand the fundamentals of various cultures and cultural interactions, and (3) translate this understanding into personal behaviors and organizational expectations (TMC/Berlitz, 2009). Awareness of culture at the individual, group, and organization levels can help a Change Coach observe and work with a client on specific behaviors or attitudes that impact his success, both positively and negatively. Table 10.1 suggests ways

Table 10.1 Challenges for Cross-Cultural Change Coaching

	INDIVIDUAL	GROUP	ORGANIZATIONAL
Performing	• Developing the ability to lead or succeed in a diverse multicultural environment (skills such as interviewing, performance management, conflict handling, delegation, etc.). • Improving awareness or behavior in interpersonal communications and inclusion. Effective performance in diverse, multicultural team. • Improving critical business skills in a diverse, global context (such as negotiation and selling skills, building and sustaining client relationship, etc.).	• Improving team performance in diverse, multicultural or global settings. • Leveraging the effectiveness and business relevance of employee networks or resource groups. • Enhancing performance and innovation through expanded team membership (or alliances). • Increased awareness of team members' differences, capabilities, and contributions, leading to improved effectiveness or productivity.	• Improving engagement, commitment, and loyalty of specific employee groups as demonstrated by increased productivity or results. • Improved and expedited merger and acquisition integration. • Ensuring successful organization-wide change that results in process improvement, ROI, growth, new-product innovation, or other bottom-line benefits.
Developing	• Developing global leadership capabilities and building global mindsets. • Strategic and increasingly global thinking. Building effective networks and strategic relationships. • Examining "self as instrument of change." • Identifying "stretch" opportunities. • Enhancing individual fit and performance in cultural transitions.	• Leading global teams. Developing and sustaining effective team norms. • Developing or leveraging more-effective stakeholder relations/alliances with other teams or groups. • Enabling virtual cross-functional collaboration and teamwork. Exploring team "self management" (i.e., leaderless teaming).	• Building a diverse talent pipeline. • Building capacity and capability for change and transition. • Enabling effective international expatriation and international assignments to encourage global growth. • Ensuring effective international outsourcing.
Transforming	• Ability to notice and adapt to a variety of cultures and environments, to easily and quickly fit in and contribute at all levels of an organization. • Build capacity and bandwidth to successfully function with higher levels of responsibility and power. • Demonstrating successful contribution or leadership in a new or different arena (level, region, customer, or product type, etc.).	• Building an effective global strategy. Establishing effective alliances, collaboration and teamwork at the transorganization, multicountry, or cross-industry levels.	• Enhancing merger and acquisition due diligence. • Enhancing joint venture and supplier relationships. • Ensuring successful organization-wide change and cultural transformations. • Partnering with other countries, governments, or supporting research across industry or global boundaries to facilitate breakthroughs in resources, products, or other offerings.

Adapted from the TMC/Berlitz paper, "The Concept of Culture" (2009)

that the Change Coach can successfully support individuals, groups, and organizations in a wide range of changes. This table is not intended as an exhaustive list of options but can guide the Change Coach to observe and facilitate ways to broaden the cultural awareness and understanding of the client.

Chapter Summary

In this chapter, the authors defined the concept of culture at the individual, group, and organization levels, as well as its importance and application to coaching for change. Examples of cultural dimensions have been cited, as well as specific tools and coaching challenges for working in and across cultures.

Knowledge Check

1. Define "culture" and "cultural bias."
2. What are four dimensions of culture that could be important in change coaching?
3. What are four ways to learn about and address cultural biases?
4. Describe two examples of how a coach would leverage cultural differences or similarities to support change.
5. List three potential cultural biases that could influence your coaching.

Learning Activities

Learning Activity #1: Elements of Culture

In writing, describe three different organization or groups cultures and identify the elements of each that provide the differences (age, industry or profession, country, values, etc.).

Learning Activity #2: Identifying the Personal Culture

In writing, describe your own personal culture (values, assumptions, preferences, socialization, education, family history, language, background). Identify four new experiences that would help broaden understanding of different cultures (e.g., traveling to another country, reading a book, interviewing or shadowing a person who is significantly different from yourself, working in another organization or division—even as a volunteer, etc.). Commit to a goal that will broaden your cultural understanding in at least three ways within the next six months.

Learning Activity #3: Reflection on Personal Culture

Using your results from a personality or preference assessment like Myers-Briggs Type Indicator, DiSC, Hogan, WorkPlace Big 5, or Herrmann Brain Dominance Instrument, reflect on the cultural aspects of your preferences and how they can facilitate or constrain interactions with others.

Learning Activity #4: Cultural Flexibility Assessment

Test your cultural flexibility using the assessment in Raines and Ewing (2006).

Learning Activity #5: Influence of Leadership Culture

Think of a well-known leader in your field and reflect on how he or she has shaped the organization or group culture through leadership. What are the positive and negative consequences of the leader's influence on the culture?

Learning Activity #6: Cultural Impact in Mergers and Acquisitions

Recall a case of a merger or acquisition. What were the implications of culture in that integration? How early in the process were these implications discovered or identified? What has been the result? How has culture been a force promoting or inhibiting the successful integration (or both)?

Learning Activity #7: Cultural Perspectives in Coaching

Develop an awareness of coaching models from a cultural perspective, and scrutinize the theoretical foundations of the models to detect biases that might affect your coaching. As Lennard (2010) notes "a focus on your individual cultural orientation becomes an integral part of developing your own coaching model" (p. 5). Examine the selected coaching models to ensure they are appropriate and flexible enough to adapt to differences.

References

Abbott, G. (2010). Cross cultural coaching: A paradoxical perspective. In E. Cox, T. Bachkirova, & D. Clutterbuck (Eds.), *The complete handbook of coaching* (pp. 324–339). London: Sage.

Abbott, G., & Rosinski, P. (2007). Global coaching and evidence based coaching: Multiple perspectives operating in a process of pragmatic humanism. *International Journal of Evidence Based Coaching and Mentoring, 5*(1), 58–77.

Argyris, C. (1977). Double loop learning. *Harvard Business Review, 55*(5), 115–125.

Burke, W. (2011). *Organization change.* (3rd ed.). Thousand Oaks, CA: Sage.

Cameron, K. S., & Quinn, R. E. (2009). *Diagnosing and changing organizational culture: Based on the competing values framework* (rev. ed.). San Francisco, CA: Jossey-Bass.

Culture. (n.d.). In Merriam-Webster's online dictionary (11th ed.). Retrieved from www.merriam-webster.com/dictionary/culture

Culture. (n.d.). In Dictionary.com online. Retrieved from http://dictionary.reference.com/browse/culture?s = t

Denison, D. (n.d.). Organizational culture model. Retrieved from www.denisonconsulting.com/model-surveys/denison-model

Denison, D., Hooijberg, R., Lane, N., & Leif, D. (2012). *Leading culture change in global organizations: Aligning culture and strategy.* San Francisco, CA: Jossey-Bass.

Gardenswartz, L., & Rowe, A. (1994). *The managing diversity survival guide: A complete collection of activities, checklists and tips.* Burr Ridge, IL: Irwin Professional Publishers.

Gardenswartz, L., & Rowe, A. (2003). *Diverse teams at work: Capitalizing on the power of diversity.* Alexandria, VA: Society for Human Resource Management.

Hicks, M. D., & Peterson, D. B. (1999). Leaders coaching across borders. In W. H. Mobley, M. J. Gessner & V. J. Arnold (Eds.), *Advances in global leadership* (Vol. 1, pp. 295–314). Stamford, CT: JAI Press.

Hofstede, G., Hofstede, G. J., & Minkov, M. (2010). *Cultures and organizations: Software of the mind* (3rd ed.). New York, NY: McGraw-Hill.

International Coach Federation. (2012). *Global coaching study—Executive summary.* Lexington, KY: International Coach Federation.

Jenkins, J. (2006). Coaching meets the cross-cultural challenge. *Leadership in Action, 26*(5), 23–24.

Kotter, J. (1996). *Leading change.* Cambridge, MA: Harvard Business School Press.

Lennard, D. (2010). *Coaching models: A cultural perspective: A guide to model development for practitioners and students of coaching.* New York, NY: Routledge.

Loden, M. (1995). *Implementing diversity.* New York, NY: McGraw-Hill.

Marshak, R. (2006). *Covert processes at work: Managing the five hidden dimensions of organizational change.* San Francisco, CA: Berrett-Kohler.

Maurer, R. (2010). *Beyond the wall of resistance.* Austin, TX: Bard Press.

Passmore, J. (2009). Introduction. In J. Passmore (Ed.), *Diversity in coaching: Working with gender, culture, race and age* (pp. 1–3). London: Kogan-Page.

Passmore, J., & Law, H. (2009). Cross-cultural and diversity coaching. In J. Passmore (Ed.), *Diversity in coaching: Working with gender, culture, race and age* (pp. 4–16). London: Kogan-Page.

Peterson, D. (2007). Executive coaching in a cross-cultural context. *Consulting Psychology Journal: Practice and Research, 59*(4), 261–271.

Raines, C., & Ewing, L. (2006). *The art of connecting: How to build rapport, overcome differences and communicate effectively with anyone.* New York, NY: AMACOM.

Rojon, C., & McDowell, A. (2010). Cultural orientations framework (COF) assessment questionnaire in cross-cultural coaching: A cross-validation with wave focus styles. *International Journal of Evidence-Based Coaching and Mentoring, 3*(2). Retrieved from http://www.business.brookes.ac.uk/research/areas/coachingandmentoring/

Rosinski, P. (2003). *Coaching across cultures: New tools for leveraging national, corporate & professional differences.* London: Nicholas Brealy.

Schein, Ed. (1994). Organizational culture. In W. French, C. Bell, & R. Zawacki (Eds.), *Organization development and transformation: Managing effective change* (4th ed.). Chicago, IL: Irwin.

Schein, E. (2010). *Organization culture and leadership* (4th ed.). San Francisco, CA: Jossey-Bass.

TMC/Berlitz. (2009). *The concept of culture.* Unpublished article.

TMC/Berlitz. (2010). *Cultural orientations approach (COA) certification participant manual.* New York, NY: TMC/Berlitz.

Weick, K. (1995). *Sensemaking in organizations.* Thousand Oaks, CA: Sage.

Weston, M. (2001). Coaching generations in the workplace. *Nursing Administration Quarterly, 25*(2), 11–21.

11

FIVE ROLES OF CHANGE COACHING

Given the significant and special roles that leaders and others play in the change process, as described in Chapter 3, there are many applications of coaching. This chapter will provide information about five specific applications of coaching for change in organizations today. As shown in Figure 3.1, change coaching is based on numerous disciplines and several different professional helping practices, and it manifests through a variety of applications/roles, including internal coach, external coach, peer coach, **manager-as-coach**, and group coaching. In this chapter, we consider each of these five applications, first by introducing the application and then by explaining reasons for using that approach. Also included in the chapter discussion are the knowledge, skills, and abilities required; issues related to contracting; challenges that may be encountered and possible solutions; and, finally, ways in which the application can be used to support change. In addition, we address the following questions:

- What are five roles of coaching for change?
- What is the focus of each?
- How do they differ?
- When is each appropriate to use?
- What knowledge, skills, and abilities are particularly important for each?
- What are the contractual considerations of each?
- What challenges might the coach encounter with each approach and what are possible solutions to those challenges?
- How do the approaches support change at the individual, group, and organization levels?

Internal Coach

Coaching is an essential staple for developing business leaders in corporate America. For the past few decades, corporations have regularly contracted with external executive coaches to develop their executives' leadership skills and improve performance (Bennett & Bush, 2009; Cox, Clutterbuck, & Bachkirova, 2010; Underhill, McAnally, & Koriath, 2007). At the same time, internal coaching has become a vital method for employee growth in the workplace and should be considered less a competitor and more a complement to external executive coaching.

Internal coaching emerged from the acceptance of executive coaching within the workplace, developing out of the need for a professional within organizations whose main responsibility is to coach executives and management. While external coaches are often preferred for work with senior-level executives, internal coaches offer services to all levels in the organization. Most often, the internal coach works with directors, supervisors, and other employees. The rise of internal coaches parallels the increased demand for organizational coaching as a whole and is generally considered to be a cost-effective strategy for offering the benefits of coaching at all levels.

An *internal coach* is someone who is a full- or part-time employee of the client's organization (Battley, 2006). Often, internal coaches work in organization development or human resources departments and are available to coach any leaders, managers, and supervisors. In a survey of 55 predominately large companies (the median number of employees was 34,000), 60 percent of respondents employed internal coaches, while 100 percent of respondents reported contracting with external coaches. In organizations that use both internal and external coaching, senior-level executives, senior managers, and senior vice presidents accounted for 40 percent of the external coaching engagements (McDermott, Levenson, & Newton, 2007).

One important and obvious difference between internal and external coaching is that the internal coach is a fellow employee of the person being coached. Frisch (2001) noted, "Internal coaching is a one-on-one developmental intervention supported by the organization and provided by a colleague of those coached who is trusted to shape and deliver a program yielding individual professional growth" (p. 242). There are many applications of internal coaching, including helping individuals realize their own potential by way of career and skills development, onboarding new managers, helping improve employee relationships, and supporting an organizational change initiative.

Several key factors determine the role of the internal coach and the interaction with the peer employee. The coach is outside of the usual chain of command, which helps to differentiate between the regular job coaching that would be performed by the manager. The internal coach can also develop a flexible plan since she already has background information on the employee, which allows her to more readily develop a customized plan for targeted development (Frisch, 2001). Coaches will also distinguish their coaching from other human resources-related functions such as recruiting, compensation, employee relationships, and training.

Why Use Internal Coaches?

More organizations are moving to employing individuals with either part-time or primary responsibilities as internal coaches. Advantages of using internal coaches include:

- Supporting a coaching culture
- Ready access to coaching resources
- Possible cost savings (compared to using external coaches)
- Integration of coaching services with performance and talent management systems
- Developing existing human capital throughout all levels of a group or organization
- Aligning coaching engagements with strategic goals
- Understanding of the existing and desired organizational culture and resources
- More readily accessible coaches to meet busy schedules and to provide observations and feedback (Carter, 2005; Frisch, 2001; McKee, Tilin, & Mason, 2009; Rock & Donde, 2008; Underhill et al., 2007; Weiss, 2009).

The increased interest in internal coaching and how this phenomenon will continue to increase in popularity has provided the means for dedicated research in the field of internal coaching. Research suggests that to have a successful coaching experience, three critical factors must be considered: the position level of the employee who is being coached, the time commitment that will be invested by the coach, and the cost (Underhill et al., 2007). Research highlights several reasons why internal coaching is beneficial in the workplace. Underhill et al. (2007) considered internal coaching to have the same high level of execution and results as external coaching, and internal coaching has a lower cost. In addition, internal coaching can provide more-beneficial coaching practices by assigning coaching to specific assignments, while incorporating an organization's unique corporate culture.

Knowledge, Skills, and Abilities

Weintraub, Eisenman, and Perkins (n.d.) identified nine skills and abilities that internal coaches need in order to be successful:

- Credibility
- Integrity
- Conceptual knowledge
- Engagement
- Presence
- Insight
- Political savvy
- Objectivity
- Coaching skills.

Credibility is the most important factor of any skill or ability a coach can demonstrate. External coaches are often automatically assumed to be credible, because they are hired from outside the organization. Internal coaches, on the other hand, are considered credible only when they have sustained experience and knowledge of the business and of the practice of coaching. It can, therefore, be difficult for relatively new internal coaches to be considered credible by those with whom they work. This challenge can be solved by assigning internal coaches to less-senior-level clients, and by these coaches then demonstrating good coaching performance over a sustained period of time.

Internal coaches exhibit integrity when they are considered **trustworthy** and when they demonstrate that their interest in the client and the organization is their top priority. Trust is paired with confidentiality, and a client must trust that his coach will not divulge sensitive information that falls outside of the coaching contract. Trust is gained over time with the coach's demonstration of high ethical standards. Conceptual knowledge is demonstrated when a coach has basic knowledge of adult learning theory, coaching theory, and organizational behavior and development, learned through training.

A coach exhibits engagement when committing to the client through words and tone, developing an emotional connection, and feeling empathy for the client. Presence is demonstrated when coaches appear confident they can help the client, which facilitates an authentic connection with the client. A coach's presence comes from her experience, willingness to work toward a positive outcome, and a feeling of competence and skill. A coach with insight is one who can understand a client's behavior, read between the lines, and make sense of disparate pieces of information to see the bigger picture and lead to a positive impact for the client.

Internal coaches have to be politically aware and astute when dealing with internal clients who are dealing with organizational culture, challenging work situations, or understanding the impact of a client's behavior in the wider organization. The power of internal coaches is that they understand the organizational culture and political landscape, since they are a part of it. Another challenging and important attribute for an internal coach to possess is objectivity, that is, being able to observe and diagnose an issue in an unbiased way. This skill is easier for external coaches since they typically have no ties to the organization; internal coaches often bring their own assumptions and perceptions of the organization and its employees, and they must watch for biases. Last, all coaches need foundational coaching skills like asking questions, reflecting on what is (and is not) being said, clarifying or restating the important points, active listening, maintaining coaching relationships, and successfully applying appropriate coaching models.

Contracting Issues

Even though internal coaches support the organization from within, contracting is just as important for internal coaches as it is for external coaches, because all involved parties (e.g., client, coach, manager) need to understand the parameters of the coaching engagement. There may be a tendency in the case of internal coaches for contracting to be more informal. While informality may be appropriate, the need to clarify expectations, roles, boundaries (including issues of confidentiality), and process is essential. In addition, the need for agreement between key stakeholders (e.g., client, coach, manager, and coaching practice manager) should not be overlooked. Since internal coaches often perform the coaching role as part of or in addition to their other duties (i.e., internal organizational consultant or human resources generalist), internal coaches must be clear with their own management about job priorities and how much time they will allot to coaching.

Challenges and Solutions

While there are many cited benefits and advantages to internal coaching, there are also challenges. Table 11.1 includes some of the challenges that may be encountered when internal coaching, as well as possible solutions.

Table 11.1 Internal Coaching Challenges and Solutions

CHALLENGES	POSSIBLE SOLUTIONS
Credibility: Competence as a coach; too theoretical; lack leadership experience; stereotyping based on prior experience	Focus on objectivity; knowledge of the organizational, cultural, and strategic priorities; coaching competence and experience
Confidentiality: Sharing information about the coaching engagement and the content of the coaching sessions within the organization	Define boundaries of the coaching engagement and relationship related to confidentiality; review the organization's policies concerning confidentiality during a coaching engagement; define what is and what is not confidential; define the role of the client in sharing information with his manager
Background and credentials: Lack coaching competence	Educate and train coaches in essential coaching competencies; support ongoing professional development for coaches; use coaches with backgrounds and experiences that will support their effectiveness with internal clients; provide feedback to the coaches about the coaching services they are providing
Internal support: Sharing information, accesses internal and external resources to support client, knowledge and skill development, current focus and trends in the business of the organization	Offer ongoing support to internal coaches in the form of coaching supervision or monthly meetings as a group to discuss issues or trends seen in coaching, and offer skill-building activities. Conduct quarterly or annual workshops for coaches (including external coaches) to share the organization's strategy and goals and get feedback about all aspects of the coaching program. It is also a good idea to have someone managing or overseeing the internal coaching engagements in an organization, so that the resources are used strategically and equitably.
Internal conflicts of interest: While internal coaches are members of the same organization as their clients, it is important to ensure that internal boundaries of security and information sharing are honored in the same way as if the coach were external	Ensure that coaches are appropriately assigned to clients or internal projects with the right levels of security clearances and appropriate access to shared information.

(Carter, 2005; Underhill et al., 2007; Weintraub et al., n.d.; Weiss, 2009)

Internal Coaching to Support Change

As organizations continue to confront and experience constantly changing environments, coaching has gained interest as an effective action supporting change and development (Ratiu & Baban, 2012). The best results of internal coaching come about when they involve proactive individuals who are open to change and willing to cooperate. "Participants involved in the coaching process will have results, enhanced competencies of leadership, a balance between goals in life and professional goals and will show higher adaptability" (Ratiu &

Baban, 2012, p. 157). Therefore, in order for participants to experience a positive change, they must stay proactive and be willing to maintain an open mind toward the learning process of coaching. The following are examples of ways in which internal coaching can support change:

- Clarify the role the leader will play in a change initiative
- Help the client process his own reactions to a change initiative and deal with any resistance or concerns so that he can be a positive advocate for the change
- Help the client develop a change initiative including the vision, a case for change, ways to involve others, and a strategy for the change
- Help a client understand how she can support a larger, organizational change in terms of using the influence of her role as well as carrying out specific actions
- Support a group in deploying or sustaining a change initiative, including gathering data on progress, stakeholder acceptance, and how well the change is being integrated with the organization's other systems, policies, processes, and structures.

External Coach

If the coach is not on the permanent payroll of the client's company, then he or she is an external resource. *External coaches* are engaged by organizations or by specific individuals, and they may represent their own businesses or be members of coaching or consulting firms. An external coach may have multiple coaching engagements with an organization, potentially resulting in conflicts of interest that must be addressed (Battley, 2006). External coaches may be hired directly by the individual client or by the client's organization, or be employed or contracted by a coaching service provider. Service providers have a contract with the client's organization for coaching services.

External coaches are often referred to as "executive coaches," so it is important to clarify what is meant by "executive coach" and "executive coaching." No universally accepted definition of *executive coaching* exists. Various descriptions of executive coaching focus on determining the relationship between the coach and client, recognizing an executive's capacity for improvement, or effecting organizational change by improving leadership skills (Brennan & Prior, 2005; Thomas & Pirtle, 2010).

Most definitions of executive coaching assume an understanding of who qualifies as an executive, but, ultimately, the term "executive" varies from company to company. A vice president at one firm may be accountable for an entire line of business and lead several layers of middle management, while a vice president at another organization may have a small scope of responsibility and no direct reports. "Executive coaching" may therefore be used to refer to the broad application of coaching leaders or coaching senior- and executive-level leaders of an organization.

Why Use External Coaches?

Battley (2006) suggested that external coaches lend an independent perspective, senior leadership credibility/experience, and a higher degree of confidentiality than do internal coaches. In addition, external coaches have greater financial motivation to succeed with their clients than do internal coaches, who will remain employed with the company after the engagement is over. External coaches are able to engage in truth-telling with fewer consequences than internal coaches (Thomas & Pirtle, 2010).

There are many key advantages to employing an external coach, including the client's ability in many cases to choose his or her own coach; an increased sense of confidentiality based on the nature of the coaching engagement being external from the organization; and greater motivation on the part of the coach, as he is often more highly motivated to assist the client to find a positive outcome in order to establish or maintain a reputation for impact.

There are, however, potential conflicts when an external coach is involved. There is often ambiguity about "who is the client." Is the actual client the "coachee," or the "target"? Is his manager the "client," or the "banker" funding the engagement? Is the Human Resources partner the actual "client," or simply the coordinator of the company's external coaching program?

Multiple stakeholders can muddy the waters and confuse the contracting terms with the client, making it all the more important to have an explicit contract. Cost can also be an issue with external executive coaching, even when there is no question about who should pay. Last, external executive coaching is difficult when it is "forced" on an employee, without engaging him in the selection of the coach, or allowing her to commit to the process freely. This situation requires a coach skilled in engagement techniques who is able to sense the situation, build good rapport, and help increase the client's motivation.

External coaching is a valuable asset to organizations that carefully establish a context for services and communicate with multiple stakeholders successfully. Understanding and avoiding potential conflicts by examining external coaching from all stakeholders' perspectives is essential. Ultimately, executive coaching engagements will not be successful for a company unless the client does the work necessary for change and then transfers that learning to the organization. In a study of 20 Norwegian executives from Fortune 500 companies, researchers reported significant positive change in self-efficacy as a result of executive coaching. If a leader is better able to access and apply his or her professional skills, then he or she has the opportunity to exert further positive influence on the organization. Leaders' self-efficacy is important because it affects attitudes and performance of their followers and their followers' commitment to organizational tasks (Moen & Federici, 2012). The type of change and its effect on organizations depends on the goals of the coaching engagement and on the way all involved stakeholders measure growth after the engagement.

Knowledge, Skills, and Abilities

Little data is available on how executive coaches become qualified for their craft, because there is no requirement for coaches to have licenses to practice. In a study that reported the types of graduate degrees held by 130 coaches, 46.9 percent had counseling-related degrees, 31.5 percent had business-related degrees, and 21.5 percent had other types of degrees. Forty percent of respondents had identified themselves as executive coaches for more than 10 years (Newsom & Dent, 2011). Although professional credentialing and educational backgrounds vary tremendously, coaches' practice behaviors should be aligned with expectations stated by client company purchasers and executive clients (Liljenstrand & Nebeker, 2008; Sanson, 2006). Newsom and Dent (2011) note that the most frequent coaching behaviors reported by coaches are establishing trust, honesty, and respect; using open-ended questions; and clarifying and understanding client concerns and challenges.

Those who purchase external coaching services with company funds expect to see behavioral change in the client that can positively impact organizational culture as a result of coaching engagements (Dagley, 2010). In a survey of 20 professionals with extensive purchasing experience, coaching capabilities were linked with three common themes that respondents identified as necessary for positive coaching outcomes: engagement, deeper conversations, and insight and responsibility (see Table 11.2).

Table 11.2 Executive Coaching Capabilities

EXECUTIVE EXPERIENCE	COACHING CAPABILITIES
Engagement	• Credibility • Empathy and respect • Holding the professional self
Deeper conversations	• Diagnostic skill and insight • Approach flexibility and range
Insight and responsibility	• Works to the business context • A philosophy of personal responsibility • Skillful challenging

Adapted from Dagley (2010)

Contracting Issues

Understanding Coaching Potential clients should understand what a coach can and cannot do. Clients must be made aware of how they can benefit from the coaching process, as well as what coaching entails, in order to be fully committed to the coaching process (Bush, 2005). An unprepared client may not understand expectations, time commitments, or even what executive coaching entails. Some potential clients might not realize how long they will have access to coaching services or understand how coaching differs from therapy (Underhill et al., 2007).

If clients are not prepared for coaching, the coach will have to establish the context for the connection, inform the client how coaching can help her, and then seek to build trust and begin working on issues. If the first meeting between the coach and client begins with the client asking, "What is a coach? Is it like a motivational speaker?" then the executive coach will have a difficult first session (Underhill et al., 2007, p. 42). It is also possible that an unprepared executive client will feel unnecessary vulnerability and/or stress. General information about coaching, coaching qualifications, and coaching practices should be readily available to senior leaders. Clients may become disengaged from the coaching process for a variety of reasons during a coaching engagement, but that does not diminish the importance of establishing a proper context for coaching services within organizations.

Purchasing Coaching Often, a variety of stakeholders with differing agendas are involved in hiring an external executive coach. Coaches must be considered qualified by their clients, the purchasers of external coaching services, and by the consultancy firms that hire the coaches to send to clients (in cases where the coaches are not self-employed). Purchasers highly value an external coach who works well with the client's business context and agenda. Purchasers are likely to be more sensitive to the company's needs because they are responsible for contracting the coaching relationship (Dagley, 2010).

Interestingly, business acumen and leadership experience are not listed as necessary skills by the purchasers surveyed. Research by Underhill et al. (2007) did not indicate how purchasers determined whether an executive coach possessed these necessary skills. No evidence is available to support why these skills are unique to executive coaches. The tools seem to be necessary for all types of business-related coaching.

No matter how qualified and experienced a coach may be according to the purchaser at the company, the coach/client relationship will not be successful if the two professionals cannot form a positive working relationship. *Fit* is an ambiguous term that is difficult to describe and quantify, but necessary to discuss and understand. If the potential client has negative feelings about the potential coach's persona, qualifications, or communication style, he or she may not trust the coach enough to provide personal information and to explore change. The relationship of trust between coach and client is a complex relationship determined by variables such as the coach, the client, and the similarity and difference of values between the coach and client. When a relationship of trust does not develop, the coaching process may be hindered and the coaching goals not be achieved (Augustijnen, Schnitzer, & Esbroeck, 2011).

The client's perception of the coach sometimes matters more than the coach's resume (Bush, 2005). A coach who appears to be a good fit on paper may not click with an executive in person if the coach is unable to establish an atmosphere of mutual respect, open communication, and trust (Bennett & English, 2011; Flaherty, 1999), and it is a good practice to offer executives a selection of three or four potential coaches from whom to choose. Some professionals recommend that the coach and client meet privately before the first scheduled coaching session to establish rapport and assess the client's readiness for coaching (Zeus & Skiffington, 2001).

Who Should Pay for Coaching? Should executives hire a coach using private funds or engage with a coach paid for by their employers? Leaders must contemplate their goals and ethics before making a decision. Self-pay coaching provides the highest level of confidentiality, the broadest flexibility for the client, and can continue if the client's employment situation changes. Battley (2006) suggested other important questions leaders should consider: (1) Does the executive plan to stay with the company and use the leadership knowledge he/she gains for the business; (2) Must executives notify their employers if they hire a coach; and, (3) What problems may arise with divulging proprietary company information?

Leaders who know they want to change companies have multiple ethical considerations to face if they are sure that knowledge or value gained from company-provided coaching will have no impact on their current organizations. Proprietary considerations vary according to industry and organization, as do competition clauses in employment contracts. Executives should consider their legal obligations to their employers when deciding what they are able to share with coaches hired privately by executives. Coaches are ethically prohibited from disclosing client information but not legally bound to confidentiality in the same way attorneys and therapists may be. Before engaging in a coaching relationship, stakeholders must identify their goals and values prior to making complex decisions based on budgets, staffing, client requests, client needs, and multiple additional factors.

If a client begins work with an employer-provided coach and then decides to leave the company as a result of discoveries or insights made during the coaching sessions, the authors would argue that no ethical violations have occurred, because the leader's actions were not premeditated or designed to take advantage of the employer. When organizations pay for coaching, sometimes the client's department pays for the services out of its budget. In other situations, coaching is financed through a company-wide leadership development fund (Underhill et al., 2007).

Purchasers of coaching services should identify stakeholders other than the client who will be involved in the coaching process and define their roles, especially concerning communication and confidentiality, record keeping, and information access (Bennett, 2008). Multiple positions exist on how involved a client's boss or purchaser should be in the coaching process, but all positions agree that clear contracting up front will help prevent misunderstanding and miscommunication.

Challenges and Solutions

While there are many cited benefits and advantages to external coaching, there are also challenges with this type of coaching. Table 11.3 describes some challenges that may be encountered when external coaching, as well as possible solutions.

External Coaching to Support Change

External coaches can often be instrumental in supporting change at the individual, group, and organization levels. The following are examples of ways in which external coaching can support change:

Table 11.3 External Coaching Challenges and Solutions

CHALLENGES	POSSIBLE SOLUTIONS
Credibility: Ensure that potential coaches have the appropriate background, credentials, and experience to be successful with clients in a particular organization (or part of the organization, such as the sales group or the engineering group)	Source coaches from professional associations, especially from function- or discipline-related groups, to ensure specific background or experience; check credentials and references; interview potential coaches for fit within the organization or with a particular client
Working with limited contextual knowledge: Entering the organization with limited knowledge about the organization; not having technical knowledge related to the client's work; not being familiar with the organization's history and strategic priorities	Orient the coach to the company culture, history, financials and strategy; hold regular meetings for external coaches to keep them abreast of what is happening in the company or industry; ensure that the coach is paired with an internal resource (the client's manager, or human resource specialist) during the coaching engagement
Confidentiality: Gaining knowledge about the company that, if shared, would be unethical or illegal; learning the client's plans for a career change	Have external coaches sign nondisclosure agreement; only work with coaches who have professional liability insurance; check references for potential coaches; ensure that potential coaches have specific clearances needed
Understanding of coaching: The client may not be familiar with coaching (how it is different from other helping practices, strategies for selecting a coach; leading practices for working with a coach; in what, if any, ways to involve the client's manager)	Orient the client about coaching; set specific conditions for the coaching engagement, including length, frequency and duration of sessions, cost, measurement processes and outcome tracking; assist the client in selecting a suitable external coach; ensure that the client and coach are aligned with the client's manager and/or human resource specialist in establishing goals for the engagement; follow up on the progress of the coaching at regular intervals (monthly or quarterly)

(Bennett, 2008; Bush, 2005)

- Help a client gain a broader perspective concerning the business, a role, or change
- Offer examples of similar changes undertaken in other businesses or by other individuals (within the bounds of confidentiality) and provide industry or market intelligence to inform the planned change
- Help the client stay focused on the change while addressing the personal, social, political, and career impacts it may have on his or her life
- Ensure that the client identifies and addresses potential stakeholders outside the business, including international partners or competitors, boards, and professional associations
- Help members of an executive group collaborate effectively to make the change successful and to learn how to leverage resources across the organization, not just in their own functions or departments

Peer Coaching

Coaching roles are characterized by the specific relationship between coach and client. Looking at the full spectrum of coaching, peer coaching is the only genre that is driven and led by individuals of equal status. The primary function of peer coaching is to improve performance and skills in an open, trusting, and nonevaluative environment (Ladyshewsky, 2010b).

Peer coaching has been defined as "a type of helping relationship in which two people of equal status actively participate in helping each other on specific tasks or problems with a mutual desire to be helpful" (Parker, Hall, & Kram, 2008, p. 499). This equality lends itself to establishing trust and rapport as a foundation to foster deeper conversations, which enhance skill building and learning. The relationship between two people who have similar skills and training helps to remove the evaluative and corrective component of the conversations (Ladyshewsky, 2002). This nonevaluative aspect is one of the greatest benefits of peer coaching (Carroll, Hunt, & Weintraub, 2007). Removing the evaluative component encourages clients to assess their own strengths and development needs through discussion and self-reflection, which builds confidence and commitment.

While the terms "peer coaching" and "mentoring" are sometimes used interchangeably in the literature, they are distinct and separate methods to improve performance and develop skills. Coaching focuses on developing knowledge or skills that are currently needed, while mentoring has a longer-term career focus (Smits, 2010). Peer coaches encourage more experiential learning; mentors are expected to have a higher level of knowledge that they can pass on to the protégé (Ladyshewsky, 2004; Waddell & Dunn, 2005). Mentors often demonstrate their subject matter expertise by telling stories or sharing their experiences with protégés. This act of "telling" is counter to the coaching practice of asking questions to guide the conversation without providing solutions. Depending on the specific needs of the learner, peer mentoring may be more effective than peer coaching, and vice versa.

Why Use Peer Coaching?

Peer coaching can be used in any environment where individuals need and want to build skills and enhance performance. Peer coaching began in the fields of education and clinical/therapeutic practice; however, the benefits easily translate to a corporate environment as a low-cost option for staff development (Carroll et al., 2007). Coca-Cola Enterprises created a formal peer coaching program that engaged new employees and their managers and peers with a structured program for a repeatable, high-impact, effective on-boarding process (Fritz, Kaestner, & Bergmann, 2010). A program implemented at Citizen's Financial Group paired peers who were well versed in the tangible skills and intangible cultural knowledge needed for success (Carroll et al., 2007). Given the proven results in the cited studies, peer coaching is a potent tool for closing performance gaps in an organization.

There is one environment in which peer coaching is not a good fit, and that is in the realm of executive coaching. Peer coaching can increase the participants' skills, including executives involved in peer coaching. However, in an executive environment, competition between peers becomes increasingly prevalent and the participants' ability to maintain equality is reduced or eliminated altogether. When peers perceive themselves to be unequal, the coaching engagement will be less successful. Coaching for executives should therefore be provided through another coaching genre (Ladyshewsky, 2010b).

Peer coaching is usually driven by the client's need to develop a specific skillset and improve overall performance or competency. With the support of a peer coach, clients have the opportunity to apply and experiment with the knowledge they develop through traditional learning channels to gain mastery of that knowledge (Ladyshewsky, 2010b; Waddell & Dunn, 2005). When used in combination with other forms of peer-assisted learning, novice learners have shown marked improvement over those without such a support strategy (Ladyshewsky, 2002). Peer coaching provides more opportunity to practice skills and integrate them into daily processes and routines. The fact that peers are coaching one another provides added benefits to organizations in terms of a low-to-no-cost operation for a formalized program as well as the increased knowledge and productivity of more team members (Carroll et al., 2007; Parker et al., 2008). Whereas executive or internal coaching impacts only a single individual, peer coaching impacts twice as many participants because both participants develop skills when coaching is peer to peer.

Peer coaching is effective for faculty development across the education field. The research has extended and expanded into clinical healthcare and medical education, where studies have shown that peer coaching and interaction promote cognitive development as well as feelings of empowerment (Ladyshewsky, 2002; Waddell & Dunn, 2005). In more recent years, corporations have begun to develop and use peer-coaching programs (Carroll et al., 2007; Fritz et al., 2010; Hunt & Weintraub, 2002). The use of peer coaching in corporate settings supports skill development and career growth.

Peer coaching is used in a variety of settings to accelerate skill and career development. Within corporate settings, peer coaching has been used as part of on-boarding, on-the-job-training, staff development, and leadership development programs. Case studies at Citizen's Financial Group, Coca-Cola Enterprises, and Bristol-Myers Squibb showed the successful use of peer coaching as a component of larger leadership programs, which ultimately supported a culture of learning and development (Carroll et al., 2007; Derven & Frappolli, 2011; Fritz et al., 2010). Peer coaching enables learners to refine their skills, reflect on their goals and progress, and take ownership of their career paths.

As suggested by its name, the most successful peer coaching programs are driven by the individuals themselves working together. According to Carroll et al. (2007), "informal peer coaching has probably been the single most important source of learning through the ages" (p. 206). Waddell and Dunn (2005) discussed that in a partnership focused on improving performance, peer coaching can be initiated by a learner or observer. When initiated by a learner, the focus is on asking questions or requesting feedback, whereas an observer may begin by highlighting successes or strengths as well as areas needing improvement (Ladyshewsky, 2010b; Waddell & Dunn, 2005). In contrast, a formal peer-coaching program begins with a solid business case that explains how the individual and/or organization will improve performance through the use of peer coaching (Carroll et al., 2007). Formal peer coaching should include some form of education about coaching and a framework to keep the client clear on goals, as well as provide the client with the opportunity to demonstrate new skills or behaviors. In both formal and informal peer-coaching scenarios, reflection and self-assessment enable clients to gauge their own progress in closing perceived skill gaps.

Knowledge, Skills, and Abilities

Peer coaching requires the same knowledge and skills as other forms of coaching. As with all types of productive coaching relationships, the coach should use effective listening skills, ask exploratory questions, build trust, and maintain tact, confidentiality, and diplomacy. Establishing a safe, nonjudgmental, and encouraging environment enables the client to explore all areas of development without fear of evaluation.

When dyads are established, peers should be paired based on equal statuses in job type, experience, and position. As the relationship deepens through the coaching engagement, it becomes the responsibility of the twosome to preserve equality.

Equality is maintained by the peers providing nonevaluative feedback to each other (Ladyshewsky, 2010b). Peer-coaching participants must actively work on the act of nonevaluation to achieve and sustain that environment throughout the engagement.

The ability to practice new learned behaviors is also critical to peer coaching's success. A peer-coaching program that provides practice opportunities amongst the peer group will also further establish and reinforce a sense of trust, because the participants serve as both observers and learners (Trautwien & Ammerman, 2010; Waddell & Dunn, 2005). The opportunity to practice and reinforce new skills leads clients toward mastery.

Contracting Issues

There is a lack of formal research specifically regarding contracting within peer coaching; however, as with all coaching relationships, contracting is a critical activity to ensure a successful coaching engagement. Despite this lack of contracting-specific literature, a key assumption can be made regarding the nature of peer coaching contracting. It can be inferred that contracting issues would be more prevalent in informal peer coaching engagements due to lack of awareness of this critical activity. Since the goal of peer coaching is to address a specific development need, peer coaches should work together to create **individual development plans** (**IDP**), including metrics, goals, and engagement length. This process is more apt to occur within more-formal peer coaching programs, as there is a higher likelihood that formal programs would provide coach training, including creating a development plan (Smits, 2010; Waddell & Dunn, 2005), setting measurable goals (Ladyshewsky, 2010b; Showers & Joyce, 1996), and developing coaching methods, such as questioning and non-evaluative feedback (Cureton, Green & Meakin, 2010; Fritz et al., 2010). The true challenge arises in informal settings where peers are unaware of coaching methods. Informal engagements can still be helpful to participants; however, it is more likely it will be an "accidental success" (Bennett, 2008, p. 7) rather than the attainment of clearly defined goals accomplished using proven coaching practices and techniques.

Challenges and Solutions

While there are many cited benefits and advantages to peer coaching, there are also challenges confronting this type of coaching. Table 11.4 presents some of the challenges that may be encountered when peer coaching, as well as possible solutions.

Table 11.4 Peer Coaching Challenges and Solutions

CHALLENGES	POSSIBLE SOLUTIONS
Trust: Lack of trust between the peers	Develop a mutually supportive relationship based on trust and respect
Knowledge, skills, and abilities: Lack of coaching competence; poor self-awareness or interpersonal skills leading to dominance or manipulation of the partnership; not understanding goal setting and measurement.	Provide training to participants on how to provide constructive, non-evaluative feedback; establish and measure progress towards goals; maintain equality in the coaching partnership.
Multiple roles: Dual roles of peer-peer and peer-coach	Clarify the work that will be a part of the coaching relationship; establish boundaries for the coaching; keep the coaching work in the setting of established coaching sessions; ensure regular "check ins" to assess the peer-coaching process and make adjustments as needed.
Inequality: The peer-peer relationship is impacted by the peer-peer/coach roles in the relationship; interactions will shift from peer-peer to peer-coach.	Ensure both participants are equal in role, tenure, and/or experience; allow participants to select a peer with perceived equivalence; ensure that sessions are divided equally in terms of time and attention to each partner's issues, and that coaching goals are similar in scope and duration; offer observation or supervision by a trained coach if the partners are concerned about equality issues.
Coaching process: Ensure that both partners are knowledgeable about coaching and committed to the process to form strong, trust-filled peer-coaching bonds.	Provide foundational coaching skills training. Allow peer coaching participants to select their own equal coaching partners; have peers complete a pre-coaching self-assessment to uncover the goals expected to be met during their peer coaching experience; pair peers with similar goals and expectations to be partners; ensure that there are regular "process checks" built into the coaching process, and opportunities for both partners to discuss what is going well and what needs to be improved about the interaction.

(Bennett, 2008; Carroll et al., 2007; Ladyshewsky, 2010a, 2010b; Parker et al., 2008; Smits, 2010; Waddell & Dunn, 2005)

Peer Coaching to Support Change

Peer coaching can be ideal as a support to change, since the peers are often from the same organizational setting or environment and are aware of the contextual challenges and opportunities. The following are examples of ways in which peer coaching can support change:

- Peer coaching can exist at multiple levels within an organization. As such, peer coaching can effect and support change on the individual level in one-on-one coaching relationships, as well as at the micro level of groups and the macro level of the entire organization. As peer coaching is skills based, it is a powerful source of learning. This learning can be applied to job-specific proficiencies as well as leadership competencies, thus improving a client's overall performance and increasing the opportunity to excel (Parker et al., 2008).

- Peer coaching is a mutually beneficial and cost-effective engagement, as it facilitates growth and development for both individuals involved and uses existing resources to serve as coaches.
- Peer coaching's reach can extend beyond the relationship of the two individuals and afford groups the opportunity for collective change from knowledge transfer and behavioral modeling (Bush, 2005; Holliday, 2001; Parker et al., 2008; Showers & Joyce, 1996).
- Peer coaching groups have been shown to more effectively support a team's change and success than coaching from the team leader or from someone external to the organization (Clutterbuck, 2007).
- Peer coaching has been shown to accelerate group or organizational change and create a self-sustaining coaching organization in which experienced individuals are coaching new individuals as they enter the organization (Smits, 2010).

Managers as Coaches

Coaching has become a popular approach for managers in the workplace to help motivate, engage, and support employee performance. "Manager-coaches" provide relationship-based, on-the-job learning and feedback in order to develop employees experiencing job transition and displacements due to downsizing; engage and motivate their employees; and retain their top or key organizational talent (Wright, 2005). A "manager-coach" is a manager who uses coaching-related knowledge, approaches, and skills to coach a person (a "direct report") who reports to him within the organizational structure. Coaching in any setting can only be truly effective when the client is willing and open to change. The role of the manager-coach is to assist in creating that awareness and support behavioral change. An organizational-coaching culture is developed when managers adopt coaching skills to address performance at the individual or group level.

The difference between a "manager-coach" and other coach roles is that the manager also has impact on the employee's finances and career. This dual role can impact the coaching process both positively and negatively: the manager's awareness of the employee's situation, performance, and function can serve to clarify coaching goals and development but can also promote suspicion, mistrust, and resistance to change. In addition, it can be difficult for the manager to negotiate between the roles, since managing often requires "telling" or "directing," while coaching is about discovery, creating possibilities, and taking action in order to produce desired results. Managers (similar to coaches) often encourage employees to consider different models or perspectives, envision different possibilities, and reflect and prospectively think.

Managing involves achieving results through others, communicating information about employee performance upward in the organizational structure, communicating information from higher in the organizational structure down to employees, creating a team from individuals, developing an environment of trust, directing others so that their work meets the expectations of the organization, evaluating individual and team performance against the plan, planning the work of others, and staffing people to specific projects or tasks. Coaching involves strengthening employees by encouraging them to find their own solutions, engaging in candid and collegial open conversations, giving non-judgmental feedback, guiding reflection on new experiences or skills, helping others reframe challenges, helping others reframe beyond their own expectations, helping others accept and learn from failure, providing assignments that stretch employees, providing experience-based insights, reinforcing positive behavior and work strengths to leverage better results, and serving as a trusted sounding board for new ideas. These roles are complementary, not contradictory. Hamlin, Ellinger, and Beattie (2006) wrote that "truly effective managers and managerial leaders are those who embed effective coaching into the heart of their management practice" and "coaching is an essential core activity of management and leadership" (pp. 326–327).

Managers and organizations desiring to transform the manager role from a more-traditional approach of implementing employee action plans, enforcing policies and procedures, and ensuring employees are effectively trained to complete their jobs can choose to embrace the role of manager as coach. However, because the role of manager-coaches the manager-coach differs from the traditional manager role in approach and purpose, it is important to understand unique points to consider when coaching as manager.

Why Use Managers as Coaches?

Organizations have a number of reasons to institute coaching. The reasons range from leadership skill development to goal setting to work–life balance. The manager as coach can support all points along the continuum (Mukherjee, 2012). While these activities, in addition to career counseling and performance appraisals, can be addressed through the role of manager as coach, the role is characterized as the day-to-day aspect of helping employees expand their capabilities and improve their performance. Unlike the traditional manager, who may use a one-on-one session to talk about an employee's performance issue, the manager-coach transitions from one-on-one sessions to coaching sessions in which coaching is used as a tool for ongoing developmental purposes versus one-time problem solving. In doing so, a manager-coach helps team members maximize their potential or advance their performance to outstanding levels of achievement (Orth, Wilkinson, & Benfari, 1987). Definitions of manager-as-coach coalesce around the thought that the role of a manager-coach is to empower employees, help improve individual and team performance, develop employees to increase their ability to achieve career goals, improve work quality, and retain top performers within organizations (Joo, Sushko, & McLean, 2012). The influence a manager wields over an employee can create a harmful power dynamic if not managed (Murphy, 2005).

While tracking and managing employee performance is the manager's primary role in the success of the business, coaching skills can be helpful in addressing problems and skill deficits that affect performance. Managers can also coach employees on business acumen, political correctness, influential communication, teaming, and other behavioral issues. The difference is that performance management is the manager's responsibility, while coaching is offered at the request and agreement of the employee. Coaching is optional for the employee—management is not.

The employee-manager coaching relationship has been described as a "working partnership between an employee and his or her direct supervisor that is focused on addressing the performance and development needs of that employee" (Gregory & Levy, 2011, p. 67). The prominence of managers as coaches has increased and will continue to thrive as organizations recognize the benefits of coaching and begin to integrate methodologies into their management and leadership-development structures. The function of managers as coaches can pose certain unique challenges; however, the benefits to the individual, group, and overall organization are entirely worthwhile endeavors. "Effective coaching will lead to your ultimate role of achieving results through and with others" (Ellis, 2004, p. 115).

Knowledge, Skills, and Abilities

Coaching is about learning and draws heavily on principles of learning theory and adult learning. Relevant aspects of the theories include (a) the learner is always actively seeking out stimuli, (b) knowledge has to be propagated from within, and (c) motivation has to be innate (Zeus & Skiffington, 2001). With this in mind, certain knowledge and skills are essential for the manager-coach. These include specialized training in employee development, leadership styles, emotional intelligence, and basic coaching skills.

Training in employee development is required for the coaching manager to be effective. Coaching managers are expected to motivate, develop, and support employees within the organization. The training should introduce development practices, build the organizational learning culture, and foster positive relationships between managers and employees (Joo et al., 2012). These are necessary components for improving quality of work and retaining employees.

Emotional intelligence, and more specifically self-awareness, is required to be effective as a manager when coaching direct reports. A manager could be contributing to the problems or behaviors of the employee (McManus, 2006). Keen emotional intelligence is also necessary to recognize emotions as well as express them in a reasonable manner. A coaching manager must be cognitively and socio-emotionally more mature than the employee to be effective and have a positive impact (Clutterbuck & Megginson, 2010). Depending on the situation, a manager can be in a position of control that leads to too much advocacy of her own ideas, suggestions, or agendas, which would reduce or inhibit trust.

Manager coaching enhances employee engagement and performance, and it helps employees learn and improve proficiencies by providing guidance, encouragement, and support (Grant, 2010). This ongoing process allows employees to recognize opportunities to improve their effectiveness and capabilities and guides them to exceed prior levels of work through constructive feedback that shows they are respected and valued. Employees are empowered to make their own decisions, unleashing their potential, enabling learning, and improving performance (Joo et al., 2012).

Employees should be coached to succeed. All people want to be successful and feel that they have made a contribution (Champy & Nohria, 1996). These outcomes are achieved through regular, constructive, and significant feedback from managers, which identifies effective or ineffective performance so that employees know if they are meeting the expectations of their managers, supervisors, and customers (Joo et al., 2012).

A manager as coach has many preferred skills and behaviors, including listening skills, analytical skills, effective questioning techniques, observation, giving and receiving performance feedback, and creating a supportive environment. A manager should know his employees and how to work best with a variety of personalities. Managers who are also coaches should be direct communicators and results oriented (Champy & Nohria, 1996). These managers create a climate of communication, support, trust, acceptance, and commitment for improving performance and developing employees' capabilities (Joo et al., 2012).

In addition to open communication and valuing people over tasks, it is crucial to have clear goals and clarity about all issues being addressed. If a company unites itself with vision and values, people know where they are going, and are more likely to be effective and adopt the firm's principles (Champy & Nohria, 1996). It is also important that managers help foster and support organizational change. Manager-coaches need to be skilled at developing rapport in order to engage in collaborative goal setting (Grant, 2010).

Contracting Issues

While managerial coaching is often informal, contracting is still important. Employees being coached must be open to improvement, eager to learn from their mistakes, and willing to try new approaches (Murphy, 2005). The manager must be able to build trust and leverage adequate dialogue and respectful feedback. Without this foundation, the manager may encounter resistance to feedback and ultimately resistance to change. It is crucial for the coaching relationship to be developed within a safe environment grounded in trust, credibility, and confidentiality (Murphy, 2005). This environment can best be described as the "coaching-friendly context" in which employees "feel more able to talk frankly with others about their development, challenges, and mistakes" (Hunt & Weintraub, 2007, pp. 7–8).

In the manager-coach role, the manager is often responsible for evaluating the performance of that employee. There are inherent conflicts that exist within this relationship because "the process of evaluation tends to inhibit the degree to which direct reports will be open about their concerns, problems, mistakes " (Hunt & Weintraub, 2007, p. 16). The employee has the desire to make a good impression so that he can minimize any negatives to his performance reviews (Murphy, 2005). The manager also opens the door to criticism of her past actions that may contradict present actions (Bennett, 2008). Direct reports may be hesitant to bring up any mistakes or perceived shortcomings to their manager, because it could adversely affect their performance reviews. An emphasis on creating an atmosphere of trust between the manager and employee can help mitigate the obstacles (McManus, 2006).

Coaching as a manager can occur formally or informally. By the nature of a manager's role it is likely to occur in an informal manner as the need or opportunity arises (McManus, 2006). It may not be appropriate for a manager to utilize a coaching approach if the employee is new or inexperienced and requires explicit instructions to perform at a satisfactory level. In addition, if no improvements have been observed after several coaching sessions, a managerial intervention may be necessary. Of course, it is important to acknowledge that results are rarely seen in a single session (McManus, 2006). Zeus and Skiffington (2001) point out that the learning process is just as important as the knowledge and skills gained. A distinction between the manager role and the coach role is important. Although a manager-as-coach approach may be employed routinely to develop relationships and improve performance, there are situations in which a coaching approach will not be appropriate or effective. Ultimately, the manager must consider his own adequacy of training, skillset, value system, and motivation (Gilley & Gilley, 2007).

The manager-coach may find herself conflicted between the employee and stakeholders. The stakeholders in a manager-as-coach scenario are usually individuals within the organization who have a vested interest in the development of that employee and the company. They generally favor progress reports on the coaching experience, which may cause an ethical dilemma for the coach. The idea of client confidentiality fundamentally contradicts reporting progress to outside parties.

Challenges and Solutions

While there are many cited benefits and advantages to managers providing coaching, there are also challenges. Table 11.5 enumerates some of the challenges that may be encountered when managers coach, as well as possible solutions.

How Managers Coaching Can Support Change

The following are examples of ways in which managers coaching can support change:

- Helping a direct report develop a career plan or get additional training for improvement
- Helping a direct report understand the importance of an organizational change initiative and take action in the role of a change agent
- Coaching a group to identify key stakeholders for a change, and develop an action plan to influence them in supporting the change

Table 11.5 Managers-as-Coaches Challenges and Solutions

CHALLENGE	POSSIBLE SOLUTIONS
Managing multiple roles: The manager serving as coach continues to hold the role of manager.	Clarify roles and expectations with the employee/client: make a clear distinction in discussions when being a manager versus a coach; focus on goals and behaviors; ask, "Is this a performance issue or a coaching issue?"; identify any competing agendas that may exist between manager-employee-organization and ask, "Who is the client?"
Building trust: The manager or client lack trust in each other; client may lack trust in the organization or senior leaders.	Consider the quality of the current manager-employee relationship when introducing manager-coaching (not all are ready to be coaches, or be coached); offer some guidelines on building trust, and have ground rules about what to expect and how to give feedback if there is a problem; ensure that there are regular "process checks" built into the coaching process, and opportunities for both partners to discuss what is going well and what needs to be improved about the interaction.
Developing knowledge, skills, and abilities: Managers may lack coaching competence.	Define the scope and role of manager-coaches; assess managers to identify appropriate manager-coaches and offer development and ongoing support for them; offer orientation to prepare employees to engage effectively in coaching with their managers.
Differentiating between coaching and performance-management issues: Ensuring that manager-coaches use clear direction, tracking, and assessment to address performance-related issues while offering the option of coaching for development and other behavioral issues.	Discussing the difference (in role and approach) with employees; clarifying which issues are which; adopting and communicating standard performance-management systems and processes; asking employees to request coaching when it is wanted; encouraging an environment of safety and openness; practicing giving respectful feedback.

(Bennett, 2008; Murphy, 2005)

- Coaching an employee to identify and work toward additional goals or projects that would gain additional visibility or lead to promotion in the organization.
- Supporting an individual or group in taking on a new level of responsibility or a developmental experience that is not required, but that will benefit the organization and offer recognition.

Group/Team Coaching

The definition of group or team coaching can be similar to individual coaching. Whitmore (2002) defined it as "unlocking a team's (formerly individual) potential to maximize their own performance. It is helping them to learn rather than teaching them" (p. 8). It can be described as a group of people assembled for purposes of learning, self-awareness, professional growth, and team building to achieve personal and organizational objectives and goals. Group/team coaching generates an enhanced experience because it is facilitated by a professional coach in a group where each person adds to the experience of others in the group toward the desired outcome (Britton, 2010).

The terms "team" or "group" coaching may be used interchangeably for coaching that involves more than one client meeting together with the coach in a collective setting. Group coaching often refers to a small assembly of people gathered for holistic goals or tasks. Team coaching is more likely to refer to a group of people gathered for a specific coordinated purpose, which is usually task oriented. It focuses on using collective talents and resources to accomplish the team's work (Hackman & Wageman, 2005). Since the uses of group coaching tend toward more therapeutic, learning, and social applications, this section focuses primarily on team coaching. The principles outlined can apply to either.

Team coaching is defined by purpose and coaches are explicit about their method and approach so that the people in the team or group know what to expect from themselves, the coach, and others. A team coach is effective if the team understands what the coach is there to do (Dunlap, 2006). Clutterbuck (2007) described team coaching as "helping the team improve performance, and the processes by which performance is achieved, through reflection and dialogue" (p. 77).

Knowledge, Skills, and Abilities

According to Britton (2010), team coaching is more directive than individual coaching. A coach needs to have knowledge of the client's agenda, be able to identify behaviors, and discern if there is a desire to change those behaviors. Many of the skills needed are the same as those for individual coaching. A key difference is the capacity to be able to notice enough of what is happening in the group without noticing so much that the coach is rendered ineffective by information overload (Clutterbuck, 2007). The role of group and team coaches is to protect the boundaries of the group, observe the group's interactions, represent authority or experience in the group, limit destructive behavior, and attend to the group's system administration such as preparing the setting (Thornton, 2010).

Knowledge of team dynamics, combined with practical experience, is important. While coaching skills are essential, a coach's ability to be self-aware and introspective is crucial. Possibly the most challenging skill of a team coach is the coach's ability to transition the group to coach itself. Individual and group honesty is a challenge that needs to be incorporated for this quality result. Clutterbuck (2007) and Zeus and Skiffington (2001) suggest that the coach monitors the team in designing goals and addressing both wins and obstacles. In addition, the coach coordinates the team by design of group activities, teaching, and communicating with the management liaison. This type of coach will have a clear alliance to the managing client.

Another important skill is that of noticing group behaviors that enhance and impede group work (Hackman & Wageman, 2005). By feeding this information back to the group, the team can reflect and attempt to interpret and make meaning of its behaviors. The coach follows up by helping group members decide if and how they wish to change behaviors. Knowledge of appreciative inquiry can help the coach start with solutions and an emphasis on what is working well (Clutterbuck, 2007; Orem, Binkert, & Clancy, 2007).

Contracting Issues

Working with groups in a coaching relationship presents some special contracting needs. First, consider that the client comprises both the individuals who are a part of the group and the group as a unit. Managing interpersonal dynamics with a team helps it collectively deal with conflict, build collective emotional intelligence, and manage stress. These elements help establish and maintain a healthy coaching environment.

Contracting is best treated as a business agreement, describing what can be expected by the negotiating entities. The agreement consists of payment, including amount, due date, and the responsible authorizing agent; team membership (criteria and names); sponsors; any deadline dates; and cancellation policies. Logistics such as venue, which covers the environment—including room layout, equipment, and furnishings—must be addressed. The number of participants and the meeting specifics like time and day should be noted. Ideally, there should be agreement about content, materials used, and outcome measures. Finally, areas such as insurance, liability, meals, break room service, and any other participant comforts need to be included as contract items (Britton, 2010).

Challenges and Solutions

While there are many cited benefits and advantages to group coaching, there are also challenges confronting this type of coaching. Table 11.6 summarizes some of the challenges that may be encountered when coaching groups, as well as possible solutions.

Table 11.6 Group Coaching Challenges and Solutions

CHALLENGES	POSSIBLE SOLUTIONS
Focusing the agenda: With multiple participants in the group-coaching engagement it may be difficult to establish agreement about the coaching agenda.	Use consensus-building tools to develop a shared focus for the group and for the coaching.
Maintaining a coaching approach: The coach does not need to be an expert in all areas nor should this be expected by participants. The coach is there to uncover the group's capacity.	Call on experiences and knowledge from all participants; lay out the space in a circular or half-circle fashion to create a sense of equality and inclusion which can create a user-friendly environment for participants opening up to others; implement checkpoints along the course of the session to help the coach stay on target; use evaluation forms for group feedback to aid the coach in developing skills.
Working at multiple levels: Working with a group of individuals as well as the dynamics of the group	Employ collaborative and collective goal setting methods, and assess increasing capacity for successful task completion and problem solving; periodically evaluate coaching impact on the team and provide feedback for the coach on what is most helpful; foster diversity on the team—a homogenous team may have a high degree of affinity for one another but a highly diverse team has greater potential for creativity.
Keeping the group together: Capacity to manage various levels of relationships within the team; ensuring that the group interaction is stimulated and sustained, even over distance and virtual media; addressing competing priorities and constraints	Develop the team's capacity for engagement and participation; work virtually if necessary so all members do not need to be physically present for coaching sessions. Research shows that virtual teams perform better if they have a face-to-face meeting in the first 90 days.
Building trust, credibility, and respectful interaction: Good boundaries must be maintained so if a member of the team shares something with the coach, that team member can trust the coach to maintain confidentiality.	Identify ground rules for group sessions up front and address any situations that arise; before meetings, ensure that agendas and any pre-reading is sent out; start each meeting with a "check in" to give each member a minute to share an individual perspective.
Team support and structure: Resources, support, and clarity of purpose are crucial to success so that the team has what it needs.	Contract for regular meetings averaging one-to-three hours, and engagements lasting between three-to-six months. Groups function best with 3 to 12 participants; smaller groups tend to be more effective; groups larger than 12 have a higher dropout rate. Ensure that the group has the authority to act on its ideas.

(Britton, 2010; Clutterbuck, 2007; Derosa & Lepsinger, 2010; Hackman, 2011; Whitcomb, 2008)

Group Coaching to Support Change

Change is supported by improving a client's bottom line. Clutterbuck (2007) argues that team coaching increases efficiency. In addition, retention is affected by reducing conflict within and between teams. The quality of communication between teams and stakeholders is improved and the overall knowledge is increased. Leadership qualities become more evident, which helps with an organization's succession planning. Team coaching is more cost effective because a larger number of people can be coached for the same amount of money as one person; the ROI has been demonstrated (Britton, 2010).

The following are examples of ways in which team coaching can support change:

- Coaching leadership teams to develop a common vision and case for change
- Ensuring that change guiding teams include representative perspectives from all key stakeholder groups
- Supporting change-implementation teams to develop action plans, stakeholder analyses, and measures for the success of the change
- Facilitating change teams (guiding teams, integration teams) to collaborate in planning action, addressing conflict over resources and resistance to change, and celebrating successes for the change
- Fostering effective communication to build understanding between change teams at different levels in the infrastructure (sponsors, guiding teams, integration teams, and implementation teams).

Chapter Summary

There are five roles of coaching for change, each with their own unique set of advantages and disadvantages. The five roles include, internal coach, external coach, peer coaching, manager-coach, and group/team coaching. An *internal coach* is someone who is a full- or part-time employee of the client's organization, often in the organization development or human resources department. An *external coach* is someone who is not on the permanent payroll of the client's company. *Peer coaching* (not the same thing as mentoring) is when two people of equal status actively participate in helping each other on specific tasks or problems with a mutual desire to be helpful. A *manager-coach* is someone who manages or supervises the client, who is the manager's employee. Group/team coaching is coaching that involves multiple clients meeting together with the coach in a collective setting to address a shared agenda.

Knowledge Check

1. What are the five roles of change coaching described in this chapter? How are they similar? How are they different?

2. Identify 3–5 differences of working as an internal versus an external coach.
3. How can the skills of effective managers be developed and applied in coaching conversations?
4. What are the best practices for manager-coach skill and mindset development?
5. How can effectiveness be assessed for each of the roles?
6. List three considerations for managers serving as coaches. List three considerations for peers serving as coaches.

Learning Activities

Learning Activity 1: Manager-as-Coach Scenarios

Think of an effective manager that you had or have heard about. In what ways did he or she act as a coach? Was the manager a good coach? In what ways? How did the manager differentiate between coaching and performance management? What were some of the results—for individuals, the group, and the organization? Write any reflections in the form of a short essay or journal entry.

Learning Activity 2: Observing Coaching

Watch one of the following movies:

- *Avatar* (2009)
- *Moneyball* (2012)

Observe the ways in which coaching relationships and skills are used, for example:

- What applications of coaching were used?
- What skills were used?
- What challenges are faced? What solutions were used? How effective were the solutions?
- How did coaching support change at the individual, group, and/or organization levels?
- What did you observe that would influence your coaching?

Learning Activity 3: Your Experience

List each of the five coaching roles you have personally experienced (either as coach or client). For each, make a note of the following:

- What was the change goal for the coaching?
- How effective was the coaching (in getting to the goals)? Why?
- Describe the contracting process—what was covered? What was missing? What would you have done differently?
- What challenges did you experience and how did you (or the coach) address them?
- Was there an evaluation process for the coaching? What did it include?
- Was this the optimal coaching role for the change scenario? Could the coaching have been equally effective if addressed with a different role? (For example, if this experience was with internal coaching, would it have been equally effective as a peer coaching, group coaching, or manager-coaching engagement?)

Learning Activity 4: Preparation

Consider planned roles and professional relationships in which you are involved. These might include: manager, peer, internal, or external coach. Select one role and identify how you will approach the application of coaching:

- Who is the client?
- What relationship do you have with the client?
- Who are the stakeholders?
- What challenges can you anticipate? What are some possible solutions?

References

Augustijnen, M. T., Schnitzer, G., & Van Esbroeck, R. (2011). A model of executive coaching: A qualitative study. *International Coaching Psychology Review, 6*(2), 150–164.

Battley, S. (2006). *Coached to lead: How to achieve extraordinary results with an executive coach.* San Francisco, CA: Jossey-Bass.

Bennett, J. L. (2008). Contracting for success. *International Journal of Coaching in Organizations, 6*(4), 7–14.

Bennett, J. L., & Bush, M. W. (2009). Coaching in organizations: Current trends and future opportunities. *OD Practitioner, 41*(1), 2–7.

Bennett, J. L., & English, J. (2011). Executive coaching style: In search of a vocabulary. In I. O'Donovan & D. Megginson (Eds.), *Developing mentoring & coaching research and practice* (pp. 82–96). Marlborough, Wiltshire, UK: European Mentoring and Coaching Council.

Brennan, D., & Prior, D. M. (2005). The future of coaching as a profession: The next five years 2005–2010. Lexington, KY: International Coach Federation.

Britton, J. (2010). *Effective group coaching.* Mississauga, ON: Wiley and Sons Canada Ltd.

Bush, M. W. (2005). *Client perceptions of effectiveness in executive coaching.* Doctoral dissertation. Pepperdine University.

Carroll, P. A., Hunt, J. M., & Weintraub, J. R. (2007). Peer coaching at Citizen's Financial Group (CFG). In J. M. Hunt & J. R. Weintraub (Eds.), *The coaching organization: A strategy for developing leaders* (pp. 205–214). Thousand Oaks, CA: Sage.

Carter, A. (2005). *Providing coaching internally: A literature review.* Retrieved from Institute for Employment Studies website: www.employment-studies.co.uk/pdflibrary/mp43.pdf

Champy, J., & Nohria, N. (1996). *Fast forward: The best ideas on managing business change.* Boston, MA: Harvard Business School Publishing.

Clutterbuck, D. (2007). *Coaching the team at work.* London: Nicholas Brealey.

Clutterbuck, D., & Megginson, D. (2010, December). Coach maturity: An emerging concept. *International Journal of Coaching and Mentoring, XIII*(1), n.p.

Cox, E., Clutterbuck, D., & Bachkirova, T. (2010). Introduction. In E. Cox, D. Clutterbuck, & T. Bachkirova (Eds.), *The complete handbook of coaching* (pp. 1–20). Los Angeles, CA: Sage.

Cureton, D., Green, P., & Meakin, L. (2010). Peer mentoring for staff development in a changing work environment. *International Journal of Evidence Based Coaching and Mentoring, 8*(2), 79–89.

Dagley, G. R. (2010). Exceptional executive coaches: Practices and attributes. *International Coaching Psychology Review, 5*(1), 63.

Derosa, D., & Lepsinger, R. (2010). *Virtual team success: A practical guide for working and leading from a distance.* San Francisco, CA: Jossey-Bass.

Derven, M., & Frappolli, K. (2011). Aligning leadership development for general managers with global strategy: The Bristol-Myers Squibb story. *Industrial & Commercial Training, 43*(1), 4–12.

Dunlap, H. (2006). An exploratory investigation into the perceived effects of team coaching in the construction sector. *The International Journal of Mentoring and Coaching, IV*(2), 24–44.

Ellis, C. W. (2004). *Management skills for new managers.* New York, NY: AMACOM.

Flaherty, J. (1999). *Coaching: Evoking excellence in others.* Boston, MA: Butterworth-Heinemann.

Frisch, M. H. (2001). The emerging role of the internal coach. *Consulting Psychology Journal: Practice and Research, 53*(4), 240–250.

Fritz, K., Kaestner, M., & Bergmann, M. (2010). Coca-Cola enterprises invest in on-boarding at the front lines to benefit the bottom line. *Global Business & Organizational Excellence, 29*(4), 15–22.

Gilley, J. W., & Gilley, A. (2007). *The manager as coach.* Westport, CT: Praeger Publishers.

Grant, A. M. (2010). It takes time: A stages of change perspective on the adoption of workplace coaching skills. *Journal of Change Management, 10*(1), 61–77.

Gregory, J. B., & Levy, P. E. (2011). It's not me, it's you: A multilevel examination of variables that impact employee coaching relationships. *Consulting Psychology Journal: Practice and Research, 63*(2), 67–88.

Hackman. J. R. (2011). Six common misperceptions about teamwork. http://blogs.hbr.org/cs/2011/06/six_common_misperceptions_abou.html

Hackman, J. R., & Wageman, R. (2005). A theory of team coaching. *Academy of Management Review, 30*(2), 269–287.

Hamlin, R. G., Ellinger, A. D., & Beattie, R. S. (2006). Coaching at the heart of managerial effectiveness: A cross-cultural study of managerial behaviours. *Human Resource Development International, 9*(3), 305–331.

Holliday, M. (2001). *Coaching, mentoring & managing: Breakthrough strategies to solve performance problems and build winning teams.* Franklin Lakes, NJ: Career Press.

Hunt, J. M., & Weintraub J. R. (2002). *The coaching manager: Developing top talent in business.* Thousand Oaks, CA: Sage.

Hunt, J. M., & Weintraub, J. R. (2007). *The coaching organization: A strategy for developing leaders.* Thousand Oaks, CA: Sage.

Joo, B. K., Sushko, J. S., & McLean, G. N. (2012). Multiple faces of coaching: Manager-as-coach, executive coaching, and formal mentoring. *Organization Development Journal, 30*(1), 19–38.

Ladyshewsky, R. K. (2002). A quasi-experimental study of the differences in performance and clinical reasoning using individual learning versus reciprocal peer coaching. *Physiotherapy Theory and Practice, 18,* 17–31.

Ladyshewsky, R. K. (2004). Impact of peer-coaching on the clinical reasoning of the novice practitioner. *Physiotherapy Canada, 56*(1), 15–26.

Ladyshewsky, R. K. (2010a). Building competency in the novice allied health professional through peer coaching. *Journal of Allied Health, 39*(2), e77–e82.

Ladyshewsky, R. K. (2010b). Peer coaching. In E. Cox, T. Bachkirova, & D. Clutterbuck (Eds.), *The complete handbook of coaching* (pp. 284–296). Thousand Oaks, CA: Sage.

Liljenstrand, A., & Nebecker, D. M. (2008). Coaching services: A look at coaches, clients, and practices. *Consulting Psychology Journal: Practice and Research, 60*(1), 57–77.

McDermott, M., Levenson, A., & Newton, S. (2007). What coaching can and cannot do for your organization. *Human Resource Planning, 30*(2), 30–37.

McKee, A., Tilin, F., & Mason, D. (2009). Coaching from the inside: Building an internal group of emotionally intelligent coaches. *International Coaching Psychology Review, 4*(1), 59–70.

McManus, P. (2006). *Coaching people.* Boston, MA: Harvard Business School Publishing Corporation.

Moen, F., & Federici, R. (2012). The effect from external executive coaching. *Coaching: An International Journal of Theory, Research & Practice, 5*(2), 113–131.

Mukherjee, S. (2012). Does coaching transform coaches? A case study of internal coaching. *International Journal of Evidence Based Coaching and Mentoring, 10*(2), 76–87.

Murphy, S. A. (2005). Recourse to executive coaching: The mediating role of human resources. *International Journal of Police Science and Management, 7*(3), 175–186

Newsom, G., & Dent, E. B. (2011). A work behaviour analysis of executive coaches. *International Journal of Evidence Based Coaching & Mentoring, 9*(2), 1–22.

Orem, S. L., Binkert, J., & Clancy, A. L. (2007). *Appreciative coaching: A positive process for change.* San Francisco, CA: John Wiley & Sons.

Orth, C. D., Wilkinson, H. E., & Benfari, R. C. (1987). Facilitating natural supports in the workplace: Strategies for support consultants. *Organizational Dynamics, 15*(4), 66–69.

Parker, P., Hall, D. T., & Kram, K. E. (2008). Peer coaching: A relational process for accelerating career learning. *Academy of Management & Learning, 7*(4), 487–503.

Ratiu, L., & Baban, A. (2012). Executive coaching as a change process: an analysis of the readiness for coaching. *Cognition, Brain, Behavior, 16*(1), 139–164.

Rock, D., & Donde, R. (2008). Driving change with internal coaching programs (Rep.). Retrieved from Results Coaching Systems website: www.davidrock.net/files/Driving _Organisational_Change_with_Internal _Coaching_Programs.pdf

Sanson, M. (2006). *The supply of executive coaching services* (Doctoral dissertation). University of St. Gallen, Switzerland.

Showers, B., & Joyce, B. (1996). The evolution of peer coaching. *Educational Leadership, 53*(6), 12–16.

Smits, S. J. (2010). Extending the journey: Leadership development beyond the MBA. *Poznan University of Economics Review, 10*(1), 62–77.

Thomas, R., & Pirtle, J. (2010). Developing leaders: An analysis of the efficacy of executive coaching. *Leadership & Organizational Management Journal, 2010*(3), 106–112.

Thornton, C. (2010). *Group and team coaching: The essential guide.* New York, NY: Routledge.

Trautwein, B., & Ammerman, S. (2010). From pedagogy to practice: Mentoring and reciprocal peer coaching for preservice teachers. *Volta Review, 110*(2), 191–206.

Underhill, B. O., McAnally, K., & Koriath, J. J. (2007). *Executive coaching for results: The definitive guide to developing organizational leaders.* San Francisco, CA: Berrett-Koehler.

Waddell, D.L., & Dunn, N. (2005). Peer coaching: The next step in staff development. *The Journal of Continuing Education in Nursing, 36*(2), 84–89.

Weintraub, J. R., Eisenman, E., & Perkins, S. (n.d.). The internal coach playbook. *Babson Insight.* Retrieved from www.babson.edu/executive-education/thought-leadership/babson-insight/Articles/Pages/The-Internal-Coach-Playbook.aspx

Weiss, A. (2009). Practicing internal OD. In W. J. Rothwell, J. M. Stavros, R. L. Sullivan, & A. Sullivan (Eds.), *Practicing organization development: A guide for leading change* (pp. 185–203). San Francisco, CA: Pfeiffer.

Whitcomb, J. (2008). Action learning: An approach to team coaching. In C. Wahl, C. Scriber & B. Bloomfield (Eds.), *On becoming a leadership coach: A holistic approach to coaching excellence* (pp. 199–208). New York, NY: Palgrave McMillan.

Whitmore, J. (2002). *Coaching for performance* (3rd ed.). Boston, MA: Nicholas Brealey.

Wright, J. (2005). Workplace coaching: What's it all about? *Work: A Journal of Prevention, Assessment and Rehabilitation, 24*(3), 325–328.

Zeus, P., & Skiffington, S. (2001). *The complete guide to coaching at work.* Sydney, Australia: McGraw-Hill.

12

Ethical Considerations of Change Coaching

This chapter will explore some of the ethical frameworks that can be applied when coaching for change, including some of the most common ethical dilemmas that coaches face. Suggestions are offered on how to become aware of an organization, group, or individual's ethical framework, and how to deal with typical ethical dilemmas as a coach. In this chapter, the authors will address the following questions:

- What are the ethical frameworks that inform coaching for change?
- What are some common ethical dilemmas faced by a coach?
- How would a coach gain an understanding about the ethics in an organization, group, or individual which he or she is coaching?
- How do coaches deal with ethical dilemmas?

People have considered the nature of ethics for thousands of years—most notably beginning with the teachings of the ancient Greek philosopher Socrates, and later Plato and Aristotle. Ethics and their close relatives values, codes, and standards of behavior remain active topics for debate and discussion even today.

Ethics are moral principles adopted by an individual or group to provide rules for appropriate conduct by members of the group in given situations. *Values,* on the other hand, are focused on what is good and desirable. Ethics are contextual based on values. *Ethical codes* or *codes of conduct* represent the ideal standards set by a professional organization or group of organizations and agreed upon by those who accept membership in those organizations. Therefore, what is ethical in one part of the world or in one organization may not be in another.

While ethics and values are generally beliefs and principles that reside internally within a person or group of people, and are enforced at their own discretion, *laws* are externally imposed rules of behavior established by legislation and courts in order to define minimum standards for a society to operate in an orderly manner. Perhaps not surprisingly, what authorities interpret as legal may not always be ethical.

Ethical Frameworks That Inform Change Coaching

Currently, there is no universal code of conduct or code of ethics for coaches—those practicing coaching professionally or those using coaching skills as part of their helping role. The ethical behaviors of coaches instead "are guided by community standards and practices, moral expectations based on cultural patterns or religious beliefs, and local, state [provincial], and federal laws" (Brammer & MacDonald, 2003, p. 153). Passmore and Mortimer (2011) argued, "Codes can never offer a solution for all situations, but only principles to consider when making a decision. The alternative route is to help practitioners develop ethical decision-making frameworks which can guide them in making more conscious and informed ethical decisions" (p. 219).

Western European and American values that frequently inform ethics include:

- Respect for others—their dignity, autonomy, integrity
- Veracity—telling the truth, or just not lying
- Honoring one's promises
- Equity—treating others fairly
- Beneficence—making things better
- Non-malfeasance—not making things worse
- Integrity
- Fidelity/loyalty
- Fairness
- Caring for others
- Pursuit of excellence
- Accountability.

There are multiple approaches to ethical decision making, and it is important to remember that in most cases no one approach is absolute. Each way—each approach—has an alternative path, a counterargument, and potentially its own set of dilemmas. For example, when pursuing the common good, say by condemning a neighborhood using the power of eminent domain to make room for a new, publicly funded football stadium, the individual's good or benefit may be sacrificed.

An individual's quest is to find the one approach that is right for *himself* or *herself*, in this place and at this time. The *individual* gets to decide what is important and what has priority. The *individual* gets to decide whether to act in compliance with the norm or to challenge it. And the *individual* receives the consequences—both positive and negative—that result from his or her decisions.

Recognizing the trans-disciplinary nature of coaching and the multiple helping-related professional practices from which coaching draws—as well as the multiple roles that coaches may play, and the professional associations or licensing boards that serve those who practice coaching—it is difficult to identify a single set of ethical guidelines for coaches. Take, for example, the manager who is also a professional accountant. This manager would, of course, be expected in her role as a professional accountant to comply with the code of conduct for accountants. And, when coaching, this same manager would be expected to comply with any related ethical guidelines for coaching. But that is not all. Assuming that the manager works in a company, she would also be expected to comply with the standards of ethical conduct for the business. In addition, these standards might differ somewhat, depending on the country, or countries, in which the company does business.

Consider another example for an external coach working for a coaching service provider who serves clients in a company. The coach would, of course, be expected to comply with the coaching guidelines as well as guidelines established by the service provider for which he works—all while functioning in the context of a particular client organization that has its own standards of ethical conduct. In addition, the coach may also hold a professional credential or license, which likely has its own guidelines.

In both examples, the coach may be confronted with ethical dilemmas and the need to consider them through multiple frames of reference: ethical guidelines and codes of conduct originating from the client organization, one's professional association, and/or one's licensing board.

A variety of formal, standardized codes of conduct or ethical standards have existed for coaches for some time—for example, the International Coach Federation's code of conduct, last updated in 2008. Even if there were a universal professional code of conduct, there are no mechanisms to enforce compliance by preventing someone from practicing the art and science of coaching. There is no organization yet charged with the duty of checking a coach's credentialing documents or association memberships.

In an effort to lay a firm foundation of ground rules, establish markers of good practice, and pave the way to self-regulation, in 2011 the International Coach Federation (ICF) and the European Mentoring and Coaching Council (EMCC) joined forces to draft and agree upon a common code of conduct for coach and mentor practitioners, and for their representative industry bodies. In addition, the Association for Coaching (AC) has also partnered and signed on to this effort. The code of conduct was not meant to replace the ICF code of conduct, but rather to be used in conjunction with the existing code of ethics. The code establishes a set of guidelines that are a benchmark for ethics and good practice in coaching and mentoring. The guidelines form the basis for the development of self-regulation for the coaching and mentoring profession.

Ethical Decision-Making Rationalizations

Making ethical decisions is not always a clear, easy, or black-and-white proposition; often, it's none of these things. Individuals, groups, and organizations may have their own unique ethical beliefs and cultures, and the right answer for one person may be the wrong answer for someone else.

Business people are often under pressure to do what is faster, or less expensive, or more profitable at the expense of ethical considerations. Here are some of the questions that can and should be asked by coaches when attempting to divine what is the right and good thing to do in a particular decision-making situation:

- If it is legal, is it ethical?
- If it is necessary, is it ethical?
- If it is part of the job, is it ethical?
- If it is for a good cause, is it ethical?
- If it is the way business is done, is it ethical?
- If everyone is doing it, is it ethical?
- If I don't gain personally, is it ethical?
- If no one gets hurt, is it ethical?
- If it conforms to principles and values of the organization, is it ethical?
- If it satisfies my personal definition of right and wrong, is it ethical?

Ethical Challenges Coaches Might Encounter

Because coaches may at times become trusted advisors and confidants—to employees, and to the organizations for which they work—and because they may have access to proprietary or confidential information not generally known to the public, the business's competitors, or to many of the organization's employees, a variety of ethical challenges may arise. As a result, coaches must constantly be on the alert for such challenges and be prepared to prevent them whenever possible—or, if they cannot be prevented, head them off immediately.

Passmore and Mortimer (2011) claimed that there are four main sources of ethical dilemmas for coaches: issues with the coachee, issues with the coach, boundary issues, and issues with the multiple relationship nature of coaching in organizations. Brennan and Wildflower (2010) offered similar potential ethical issues, including contracting, confidentiality/boundary management, misrepresentation, conflict of interest, dual and multiple relationships, competence, and self-management. Other ethical challenges could be the direct result of physical contact with the client, aggressive marketing practices, and improper use of the client's property or technology.

Suggestions for Internal and External Coaches

Coaches who are internal to an organization have different concerns than do coaches who are external to an organization. While the guidelines for coaching are similar in many ways, they can also be subtly different. Consider these suggestions for people who are working as internal and external coaches.

Internal Coaches

- Do no harm.
- Know the code for ethical behavior of the organization.
- Develop a professional relationship with someone who can help assess ethical dilemmas that may arise. Many organizations have an ethics office or legal counsel with whom to consult. If not, engage a Human Resources business partner with any questions or concerns.
- Operate within the ethical guidelines of one's professional association(s) and professional licensing board(s).
- Operate within the ethical guidelines for coaching, if established by the organization.
- Confront observations of unethical behavior by clients in a manner that provides them the opportunity to address them before reporting them (as appropriate).
- Avoid dual relationships with clients.

External Coaches

- Do no harm.
- Know the ethical guidelines for conduct within client organizations.

- Operate within the ethical guidelines of one's professional association(s) and professional licensing board(s).
- Communicate with clients on how perceived ethical dilemmas that may arise during the coaching engagement will be dealt with.
- Develop a professional relationship with someone that can help assess ethical dilemmas that may arise.
- Avoid personal relationships with clients while engaged in coaching engagements.
- Acknowledge and clarify situations where multiple relationships with a client exist.
- Establish a consistent price and disclose the full price of services before they are begun.
- Have agreements for services in writing approved by both parties before beginning the work.

Steps to Take When Dealing With an Ethical Dilemma

Every coach will, from time to time, confront ethical dilemmas—some minor and others more serious. Ethical dilemmas will occur in any organization, despite the best efforts of all concerned to avoid them. As a coach, it is important to be on the alert for such ethical dilemmas and then take immediate steps to deal with them. Here is a suggested procedure for addressing ethical dilemmas when they occur:

1. Stop all activities.
2. Gather facts about the situation.
3. Review codes of ethics and conduct that apply.
4. Consult a professional who is knowledgeable about the codes of ethics and conduct that apply; seek his counsel.
5. Discuss the situation with those involved, if possible and practical.
6. Make a decision and act according to standards of ethical practices.

Chapter Summary

Ethics and coaching go hand in hand. For a coach to be effective, he or she must be ethical. *Ethics* are moral principles adopted by an individual or group to provide rules for appropriate conduct by members of the group in given situations, while *values* focus on what is good and desirable. Western European and American values that often inform ethics include such things as respect for others, veracity, equity, integrity, fairness, caring for others, accountability, and more.

Coaches should avoid the kinds of ethical challenges that result from multiple relationships, physical contact with clients, coach limitations, unclear understanding of what information will be shared with whom and when, and personal conflicts of interest.

Knowledge Check

1. Define "ethics." Do ethics differ from values? If so, how?
2. Name two professional associations that provide codes of conduct for coaches.
3. What are the six steps for addressing an ethical dilemma?
4. What are five of the recommended considerations for internal and external Change Coaches regarding ethical conduct?

Learning Activities

Learning Activity 1: Explore Ethical Decisions

Read each statement and consider under what circumstances the situation could be a breach of ethics.

- Accepting a client's major competitor as a client
- Telling an employer that the employee being coached is planning to quit, in the absence of an agreement to disclose that information
- Altering the agreement for coaching services without the knowledge and consent of all parties
- Using a professional association's database to mail solicitations or announcements without authorization
- Overstating or inflating the benefits of coaching; making promises for the outcomes of coaching
- Asking a client to make a financial donation to your favorite civic or community organization while the person is a client
- Receiving a fee for referring a client without disclosing it
- Identifying a client's problem and telling her how to solve it
- Getting romantically involved with a current coaching client

- Disclosing information gained from an **anonymous** interview with a client's peer in such a way that the client is able to link the information with the source
- Making an investment decision involving a client company based on confidential and proprietary information gained from an executive through a coaching engagement
- Using a proprietary model developed by another coach or company in your own coaching practice without attributing it to the source or gaining permission to use it.

Learning Activity 2: Ethical Dilemmas

Discuss each of the following numbered situations. Use these questions to guide the discussion:

- What is the coach's role?
- Who is involved?
- What is the ethical dilemma/challenge?
- What are the options?
- How will the dilemma/challenge be resolved?
- What is the basis for action?

The coach is asked to work with a coaching client in his role as an employee of a coaching services provider. The client organization to which the coach is assigned is an abortion rights advocacy agency.

A client tells the coach he has embezzled money from his employer. Does the coach tell the police? The employer?

1. A coach and a colleague are asked to provide a workshop for a client. The coach will be paid for the engagement. As the coach prepares the program materials, she discovers a program available on the web. The coach decides to copy some of the material for use in her workshop. The coach's colleague believes she should not use it because it is not her material.
2. Someone is asked to coach a friend's partner/spouse. The friend believes this will be good because she has shared a great deal of information about the difficulties of the relationship.
3. A coach is being paid by an organization to coach a manager/leader. The person being coached recently completed several assessments (personality and multi-rater). Following the coaching session in which the coach

debriefed the assessments and began focusing on coaching priorities, the senior HR manager called. She said, "*Your client* told the CEO that he had nothing to work on. The feedback indicated he was perfect and that you (the coach) told him so. What did you say? What were the results of the assessments? What coaching goals has the client established for himself?"

Learning Activity 3: Ethical Dilemma A

A coach was coaching a senior leader as part of his duties with a global talent management firm, while also working as a part-time faculty member at a university. After leaving the firm, the coach returned to the university as a full-time member of the faculty and continued to work with clients through the consulting firm on a contractual basis. The university has a leadership-development practice through which members of the faculty work with clients. The university was in the process of soliciting business from the coaching client's company. This coach was not involved in the business-development activities. A local boutique-consulting firm with a relationship with the client and the client's company asked the coach to consult with the client's team.

Considerations:

- What are the ethical issues involved in this situation?
- What solutions would be considered?
- What elements of a code of conduct (the coach's or the organization's) would provide guidance in handling this situation?

Learning Activity 4: Ethical Dilemma B

Assume you are an internal coach in a large Fortune 500 company, coaching a director, Derek, as part of your role in the HR/organization development department. You have been working with Derek for a year now, and he is on the fast track to higher levels of leadership within the company. The coaching focus is to help Derek develop as a leader. He is bright, energetic, innovative, works well with others, and is an expert in a very sought-after technical field. He is 36 years old and has been with the company since graduating with his master's degree. Derek is currently being offered all of the leadership-development opportunities the company has: He is a member of an exclusive leadership-development program, sits on two high-level internal review boards that afford him increased visibility with executives, and the company has recently invested a large sum to send him to a high-profile executive education program in an Ivy League school on the East Coast. In the first session after Derek returns from the executive program, he is brimming over with excitement about what he learned and whom he met. He has seen the world and the industry through a larger lens because of the executive experience and is now considering an offer from one of the participants for a senior director role at another company.

Considerations:

- What are the ethical issues involved in this situation?
- What solutions should be considered?
- What elements of a code of conduct (the coach's/yours or the organization's) would provide guidance in handling this situation?

Learning Activity 5: Defining Ethical Practices

Write a statement of ethical beliefs and personal values. Discuss these with a professional colleague and refine the statement. Consider codes of conduct from relevant professional organizations as the statement of ethical beliefs is refined. If in an internal coach or manager-coach position, consider the employer's code of conduct.

Learning Activity 6: Compare Codes of Ethics

Compare and contrast the codes of ethics from two professional/practice associations.

- What do they have in common? What is substantively different?
- What, if any, elements do you disagree with or consider not to be applicable to your own practice? Why?
- Which elements would be adopted for your own personal code of ethics for change coaching?

Additional Resources

The following are coaching and coaching-related organizations and links to their codes of conduct and ethical guidelines:

- American Psychological Association (APA)
- Asia Pacific Alliance of Coaches (APAC)

- Association for Professional Executive Coaching & Supervision (APECS)
- Australian Psychological Society (APS)
- British Psychological Society (BPS)
- Center for Credentialing & Education (CCE)
- Chartered Institute of Personnel and Development (CIPD)
- Coaches and Mentors of South Africa (COMENSA)
- European Mentoring and Coaching Council (EMCC)
- Institute of Management Consultants (IMC-USA)
- International Association of Facilitators (IAF)
- International Coach Federation (ICF)
- Society for Human Resource Management (SHRM)
- Society for Industrial and Organizational Psychology (SIOP)

References

Brammer, L. M., & MacDonald, G. (2003). *The helping relationship: Process and skills* (8th ed.). Boston, MA: Allyn and Bacon.

Brennan, D., & Wildflower, L. (2010). Ethics in coaching. In E. Cox, D. Clutterbuck & T. Bachkirova (Eds.) (pp. 369–380). *The complete handbook of coaching*. Los Angeles, CA: Sage.

Passmore, J., & Mortimer, L. (2011). Ethics in coaching. In G. Hernez-Broome & L. Boyce (Eds.) (pp. 205–228). *Advancing executive coaching: Setting the course for successful leadership coaching*. San Francisco, CA: Jossey-Bass.

13

Measurement and Evaluation

As in other professions, coaches and change-management practitioners require ongoing development to function at their highest levels. This chapter will explore the impacts of coaching, and offer ways of assessing those impacts. In this chapter, we will address the following questions:

- What about coaching can be measured and evaluated?
- What are the challenges associated with assessment of coaching and what strategies can be used to address them?
- What are the most effective approaches to impact measurement?
- What is the impact of coaching?

Assessing the Benefits of Change and Coaching

While most companies are concerned about minimizing costs, recent years have signaled a worldwide trend in even closer management of business expenses. Employees have had to accomplish more with less as competition for profits and pressure from management and shareholders have intensified. Now, more than ever, justification of every business expense is highly scrutinized. Functions not clearly and directly linked to generating revenue are typically the first to be cut in a downturn, with particular emphasis on training and development initiatives, including, but not limited to, coaching and change.

Both coaching and change have come under this scrutiny and share many of the attributes that make assessment and evaluation difficult. Levenson (2009) wrote:

> The main reason why it is difficult to link executive coaching to business performance is a line-of-sight problem between the individual and business impact. Although leaders often are credited with or blamed for the performance of their piece of the business,

> the reality is much more complex. With a host of factors contributing to business success and failure, it typically is asking too much to require careful measurement of business impacts as the main yardstick to evaluate executive coaching. (p. 104)

Levenson's point about coaching also applies to change projects. While it can be relatively easy to evaluate the success of change (Did it happen? Did it meet the objectives?), it is not as straightforward a proposition to evaluate the success of change coaching. A successful professional coach would be well served by articulating a value proposition that can appropriately quantify results. Demonstrating value should be a priority for all change coaching roles, from the manager who uses coaching skills, to a colleague who coaches a peer. New clients may be more inclined to partner with a Change Coach who can correlate his or her services to value than with another coach who is not able to articulate the benefits of change coaching.

Establishing the values that are important for the client may help coach and client more clearly define the scope of the coaching engagement. Levenson (2009) suggested tying the coaching outcomes to changes "that are the focus of the coaching have to matter to the business either strategically, financially, or both" (p. 104). Furthermore, a coach who is inclined to calculate value may be able to more quickly mitigate any initial skepticism about change coaching. In doing so, the coach may establish credibility early on, thus facilitating a deeper, more-fruitful coaching engagement. Successful delivery of promised returns may also result in additional future business from satisfied clients.

The practice of coaching has proliferated in recent decades, and this boom has been attributed to changes in the global business environment that have created a shift in emphasis toward human capital, a move from wanting to develop "managerial" skills to "leadership" skills, as well as a need for more flexible and adaptable development processes (Frisch, 2005).

Executives report finding coaching beneficial and believe they have received a high return on investment from their coaching experience (Hall, Otazo, & Hollenbeck, 1999). However, there is very little empirical evidence to support these claims, and, in fact, there is some indication that executive coaching can occasionally *harm* executives and their organizations (Berglas, 2002), and that change most often fails (Jørgensen, Owens, & Neus, 2008; Kotter, 2007). In response to the popularity of coaching, serious attempts are being made to identify ways of examining both change and coaching, and to identify critical success factors for the implementation of each. At present, there are as many questions as answers about this important work, and it remains a significant opportunity for further study in both disciplines.

The main focus of this chapter is on evaluation and measurement for coaching; examples are also offered about evaluating change success. It must be noted that, given the complexities of change—especially at the organization level—it is possible that the change coaching is evaluated positively, while the change project itself is not successful or completed. Cases such as these, while disappointing for both coach and client, should be reflected on with a "long view." It may be that the influence of the client, or even the coach, is not felt or acted on immediately and will be understood or leveraged more strongly over time. Alternatively, it may be that the client's position or role in the system was not powerful enough to implement the change completely. These situations call for reflection and self-assessment, as well as evaluation of the change and coaching processes. If nothing else good comes from it, at least both the coach and client can take away some valuable insights and lessons learned.

Why Assess?

Evaluation is a tool to provide valuable data about a subject or field. The qualitative and quantitative data obtained from evaluation can be used to prove the benefits of coaching. Coaching also needs evaluation to help understand the impact coaching has on people and organizations (De Meuse, Dai, & Lee, 2009). Leaders of companies want to know the benefits of programs and initiatives being used in their organizations, and assessment can provide them with the type of information that details the value and change occurring within the organization as a result of coaching.

Organizations are under pressure to justify the expense of coaching engagements and to ensure the individuals being coached are getting an experience that is of high enough quality to be worthy of the time, money, and other resources invested. Organizations have enhanced their structures for programs to go beyond purely managing employees and are now working to develop them as an investment in the future of the company (Phillips & Phillips, 2010). Beyond the anecdotal data of program participants, internal learning and development practitioners need tools to be able to tie the impact of coaching and other development programs to business results. Internal studies can be done but are limited to the company itself. Learning and development practitioners will be able to garner more support for the program if evaluative measures are available beyond the walls of the organization.

In summary, there are many reasons to measure the impact of change and coaching, including:

- Demonstrate results of the change
- Show the value of coaching as an intervention
- Illustrate the application (results) of coaching
- Promote the use of coaching for change projects.

As varied as the approaches are for measuring the impact of coaching, the benefits and challenges that can result from applying these approaches are equally varied. As DeMeuse et al. (2009) noted, coaching is perceived as a successful and effective practice, though the evaluative study of the work has not advanced as progressively as the practice itself. It has been acknowledged that, while a large degree of formal measurement of coaching efficacy has not been conducted, there is a need for this work to be done to benefit the practice and the consumers (Thomas & Pirtle, 2010). Perhaps it is because of the challenges involved in establishing a consensus for measurement that the evaluation has lagged behind the execution.

Challenges and Strategies

Evaluating the ROI of coaching is not an easy proposition. The challenge in evaluating change coaching ROI likely depends on:

- Organizational level of person being coached
- Intensity of the coaching intervention at 3, 6, and 12 months
- Receptivity of the manager receiving coaching
- Quality of the coach
- Holding the manager accountable to improve
- Aligning coaching to business strategy.

It can be concluded that, yes, standards of evaluation would be beneficial to all stakeholders involved in the coaching profession. However, even though this is generally accepted, a satisfying standard measure does not yet exist. There are, however, variations of measurement tools and indicators that can complicate establishing a consensus. Yet even if a standard measurement is agreed on, gathering the data to evaluate the work is challenging.

There are two aspects that conspire to create this challenge: the intangible and subjective nature of coaching, and the near impossibility of isolating the impact of a coaching engagement. While these are challenges to contend with, they are not insurmountable.

The debate between a pure measurement of ROI and an anecdotal acceptance of coaching as a good thing demonstrates that neither end of the spectrum is satisfactory in accounting for the tangible and intangible results that coaching can produce. Phillips, Phillips, and Edwards (2012) took this into account when they outlined the ROI Institute's ROI Methodology™ to include not only the pure ROI measurement but also the framework for evaluation, a process for determining the ROI, articulation of the operating standards, an explanation of how the measurement will be applied, and then the actual implementation and communication of the results to represent the full picture of the impact of coaching.

Even if the intangible and tangible factors were sufficiently addressed in an evaluative process, the truth is that even these can be quite subjective in nature. Pre- and post-engagement feedback can be collected from participants and managers, but these are still based on the perception of each individual regarding the specific engagement (DeMeuse et al., 2009). Coaching engagements are, by nature, both confidential and personalized. Both of these components contribute to the challenge behind establishing "controlled trials" (MacKie, 2007, p. 310), which is the point to where the psychotherapy field has evolved in evaluating effective engagements. Even if case studies had been developed based on individual coaching engagements, they have not yet been developed in a way in which they can be replicated to further the study of the field. MacKie (2007) acknowledged all of these challenges but still concluded there is enough potential for the field to establish common "outcome domains" (p. 316) so that comparisons could be made across varying interventions.

In addition to the complications of tangible and intangible results, it is also a challenge to isolate the effect of coaching engagements to draw the conclusion that solely the coaching experience brought about the positive (or negative) impact. Fillery-Travis and Lane (2006) pointed out that many factors in the life of a person being coached (coachee) can influence the effect of the coaching engagement, and it is subjective in defining what an effect truly is—whether the effect is simply raising the awareness of the coachee, or catalyzing an actual change in his or her behavior. Often a coaching engagement is a component of a development program, and the impact of the coaching could be easily blended holistically with the results of the development program.

While skill-building coaching and training can be easily isolated and measured for impact (especially financial impact), other types of coaching, such as executive coaching, life coaching, and transformational coaching, are, by definition, intertwined in everyday actions and other factors such that crediting or blaming coaching for a particular effect would be shortsighted (DeMeuse et al., 2009). Quite simply, a client cannot be put in a box and be completely isolated from influences other than his coach for the duration of the coaching engagement. Coaching often works because of the real-world opportunities that afford practice of the strategies developed during the course of the coaching engagement.

The first step toward overcoming the challenges of evaluating change coaching is an acknowledgment and acceptance of the challenges. If practitioners can arrive at specific standards to use as part of an evaluative process, the arguments of the variation in coaching types and processes can be eliminated. As MacKie (2007) suggested, "outcome domains" (p. 316) can provide the framework necessary to be able to evaluate coaching, in spite of the differences of the field.

In addition to being broader and specific for evaluative purposes, it should be understood that both tangible and intangible results are important and should be incorporated into the evaluation process. A pure ROI figure does not describe the full value of the coaching engagement, and it is a disservice to all involved to boil the impact down to a calculated figure (Phillips et al., 2012). ROI is a portion of the story of the impact, but it is not the complete measure.

Finally, practitioners need to be more strategic in planning their evaluative efforts. Retrospective studies provide only half of the story for the engagement (DeMeuse et al., 2009); having a representation of expectations—while subjective—provides a baseline for the study of the success of the work being done. Coaches must go into the engagement with the intention of evaluating their work before they conduct even their first contracting session. Some aspects to consider for evaluation of change coaching include:

- Success of the change (Was it completed? Did it accomplish its documented objectives? Did the deployment meet schedule and budget commitments?)
- Readiness of the system, the client, and other stakeholders to change
- The client's role in the change, and his or her ability to impact the change in a significant way in that role

- Robustness of the change plan and infrastructure deployment
- The client's actions in building stakeholder engagement, driving action, and addressing risks and opportunities
- Implementation of the coaching process per the contracted agreement.

Researchers and practitioners face many challenges related to assessing the impacts of coaching for change at the individual, group, and organization levels. The following is a summary of challenges that may be encountered and that should be considered when designing and conducting impact assessments.

- Access to clients and coaches
- Ability to isolate coaching as an intervention
- Ability to conduct longitudinal studies
- Ability to conduct control studies
- Various definitions of coaching
- Various approaches to coaching
- Standardizing the delivery of coaching services in the dynamic
- Estimating the cost benefit of conducting the evaluation
- Identifying what to measure (process, impact, results)
- Aligning assessment with the three focal areas of coaching (performance, development, and transformation)
- Linking coaching with change efforts at the group and organization levels.

Assessing Impact

Approximately half of organizations globally evaluate change, and far fewer evaluate coaching. According to DeMeuse and Dai (2008), approximately 10 percent of companies in the United States and 19 percent in the United Kingdom measure the impacts of coaching. The assessments are frequently focused on affective reactions, "perceptions" of success, and have a short-term focus. Consulting firms that provide the coaching services conduct much of the assessment work.

One study found that half of the participant organizations measured change-management effectiveness as well as individual change (Creasey & Hiatt, 2012) using surveys, implementation reviews, interviews, focus groups, and assessments. Measurement occurred at several points in the process, including pre- and postimplementation, and at key milestones. Some of the study organizations measured change effectiveness continually throughout the change process. The criteria used to determine effectiveness included such things as:

- Adoption, usage, acceptance, adherence—these evaluations focused on employee behaviors and processes, evaluating if employees were performing as required by the project or initiative
- Project performance—overall project successes, benefits, realization, data on project metrics and KPIs (key performance indicators), performance against deliverables, schedule adherence, and timeliness
- Engagement and commitment—level of employee engagement and commitment to the change
- Awareness and understanding—level of employee awareness of the need for change
- Perception and attitude—measuring and evaluating the overall attitude about the change and perception issues
- Change-management activities—completion and effectiveness of key change-management activities including communications delivered and training delivered
- Indicators of change not occurring—including calls to a help desk, resistance issues surfaced, unexpected obstacles, turnover, absenteeism, and error rates (Creasey & Hiatt, 2012, pp. 128–129).

In addition, the study reported measures that tracked individual transition, including direct feedback, tracking performance, supervisor and management feedback, feedback from change agents, and evidence of concerns, questions, and change not occurring. Change project metrics that were tracked included:

- Adherence to schedule and budget
- Achievement of intended outcomes
- Employee usage
- User response
- Achievement of interim milestones
- Error tracking
- Engagement measures: user perceptions and attitudes about the change.

Respondents with above-average change-management programs showed higher rates of effectiveness with regard to speed of adoption, rate of utilization, and high levels of proficiency, as compared to those with poor change-management programs. "Poor change management resulted in slower speed of adoption, less utilization and lower proficiency" (Creasey & Hiatt, 2012, p. 131).

There is a need for more objective, behaviorally focused, change-oriented assessments to support change coaching:

> Unlike most business processes, which tend to reduce information to abstractions, executive coaching engages people in customized ways that acknowledge and honor their individuality. It helps people know themselves better, live more consciously, and contribute more richly. The essentially human nature of coaching is what makes it work—and also what makes it nearly impossible to quantify. (Sherman & Freas, 2004, p. 2)

Before determining how to measure the impact of change coaching, consider what you are seeking to assess. Identify measures that can potentially show the impact of coaching on:

- Knowledge and awareness
- Behaviors
- Financials
- Business outcomes (including the success of the change itself)
- Improved relationships

Then, consider ways to conduct the assessment. Examples include:

- Self-rated assessments or inventories—e.g., viaEDGE™ (learning agility), Watson Glaser™ Critical Thinking
- Multi-rater feedback—e.g., LEA 360™, Benchmarks, Voices®, performance assessment
- Accomplishment
- Personal observation and reflection
- Pre- and post-testing of learning, performance, and behaviors related to the desired change (i.e., change readiness assessment, stakeholder analysis, performance per change plan, schedule, and budget)
- Interviews
- Business outcomes and financial performance—e.g., return on investment, **cost-benefit analysis**, error rates, help desk call volume
- Readiness for promotion or expanded role
- Anecdotal stories and stakeholder feedback
- Case studies
- Comparison to other studies
- Observation of group interactions or client behaviors
- Knowledge and/or skill tests.

Combining the "what" to assess with "how" to assess it provides a framework for impact assessment (see Table 13.1).

Table 13.1 Focus and Approaches to Impact Assessment

FOCUS OF ASSESSMENT	APPROACHES TO ASSESSMENT
Financial investment	• Business outcomes and financial performance
Impact on specific behavioral indicators	• Self-rated assessments or inventories • Multi-rater feedback • Personal observation and reflection • Readiness for promotion or expanded role • Anecdotal stories • Interviews • Pre- and post-testing of learning, performance, and behaviors • Knowledge and/or skill tests
Impact on business outcomes	• Business outcomes and financial performance • Comparison to other studies • Case studies • Anecdotal stories and stakeholder feedback
Impact on relationships (interpersonal/team)	• Self-rated assessments or inventories • Personal observation and reflection • Interviews • Anecdotal stories and stakeholder feedback • Observation

The following 10 questions can be used to gather basic information about the impact of coaching. The client can use these questions to help determine the impact of the change coaching.

1. What can I now do more/less of?
2. What have I stopped/started doing?
3. What can I now do that I could/would not do before?
4. What benefits do other people now get from me?
5. How much value have I added?
6. How much time, material, and money have I saved?
7. What can I now do more easily/effectively?
8. What can I now do to a higher standard?
9. How have my experience and my self-awareness and self-management changed?
10. How do others now experience me?

In addition, it is useful to enquire or gather data about the impact of change coaching at the systems level with questions such as:

- Adherence to schedule and budget, or achievement of interim milestones
- Achievement of intended change outcomes

- User response to the change (acceptance, resistance as measured in surveys, interviews, focus groups, communications, or meetings)
- Employee usage of changed systems, processes, or procedures
- Error tracking and process improvements
- Risks averted and/or opportunities maximized during the change.

There may be some situations where a formal evaluation is not required. In such cases, the documented reaction and opinion of others can be used to support coaching as an effective intervention. After all, there is agreement that coaching is beneficial, and the use of coaching continues to become more prevalent in organizations (DeMeuse et al., 2009). However, other than a general (and largely unproven) idea that coaching works, there is little consistency in approaches to assessing the impact of coaching.

One primary difference is in the purpose of evaluating coaching. Not all organizations are concerned with the economic returns of coaching. Instead, they are focused on coaching as it relates to their businesses' missions (Schlosser, Steinbrenner, Kumata, & Hunt, 2006). The lack of consistency in deploying coaching may be another cause for differences in evaluation. Organizations are different, as are their purposes for using coaching as an intervention to support the organization. The agreement that "coaching works" may be the only data needed to validate the use of coaching in an organization.

Evaluation Methods

A return-on-investment evaluation is just one method that has been used to evaluate coaching programs. We know that coaching works, but organizations want to evaluate a program such as coaching by more than simply whether or not it works (Peterson & Kraiger, 2004). Many argue that since a business's main objective is to make money, the impact of coaching should be measured by its financial benefits (Grant, 2012). In addition, companies may have limited budgets, and initiatives that can prove results may get the limited funds in the budget. An ROI evaluation can provide a business with the financial information needed to determine the overall financial benefit of the coaching venture to the organization.

To calculate the ROI of coaching, or any training program, divide the net income by the costs, and then express this figure as a percentage (Grant, 2012). This calculation weighs the financial gains against the costs to determine the financial success of the program, based on the total funds invested in the program.

The ROI method of evaluation provides only one piece of data about coaching, and some situations might require a comprehensive look at the coaching program. Kirkpatrick's (1998) model for evaluating training programs is much more in depth than a simple ROI calculation. Kirkpatrick has approached the concept of measuring learning from four different perspectives, or levels. He states, "Learning has taken place when one or more of the following occurs: Attitudes are changed. Knowledge is increased. Skill is improved. One or more of these changes must take place if a change in behavior is to occur" (p. 21). Past studies have been conducted on training interventions that evaluate the interventions at these different levels of analysis (DeMeuse et al., 2009). These studies provided a comprehensive look at the coaching engagement. The other levels of evaluation include reaction, learning, behavior, and business impact (Phillips, 2002).

The following is a summary of the Phillips five-level model:

- Level 1: Reaction (affective perspective about the experience)
- Level 2: Learning (awareness and acceptance of insights)
- Level 3: Application (behavior shift)
- Level 4: Impact (results of behavioral change)
- Level 5: Return on investment (ROI).

The higher the level of evaluation (level 1 to level 5), the more useful the data and the more difficult to obtain. Each of these levels of evaluation can provide different information about the coaching engagement.

The first level, reaction, evaluates the feelings about the coaching engagement (Phillips, 2002). The reaction can be measured on the part of the coach, client, or participating organization. If a coaching program is evaluated, most of the time it is done at the reaction level alone (Fairhurst, 2007). Measuring the reaction of coaching will not provide much useful data about the effectiveness of coaching in helping a client achieve his or her objectives. Instead, coaches must rely on the other levels to provide useful data.

The second level, learning, measures the growth in knowledge or attitude as a result of the program (Phillips, 2002). Coaching is different from the typical training program in that usually there is not specific knowledge to be learned during the program. De Meuse et al. (2009) argued that coaching does not provide a client with additional knowledge; therefore, learning cannot be measured. If a learning objective is set at the onset of the engagement, learning can be measured. The third level measures changes in behavior and progress with application. The impact level (fourth level) takes into account the change in behavior after the coaching arrangement (Phillips, 2002).

Finally, the fifth level, the business impact level of evaluation, measures the results of coaching to the business objectives resulting in a return on the investment (Phillips, 2002). The data from this level of evaluation will be valuable to the entire organization, as it can be crucial in validating the service of coaching. A coach can be hired for a variety of reasons, and the ultimate outcome from the coaching services is to improve a company or organization through the individual or group being coached.

Steps in the Assessment Process

A roadmap of the assessment process is of clear value to anyone who hopes to take on this task effectively and efficiently. The following steps will serve to guide the assessment of coaching:

1. Why conduct the assessment? (e.g., impacts, justification for expenditure, process improvement)
2. Who will sponsor and support this assessment? (e.g., coaching service provider, client organization, human resources department)
3. What is the scope of the assessment? (e.g., accounting for factors impacting results, focusing on the coach and/or client)
4. What is being assessed? (e.g., behaviors, changes, learning, impacts)
5. What is/are the best method(s)? (e.g., survey, interviews, performance measures)
6. Who are the key stakeholders? (e.g., client, coach, manager, human resources staff)
7. What is the plan for assessment? (e.g., who will do what by when and how?)
8. How will data be processed and analyzed? (e.g., data recording and analysis)
9. How will meaning be made of the data gathered and analyzed? (e.g., compare to desired outcomes and established research findings)
10. How will I report the findings? (e.g., presentation, publication, written report)

Examples of Coaching Impact Studies

The following examples of completed coaching impact studies are intended to demonstrate a variety of approaches and outcomes. According to international consulting and coaching firm Drake Beam Morin (DBM, 2008), 77 percent of study respondents who calculated ROI believed that executive coaching provided their organizations with a solid return. These individuals estimated levels ranging from a minimum ROI of 100 percent to a return of more than 500 percent.

Coaching has been attributed with impacting or being the primary cause for many qualitative and quantitative changes, including:

- Increased executive output such as sales revenue and productivity
- Quality improvements such as increased reliability or decreased defects
- Cost savings
- Reduced employee turnover
- Achievement of agreed-upon development objectives
- Anecdotal evidence of success
- Other people's perceptions of the client
- Client's ability to be promoted or to take on new responsibilities.

According to Schlosser, Steinbrenner, Kumata, and Hunt (2007), the impact of coaching varies based on the perspective from which it is viewed. They considered the perspectives of the coach, the client's manager, and the coachee (client) (see Table 13.2).

Jarvis, Lane, and Fillery-Travis (2006) suggested that coaching helps to improve performance by increasing understanding of the desired performance, how to achieve the desired results, the skills required, the models of problem solving that hinder and support performance, and competence for the future. According to a study done by the Institute for Corporate Productivity for the American Management Association, coaching results in:

- Improved individual performance and productivity
- Addressing leadership development/succession planning

Table 13.2 Perceptions of Impact of Coaching

COACH	MANAGER	COACHEE (CLIENT)
Internal customer satisfaction/ relationships	Employee engagement	Promotion/promotability
Employee engagement	Base of committed followers	Employee engagement
Promotion/promotability	Promotion/promotability	Productivity
Alignment with business priorities	Employee satisfaction	Base of committed followers
Productivity		Employee alignment

- Increased worker skill levels
- Improved organizational performance
- Addressing specific workplace problems
- Enhanced employee engagement (Thompson, Bear, Dennis, Vickers, London, & Morrison, 2008).

In addition, Kombarakaran, Yang, Baker, and Fernandes (2008) identified five areas of improved executive performance as a result of coaching. These include:

1. effective people management, which includes increased insights into how colleagues perceive the leaders actions and decisions, better self-awareness and understanding of personal strengths, and better results managing direct reports and internal customers;
2. better relationships with managers, which involves productive relationships with better communication and feedback;
3. improved goal setting and prioritization, which includes better ability to define performance, better ability to define business objectives with direct reports, and increased insight into the business drivers of decisions and their impact on others;
4. increased engagement and productivity, which involves ability to adapt to the work environment and more-productive and satisfied employees; and
5. more-effective dialogue and communication, which includes increased partnership and dialogue between managers and executives.

Table 13.3 summarizes a few coaching-impact studies. The purpose or coaching agenda—performance (P), development (D), and transformation (T)—is identified, along with the focus of the study, methodology used, results, and the citation.

Techniques to improve performance have different impacts on organizations; therefore, an evaluation plan should be designed to fit the program of that specific organization. The evaluation plan must be well thought out, considering various components involved in the process. It is important to determine an audience for the results when designing an evaluation. An evaluation for a chief executive officer may look different than one for a coach looking to identity opportunities for professional growth.

Determining the audience can help to identify the purpose of the evaluation. Specific objectives for evaluation are derived directly from the program (Phillips, 2002). The objective of coaching for the company should also be considered,

Table 13.3 Examples of Impact Studies

FOCUS	FOCUS	METHODOLOGY	RESULTS	CITATION
D	Examine executive coaching effectiveness by investigating whether executive coaching has an impact on client performance outcomes as well as individual outcomes as manifested by self awareness, career satisfaction, job affective commitment, and job performance	Quasi-experimental field pre-post design with an untreated control group; 197 participants	Executive coaching may be a mechanism by which executives could be helped in improving and maintaining a high level of career satisfaction	Bozer, G., & Sarros, J. C. (2012). Examining the effectiveness of executive coaching on clients' performance in the Israeli context. *International Journal of Evidence-Based Coaching and Mentoring, 10*(1), 14–32.
T	Impact of a 10-week coaching intervention program based on Epstein's CEST theory on transformational leadership among 14 secondary school principals	Pre-test, post-test control group Qualitative and quantitative	There was a significant difference between the pre-test and post-test scores for the intervention group, as rated by the school staff. The control group remained unchanged. The school principals became more reflective about their thinking processes and leadership practices. Changing information-processing styles can influence leadership style.	Cerni, T., Curtis, G. J., & Colmar, S. H. (2010). Executive coaching can enhance transformational leadership. *International Coaching Psychology Review, 5*(1): 81–85.
D, T	To evaluate executive coaching for members who were on a High Potential Development Scheme within the Ministry of Defense (MoD).	A multi-method approach was taken which comprised the use of questionnaires to survey scheme member's perceptions, a Return on Investment (ROI) study and a follow-up of members to determine their	All participants (10) who had been coached rated their experience positively. All rated their own progress within the Development Scheme as high, and in particular they perceived it was their leadership skills	Feggetter, A. J. W. (2007). A preliminary evaluation of executive coaching: Does executive coaching work for candidates on a high-potential

(*Continued*)

Table 13.3 (*Continued*)

FOCUS	FOCUS	METHODOLOGY	RESULTS	CITATION
		success in gaining promotion Participants: 10	that had benefited. A preliminary ROI calculation also indicated that the benefits exceeded the costs. Other benefits included promotion, broader leadership skills, and skills transfer within the Ministry of Defense. The results indicate that within the context of the Development Scheme, coaching provides a potential financial ROI. The findings show that coaching impacts positively on scheme members such that they are highly committed to demonstrating and exhibiting leadership behaviors and that there is some evidence of a broader impact on the Department as a whole with generalized skills transfer.	development scheme? *International Coaching Psychology Review, 2*(2): 129–142.
D	The impact of a one-year executive-coaching experiment on intrapersonal causal attribution.	Pre- and post-test control group design Participants: 22 executives in a Norwegian Fortune 500 company	Executive coaching had significant effects on the executives' causal attributions. Causal attributions of successful achievements to strategy, ability, and efforts increased while attributions of unsuccessful achievement to ability decreased as a result.	Moen, F., & Allgood, E. (2009). Coaching and the effect on self-efficacy. *Organization Development Journal, 27*(4): 69–82.

Table 13.3 (*Continued*)

FOCUS	FOCUS	METHODOLOGY	RESULTS	CITATION
P	The impact of multisource or 360-degree feedback on management performance	Meta-analysis of 24 longitudinal studies	Improvements in the performance of managers, as evaluated by subsequent multisource feedback, were small in size. The assessments derived from subordinates, often called direct reports in this context, and supervisors revealed only a small improvement in performance.	Smither, J. W., London, M., Flautt, R., Vargas, Y., & Kucine, I. (2003). Can working with an executive coach improve multisource feedback ratings over time? A quasi-experimental field study. *Personal Psychology,* 23–44.
D	Examine the relative effectiveness of external, peer, and self-coaches on the performance of participants in two MBA programs.	A one-factor, between-group, repeated-measures design was used.	In both studies, an external coach was perceived by the participants to have higher credibility than their peers. Self-coaching was perceived to be more credible than coaching from peers. Those who were coached by an external coach or were self-coached had significantly higher grades than those who were coached by a peer. And, satisfaction with the coaching process was highest among the managers who worked with an external coach.	Sue-Chan, C., & Latham, G. P. (2004). The relative effectiveness of external, peer, and self-coaches. *Applied Psychology: An International Review, 53*(2), 260–278.

(*Continued*)

Table 13.3 (*Continued*)

FOCUS	FOCUS	METHODOLOGY	RESULTS	CITATION
P, D	The after-coaching leadership skills of management that affect direct reports.	Hermeneutic phenomenological study	Improvements in manager behaviors and results: motivated environment, safe work environment, depth of communication, and self-reflection.	Wenson, J. E. (2010). After-coaching leadership skills and their impact on direct reports: recommendations for organizations. *Human Resource Development International, 13*(5), 607–616.
P, D, T	Focused on how the adoption of coaching behaviors by line managers contributed to the achievement of organizational goals.	Organizational case study	– The adoption of coaching by line managers does contribute to the achievement of organizational goals – Coaching can form part of the "how-to" toolkit of customer service improvement The following factors could increase the efficacy of the coaching activities: – Alignment of personal and organizational values – Increasing line managers' confidence in their coaching abilities – Improving the consistency of management culture across the organization	Wheeler, L. (2011). How does the adoption of coaching behaviors by line managers contribute to the achievement of organizational goals? *International Journal of Evidence-Based Coaching & Mentoring, 9*(1), 1–15.

Table 13.3 (*Continued*)

FOCUS	FOCUS	METHODOLOGY	RESULTS	CITATION
P	High-potential African American executive who is faltering in his leadership role	Case study	– Effective executive leadership results from the interaction between the person-specific attributes and capabilities of the executive and the context in which the executive is operating – Reaffirms the importance of achieving candor and alignment between the individual being coached and key organizational stakeholders regarding the purpose, method, and desired outcomes of the coaching work. – Case teaches the importance of incorporating proactive developmental support in the career planning and placement of high-potential executives.	Winum, P. C. (2005). Effectiveness of a high-potential African American executive: The anatomy of a coaching engagement. *Consulting Psychology Journal: Practice and Research, 57*(1), 71–89.

assuming there is an objective in mind. Understanding the objectives for the coaching engagement helps build an evaluation that specifically measures those objectives.

The evaluation plan must be designed before the beginning of the coaching engagement. Understanding the purpose and planning the evaluation ahead of time will ensure that the correct information is collected during the coaching engagement to perform an evaluation after the coaching engagement (Petersen & Kraiger, 2004). Not only will planning ahead of time create a better evaluation process, but it may also create one that is less expensive. A six-month coaching engagement can cost up to $75,000 (De Meuse et al., 2009). A carefully planned evaluation will appropriately allocate valuable time and resources of a company to ensure they are not wasted on the evaluation process of coaching.

Case Examples

The issue that faces today's business coach is that there are very few studies that can accurately show a bottom-line ROI for every dollar spent on executive coaching. Furthermore, it has proven even more difficult to create a study that can be consistently replicated. In this section, we present two case studies. The first study shows a direct return on investment for executive coaching. The second study shows that not every return to the organization can be quantifiably measured; yet, the findings of this study are just as valuable to the health and culture of the organization as is the ROI.

Internal coaching has been proven to have a positive overall impact for the coach, the client, and the organization at large. Mukherjee (2012) surveyed coaching managers after they completed coaching sessions with their clients and found a majority (60 percent) of the clients had improved interpersonal skills, and they became more effective in dealing with their peers, direct reports, and senior staff. Thirty-nine percent said they became better listeners, 33 percent said their work-life balance improved, and 25 percent said they had increased confidence. Coaching has a positive effect on the client and also on the coaches themselves.

In a study of the impact on coaching within American Insurance Group Retirement Services (AIG RS), Donde and Rock (2008) found that clients received immense benefits from the coaching engagement, including feeling a sense of increased loyalty, value to the company, and trust of their fellow employees, as well as being more proactive and productive at work. Intangible benefits included greater job satisfaction, more employee commitment, stronger networks across the organization, greater communication, and improvement in skill development and retention. Donde and Rock (2008) also demonstrated one incredible example of coaching's return on investment to AIG RS. The client showed an increase in retention (19 percent) and engagement (13 percent), and the client's subordinates also showed an even greater increase in retention (28 percent) and engagement (21 percent). The company asked for a financial ROI of 15 percent and instead received an incredible ROI of 1,700 percent—a 17:1 ratio—based on the first round of internal coaching, equaling a monetary value of $2.5 million (Donde & Rock, 2008). ROI further increased with subsequent rounds of coaching. While most organizations will not see a return on investment quite this impressive, any number between 1 and 1,700 percent would be seen as a positive investment. The financial savings, combined with greater employee satisfaction, retention, productivity, and stronger interpersonal relationships easily demonstrates that internal coaching has a measurable and positive impact throughout an organization.

A third example is from Nations Hotel Corporation, which set out to create a coaching program that could demonstrate the financial benefits of coaching on the organization. The company randomly selected 25 executives who were in vice president positions or above. These participants were measured in five priority areas: revenue growth, retention, direct cost savings, productivity, and efficiency. The ROI was then calculated in two ways: benefit cost ratio (BCR) and return on investment. Nations Hotel's internal group that designed and measured this program, Nations Hotel Learning Organization—Coaching for Business Impact, found a BCR of 3.21:1. In other words, for every dollar invested in coaching, $3.21 was generated in benefits to the corporation. The ROI showed a return of 221 percent. That is, for every dollar invested in the coaching program, the invested dollar was returned plus $2.21 (Phillips & Phillips, 2008). These results show a very strong case for executive coaching, and this evaluation was possible because of careful planning and a strong attention to detail by the coaching service provider, organization in which coaching occurred, and the evaluators.

These are very exciting returns for the executive coaching community, which can show an ROI-focused corporate executive that there can be major returns to a corporation that invests in its people. However, for every bottom-line ROI study, there are many more that can show the relationship in an intangible, value-based return to the corporation.

Another study examined more closely the qualitative effects of executive-based coaching. McDermott, Levenson, and Newton (2007) surveyed the impact of executive coaching on multiple organizations through interactions with learning and development professionals. The authors conducted initial interviews with 10 companies, which allowed them to craft a survey that would provide information on how they manage and measure coaching and feedback tools. Next, they online surveyed a sample of 55 companies, targeting individuals within the companies responsible for leadership and organization development. The typical survey respondent was the person responsible for coaching initiatives in his or her organization, with a title of manager, director, or vice president of HR in leadership development, talent management, or organization development. The findings of the survey demonstrated that coaching did have a qualitative impact, with the largest impact being seen at the individual level, "such as developing future leaders and improving leadership behaviors and individual employees performance" (McDermott et al., 2007, pp. 32–33). However, at the organization level, the survey respondents did not report systemic changes that were as great as those at the micro level. Organizational impact was noted, but not as deeply as the impact on the individual (McDermott et al., 2007). These survey findings are consistent with the benefits and challenges outlined earlier; yet, the conclusion still remains that coaching has a positive impact.

In another example, Haug (2011) looked at whether the introduction of a coaching model with a large international organization in Germany would be an effective intervention for its financial crisis. The research question was, "Can coaching interventions support team effectiveness?" (Haug, 2011, p. 89). The project lasted six months, with 20 weekly meetings, each attended by four to five participants. Haug observed three meetings and realized she would need to meet individually with team members if there was to be any progress. Haug (2011) used several tools to guide both her team and individual work, including Zeus and Skiffington's (2001) coaching cycle, the Subjective-Objective-Analysis-Plan (SOAP) technique for critical reflection, and the Work-Life-Balance Wheel. She used the individual sessions to support personal and team objectives. This approach resulted in a greater sense of investment in the team objectives. By using enhanced communication skills gained from the individual sessions, greater productivity resulted in the group. By meeting individually, she enabled team members to more effectively contribute in a group setting. She learned that the team members had unconsciously been following different objectives, even though they explicitly shared a common team objective.

Chapter Summary

In these times of tightened budgets, it is more important than ever for coaches to clearly demonstrate their value to organizations. However, while the success of making an organizational change can be readily demonstrated, it is not so easy to demonstrate the success of change coaching. While executives report that coaching was beneficial—and that they received a high ROI—there is little empirical evidence to support these assertions. Regardless, clients are more inclined to partner with Change Coaches who can demonstrate their value to the organization.

Evaluating the ROI of coaching is challenging for a variety of reasons, including the organizational level of the client/coachee, the intensity of the coaching intervention, the quality of the coach, and more. In addition, it can be difficult to isolate the impact of coaching from the many other factors in an organization that have an influence on the client/coachee and play some role in determining his or her effectiveness. As a result of these challenges, only half of organizations evaluate change, while far fewer evaluate coaching.

However, those organizations that do evaluate coaching are likely to identify a variety of positive qualitative and quantitative changes, including increased executive output (sales revenue and productivity), quality improvements, cost savings, reduced employee turnover, and more. To be most effective, an evaluation must be well thought out, and it must consider the various components involved in the process.

Knowledge Check

1. What are four known impacts of coaching that are useful to measure?
2. What are four known aspects of change coaching that are useful to measure?
3. Why is it important to link change coaching to the outcomes of a change project?
4. What is one method to assess the impact of coaching and/or change? What are three challenges to assessing the impact of coaching and strategies for addressing each?
5. What are the steps to consider when preparing for and conducting an impact analysis?

Learning Activities

Learning Activity 1: Evaluation

Develop an impact analysis using either a return on investment, observable behavior shift, change master, or learning model. Apply the approach to your own coaching. Use the results to gain insights that can improve or enhance your coaching practices.

Learning Activity 2: Feedback

Ask at least three current or recent coaching clients to provide feedback about your coaching and their experience. Ask:

- What changed?
- What aspect(s) of the coaching experience are most helpful for you?
- What aspect(s) of the coaching experience are least helpful for you?
- Reflecting on the role I played as your coach, what did I do (or not do) that was most useful?
- What, if anything, would you like to see me change to improve my coaching?
- What has been/was the impact (what changes have your implemented) of the coaching I provided you?

Learning Activity 3: Linking Coaching Evaluation to Change

Review the change frameworks and skills outlined in earlier chapters of this book to identify which would be the most useful in developing a strategy for linking coaching evaluation to change. Choose at least three of the above to develop a generic evaluation plan that could be used in a change coaching engagement. Include aspects such as the timing and frequency of the evaluation(s), change factors to assess, data-gathering tactics, target stakeholders or populations, and a strategy for reporting the findings. Use this plan to create a template for implementation and reporting. Adapt the template so that there are different versions to use for change coaching evaluation at the individual, group, and organization levels.

References

Berglas, S. (2002). The very real dangers of executive coaching. *Harvard Business Review, 80*(6), 86–92.

Creasey, T., & Hiatt, J. (2012). *Best practices in change management.* Loveland, CO: Prosci.

DeMeuse, K. P., & Dai, G. (2008). *Coaching effectiveness: How do we know? A meta-analytic answer.* Paper presented at the Academy of Management, Anaheim, CA.

DeMeuse, K. P., Dai, G., & Lee, R. J. (2009). Evaluating the effectiveness of executive coaching: Beyond ROI? *Coaching: An international journal of theory, research & practice, 2*(2), 117–134.

DBM. (2008). *Trends in executive coaching: New research reveals emerging best practices.* New York, NY: DBM.

Donde, R., & Rock, D. (2008). Measuring the effectiveness of training internal coaches: American Insurance Group Retirement Services in collaboration with Results

Coaching Systems (Rep.). Retrieved from Results Coaching Systems website: http://www.resultscoaches.com/files/Measuring-Effectiveness-Internal-Coaches-Paper-A4.pdf

Fairhurst, P. (July 2007). Measuring the success of coaching. *TJ.* 52–55.

Fillery-Travis, A., & Lane, D. (2006). Does coaching work or are we asking the wrong questions? *International Coaching Psychology Review, 1*(1), 23–36.

Frisch, M. H. (2005). Coaching caveats. *Human Resource Planning, 28*(2), 13–15.

Grant, A. (2012). ROI is a poor measure of coaching success: Towards a more holistic approach using a well-being and engagement framework. *Coaching: An International Journal of Theory, Research & Practice, 5*(2), 74–85.

Hall, D. T., Otazo, K. L., & Hollenbeck, G. P. (1999). Behind closed doors: What really happens in executive coaching. *Organizational Dynamics, 27*(3), 39–53.

Haug, M. (2011). What is the relationship between coaching interventions and team effectiveness? *International Journal of Evidence Based Coaching and Mentoring, Special Issue No. 5,* 89–101.

Jarvis, J., Lane, D. A., & Fillery-Travis, A. (2006). *The case for coaching: Making evidence-based decisions on coaching.* London: Chartered Institute for Personnel Development.

Jørgensen, H. H., Owens, L., & Neus, A. (2008). Making change work (G. Services, Trans.) (p. 48). Somers, NY: IBM Corporation.

Kirkpatrick, D. L. (1998). *Evaluating training programs: The four levels* (2nd ed.). San Francisco, CA: Berrett-Koehler.

Kombarakaran, F. A., Yang, J. A., Baker, M. N., & Fernandes, P. E. (2008). Executive coaching: It works! *Consulting Psychology Journal: Practice and Research, 60*(1), 78–90.

Kotter, J. P. (January 2007). Leading change: Why transformation efforts fail. *Harvard Business Review*, 96–103.

Levenson, A. (2009). Measuring and maximizing the business impact of executive coaching. *Consulting Psychology Journal: Practice and Research, 61*(2), 103–121.

MacKie, D. (2007). Evaluating the effectiveness of coaching: Where are we now and where do we need to be? *Australian Psychologist, 42*(4), 310–318.

McDermott, M., Levenson, A., & Newton, S. (2007). What coaching can and cannot do for your organization. *Human Resource Planning, 30*(2), 30–37.

Mukherjee, S. (2012). Does coaching transform coaches? A case study of internal coaching. *International Journal of Evidence-Based Coaching and Mentoring, 10*(2), 76–87.

Peterson, D. B., & Kraiger, K. (2004). A practical guide to evaluating coaching: Translating state-of-the-art techniques to the real world. In J. E. Edwards, J. C. Scott & N. S. Raju (Eds.), *The human resources program evaluation handbook* (pp. 262–282). Thousand Oaks, CA: Sage.

Phillips, J. J., & Phillips, P. P. (2008). Measuring ROI in business coaching: Nations hotel. In J. J. Phillips & P. P. Phillips (Eds.) (pp. 251–271). *Proving the value of HR: ROI case studies* (2nd ed.). Birmingham, AL: ROI Institute.

Phillips, J. J., & Phillips, P. P. (2010). *Measuring for success: What CEOs really think about learning investments.* Alexandria, VA: ASTD Press.

Phillips, P. P. (2002). *The bottomline on ROI: Basics, benefits, & barriers to measuring training & performance improvement.* Atlanta, GA: CEP Press.

Phillips, P. P., Phillips, J. J., & Edwards, L. A. (2012). *Measuring the success of coaching: A step-by-step guide for measuring impact and calculating ROI.* Alexandria, VA: ASTD Press.

Schlosser, B., Steinbrenner, D., Kumata, E., & Hunt, J. (2006). The coaching impact study: Measuring the value of executive coaching. *International Journal of Coaching in Organizations, 4*(3), 8–26.

Schlosser, B., Steinbrenner, D., Kumata, E., & Hunt, J. (2007). The coaching impact study: Measuring the value of executive coaching with commentary. *International Journal of Coaching in Organizations, 5*(1), 140–161.

Sherman, S., & Freas, A. (2004). The wild west of executive coaching. *Harvard Business Review, 82*(11), 82–90.

Thomas, R. E., & Pirtle, J. (2010). Developing leaders: An analysis of the efficacy of executive coaching. *Leadership & Organizational Management Journal, 2010*(3), 106–112.

Thompson, H. B., Bear, D. J., Dennis, D. J., Vickers, M., London, J., & Morrison, C. L. (2008). *Coaching: A global study of successful practices: Trends and future possibilities 2008.* New York, NY: AMACOM.

Zeus, P., & Skiffington, S. (2001). *The complete guide to coaching at work.* Sydney, Australia: McGraw-Hill.

14

Developing Change Coaching Mastery

The ongoing development of knowledge, skills, and abilities is essential to professional practice. This ongoing need also applies to change coaching. Developing mastery involves assessment, change, and reflection—not only for clients, but for coaches, as well. In addition, it has a positive impact on clients when clients see coaches "walking the talk," being open to feedback and observation about their practice and demeanor.

The Mastery Model was introduced in Chapter 6 as an approach to capacity-building for all levels of change clients—individuals, groups and organizations. The same model can be applied to the development of mastery in coaching. In this chapter, the authors consider the development of coaching mastery, explore the tools available to coaches for their ongoing development, and address the following questions:

- Why is it important to develop coaching mastery?
- How does the Mastery Model apply to coach mastery?
- How can a change coach leverage tools to support ongoing development as a coach?

Change Coaching Mastery

Being able to identify the qualities of a skilled coach is a precursor to becoming one, educating one, or hiring one. A great deal has been written on the processes, techniques, and models to help executive coaches find ongoing success (Bush, 2005; Crane, 1998; Dotlich & Cairo, 1999; Fitzgerald & Berger, 2002; Hargrove, 1995; Kilburg, 1996, 2000; Laske, 2004; O'Neill, 2007; Zeus & Skiffington, 2001). While the precise skills, qualifications, attributes and requirements for professional coaches and those who use coaching skills in other practices (e.g., manager, consultant, parent) are not widely agreed upon, a number of skills have been identified and are generally accepted as necessary for skilled coaching practitioners. These include:

- Giving feedback
- Being present and listening actively
- Building trusting relationships
- Understanding context and culture of executives
- Being aware of business/management goals/impacts
- Creating a commitment for change
- Fostering self-awareness/reflection
- Acting on intuition with courage
- Being a reflective practitioner (Bennett & Rogers, 2013).

Hargrove (1995) asserted that "a coach is something that you 'be'" (p. 39). He identifies the coach as being who one *is,* as opposed to an approach or model that one must follow step by step. The coach's self-awareness, confidence, and focus allow a coaching engagement to be what it needs to be to meet the needs of the client.

Mastery in change coaching requires a high level of competence in, and application of, coach interpersonal and intrapersonal skills in the service of clients' needs in the coaching relationship (O'Broin & Palmer, 2010). It requires actively pursuing self-awareness and self-management to recognize and challenge unhelpful beliefs, perceptions, feelings, and behaviors about self, clients, and the coaching process. This reflection can be used as part of the coach's self-development process. As Riley & Frost (2008) noted, "Wanting to change, wanting to become a more essential you requires you to become aware and awake—requires the claiming of your interior knowing" (p. 16). They ask us to ask ourselves, "Why do you do what you do, feel as you feel, think what you think? What is in you that you know . . . and what about you do you need to discover?" (p. 16). During change coaching sessions, a coach can practice observing herself interacting with the client, to hone the skill of self-awareness. Outside of coaching sessions, tools such as self-reflection, coaching supervision, self-management frameworks (Kemp, 2008), self-supervision, peer discussion, and feedback from clients can be leveraged.

> During a coaching session, this may involve reflection in action (Schon, 1983) and where appropriate, feedback from the client . . . Mastery in coaching requires a high level of competence in and application of coach inter-personal and intra-personal skills in the service of the client's needs in the coaching relationship. (O'Broin & Palmer, 2010, pp. 138–139)

Competency models serve as an anchor in the field of coaching, providing a common language based on specific criteria. The coaching-related literature documents characteristics or competencies of expert coaching, which include components of self-awareness/self-management, listening, promoting action, and demonstrating intuition (Brotman, Liberi, & Wasylyshyn, 2000; Bush, 2005; Guthrie & Alexander, 2000; Hargrove, 1995; Whitworth, Kimsey-House, Kimsey-House, & Sandahl, 2007).

To be an effective Change Coach, one must have acquired key skills and abilities. To reach a level of mastery, however, coaches must also be aware of their knowledge, skills, and abilities in coaching and in change, and be able to apply them in both arenas. In addition, mastery requires a demonstrated level of learning agility—the willingness and ability to assess and continuously enhance one's knowledge, skills, and abilities.

Many of the models for designing and evaluating learning are rooted in Bloom's Taxonomy of learning objectives (Bloom, Engelhart, Furst, Hill, & Krathwohl, 1956) and Howell's (1982) conscious competence model. Bloom's Taxonomy includes three domains: cognitive, affective, and psychomotor—more commonly known as think, feel, and do. A key premise of Bloom's Taxonomy is that mastery must be achieved at each level of a domain before advancing to the next.

Awareness is a significant factor in skill acquisition and may be used, in part, to describe a learner's level of consciousness. Building on Bloom's model, Krathwhol's (2002) model begins with a level of imitation and advances to a level described as naturalization. Once a learner (in this case, the coach) achieves the level of naturalization, the learner has become automated, in a sense, and the activity is subconscious (often referred to as an "unconscious" state). This progression of repeating a process before gaining precision and achieving mastery can be compared with Howell's (1982) conscious competence model.

Howell (1982) described a sequence of learning in which the learner starts in an unconscious incompetent state. At this stage, the individual may be unaware of or unconcerned about the skill. Next is conscious incompetence. At this stage, the individual becomes aware of the skill that is lacking and gains an understanding of how to improve the skill. Next is the stage of conscious competence; the learner is now demonstrating the knowledge needed and can perform reliably. And, finally, the learner reaches an unconscious competence and is performing the skill as a second nature, or intuitively.

Taylor (2007) offered a fifth stage, naming it "reflective competency." This stage involves being conscious of unconscious incompetence. By continually self-challenging in the fifth stage with self-study and peer review, evolved learners cycle back through the stage of unconscious incompetence, where new enlightenment reveals something else they did not know. With the addition of the fifth stage, Howell's model becomes much more cyclical and dynamic, reminiscent of Argyris's concept of double-loop learning. Argyris coined this term to describe the process of examining how personal behavior may impact outcomes. He says of consultants: "They need to reflect critically on their own behavior, identify the ways they often inadvertently contribute to the organization's problems, and then change how they act" (Argyris, 1991, p. 4). This advice is appropriate for Change Coaches, as well.

A reflective practitioner is "someone who lives reflection as a way of being" with reflection defined as "awareness of self within the moment, having a clear mind so as to be open to possibility of that moment" (Johns, 2009, pp. 3–4). While an effective practitioner must have acquired knowledge, a reflective practitioner understands that no two experiences are alike, and therefore, he cannot simply rely on learned paradigms. Knowing and applying evidence-based practices and theoretical models are essential to contextualizing the human situation, yet are inadequate without the practitioner's intuitive response (Johns, 2009). Through reflection, practitioners develop their intuitive processes, and they become conscious of their competencies and incompetencies, resulting in further enlightenment (Bennett & Rogers, 2013).

Dreyfus and Dreyfus (1980, 1986, 2004) and S. Dreyfus (2004a, 2004b) developed a model of skill acquisition based on situated performance and experiential learning. Hunt and Weintraub (2007) identified the Dreyfus model of skill acquisition as "one of the most 'user-friendly' developmental frameworks" (p. 40). The Dreyfus model is comprised of five stages: novice, advanced beginner, competent, proficient, and expert. The model describes the stages through which an individual must progress to achieve mastery of a particular skill, advancing from abstract principles needed in a novice stage to a more intuitive, less self-conscious state in an expert stage (Benner, 2001; Dreyfus & Dreyfus, 1980, 2004; Hunt & Weintraub, 2007).

The Dreyfus model distinguishes the skill acquisition of learning theory in an instructional setting from the context-dependent decisions and choices one makes in lived experience (Dreyfus & Dreyfus, 1980, 1986, 2004). This model has been applied in a variety of disciplines, including nursing (Benner, 2001), engineering (Vanderburg, 2004), teaching (Berliner, 2004), the development of motor skills in sports (Moe, 2004), and the treatment of anorexia nervosa (Duesund & Jespersen, 2004). Duesund and Jespersen (2004), in their work in treating anorexia nervosa with the Dreyfus model, offered two important insights: a movement from reliance on abstract principles to use of past concrete experience, and a passage from detached observer to involved performer in the situation. The distinctions noted by Duesund and Jespersen articulate the space between novice and expert. Applying this distinction to coaching, a novice coach is still observing and imitating experiences seen by coaches who have more-evolved competence, whereas an expert coach is fully "being" in the moment with a client, as Hargrove (1995) described the masterful coach (Bennett & Rogers, 2013).

Beginning in the 1980s, Benner (2001, 2004, 2010) applied the Dreyfus model of skill acquisition. She wanted to know if differences could be attributed or understood, and how those differences might be identified in the stages of the Dreyfus model (Dreyfus & Dreyfus, 1980). According to Benner (2001), nurses display characteristic traits identified in the Dreyfus model. As the nurse practitioner's expertise grew, there was a connection between the skill of involvement and the ability to affect and influence situations. In addition, some nurses would not go on to become expert nurses if they were unable to show capabilities with interpersonal skills and problem engagement, and if they had difficulty with understanding what she called "the ends of practice" (Benner, 2004, p. 198). Nurses who did not show a progressive development into a mastery-level skillset continued to rely on their logic and rationality, in contrast to an experiential, intuitive-based process. Moreover, Benner (2004) stated, "the most qualitatively distinct difference lies between the competent and proficient level, where the practitioner begins to read the situation" (p. 188). Benner's findings show that rational-technical skill in trained nurses must be accompanied by wise discernment and practice, and that experiential learning is critical for continued development.

Coaching is a discipline that requires the practitioner to be skilled in theory and practice. Coaching demands skillful judgment and decision making over time, as changes in the client and changes in the situation are ongoing. Using Benner's framework and the Dreyfus model as a foundation, Bennett and Rogers (2013) distinguished characteristic differences between the advanced beginner and expert executive coaching experiences. Furthermore, they identified ways in which expert coaches evolve their level of skill development and application to the mastery level.

In their study of executive coaches and their skill acquisition, Bennett and Rogers (2013) interviewed International Coach Federation-credentialed and non-credentialed coaches with two or more years of coaching experience. Study participants were asked to discuss a coaching experience in which the client had a shift in perspective or action. Using the Dreyfus model, participants were classified as novice, advanced beginner, competent, proficient, or expert. This same focus was applied experientially with three groups involving more than 200 professional coaches. The results were consistent.

Bennett and Rogers (2013) concluded that the Dreyfus model of adult skill acquisition applies to executive coaching. The developmental model describes the stages through which an individual must progress to achieve mastery of a particular skill—advancing from abstract principles needed in a novice stage to a more intuitive, less self-conscious state in an expert stage. As Benner (2001, 2010) discovered, the Dreyfus model describes situated practice capacities, rather than traits or talents of the practitioners.

The Dreyfus model is, therefore, a useful framework for describing the knowledge and skills needed at the various stages of executive coaching, as supported by the findings. The advanced beginner is dealing with context, beginning to understand the situation, gradually using more-sophisticated rules, and making decisions with an analytical mind, considering the actions available (Benner, 2001; H. Dreyfus, 2004; S. Dreyfus, 2004a, 2004b; Dreyfus & Dreyfus, 1980; Hunt & Weintraub, 2007). Advanced beginner coaches worked with several clients and client issues, applied a coaching conversation model with little or no assistance—yet were frequently aware of its presence, applied basic coaching skills of listening and asking questions with ease and began to use different approaches, applied additional coaching skills (e.g., reframing, metaphors), and were cautious about taking risks. On the other hand, expert coaches operated in a fluid manner, generally knew what to do and how to do it, were naturally creative, took risks, viewed problems or challenges as opportunities—not obstacles, and applied knowledge and skills to situations in different ways, as appropriate. These differences highlight the benefit of coaching skills acquired over time and the insights gained from reflecting on coaching experience over time.

Distinctions: Advanced Beginner to Expert

The self-awareness level increases for the Change Coach as the skill level increases from the advanced beginner to the expert. As the coach's skill level increases, the focus of the coaching engagement shifts from a shared focus (on coach *and* client) to a client-centered focus. Therefore, the advanced beginner is self-focused and client-aware, and the expert is self-aware and client-focused. The literature discusses coaching skills that are generally accepted as necessary for the skilled practitioner. These skills include the ability to foster self-awareness and reflection (De Hann, 2008a, 2008b; Dotlich & Cairo, 1999; Hurd, 2003; Zeus & Skiffington, 2001) and the ability to build trusting relationships (De Hann, 2008a, 2008b; Kampa-Kokesch & Anderson, 2001; O'Neill, 2007; Zeus & Skiffington, 2001).

Advanced beginner and expert coaches express high levels of self-awareness in coaching sessions, as well as an awareness of the client.

> The expert coaches used their self-awareness to benefit the coaching experience for the client, even though they appeared at times to lack the consciousness of doing so. Expert coaches were able to remain focused on the client in the engagement, without processing their own awareness consciously in the session. The advanced beginner coaches were having moments of self-awareness, were conscious of their self-awareness, and analyzed how to use it within the coaching session. (Bennett & Rogers, 2013, p. 193)

The level of confidence that a coach demonstrates and the understanding of the coach's role increase with skill level. The literature cites being able to act courageously on one's intuition as a necessary skill for change (De Hann, 2008b, Hargrove, 1995), and Hargrove (1995) asserted that "a coach is something that you 'be'" (p. 39). Therefore, "the first question to ask, then, is not 'What do I do?' but 'How do I be?'" (p. 39). Hargrove and Hudson characterize the coach as being who one *is,* as opposed to an approach or model that one must follow step-by-step. Such "being" requires the coach to have developed character and certain abilities that are possible with practice and reflection over time. This self-awareness, confidence, and focus allow a coaching engagement to be what it needs to be for the client. By being fully present and client-focused, the coach is able to listen more deeply, attend to the nuances of what the client is saying, and observe the subtleties of expression and emotion that may be present.

Both advanced beginners and experts describe having doubts and fears, though as one would expect, the lack of confidence is more pervasive in a group of advanced beginners. Often struggling with the role of coach, the advanced beginners explore their role, showing a desire to help their clients to the fullest extent of their skills. Expert coaches understand their roles as coaches and form a partnership with their clients. Advanced coaches have confidence and a sense of freedom when coaching (Bennett & Rogers, 2013).

Expert coaches seek knowledge and experience in distinct ways. The advanced beginner is still learning and weaving together his knowledge of coaching with his experience. The expert continues to evolve by experimenting and reflecting on her coaching knowledge and experience.

Taylor's (2007) addition of a fifth stage to Howell's (1982) conscious competence model—reflective competency—captures the essence of the expert in mature practice. As Taylor described it, being conscious of unconscious incompetence allows the learner to cycle back through the learning stages. Johns (2009) described a reflective practitioner as "someone who lives reflection as a way of being" (p. 3). One might conclude that this is the optimum posture for a maturing coach. It is through reflection that practitioners hone their intuitive skills, which is tied to self-awareness, and to the confidence and liberation that comes with the Hargrove's (1995) sense of "being" a coach.

Similar coaching skills present differently when comparing the advanced beginner coach to the expert coach. In other words, the same skills, when used by coaches at different developmental levels, manifest characteristically different behavior from clients, which then result in different outcomes. Coaching skills and competencies include a variety of commonly held ideas about what makes a skilled coach (Crane, 1998; De Hann, 2008a, 2008b; Dotlich & Cairo, 1999; Fitzgerald & Berger, 2002; Freas, 2000; Hargrove, 1995; Hurd, 2003; Kampa-Kokesch & Anderson, 2001; O'Neill, 2007; Zeus & Skiffington, 2001). Practical and scholarly literature does not, however, identify a universal set of credentials.

A variety of skills can be identified and associated for coaching. Advanced beginner and expert coaches self-identified similar skillsets. Advanced beginner and expert research participants identified more than 50 skills, which were sorted into groups of like meanings. While skillsets of various developmental levels of coaches are likely the same, there is a distinct difference in the way those skills are manifested in order to bring about positive client comportment and outcomes. The practice of coaching skills and the insights gained from reflecting on coaching experience over time are key elements in creating those differences between the advanced beginner coach and the expert coach. There are distinctions between the advanced beginners' and experts' descriptions of similar executive coaching experiences. "Acquiring the skills to achieve progress through the levels of development as a coach is dependent on the learner in combination with factors of knowledge and skill building, experiential learning, and reflective practice over time" (Bennett & Rogers, 2013, p. 196).

Mastery Model Applied to the Coach

Just as the Mastery Model explained in Chapter 6 can be applied to support change at the individual, group, and organization levels, it can also be used to support performance, development, and transformational change with the intent of achieving mastery by the coach. Coaches, like clients, go through the same change process in their journey toward mastery.

Awareness. Coaches become aware of strengths in their coaching-related knowledge, skills, or coaching—or of a gap between these and the needs of clients. They may also become aware of the differences between their competencies and the competencies asserted by professional associations or crediting bodies. In the awareness stage, coaches seek more information or clarity about what the change involves. They need to understand what it will mean to them, and to the way they work and interact with others. Examples of ways in which awareness may be gained include client feedback, self-reflection about coaching experiences, and credentialing exams.

Acceptance. Coaches make peace with the change and explore or seek information to find out what the change will mean to them. There may still be concerns, confusion, and skepticism at this time, yet the intention and attitude shifts from "Why should we do this?" to "How can we make this successful?" This stage can manifest on three levels: cognitive, behavioral, and affective.

Adoption. In this stage, coaches actively engage in the new mindsets, behaviors, and interactions that support the change. They acquire or develop the capabilities to perform in new ways, and they often help others understand and make the needed changes. Accomplishing this may mean starting a behavior, gaining knowledge, developing a skill, broadening a perspective, or applying a skill or behavior in a new or different way.

Integration. Coaches become used to working and interacting in the new way, and often there are results or accomplishments to show from the change that has been implemented. The change has been embedded into existing structures, systems, and processes so that it is part of the way the organization operates and is not dependent on current leadership to drive it. The change is now sustained by the organizational culture and has become "the way we do things around here."

Mastery. Coaches continue to integrate the change into other personal and professional practices. They build increased agility and resilience, demonstrating improved capacity to make additional changes. They act with more innovation and apply learning from one area of their lives into their professional practices—often without giving it much thought or consideration. Innovation and agility become second nature. And, they are able to self-challenge themselves with self-study and peer review, cycling back through the stage of unconscious incompetence where new enlightenment reveals something else they did not know.

Actions to Support Development of Mastery

Advanced beginner and expert coaches develop competency in similar, yet different, ways. Bennett and Rogers (2013) found the following similarities: coaching training programs, graduate studies, previous work and life experiences, feedback, reading and self-study, mentors, and specialized training. Expert coaches also identified the following means: experimentation, being coached, reflecting, conference participation, and teaching others. Two practices are highlighted as ways to support development of coaching mastery: feedback and reflection.

Feedback

Feedback is considered a core element of the coaching process. Coaches and clients engage in continuous, reciprocal processes of feedback delivery and reception throughout their professional relationships. Feedback is also critical for the coach's professional development. By actively seeking feedback, the coach is able to identify strengths and weaknesses, along with what is working in coaching and what is not. Therefore, understanding the influence of feedback in coaching conversations and how to apply feedback for development of coaching capacities is essential. While several existing models of the coaching process mention feedback as a core element, only a few expand on the role and function of feedback in coaching relationships.

An evolving, maturing coach must proactively seek feedback from the client as well as other stakeholders, such as the human resources purchaser of the coaching services and the client's managers. One effective approach for gathering feedback can be the coach's use of reflection during and after the coaching session. While reflection is a loose processing of thoughts, it can be modeled so that coaches can better address surprises during and after a coaching conversation. The practical implication of this approach is that as part of feedback-seeking, reflection permits coaches to examine, question, and learn from their experience.

The way that feedback is acquired and processed varies, however, according to the person's awareness. Conscious processing of feedback is most likely to occur when a coach is unfamiliar with a situation or when the feedback obtained is incongruent with expectations. Finally, how feedback is processed is important, because it influences the nature of subsequent information processing (Taylor, Fisher, & Ilgen, 1984).

Seeking feedback in coaching conversations is critically important. It involves the coach actively seeking feedback from the client by observation and listening.

The client becomes the source of feedback to the coach—part of the process of information gathering that enables the coach to determine how the coach is performing. During coaching sessions, the coach actively listens for feedback in order to make adjustments to the process and the questions being asked. Listening to and being aware of a client's feedback is part of a coach's process of relating to and communicating with clients. Feedback giving, on the other hand, occurs when the coach provides feedback to the client. The coach identifies areas for improvement in the client's behavior or performance, and the client takes action on this feedback.

A coach has a responsibility to seek feedback from the client. There are several tools the coach can use, including feedback, focused questions for the client, surveys, interviews, and the use of reflection during and after coaching sessions. In his article on contracting, Bennett (2008) highlights the need to discuss how and when the coach and the client will give each other feedback. Potential questions the coach may use to gather feedback include, "What if any changes do we need to consider making for our working agreement?" "How is our coaching relationship meeting your needs? Are there ways it can be improved or enhanced?"

When coaches consider these types of open-ended questions as they prepare for coaching sessions, they enhance the opportunity to gather important feedback from clients. These questions provoke thought without leading the client or making the feedback to the coach personal. Instead, the focus remains on the clients and how well their needs are being met.

Surveys also provide a great source of feedback for the coach. They provide a consistent measure of progress when used after each coaching engagement. Clients may feel more comfortable providing feedback when they can reflect on the coaching experience and respond to surveys more candidly than in giving on-the-spot feedback during the coaching session. To encourage clients to complete their surveys, coaches can stress how the feedback will be used and how much it is valued. Another potential source of feedback to the coach is third-party interviews with clients and stakeholders after coaching sessions have ended. Passmore (2010) used this approach in a qualitative study involving interviews with six executives who had been coached. Such interviews provide valuable feedback that can be leveraged to better understand what is important to clients.

Passmore's (2010) research helps coaches to understand key coaching attributes and behaviors valued by clients. Understanding what is valued can shape meaningful interview questions. For example, coaches would benefit from interview questions such as "Was the coach non-judgmental?" "Did the coach establish that he could be trusted and if so, how?" "Was the coach collaborative or directive?" "Did the coach stay focused on solutions?" The results of such interviews provide coaches with feedback that can be used for continued development of coaching competence.

Another approach for gathering feedback can be the coach's use of reflection during and after the coaching session. Clutterbuck (2010) offered a framework for coaches to become reflective practitioners. He called it the four "I"s: (1) Issues (What topics did we cover?), (2) Ideas (What creative thinking occurred?), (3) Insights (What did we learn?), and (4) Intentions (What will we do as a result of our learning dialogue?).

Reflection

Like feedback, reflection is an active process that can result in learning (Cooney, 1999). Reflection is the act of examining one's thinking, feelings, and actions (Newell, 1992), and thinking purposefully in order to gain new insights, ideas, and understanding (Haddock & Bassett, 1997). According to Jarvis (1992), the reflective practitioner works to ensure that the outcome of any action is close to what is anticipated by the theory and the experience combined. These definitions suggest that the reflective practice is associated with learning from experience. Obviously, reflection does not replace scientific knowledge. What reflection offers, though, is a process that facilitates the integration of theory with practice.

Reflection is a critical tool for coaches to gather feedback about their effectiveness and impact on the client. Reflection is "an active, persistent and careful consideration of any belief or supposed form of knowledge" (Dewey, 1933, p. 9). Williams, Wessel, Gemus, and Foster-Seargeant (2002) wrote that reflection is "a process where individuals think about and evaluate their experience in order to come to new understandings and appreciations" (p. 5). Refection involves awareness of thoughts and feelings, analysis of the situation—including existing knowledge—and development of a perspective of the situation.

While there are many benefits of reflecting, here are some that pertain to the development of mastery by coaches:

- Promote reflective thinking
- Provide opportunity to reflect on and share experiences
- Confirm prior knowledge
- Assist with gaining an understanding of new learning

- Consider how one may behave in the future
- Facilitate link between scholarship and practice
- Provide awareness of thoughts and feelings
- Facilitate analysis of the situation, including existing knowledge
- Promote development of a perspective of the situation developed by analysis and application of information to the experience.

Reflection is essentially a processing of thoughts and feelings about an incident, a meeting, or a day—any event or experience at all. Reflection can be loosely or closely structured to deal with surprises during and after a coaching conversation. Schön (1983) distinguished between what he termed reflection-*in*-action and reflection-*on*-action as a means of investigating how people use their experience to analyze and frame problems, propose action, and then reevaluate the experience as a result of the action (Beard, Wilson, & Irvine, 2002). For example, reflection may take place in real-time while a conversation is occurring (reflection-*in*-action), or later when there is time to stand back from the conversation (reflection-*on*-action).

Reflection-in-Action Reflection-in-action is when the coach reacts to what is happening while the coaching conversation is taking place. Reflection affects the coach's decision making and feelings at the time of the event. Best described as "thinking while doing" or "thinking on one's feet," reflection-in-action occurs without an interruption in action (Jones, 1995; Marks-Maran & Rose, 1997). Reflection-in-action is, therefore, that process that allows people to reshape what they are working on, while they are working on it. It is that ongoing experimentation that helps people find a viable solution. In reflection-in-action, coaches do not use a trial-and-error method. Rather, their actions are much more reasoned and purposeful than that. Reflection-in-action is a conscious activity. If something is not working according to expectations, then reflection-in-action can be employed to help the coach reflect in real-time.

Reflection-in-action is generally called upon when a surprise appears in the process of accomplishing a task. That surprise causes one to question how the surprise occurred given his or her usual thinking process. Therefore, coaches will reflect-in-action to determine what is different and how they can change their thinking to address this new challenge.

Thc following examples (Table 14.1) illustrate reflection-in-action.

Table 14.1 Reflection-in-Action

WHAT? (COACH NOTICES OR RECEIVES FEEDBACK)	SO WHAT? (COACH ANALYZES THE GAP)	WHAT NEXT? (COACH DECIDES & ACTS)
I just asked my client a question and instead of an answer I got a stare. My client seems to be confused.	Does this tell me I am a poor communicator?	I have not gotten through to my client. I will reframe.
I just asked my client a question and instead of an answer I got a long silence. My client seems to be thinking.	Does this tell me I hit a chord?	I will wait for my client to answer. I need to observe more.
I used my favorite metaphor, one that has worked on just about every occasion. My client did not respond.	Does this tell me that my client does not respond to metaphors?	I will not use metaphors again with this client.
I asked my client a simple question and received a response that did not match the question.	Was my question off?	I will rephrase my question.
My client just told me she skipped her homework.	Does this tell me that my client is not committed?	I will call on her. I will remind her that doing her homework is essential if she is going to get any value from coaching.
In our previous coaching session my client was bored. Today he started drifting to a new topic. I noticed energy in his voice.	Does this tell me the presenting issue was not the real issue?	I will remind him that we are on a different subject. I need to confirm what the real issue is.
My client just interrupted me. I could not get my question right.	Is this habitual? Or did my client not realize what she just did?	I will wait for my client to finish her answer and then make her aware of the behavior.

Reflection-on-Action Reflection-on-action is the act of looking back on an experience and critically examining that experience after the fact. In the context of coaching, the coach sifts over a previous coaching conversation to take into account feelings and actions taken at that time. It involves looking back on a past experience, exploring the understandings that were present at the time of the experience, and creating new understandings based on the outcomes of the original action (Marks-Maran & Rose, 1997).

Reflection-on-action is an everyday process. People reflect on a range of everyday problems and situations all the time: What went well? What didn't? Why didn't it go well? How do I feel about it? "We reflect on action, thinking back on what we have done in order to discover how our knowing-in-action may have contributed to an unexpected outcome" (Schön, 1983, p. 26).

The following examples (Table 14.2) illustrate reflection-on-action.

Table 14.2 Reflection-on-Action

WHAT? (COACH NOTICES OR RECEIVES FEEDBACK)	SO WHAT? (COACH ANALYZES THE GAP)	WHAT NEXT? (COACH DECIDES & ACTS)
My client was constantly making shifts, going from one subject to another.	Does this tell me my client is nervous? Or confused? Did I contribute to that?	I need to ask my client to confirm his understanding. I need to make sure that my questions are getting across to him.
I thought today's session was a great one. My client had solid answers. But the HR manager told me that the client did not get any value from the coaching session.	Is my client being forced into this coaching by the HR manager? Or is my client not answering my questions honestly?	I need to confirm if my client is committed to the coaching. I also need to confirm if she answers just to please me or to avoid getting embarrassed.
I offered too much of an opinion when I should have been more disciplined. But my client thanked me for my advice and replied that today's session was a great one.	Does this tell me the client is not looking for a coach but for a mentor? Does the client prefer direct communication?	I have to decide if I am serving this client well. I might need to refer her to a mentor.
My client has been talking about the same thing over and over again.	Does this tell me that my client is anxious about something?	I need to confirm whether or not the client is anxious.
My client was constantly distracted by her phone ringing and she was reaching out to her BlackBerry at the sound of every new message beep.	Is this a symptom of her lack of commitment? Is her office environment contributing to her distraction?	I will call her and insist that next time we meet it has to be somewhere outside of her office. If she continues to get distracted, I will call on her.
As I reflect on my last session, I realize I was too rough and mean with my client. I realize she is not my favorite client because of her behavior.	Does my client remind me of someone I may not like? Do I bring my own baggage to the table?	I need to decide if this client is still a good fit for me.

Rolfe's Model of Reflection Another effective approach to reflection (Rolfe, Freshwater, & Jasper, 2001) comprises three questions representing three levels of reflection:

- *What?* What is the descriptive level of reflection? It describes the situation, responses and feelings.
- *So what?* What is the theory and knowledge-building level of reflection? What has been learned about self, relationships, models, attitudes, actions, thoughts, understanding, and improvements?
- *What next?* What is the action-oriented level of reflection? What needs to be done in order to improve future outcomes and develop learning?

Coaches can record or journal reflections in order to capture them and consider them later. This process of recording events and circumstances and returning to them for sense-making can often be useful. The following series of questions based on work by Argyris and Schon (1974) and Schon (1987) and adapted from work by MacKeracher (1996) can be used to facilitate this process.

Experience

- What did I feel about what occurred?
- What did I think about but did not say?
- What did I want to do but did not do?
- What outcomes did I desire that did not occur?

Events

- What happened?
- Who was involved?
- What was said?
- What were the outcomes?

Consideration

- What is the comparison?
- What do I think in a critical sense?
- What do I honestly think?

Another approach is to describe experiences by noting key processes within the experience. The coach or client reflects on what was trying to be achieved and why, as well as consequences, and then identifies the influencing factors, such as sources of knowledge and differing facts, involved in the decision-making process. And, finally, the coach or client considers the learning that can be derived from the initial experience and reflection. This learning includes current emotions and a view in the context of historical and social processes (Johns, 2009; Platzer & Snelling, 1997).

As coaches reflect, there are several cautions to consider:

- One can only reflect on what one remembers, or chooses to remember. Therefore, selective memory limits what can be reflected on.
- When time is short, decisions have to be made quickly. Thus, reflection is limited to those who can think and react quickly.

- If reflection is most likely to occur in the presence of unexpected outcomes, it is reasonable to assume that reflection will overlook the familiar.
- People tend to focus their attention on negative experiences and highly stressed situations. As a result, expect coaches to reflect less on what went well.
- People tend to operate within the sphere of their comfort zone. Thus, coaches might tend to neglect situations that expose uncertainty or their own lack of skills.

Chapter Summary

While most anyone can call himself or herself a coach, effective and long-lasting coaching requires practitioners to develop mastery in the knowledge, skills, and abilities of coaching. Skilled coaches must master a variety of skills, including giving feedback, building trusting relationships, fostering self-awareness and reflection, and many more. Only after doing so can a coach truly *be* a coach instead of just following a script or step-by-step model.

Seeking feedback in coaching conversations can be structured, especially if done from the reflective practitioner's point of view. The main value of this type of reflection is to help coaches assess how they are coaching and allow them to make adjustments to the coaching process or the questions being asked. Coaches periodically stop and pause to think what is working, what is not working, or what they can do to improve the work they do together with their clients. They do this in a deliberate and intentional way. They look at all sources of data to be able to confirm and adjust what and how they are doing. Seeking feedback using the reflective practitioner's approach is one way to do this. This approach offers the potential to raise a Change Coach's awareness and deepen the understanding of her coaching practice.

Knowledge Check

1. What is the importance of mastery to the Change Coach? What is the importance of the Change Coach's mastery to the client?
2. What are some strategies a coach can use to develop mastery?
3. What is the role of reflection in developing mastery? Name three types of reflection and how they can they be applied to develop mastery.

Learning Activities

Learning Activity 1: Record and Review

Record your coaching sessions and review them, paying particular attention to:

- Use of a coaching model
- Application of coaching-related skills
- Identifying how theory informs your practice of coaching.

Then, develop a list of strengths and areas for development. Use this list to create a plan for your continued development.

Learning Activity 2: Professional Development Programs

Attend and participate in various professional development programs offered by professional associations, assessment providers, and universities.

Learning Activity 3: Professional Development

Identify an area for professional development. Locate books and articles related to this topic and study them. Consider designing and conducting a professional development workshop for a group of coaches.

Learning Activity 4: Mastermind Group

Participate in a mastermind group.

Learning Activity 5: Professional Dialogue

Without breaking agreements of confidentiality, discuss with a professional colleague the challenges and successes you experience with clients. Seek ideas for alternative approaches.

Learning Activity 6: Reflection and Journaling

Maintain a practice of reflection and journaling. Use the following questions related to coaching experiences:

- Before an experience . . . What is likely to occur? What are the potential impacts? What do I bring to the situation? What challenges do I face? What are my strengths? What options do I have? What choices will I make? What do I want? What do I need?
- During an experience . . . What is happening? How am I feeling? What am I thinking? What options do I have? What actions have I taken? What are the impacts? What do I want? What can I learn from this experience?
- Following an experience . . . What happened? How did I feel? What was I thinking? What options did I have? What choices did I make? What were the impacts (on me, a group, others, an organization, society)? What meaning can I make of the situation, events, etc.? What lessons did I learn?

Learning Activity 7: Graduate Education

Earn an advanced degree in coaching or a related field of study.

Learning Activity 8: Professional Certification

Gain and maintain a professional **certification** through an organization such as the Center for Credentialing & Education (CCE), European Mentoring & Coaching Council (EMCC), or International Coach Federation (ICF).

Learning Activity 9: Client Feedback

Ask clients for feedback about your coaching.

Learning Activity 10: Assessment Qualification

Develop expertise in using other assessments and instruments in your coaching practice. Examples include Thomas Kilmann Conflict Mode Instrument, FIRO-B, and Team Dimensions Profile. Earn a qualification to administer a proprietary (valid and reliable) assessment such as Hogan Personality Inventory, Myers-Briggs Type Indicator, WorkPlace Big Five, Predictive Index, Emotional and Social Competence Inventory, multi-rater feedback instruments (e.g., Benchmarks, Leadership Effectiveness Analysis), and Kolb Learning Style Inventory.

Learning Activity 11: Professional Dialogue

Engage with professionals in dialogues through blogs and LinkedIn groups. Observe how you (and others) present yourselves in writing and on your profiles. What does your observation tell you about your own "presence" and that of other members? Are there rules of engagement in your online groups? What are they? How would you describe the "culture" that is forming (or has formed) among the group virtually? How do you engage with the group to expand yourself professionally? Do you give and receive feedback online to become a better member of the community? What are the benefits to you of these online opportunities? What are you learning about yourself that applies to your development as a Change Coach?

References

Argyris, C. (1991). Teaching smart people how to learn. *Harvard Business Review, 4*(1), 4–15.

Argyris, C., & Schon, D. A. (1974). *Theory in practice: Increasing professional effectiveness.* San Francisco, CA: Jossey-Bass.

Beard, C., Wilson, J. P., & Irvine, D. (2002). *The power of experiential learning: A handbook for trainers and educators.* London: Kogan Page.

Benner, P. (2001). *From novice to expert: Excellence and power in clinical nursing practice* (commemorative ed.). Upper Saddle River, NJ: Prentice Hall. (Original work published 1984).

Benner, P. (2004). Using the Dreyfus model of skill acquisition to describe and interpret skill acquisition and clinical judgment in nursing practice and education. *Bulletin of Science, Technology & Society, 24*(3), 188–199.

Benner, P. (2010). Experiential learning, skill acquisition and gaining clinical expertise. In K. Osborn, A. Watson & C. Wraa (Eds.), *Preparation for practice* (pp. 32–44). Upper Saddle River, NJ: Pearson Education.

Bennett, J. L. (2008). Contracting for success. *International Journal of Coaching in Organizations,* (4), 7–14.

Bennett, J. L., & Rogers, K. (2013). Skill acquisition of executive coaches: A journey toward mastery. In A. F. Buono, L. de Caluwe, & A. Stoppelenburg (Eds.), *Exploring the professional identity of management consultants* (pp. 173–201). Charlotte, NC: Information Age Publishing.

Berliner, D. C. (2004). Describing the behavior and documenting the accomplishments of expert teachers. *Bulletin of Science, Technology & Society, 24*(3), 200–212.

Bloom, B. S. (Ed.), Engelhart, M. D., Furst, E. J., Hill, W. H., & Krathwohl, D. R. (1956). *Taxonomy of educational objectives: The classification of educational goals. Handbook 1: Cognitive domain.* New York: David McKay.

Brotman, L. E., Liberi, W. P., & Wasylyshyn, K. M. (2000). Executive coaching: The need for standards of competence. *Consulting Psychology Journal: Practice and Research, 52,* 201–205.

Bush, M. W. (2005). *Client perceptions of effectiveness in executive coaching.* Doctoral dissertation. Pepperdine University, Los Angeles.

Clutterbuck, D. (2010). Coaching reflection: the liberated coach. *Coaching: An International Journal of Theory, Research and Practice 3,* 73–81.

Cooney, A. (1999). Reflection demystified: Answering some common questions. *British Journal of Nursing, 8*(22), 1530–1534.

Crane, T. G. (1998). *The heart of coaching: Using transformational coaching to create a high-performance culture.* San Diego, CA: FTA Press.

DeHann, E. (2008a). I doubt, therefore I coach. *Consulting Psychology Journal: Practice and Research, 60*(1), 91–105.

DeHann, E. (2008b). I struggle and emerge. *Consulting Psychology Journal: Practice and Research, 60*(1), 106–131.

Dewey, J. (1933) *How we think: A restatement of the relation of reflective thinking to the educative process* (rev. ed.), Boston: D.C. Heath.

Dotlich, D. L., & Cairo, P. C. (1999). *Action coaching: How to leverage individual performance for company success.* San Francisco, CA: Jossey-Bass.

Dreyfus, H. (2004). What could be more intelligible than everyday intelligibility? Reinterpreting division I of being and time in light of division II. *Bulletin of Science, Technology & Society, 24*(3), 265–274.

Dreyfus, S. (2004a). The five-stage model of adult skill acquisition. *Bulletin of Science, Technology & Society, 24*(3), 177–181.

Dreyfus, S. (2004b). Totally model-free learned skillful coping. *Bulletin of Science, Technology & Society, 24*(3), 182–187.

Dreyfus, H., & Dreyfus, S. (1980). *The five-stage model of the mental activities involved in directed skill acquisition.* Berkeley, CA: Operations Research Center, University of California.

Dreyfus, H. L., & Dreyfus, S. E. (1986). *Mind over machine: The power of human intuition and expertise in the era of the computer.* New York, NY: Free Press.

Dreyfus, H., & Dreyfus, S. (2004). The ethical implications of the five-stage skill-acquisition model. *Bulletin of Science, Technology & Society, 24*(3), 251–264.

Duesund, L., & Jespersen, E. (2004). Skill acquisition in ski instruction and the skill model's application to treating anorexia nervosa. *Bulletin of Science, Technology & Society, 24*(3), 225–233.

Fitzgerald, C., & Berger, J. G. (Eds.). (2002). *Executive coaching: Practices & perspectives.* Palo Alto, CA: Davies-Black Publishing.

Freas, A.M. (2000). Coaching executives for business results. In M. Goldsmith, L. Lyons, & A. Freas (Eds.), *Coaching for leadership: How the world's greatest coaches help leaders learn* (pp. 27–41). San Francisco, CA: Jossey-Bass.

Guthrie, V. A., & Alexander, J. (2000). Process advising: An approach to coaching for development. In M. Goldsmith, L. Lyons, & A. Freas (Eds.), *Coaching for Leadership: How the World's Greatest Coaches Help Leaders Learn* (pp. 299–306). San Francisco, CA: Jossey-Bass.

Haddock, J., & Bassett, C. (1997). Nurses' perceptions of reflective practice. *Nursing Standard, 11*(32), 39–41.

Hargrove, R. (1995). *Masterful coaching: Extraordinary results by impacting people and the way they think and work together.* San Francisco, CA: Pfeiffer.

Howell, W. C. (1982). *Information processing and decision making.* Mahwah, NJ: Lawrence Erlbaum Associates.

Hunt, J. G., & Weintraub, J. R. (2007). *The coaching organization: A strategy for developing leaders.* Thousand Oaks, CA: Sage.

Hurd, J. L. (2003, November 12). *Learning for life: An investigation into the effect of organizational coaching on individual lives.* Paper presented at the Coaching Research Symposium, Denver, CO.

Jarvis, P. (1992). Reflective practice and nursing. *Nurse Education Today, 12,* 174–181.

Johns, C. (2009). *Becoming a reflective practitioner* (3rd ed.). West Sussex, UK: John Wiley & Sons.

Jones, P. R. (1995). Hindsight bias in reflective practice: An empirical investigation. *Journal Advanced Nursing, 21,* 783–788.

Kampa-Kokesch, S., & Anderson, M. Z. (2001). Executive coaching: A comprehensive review of the literature. *Consulting Psychology Journal: Practice and Research, 53,* 205–226.

Kemp, T. J. (2008). Self-management and the coaching relationship: Exploring coaching impact beyond models and methods. *International Coaching Psychology Review, 3*(1), 32–42.

Kilburg, R. R. (1996). Toward a conceptual understanding and definition of executive coaching. *Consulting Psychology Journal: Practice and Research, 48,* 134–144.

Kilburg, R. R. (2000). *Executive coaching: Developing managerial wisdom in a world of chaos.* Washington, DC: American Psychological Association.

Krathwohl, D. R. (2002). A revision of Bloom's taxonomy: An overview. *Theory Into Practice, 41*(4), 212–218.

Laske, O. (2004). Can evidence-based coaching increase ROI? *International Journal of Evidence Based Coaching and Mentoring, 2*(2), 41–53.

Mackeracher, D. (1996). *Making sense of adult learning.* Toronto, ON: Culture Concepts.

Marks-Maran, D., & Rose, P. (1997). Thinking and caring: New perspectives on reflection. In D. Marks-Maran & P. Rose (Eds.). *Reconstructing Nursing. Beyond Art and Science* (pp. 110–140). London: Bailliere Tindall.

Moe, V. (2004). How to understand skill acquisition in sport. *Bulletin of Science, Technology & Society, 24*(3), 213–224.

Newell, R. (1992). Anxiety, accuracy and reflection: The limits of professional development. *Journal of Advanced Nursing, 17,* 1326–3133.

O'Broin, A., & Palmer, S. (2010). Exploring the key aspects in the formation of coaching relationships: Initial indicators from the perspective of the coachee and the coach. *Coaching: An International Journal of Theory, Research & Practice, 3*(2), 124–143.

O'Neill, M. B. (2007). *Executive coaching with backbone and heart: A systems approach to engaging leaders with their challenges* (2nd ed.). San Francisco, CA: Jossey-Bass.

Passmore, J. (2010). A grounded theory study of the client experience: The implications for training and practice in coaching psychology. *International Coaching Psychology Review, 5,* 48–62.

Platzer, H., & Snelling, J. (1997). Promoting reflective practitioners in nursing: A review of and journals to facilitate reflection. *Teaching in Higher Education, 2*(2), 103–122.

Riley, B. E., & Frost, D. D. (2008). *Are you ready for outrageous success?* Raleigh, NC: Lulu.com.

Rolfe, G., Freshwater, D., & Jasper, M (2001). *Critical reflection in nursing and the helping professions: A user's guide.* Basingstoke, UK: Palgrave Macmillan.

Schon, D. A. (1983). *The reflective practitioner: How professionals think in action.* New York: Basic Books.

Schon, D. A. (1987). *Educating the reflective practitioner.* San Francisco, CA: Jossey-Bass.

Taylor, W. (2007). Conscious competence learning model discussion. Retrieved from www.businessballs.com/consciouscompetencelearningmodel.htm

Taylor, M. S., Fisher, C. D., & Ilgen, D. R. (1984). Individuals' reactions to performance feedback in organizations: A control theory perspective. *Research in Personnel and Human Resources Management, 2,* 81–124.

Vanderburg, W. (2004). The human skill-acquisition model of Stuart Dreyfus: Stemming the tide of confusing our humanity with machines. *Bulletin of Science, Technology & Society, 24*(3), 175–176.

Whitworth, L., Kimsey-House, K., Kimsey-House, H., & Sandahl, P. (2007). *Co-active coaching: New skills for coaching people toward success in work and life.* (2nd ed.). Mountain View, CA: Davies-Black.

Williams, R. M., Wessel, J., Gemus, M., & Foster-Seargeant, E. (2002). Journal writing to promote reflection by physical therapy students during clinical placements. *Physiotherapy Theory and Practice, 18*(1), 5–15.

Zeus, P., & Skiffington, S. (2001). *The complete guide to coaching at work.* Sydney, Australia: McGraw-Hill.

Appendix A: Competency Mapping to Coaching

INTERNATIONAL COACH FEDERATION (ICF) (NOTE 5)	BOARD CERTIFIED COACH: CENTER FOR CREDENTIALING & EDUCATION (CCE) (NOTE 4)	EUROPEAN MENTORING & COACHING COUNCIL (EMCC) (NOTE 2)	GRADUATE SCHOOL ALLIANCE FOR EXECUTIVE COACHING (GSAEC)	INTERNATIONAL ASSOCIATION OF FACILITATORS (NOTE 6)	PROFESSIONAL CHAPLAIN (NOTE 3)	INSTITUTE OF MANAGEMENT CONSULTANTS (NOTE 8)	CONFLICT RESOLUTION, NEGOTIATION & MEDIATION (NOTE 1)	HELPING SKILLS (NOTE 7)
Meeting Ethical Guidelines and Professional Standards – Understanding of coaching ethics and standards and ability to apply them appropriately in all coaching situations.	**Ethical and Professional Practice in Coaching:** These coaching work behaviors focus on codes of ethics, advocacy, continuing education, and personal barriers to the coaching process.			Model Positive Professional Attitude	Theory of Pastoral Care Competencies Identity and Conduct Competencies	Professional Ethics	Demonstrate knowledge of ethics of collaborative conflict resolution. Ability to demonstrate knowledge of the basic negotiation rules of ethics and principles of practice.	
		Understanding Self Demonstrate awareness of own values, beliefs and behaviors, recognizes how these affect their practice, and uses this self-awareness to manage their effectiveness in meeting the client's—and, where relevant—the sponsor's objectives.			Identity and Conduct Competencies			
		Commitment to Self-Development Explore and improve the standard of their practice and maintain the reputation of the profession.			Identity and Conduct Competencies			

(*Continued*)

INTERNATIONAL COACH FEDERATION (ICF) (NOTE 5)	BOARD CERTIFIED COACH: CENTER FOR CREDENTIALING & EDUCATION (CCE) (NOTE 4)	EUROPEAN MENTORING & COACHING COUNCIL (EMCC) (NOTE 2)	GRADUATE SCHOOL ALLIANCE FOR EXECUTIVE COACHING (GSAEC)	INTERNATIONAL ASSOCIATION OF FACILITATORS (NOTE 6)	PROFESSIONAL CHAPLAIN (NOTE 3)	INSTITUTE OF MANAGEMENT CONSULTANTS (NOTE 8)	CONFLICT RESOLUTION, NEGOTIATION & MEDIATION (NOTE 1)	HELPING SKILLS (NOTE 7)
Establishing the Coaching Agreement – Ability to understand what is required in the specific coaching interaction and to come to agreement with the prospective and new client about the coaching process and relationship.	**Screening and Orientation in Coaching:** These coaching work behaviors focus on client motivation level, informed consent, coach and client roles, and general parameters for establishing the coaching process.	**Managing the Contract** Establishes and maintains the expectations and boundaries of the coaching/mentoring contract with the client and, where appropriate, with sponsors.	Co-creating the coaching relationship	Create Collaborative Client Relationships	Pastoral Competencies	Consulting Skills & Behaviors: Project Management Consulting Competencies: Practice Management	Collaborative problem-solving skills Basic negotiation rules of ethics and principles of practice	
Establishing Trust and Intimacy with the Client – Ability to focus completely on what the client is saying and is not saying, to understand the meaning of what is said in the context of the client's desires, and to support client self-expression.	**Fundamental Coaching Skills:** These coaching work behaviors focus on the basic coaching alliance, helping skills, coaching plans, and other essential issues concerning the coaching process.	**Building the Relationship** Skillfully builds and maintains an effective relationship with the client, and where appropriate, with the sponsor.	Co-creating the coaching relationship	Create Collaborative Client Relationships Create and Sustain a Participatory Environment	Identity and Conduct Competencies Pastoral Competencies	Consulting Skills & Competencies: Emotional Intelligence	Basic negotiation rules of ethics and principles of practice	

INTERNATIONAL COACH FEDERATION (ICF) (NOTE 5)	BOARD CERTIFIED COACH: CENTER FOR CREDENTIALING & EDUCATION (CCE) (NOTE 4)	EUROPEAN MENTORING & COACHING COUNCIL (EMCC) (NOTE 2)	GRADUATE SCHOOL ALLIANCE FOR EXECUTIVE COACHING (GSAEC)	INTERNATIONAL ASSOCIATION OF FACILITATORS (NOTE 6)	PROFESSIONAL CHAPLAIN (NOTE 3)	INSTITUTE OF MANAGEMENT CONSULTANTS (NOTE 8)	CONFLICT RESOLUTION, NEGOTIATION & MEDIATION (NOTE 1)	HELPING SKILLS (NOTE 7)
Coaching Presence – Ability to be fully conscious and create spontaneous relationship with the client, employing a style that is open, flexible, and confident.	**Fundamental Coaching Skills:** These coaching work behaviors focus on the basic coaching alliance, helping skills, coaching plans, and other essential issues concerning the coaching process.	**Building the Relationship** Skillfully builds and maintains an effective relationship with the client, and where appropriate, with the sponsor.	Co-creating the coaching relationship	Create and Sustain a Participatory Environment	Pastoral Competencies	Consulting Skills & Competencies: Emotional Intelligence	Basic negotiation rules of ethics and principles of practice	
Active Listening – Ability to focus completely on what the client is saying and is not saying, to understand the meaning of what is said in the context of the client's desires, and to support client self-expression.	**Fundamental Coaching Skills:** These coaching work behaviors focus on the basic coaching alliance, helping skills, coaching plans, and other essential issues concerning the coaching process.		Making meaning with others	Guide Group to Appropriate and Useful Outcomes	Identity and Conduct Competencies	Consulting Competencies: Consulting Skills and Tools Consulting Skills & Competencies: Effective Communication	Demonstrate collaborative problem-solving skills	Listening
Powerful Questions – Ability to ask questions that reveal the information needed for maximum benefit to the coaching relationship and the client.	**Fundamental Coaching Skills:** These coaching work behaviors focus on the basic coaching alliance, helping skills, coaching plans, and other essential issues concerning the coaching process.		Making meaning with others	Guide Group to Appropriate and Useful Outcomes	Identity and Conduct Competencies	Consulting Skills & Competencies: Effective Communication	Demonstrate collaborative problem-solving skills. Ability to use both open and closed questions.	Leading Reflecting Challenging Interpreting

(*Continued*)

INTERNATIONAL COACH FEDERATION (ICF) (NOTE 5)	BOARD CERTIFIED COACH: CENTER FOR CREDENTIALING & EDUCATION (CCE) (NOTE 4)	EUROPEAN MENTORING & COACHING COUNCIL (EMCC) (NOTE 2)	GRADUATE SCHOOL ALLIANCE FOR EXECUTIVE COACHING (GSAEC)	INTERNATIONAL ASSOCIATION OF FACILITATORS (NOTE 6)	PROFESSIONAL CHAPLAIN (NOTE 3)	INSTITUTE OF MANAGEMENT CONSULTANTS (NOTE 8)	CONFLICT RESOLUTION, NEGOTIATION & MEDIATION (NOTE 1)	HELPING SKILLS (NOTE 7)
Direct Communication – Ability to communicate effectively during coaching sessions, and to use language that has the greatest positive impact on the client.	**Fundamental Coaching Skills:** These coaching work behaviors focus on the basic coaching alliance, helping skills, coaching plans, and other essential issues concerning the coaching process.	**Enabling Insight and Learning** Work with the client and sponsor to bring about insight and learning.	Helping others succeed	Guide Group to Appropriate and Useful Outcomes	Identity and Conduct Competencies	Consulting Skills & Competencies: Effective Communication	Demonstrate collaborative problem-solving skills	Leading Reflecting Challenging Interpreting Informing
Creating Awareness – Ability to integrate and accurately evaluate multiple sources of information, and to make interpretations that help the client to gain awareness and thereby achieve agreed-upon results.	**Fundamental Coaching Skills:** These coaching work behaviors focus on the basic coaching alliance, helping skills, and coaching. These coaching work behaviors focus on the basic coaching alliance, helping skills, coaching plans and other essential issues concerning the coaching process. **Assessment in Coaching:** These coaching work behaviors assess coaching goals, client strengths, and specific issues concerning the coaching process.	**Enabling Insight and Learning** Work with the client and sponsor to bring about insight and learning.	Helping others succeed	Guide Group to Appropriate and Useful Outcomes			Supporting competencies: Skills	Reflecting Summarizing Challenging Interpreting Informing

INTERNATIONAL COACH FEDERATION (ICF) (NOTE 5)	BOARD CERTIFIED COACH: CENTER FOR CREDENTIALING & EDUCATION (CCE) (NOTE 4)	EUROPEAN MENTORING & COACHING COUNCIL (EMCC) (NOTE 2)	GRADUATE SCHOOL ALLIANCE FOR EXECUTIVE COACHING (GSAEC)	INTERNATIONAL ASSOCIATION OF FACILITATORS (NOTE 6)	PROFESSIONAL CHAPLAIN (NOTE 3)	INSTITUTE OF MANAGEMENT CONSULTANTS (NOTE 8)	CONFLICT RESOLUTION, NEGOTIATION & MEDIATION (NOTE 1)	HELPING SKILLS (NOTE 7)
Designing Actions – Ability to create with the client opportunities for ongoing learning during coaching and in work/life situations, and for taking new actions that will most effectively lead to agreed-upon coaching results.	**Fundamental Coaching Skills:** These coaching work behaviors focus on the basic coaching alliance, helping skills, coaching plans, and other essential issues concerning the coaching process. **Coaching Approaches for Individuals:** These coaching work behaviors pertain to specific skills aimed at facilitating the client's desired goals during the coaching process, including monitoring client progress, decision making, and use of resources.		Process of Coaching	Guide Group to Appropriate and Useful Outcomes			Ability to demonstrate and identify courses of action and analyzing the consequences of each Ability to identify the elements of a sustainable agreement	Problem solving and decision making
Planning and Goal Setting – Ability to develop and maintain an effective coaching plan with the client.	**Fundamental Coaching Skills:** These coaching work behaviors focus on the basic coaching alliance, helping skills, coaching plans, and other essential issues concerning the coaching process.		Process of Coaching	Guide Group to Appropriate and Useful Outcomes			Ability to identify the elements of a sustainable agreement	Behavior changing

(*Continued*)

INTERNATIONAL COACH FEDERATION (ICF) (NOTE 5)	BOARD CERTIFIED COACH: CENTER FOR CREDENTIALING & EDUCATION (CCE) (NOTE 4)	EUROPEAN MENTORING & COACHING COUNCIL (EMCC) (NOTE 2)	GRADUATE SCHOOL ALLIANCE FOR EXECUTIVE COACHING (GSAEC)	INTERNATIONAL ASSOCIATION OF FACILITATORS (NOTE 6)	PROFESSIONAL CHAPLAIN (NOTE 3)	INSTITUTE OF MANAGEMENT CONSULTANTS (NOTE 8)	CONFLICT RESOLUTION, NEGOTIATION & MEDIATION (NOTE 1)	HELPING SKILLS (NOTE 7)
Managing Progress and Accountability – Ability to hold attention on what is important for the client, and to leave responsibility with the client to take action.	**Fundamental Coaching Skills:** These coaching work behaviors focus on the basic coaching alliance, helping skills, coaching plans, and other essential issues concerning the coaching process.	**Outcome and Action Orientation** Demonstrate approach, and use the skills, in supporting the client to make desired changes.	Process of Coaching	Guide Group to Appropriate and Useful Outcomes		Consulting Skills and Behaviors: Project Management		Problem solving and decision making
	Coaching Approaches for Individuals: These coaching work behaviors pertain to specific skills aimed at facilitating the client's desired goals during the coaching process, including monitoring client progress, decision making, and use of resources.							
	Coaching Approaches for Businesses and Organizations: These coaching work behaviors include organizational roles, mentoring, and conflict management related to the coaching process.							

INTERNATIONAL COACH FEDERATION (ICF) (NOTE 5)	BOARD CERTIFIED COACH: CENTER FOR CREDENTIALING & EDUCATION (CCE) (NOTE 4)	EUROPEAN MENTORING & COACHING COUNCIL (EMCC) (NOTE 2)	GRADUATE SCHOOL ALLIANCE FOR EXECUTIVE COACHING (GSAEC)	INTERNATIONAL ASSOCIATION OF FACILITATORS (NOTE 6)	PROFESSIONAL CHAPLAIN (NOTE 3)	INSTITUTE OF MANAGEMENT CONSULTANTS (NOTE 8)	CONFLICT RESOLUTION, NEGOTIATION & MEDIATION (NOTE 1)	HELPING SKILLS (NOTE 7)
		Use of Models and Techniques Apply models and tools, techniques, and ideas beyond the core communication skills in order to bring about insight and learning.			Pastoral Competencies	Consulting Skills & Competencies: Consulting Skills & Tools	Ability to understand the psycho-physiological and behavioral aspects of conflict. Ability to understand cross-cultural considerations in dealing with conflict. Ability to understand the basic motivational theories. Ability to understand the basic theories of individual and organizational power dynamics (i.e., the imbalance of power and impact on parties). Ability to identify personality and conflict management styles, strengths, and challenges. Ability to understand the conflict cycle (i.e., how it begins and escalates).	

(*Continued*)

INTERNATIONAL COACH FEDERATION (ICF) (NOTE 5)	BOARD CERTIFIED COACH: CENTER FOR CREDENTIALING & EDUCATION (CCE) (NOTE 4)	EUROPEAN MENTORING & COACHING COUNCIL (EMCC) (NOTE 2)	GRADUATE SCHOOL ALLIANCE FOR EXECUTIVE COACHING (GSAEC)	INTERNATIONAL ASSOCIATION OF FACILITATORS (NOTE 6)	PROFESSIONAL CHAPLAIN (NOTE 3)	INSTITUTE OF MANAGEMENT CONSULTANTS (NOTE 8)	CONFLICT RESOLUTION, NEGOTIATION & MEDIATION (NOTE 1)	HELPING SKILLS (NOTE 7)
							Ability to understand "positional vs. principled" negotiating concepts and demonstrate the appropriate skills. Ability to understand the differences between the roles, responsibilities, process, and expected outcomes of mediation, arbitration, and negotiation. Ability to understand the differences between compromise, cooperation, collaboration, and consensus building.	
		Evaluation Gather information on the effectiveness of their practice and contribute to establishing a culture of evaluation.						
				Build and Maintain Professional Knowledge		Consulting Skills and Behaviors: Personal and Professional Growth		

INTERNATIONAL COACH FEDERATION (ICF) (NOTE 5)	BOARD CERTIFIED COACH: CENTER FOR CREDENTIALING & EDUCATION (CCE) (NOTE 4)	EUROPEAN MENTORING & COACHING COUNCIL (EMCC) (NOTE 2)	GRADUATE SCHOOL ALLIANCE FOR EXECUTIVE COACHING (GSAEC)	INTERNATIONAL ASSOCIATION OF FACILITATORS (NOTE 6)	PROFESSIONAL CHAPLAIN (NOTE 3)	INSTITUTE OF MANAGEMENT CONSULTANTS (NOTE 8)	CONFLICT RESOLUTION, NEGOTIATION & MEDIATION (NOTE 1)	HELPING SKILLS (NOTE 7)
			Theory and Knowledge		Theory of Pastoral Care Competencies	Consulting Skills and Behaviors: Analytical and Proactive Thinking	Ability to understand the psycho-physiological and behavioral aspects of conflict. Ability to understand cross-cultural considerations in dealing with conflict. Ability to understand the basic motivational theories. Ability to understand the basic theories of individual and organizational power dynamics (i.e., the imbalance of power and impact on parties).	

(*Continued*)

INTERNATIONAL COACH FEDERATION (ICF) (NOTE 5)	BOARD CERTIFIED COACH: CENTER FOR CREDENTIALING & EDUCATION (CCE) (NOTE 4)	EUROPEAN MENTORING & COACHING COUNCIL (EMCC) (NOTE 2)	GRADUATE SCHOOL ALLIANCE FOR EXECUTIVE COACHING (GSAEC)	INTERNATIONAL ASSOCIATION OF FACILITATORS (NOTE 6)	PROFESSIONAL CHAPLAIN (NOTE 3)	INSTITUTE OF MANAGEMENT CONSULTANTS (NOTE 8)	CONFLICT RESOLUTION, NEGOTIATION & MEDIATION (NOTE 1)	HELPING SKILLS (NOTE 7)
							Ability to identify personality and conflict management styles, strengths, and challenges. Ability to understand the conflict cycle (i.e., how it begins and escalates). Ability to understand "positional vs. principled" negotiating concepts and demonstrate the appropriate skills. Ability to understand the differences between the roles, responsibilities, process, and expected outcomes of mediation, arbitration, and negotiation.	
							Ability to understand the differences between compromise, cooperation, collaboration, and consensus building.	

INTERNATIONAL COACH FEDERATION (ICF) (NOTE 5)	BOARD CERTIFIED COACH: CENTER FOR CREDENTIALING & EDUCATION (CCE) (NOTE 4)	EUROPEAN MENTORING & COACHING COUNCIL (EMCC) (NOTE 2)	GRADUATE SCHOOL ALLIANCE FOR EXECUTIVE COACHING (GSAEC)	INTERNATIONAL ASSOCIATION OF FACILITATORS (NOTE 6)	PROFESSIONAL CHAPLAIN (NOTE 3)	INSTITUTE OF MANAGEMENT CONSULTANTS (NOTE 8)	CONFLICT RESOLUTION, NEGOTIATION & MEDIATION (NOTE 1)	HELPING SKILLS (NOTE 7)
			Business Acumen		Theory of Pastoral Care Competencies Professional Competencies	Consulting Competencies: Business Understanding & External Awareness Market Knowledge & Capability Consulting Skills and Behaviors: Business Acumen	Demonstrate an understanding of the characteristics of conflict and how it manifests itself into interprofessional and organizational contexts.	
							Ability to understand the "casualties" of conflict (loss of morale, productivity, etc.). Ability to understand the prevalent conflict management styles and strategies. Ability to understand the positive opportunities that can be presented by conflict.	

Note 1:

http://www.campus-adr.org/cmher/reportarticles/Edition1_4/Corecomp1_4.html

William C. Warters & WSU

Campus Conflict Resolution Resources Project

Department of Communication

585 Manoogian Hall

Wayne State University

Detroit, MI 48201

Page last updated 11/27/2005

Retrieved 08/19/12

Note 2:

European Mentoring & Coaching Council

Competency Framework

September 2009

Retrieved 08/18/12

http://emccaccreditation.org/emcc/about-emcc/

Note 3:

Board of Chaplaincy Certification Inc.

An Affiliate of Association of Professional Chaplains

1701 E. Woodfield Road, Suite 400 • Schaumburg, IL 60173

bcci@professionalchaplains.org • www.professionalchaplains.org/BCCI

Phone: 847.240.1014 • Fax: 847.240.1015

Retrieved 08/18/12

Note 4:

Board Certified Coach

Application for Board Certified Coach (revised 2/2012)

Center for Credentialing & Education

Retrieved 08/19/12

http://www.cce-global.org/BCC/Reqs

Note 5:

Core Coaching Competencies

International Coach Federation

1999

Note 6:

Core Facilitator Competencies

International Association of Facilitators

Version 1.0, 2003

www.iaf-world.org

Retrieved 08/19/12

Note 7:

Helping Skills (for Understanding and Positive Action)

Brammer, L. M., & MacDonald, G. (2003). *The helping relationship: Process and skills* (8th ed.). Boston, MA: Allyn and Bacon, 24.

Note 8:

Institute of Management Consulting

www.imc-usa.org

Retrieved 08/19/12

Appendix B: Key Points for Change Coaching

Begin with the end in mind. (Steven Covey)

Never work harder than your client, yet always work as hard as your client.

Work from the premise that coaching clients have the answers they need, or can get access to them.

The presenting issue is rarely the real issue. As you coach, observe and listen for, "What is the real issue here?"

Beginning coaches often get caught up in the "information gathering" phase of the coaching conversation. Remember that the client will share more information as the coaching process unfolds.

"All organizations are perfectly designed to get the perfectly designed to get the results they get." (Hanna, 1988, p. 36)

"You cannot understand a system until you try to change it." (a concept attributed to Kurt Lewin and cited by Schein, 2010, p. 34)

Use assessment instruments when you have a clear purpose, and choose the instruments that meet that purpose.

Stay focused on the client's agenda at the macro and micro levels.

Maintain a mindset of inquiry and minimize evaluation and judgment; keep the information gathering focused on the client and the client's agenda.

Have the client summarize key learnings/insights and commitments for action at the end of each coaching session.

Facilitate the client to make meaning of information, observations, insights, and experiences; don't do the work for them or impose your interpretations.

When you don't know what to say, ask, or do next, it is probably because you were not listening to your client.

Coach your client through the Mastery Model (awareness, acceptance, adoption, integration, and mastery).

References

Hanna, D. P. (1988). *Designing organizations for high performance.* Reading, MA: Addison-Wesley.

Schein, E. H. (2010). *Organizational culture and leadership.* San Francisco, CA: Jossey-Bass.

Appendix C: Kerber-Buono Situational Change Mastery Questionnaire

1. **Briefly describe your change initiative. What is changing?**

2. **The following table summarizes some of the major distinctions among the three approaches to change:**

Dimensions	Directed Change	Planned Change	Guided Changing
Change Goals (Ends)	Tightly defined, unchanging goal	Clear goal with some modification, as needed	Loosely defined direction
Change Process (Means)	Tightly constrained	Flexible, participative	Experimental
Change Leadership (Role)	Tell, order, or command	Devise a plan to accomplish the goal	Point the way, watch over, and instruct
Changemaker Relationships	Persuasion	Influence	Collaboration
Pace of Change	Urgent, fast, "just do it"	Go slow during planning to go fast during implementation	Act quickly, improvise, learn, and act again

Circle one number on the following scale to indicate where you think your change initiative falls:

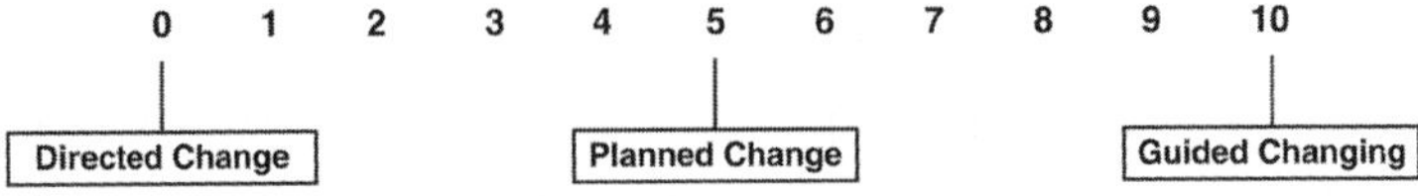

Part 1: Questions

Circle one number on each of the following 0 to 10 scales with reference to your change initiative.

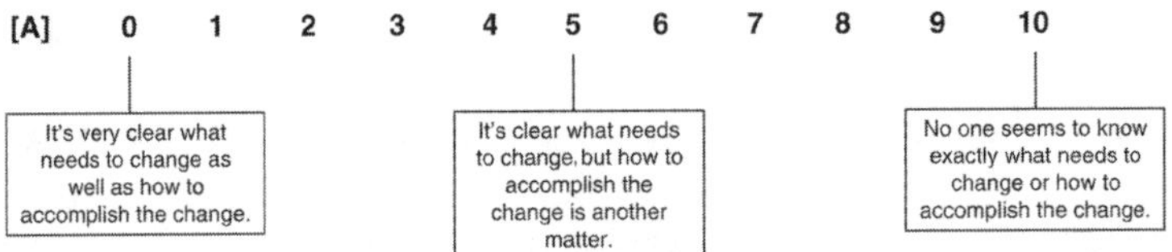

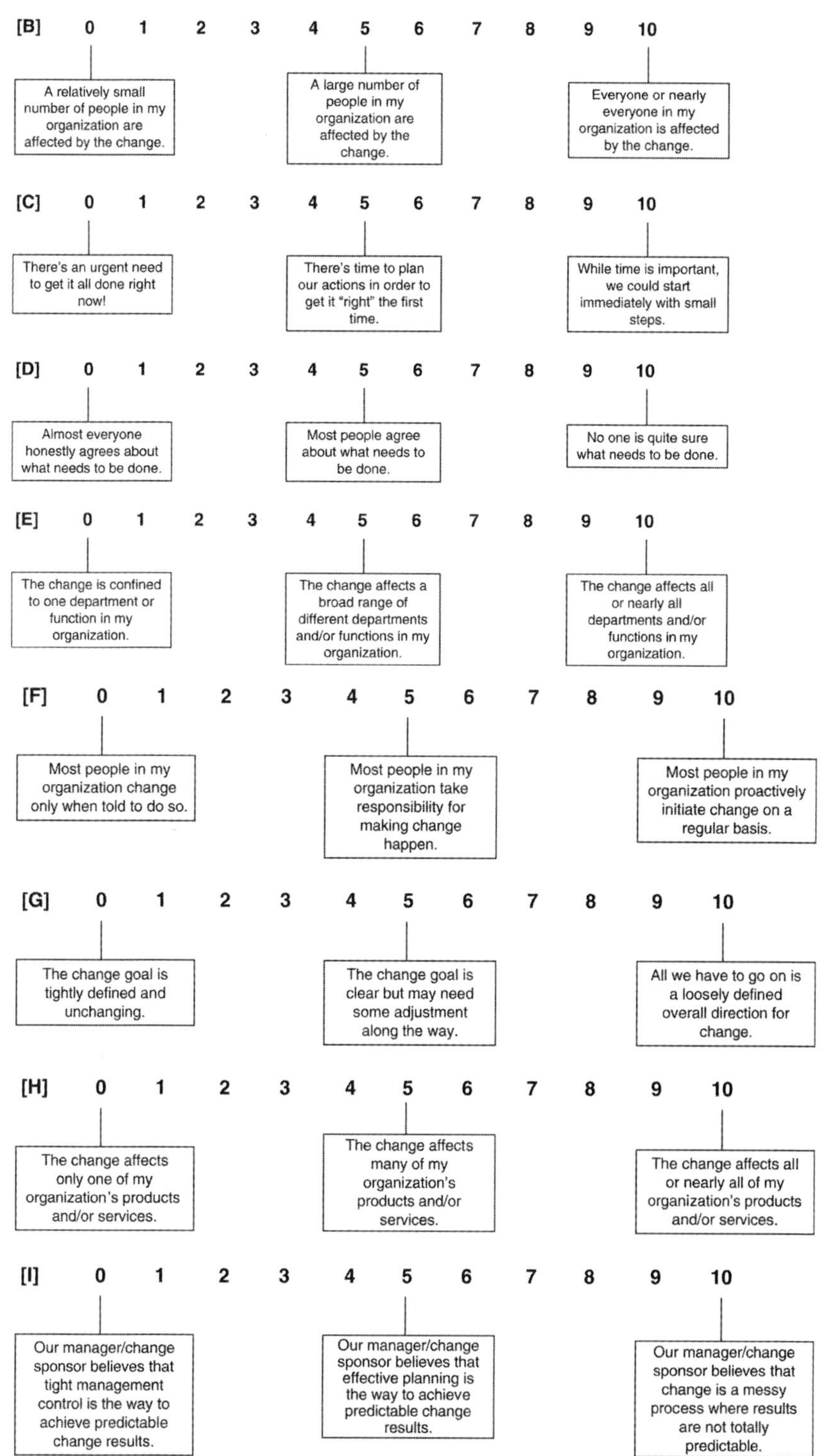
[B] 0 1 2 3 4 5 6 7 8 9 10
A relatively small number of people in my organization are affected by the change.
A large number of people in my organization are affected by the change.
Everyone or nearly everyone in my organization is affected by the change.
[C] 0 1 2 3 4 5 6 7 8 9 10
There's an urgent need to get it all done right now!
There's time to plan our actions in order to get it "right" the first time.
While time is important, we could start immediately with small steps.
[D] 0 1 2 3 4 5 6 7 8 9 10
Almost everyone honestly agrees about what needs to be done.
Most people agree about what needs to be done.
No one is quite sure what needs to be done.
[E] 0 1 2 3 4 5 6 7 8 9 10
The change is confined to one department or function in my organization.
The change affects a broad range of different departments and/or functions in my organization.
The change affects all or nearly all departments and/or functions in my organization.
[F] 0 1 2 3 4 5 6 7 8 9 10
Most people in my organization change only when told to do so.
Most people in my organization take responsibility for making change happen.
Most people in my organization proactively initiate change on a regular basis.
[G] 0 1 2 3 4 5 6 7 8 9 10
The change goal is tightly defined and unchanging.
The change goal is clear but may need some adjustment along the way.
All we have to go on is a loosely defined overall direction for change.
[H] 0 1 2 3 4 5 6 7 8 9 10
The change affects only one of my organization's products and/or services.
The change affects many of my organization's products and/or services.
The change affects all or nearly all of my organization's products and/or services.
[I] 0 1 2 3 4 5 6 7 8 9 10
Our manager/change sponsor believes that tight management control is the way to achieve predictable change results.
Our manager/change sponsor believes that effective planning is the way to achieve predictable change results.
Our manager/change sponsor believes that change is a messy process where results are not totally predictable.

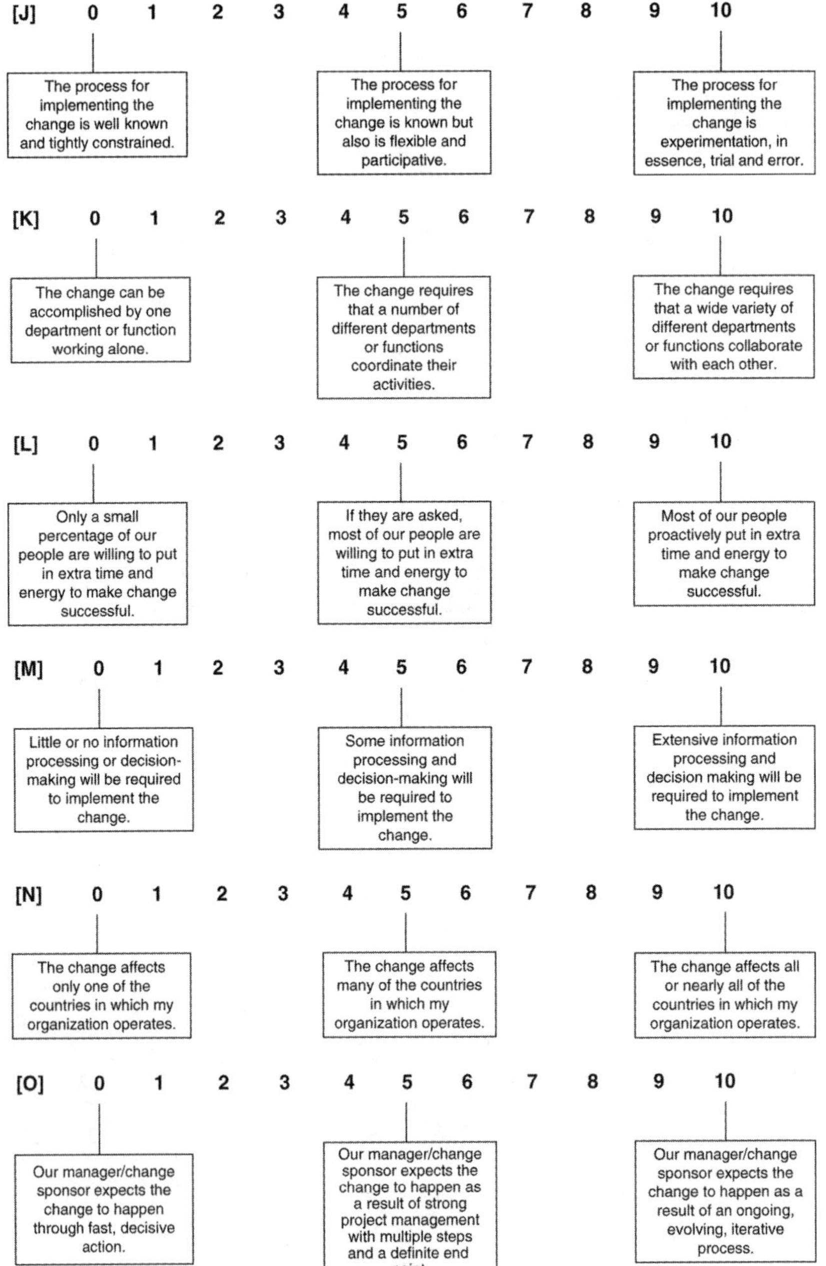
[J] 0 1 2 3 4 5 6 7 8 9 10
The process for implementing the change is well known and tightly constrained.
The process for implementing the change is known but also is flexible and participative.
The process for implementing the change is experimentation, in essence, trial and error.
[K] 0 1 2 3 4 5 6 7 8 9 10
The change can be accomplished by one department or function working alone.
The change requires that a number of different departments or functions coordinate their activities.
The change requires that a wide variety of different departments or functions collaborate with each other.
[L] 0 1 2 3 4 5 6 7 8 9 10
Only a small percentage of our people are willing to put in extra time and energy to make change successful.
If they are asked, most of our people are willing to put in extra time and energy to make change successful.
Most of our people proactively put in extra time and energy to make change successful.
[M] 0 1 2 3 4 5 6 7 8 9 10
Little or no information processing or decision-making will be required to implement the change.
Some information processing and decision-making will be required to implement the change.
Extensive information processing and decision making will be required to implement the change.
[N] 0 1 2 3 4 5 6 7 8 9 10
The change affects only one of the countries in which my organization operates.
The change affects many of the countries in which my organization operates.
The change affects all or nearly all of the countries in which my organization operates.
[O] 0 1 2 3 4 5 6 7 8 9 10
Our manager/change sponsor expects the change to happen through fast, decisive action.
Our manager/change sponsor expects the change to happen as a result of strong project management with multiple steps and a definite end point.
Our manager/change sponsor expects the change to happen as a result of an ongoing, evolving, iterative process.

Part 2: Scoring

Next to each item below, write the rating that you gave that item on the questionnaire. After you have entered your rating for each item, calculate the average score for each column.

Item Score	Item Score	Item Score
B.__________	A.__________	C.__________
E.__________	D.__________	F.__________
H.__________	G.__________	I.__________
K.__________	J.__________	L.__________
N.__________	M.__________	O.__________
TOTAL = _____	TOTAL = _____	TOTAL = _____
$\frac{\text{Total}}{5}$ = _____	$\frac{\text{Total}}{5}$ = _____	$\frac{\text{Total}}{5}$ = _____
Business Complexity	***Socio-Technical Uncertainty***	***Constraints***

Business complexity refers to the intricacy of the system (i.e., the number of different components and extent of differentiation in the organization in which the change is to be implemented. The degree of business complexity increases the more an organizational change cuts across different hierarchical levels, different work units, and different geographic locations; involves reciprocal or team interdependence; affects a range of products and services; and requires the buy-in of a number of internal and external stakeholders.

Socio-technical uncertainty refers to the amount and nature of information processing and decision making required for the change based on the extent to which the tasks involved are determined, established, or exactly known. Socio-technical uncertainty increases to the extent that there are no clearly known ways to approach the situation, no known sequence of steps that can be followed, and no identifiable set of established procedures and practices. In low socio-technical uncertainty situations, the solution to the change challenge is known, while in high socio-technical uncertainty contexts the solution is not known or fully understood. In fact, when uncertainty is high, the problem itself is not fully described or clearly understood, meaning that the search for a solution occurs simultaneously with the search for a clear definition of the problem.

Constraints refer to the extent to which the parameters of the change situation are clearly defined with little or no room for modification versus broadly defined with room for interpretation. In highly constrained situations there is little time to accomplish the change, people resist change, and the change sponsor seeks to tightly control the change process. In highly unconstrained situations, the time pressure to accomplish the change is not as great, people contribute readily to the change process, and the change sponsor has flexible expectations about the change process and outcomes.

Part 3: Identifying the Approach to Change

A. Plot your results (Total/5) for *Business Complexity* and *Socio-Technical Uncertainty* on the grid, below.

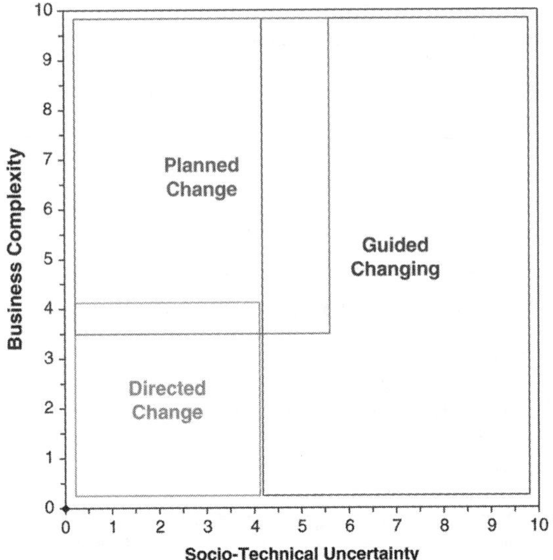

B. Plot your results for *Constraints* on the continuum below.

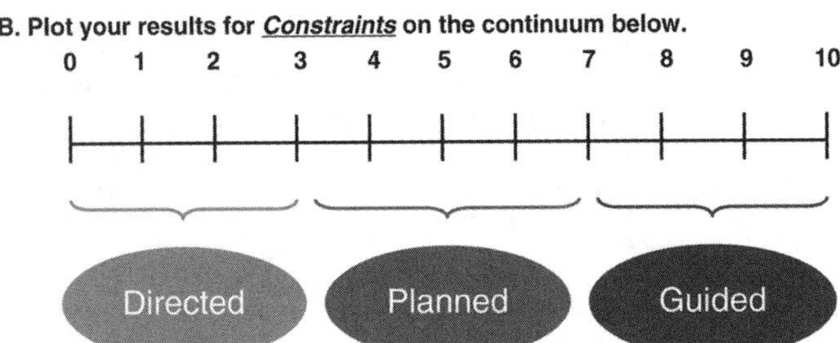

Part 4: Interpretation

1. **Where does your change fall on the Complexity/Uncertainty Grid?**
   - ☐ Directed Change.
   - ☐ Planned Change.
   - ☐ Guided Changing.
   - ☐ On the border of ____________________ and ____________________.

2. **Where does your change fall on the Constraints Continuum?**
   - ☐ Directed Change.
   - ☐ Planned Change.
   - ☐ Guided Changing.

3. **If you checked the same response to Questions 1 and 2 immediately above, the appropriate approach to change is clear. On the other hand, if your responses to Questions 1 and 2 disagree, further analysis is required.**

   a. If your change falls on the border of two approaches on the Complexity/Uncertainty Grid, use the Constraints Continuum to make your decision about the most appropriate change approach.

      i. Which approach to change is suggested by the Constraints Continuum?

      ii. Which constraints suggest that this approach makes sense?
         - ☐ Urgency of the change (Item C)?
         - ☐ People's willingness to change (Items F and L)?
         - ☐ The views of your manager/change sponsor (Items I and O)?

   b. If the results on the Complexity/Uncertainty Grid differ from the results on the Constraints Continuum:

      i. Which constraints suggest a different change approach?
         - ☐ Urgency of the change (Item C)?
         - ☐ People's willingness to change (Items F and L)?
         - ☐ The views of your manager/change sponsor (Items I and O)?

      ii. How can you attempt to modify the constraints in your situation so that the most appropriate approach to change can be used? What steps could you take?

Appendix D: Kerber-Buono Organizational Change Capacity Questionnaire

Part 1: Questions

Circle one number on each of the following 0 to 10 scales with reference to your organization.

1. We place a strong emphasis on learning and information sharing.

0 1 2 3 4 5 6 7 8 9 10
Never ---------------------------------- Sometimes ------------------------------ Almost Always

2. We hold meetings in all functions that focus on identifying and critically assessing new business opportunities.

0 1 2 3 4 5 6 7 8 9 10
Never ---------------------------------- Sometimes ------------------------------ Almost Always

3. We use a common, organization-wide framework for thinking and communicating about change.

0 1 2 3 4 5 6 7 8 9 10
Never ---------------------------------- Sometimes ------------------------------ Almost Always

4. We communicate an enduring, shared purpose that is well understood by everyone in the organization.

0 1 2 3 4 5 6 7 8 9 10
Never ---------------------------------- Sometimes ------------------------------ Almost Always

5. We designate and hold accountable an owner(s) of the goal to develop our organization's change capacity.

0 1 2 3 4 5 6 7 8 9 10
Never ---------------------------------- Sometimes ------------------------------ Almost Always

6. We select, hire, evaluate, and reward our employees based, in part, on their ability to thrive on change.

0 1 2 3 4 5 6 7 8 9 10
Never ---------------------------------- Sometimes ------------------------------ Almost Always

7. We encourage everyone in the organization to ask questions and speak the truth, especially when people perceive problems or obstacles.

0 1 2 3 4 5 6 7 8 9 10
Never ---------------------------------- Sometimes ------------------------------ Almost Always

8. We conduct low cost experiments with new ideas.

0 1 2 3 4 5 6 7 8 9 10
Never ---------------------------------- Sometimes ------------------------------ Almost Always

9. The people in our organization understand there are different approaches to change and when each is appropriate.

0 1 2 3 4 5 6 7 8 9 10
Never ---------------------------------- Sometimes ------------------------------ Almost Always

10. We encourage people to think dynamically and systematically so that strategies can change quickly.

0 1 2 3 4 5 6 7 8 9 10
Never ---------------------------------- Sometimes ------------------------------ Almost Always

11. We devote resources to scanning the external environment in search of new ideas for our business.

0 1 2 3 4 5 6 7 8 9 10
Never ---------------------------------- Sometimes ------------------------------ Almost Always

12. We create teams with maximum diversity to encourage innovation and creativity.

0 1 2 3 4 5 6 7 8 9 10
Never ---------------------------------- Sometimes ------------------------------ Almost Always

13. We encourage everyone to empathize with and value alternative viewpoints.

0 1 2 3 4 5 6 7 8 9 10
Never ---------------------------------- Sometimes ------------------------------ Almost Always

14. We recognize and reward people who support, encourage, lead, and share learning about organizational change.

0 1 2 3 4 5 6 7 8 9 10
Never ---------------------------------- Sometimes ------------------------------ Almost Always

15. We focus on developing deep expertise about how to implement organizational change.

0 1 2 3 4 5 6 7 8 9 10
Never ---------------------------------- Sometimes ------------------------------ Almost Always

16. We thoroughly examine future markets, competitors, and business opportunities.

0 1 2 3 4 5 6 7 8 9 10
Never ---------------------------------- Sometimes ------------------------------ Almost Always

17. We encourage our employees to have lots of external contact, especially with customers.

0 1 2 3 4 5 6 7 8 9 10
Never ---------------------------------- Sometimes ------------------------------ Almost Always

18. We develop, reward, and promote supervisors and managers who enable change.

0 1 2 3 4 5 6 7 8 9 10
Never ---------------------------------- Sometimes ------------------------------ Almost Always

19. We support people who take risks and apply innovative ideas.

0 1 2 3 4 5 6 7 8 9 10
Never ---------------------------------- Sometimes ------------------------------ Almost Always

20. We maintain a fluid organizational structure that allows the quick formation of new groups as needed.

0 1 2 3 4 5 6 7 8 9 10
Never ---------------------------------- Sometimes ------------------------------ Almost Always

21. We provide change coaching and consulting services to our people and departments.

0 1 2 3 4 5 6 7 8 9 10
Never ---------------------------------- Sometimes ------------------------------ Almost Always

22. We factor future scenarios into today's decisions.

0 1 2 3 4 5 6 7 8 9 10
Never ---------------------------------- Sometimes ------------------------------ Almost Always

23. We appoint a committed change sponsor for each organizational change.

0 1 2 3 4 5 6 7 8 9 10
Never.................................... Sometimes....................................Almost always

24. We work hard to enhance the personal credibility of organizational leaders.

0 1 2 3 4 5 6 7 8 9 10
Never.................................... Sometimes....................................Almost always

25. We tolerate mistakes in the interest of learning.

0 1 2 3 4 5 6 7 8 9 10
Never.................................... Sometimes....................................Almost always

26. We create systems and processes for sharing knowledge, information, and learning across boundaries.

0 1 2 3 4 5 6 7 8 9 10
Never.................................... Sometimes....................................Almost always

27. We encourage the formation of change agent networks to share best practices, tools, and research about organizational change.

0 1 2 3 4 5 6 7 8 9 10
Never.................................... Sometimes....................................Almost always

28. We focus on stringing together an ongoing series of momentary competitive advantages.

0 1 2 3 4 5 6 7 8 9 10
Never.................................... Sometimes....................................Almost always

29. We provide key change projects with enough resources to get highly visible, public successes.

0 1 2 3 4 5 6 7 8 9 10
Never.................................. Sometimes..................................Almost always

30. We listen to, encourage, and reward mavericks and trailblazers.

0 1 2 3 4 5 6 7 8 9 10
Never.................................. Sometimes..................................Almost always

Part 2: Scoring

Next to each item below, write the rating that you gave that item on the questionnaire. After you have entered your rating for each item, calculate the average score for each column.

Item Score	Item Score	Item Score
B.________	A.________	C.________
E.________	D.________	F.________
H.________	G.________	I.________
K.________	J.________	L.________
N.________	M.________	O.________
TOTAL = _____	TOTAL = _____	TOTAL = _____
$\frac{\text{Total}}{5}$ = _____	$\frac{\text{Total}}{5}$ = _____	$\frac{\text{Total}}{5}$ = _____
Business Complexity	***Socio-Technical Uncertainty***	***Constraints***

Business complexity refers to the intricacy of the system, i.e., the number of different components and extent of differentiation in the organization in which the change is to be implemented. The degree of business complexity increases the more an organizational change cuts across different hierarchical levels, different work units and different geographic locations; involves reciprocal or team interdependence; affects a range of products and services; and requires the buy-in of a number of internal and external stakeholders.

Socio-technical uncertainty refers to the amount and nature of information processing and decision making required for the change based on the extent to which the tasks involved are determined, established, or exactly known. Socio-technical uncertainty increases to the extent that there are no clearly known ways to approach the situation, no known sequence of steps that can be followed, and no identifiable set of established procedures and practices. In low socio-technical uncertainty situations, the solution to the change challenge is known, while in high socio-technical uncertainty contexts the solution is not known or fully understood. In fact, when uncertainty is high, the problem itself is not fully described or clearly understood, meaning that the search for a solution occurs simultaneously with the search for a clear definition of the problem.

Constraints refer to the extent to which the parameters of the change situation are clearly defined with little or no room for modification versus broadly defined with room for interpretation. In highly constrained situations there is little time to accomplish the change, people resist change, and the change sponsor seeks to tightly control the change process. In highly unconstrained situations, the time pressure to accomplish the change is not as great, people contribute readily to the change process, and the change sponsor has flexible expectations about the change process and outcomes.

2. **Which of the six major dimensions of change capacity is highest? Why?**

3. **Which of the six major dimensions of change capacity is lowest? Why?**

4. **Which of the six major dimensions of change capacity should be your top improvement priority? What specifically could be done to increase change capacity along this dimension?**

Glossary of Terms

Action Learning: A teaching/learning process in which people work and learn together by addressing real issues and reflecting on their actions. The emphasis is on the action taken to address the issue and on the learning that occurs while taking action at the individual, group, and organization levels.

ADKAR: A model for change developed by Jeffrey Hiatt at the Prosci Organization that involves a five-step process. ADKAR is an acronym for awareness, desire, knowledge, ability, and reinforcement.

Advocate: A person or group that informs and promotes to a leader the need for a change for the purpose of getting the leader to sponsor the desired change.

Agent: Individuals and groups that implement change.

Anonymous: Without the name or other identification available; hidden or masked.

Appreciative Inquiry: A positivist approach to change that is most often applied at the organization level and involves inquiry that appreciates the positive and engages all levels of an organization it seeks to renew, develop, and build on.

Assessment: An instrument designed (often validated) to measure knowledge, skills, behaviors, personality, learning style, etc.

Behavior: The manner in which an individual, group, or organization conducts itself.

Behavioral Change: A shift in behavior.

Being: Conscious existence.

Big Five: A five-factor personality model and various assessments, including openness, conscientiousness, extraversion, agreeableness, and neuroticism. Sometimes referred to as the NEO Big Five.

Certification: Certification represents a declaration of a particular individual's professional competence independent of certificate program providers. Certificates are issued to attest to a knowledge and experience base for coaching practitioners.

Change: The act or instance of making or becoming different; to cause something to be different, such as a process, role, or product. Change can affect individuals, groups, and organizations.

Change Agent: A person or group who drives change within the organization by championing or promoting the change, and often by managing its implementation. The role can be official or voluntary, and can help to communicate the excitement, vision, and details of the change to others within the organization.

Change Fatigue: A condition experienced by individuals who undergo too much change at once. Its impact on groups or organizations is often a drop in employee engagement or lack of participation by key stakeholders.

Client: The individual or group who receives the professional service of coaching. See also Coachee and Person Being Coached.

Coach: The individual who provides one-on-one or group coaching.

Coachability (Coaching Readiness): A person's willingness and openness to development, performance improvement, and transformation through engagement (informal or formal) with a coach.

Coachee: See Client and Person Being Coached.

Coaching: A practice of collaborating with client(s) in dialogue that is informed by skills, ethics, standards, theories, and models. Coaching seeks to co-create reflective learning experiences that support individual and collective change. (Adapted from the Future of Coaching Summit, 2012)

Coaching Service Provider: The people who use coaching-related theories, models, and skills in their work or as the basis for their professional practices.

Coaching Session: The conversations, sessions, and interventions in which coaching takes place.

Cognitive Behavioral Approach: An approach to coaching and therapy that focuses on changing beliefs, images, and thoughts in order to change behaviors.

Competence: The demonstration of knowledge and/or skills at a defined level of expertise.

Competency: The observable and/or measurable knowledge, skill, attitude, or behavior that is essential for a job or contributes to successful performance of the job, and differentiates the level of performance.

Confidentiality: Holding something in confidence, not disclosing it without the permission of the other person, group, or organization.

Consulting: A helping relationship that can be formal or informal and is established for the purpose of providing expertise, skills, and/or a process for the client.

Cost-Benefit Analysis: A method of assessing a project that takes into consideration the costs and benefits to the organization, including the revenue it generates.

Counseling: A professional helping relationship with the purpose of helping a person or group resolve an issue or challenge. Psychological methods are likely to be used, especially in collecting case-history data and testing interests and aptitudes.

Credential: A quality, skill, or experience that makes a person suited to do a task or job, usually documented to show that the person is qualified to do a particular job.

Credibility: A current estimate of the trustworthiness of a stated intention pertaining to the next transaction; believability of a person or organization's intentions in a specific situation.

Cross-disciplinary: The involvement of two or more academic disciplines.

Culture: The pattern of ideas, emotions, behaviors, and artifacts that are expected, reinforced, and rewarded by and with relationships (interpersonal, group/team, organization, society). Culture is the way things are done.

Development Coaching: Coaching that focuses on personal goals, thinking, feeling, and actions, and on how the clients can change their lives for greater personal effectiveness and/or satisfaction.

Development Plan: A formal (written) or informal (unwritten) agreement about actions that will be taken to develop knowledge, skills, and abilities within a specific period of time and with specific, defined outcomes.

Effectiveness: An estimate of the degree to which the coach's promises are fulfilled by his or her performance and recommendations. Effectiveness is usually measured in terms of goal or outcome achievement.

Emergent Change: A view of change that considers it as fluid and emerging, as well as pervasive and continuous, requiring responses and adaptation. Emergent change emphasizes the need to be responsive and adaptive. See also Planned Change.

Empathy: Understanding the situation that contributed to or triggered feelings.

Ethics: Moral principles adopted by an individual or group to provide rules for appropriate conduct. Ethics considers what is right or correct behavior in a particular situation.

Facilitation: A process in which a person helps a group improve how it identifies and solves problems and makes decisions in order to increase the group's effectiveness.

Feedback: Information about a person's behavior or performance, or the impact of behavior or performance that is delivered to the client in order to facilitate change, improvement, or achievement of desired goals. Feedback can be also be offered from the client to the coach.

Focus of Change: Three basic reasons for change at the individual, group or organization levels: performance, development, and transformation.

Goal: A desired outcome of the coaching engagement.

Hearing: The physiological sensory process by which auditory sensations are received by the ears and transmitted to the brain.

Helping Relationship: A formal or informal relationship with another person, group, or organization (the client) for the purpose of providing help, with the intent of avoiding co-dependence.

Individual Development Plan (IDP): A document created by a coaching client, based on feedback, and designed to identify goals for learning and development, actions to be taken, a timeframe for completion, and support to achieve the goals. The IDP is usually created with the coach and may include input (and sometimes approval) by a manager.

Instrument: An assessment, inventory, or survey used to gather data about a coaching client or organizational context.

Intervention: To involve oneself in a situation at the individual, group, or organization levels resulting in an alteration of the action development.

Inventory: An assessment of knowledge, skill, or preference that may be used as a pre- and/or post-test; often not determined to be statistically valid or reliable.

Key Stakeholders: Individuals or a group (can be a subset of all stakeholders) whose support is essential to the success of the change. If key stakeholders withhold or withdraw their support, the change initiative will likely fail.

Leader: The person to whom others look for guidance, direction, and vision.

Learning: The knowledge or skill acquired by instruction or study and resulting in a modification of a behavioral tendency.

Level of Change: Three arenas in which change takes place: individual or personal, group or team, and organization.

Listening: Making sense of sounds and observations.

Manager-as-Coach: The role managers play when they use coaching skills, processes, and related theories.

Master: A person eminently skilled at something.

Mastery: The act of performing at a masterful level.

Matrix Organization: A type of organizational structure in which people with similar skills are grouped together for work assignments, as opposed to being grouped by product line or geography. For example, the communications department may be in one group and report to a communications lead, while each specialist is assigned through the matrix to different change projects, each led by a different change manager. This arrangement means that each communications specialist may work on several change projects led by several different change managers.

Mentoring: A one-on-one relationship between a less-experienced person (protégé) and a more-experienced person (mentor) and intended to advance the personal and professional growth of the protégé.

Mindset: A mental attitude or disposition that predetermines a person's, group's, or organization's responses to and interpretations of situations; an inclination or habit.

Myers-Briggs Type Indicator (MBTI): A personality assessment based on the work of Carl Jung.

Novice: A person who is new to a set of knowledge or skills and who has not developed them to a level of competence, proficiency, or mastery; a beginner.

Organization Development (OD): A body of knowledge and practice that enhances individual development and organizational performance and in which the organization is viewed as a complex array of systems. OD interventions in these systems are inclusive methodologies and approaches to strategic planning, organization design, leadership development, change management, performance management, coaching, and diversity and inclusion.

Organization Transformation: A process of radical change that orients an organization in a new strategic direction and takes it to an entirely different level of effectiveness.

Organizational Culture: A collective behavior of individuals and groups who are part of an organization, team, or group and the meanings that the people attach to their actions. Culture includes the organization's values, visions, norms, working language, symbols, beliefs, and habits. "It is the way things are done." See also Culture.

Paraphrasing: A listening skill used by coaches based on a method of restating the client's basic message in a similar way, usually with fewer words, for the purpose of testing the coach's understanding of what the client has said. Paraphrasing is used to provide a concise response to the client, stating the essence of the client's content in the coach's own words.

Participant-Observer: An investigator who studies the life of a group by sharing in its activities.

Peer Coaching: The use of coaching knowledge, skills, and related theory in a formal or informal relationship with a peer.

Performance Coaching: Coaching that focuses on specific performance potential, job requirements, deficiencies, or derailers, and on how to fill performance gaps.

Permanent White Water Change: Conceived by Peter Vaill as a way to explain how organizational change is continuous and can be represented by the metaphor of white water rapids, constantly churning.

Person Being Coached: See Client and Coachee.

Person-Centered Approach: An approach to counseling, psychotherapy, and coaching based on the work of Carl Rogers. This approach is client centered and nondirective and places much of the responsibility for the process on the client, with the therapist or coach taking a nondirective role.

Planned Change: A view of change as orchestrated and planned, sequential, less dynamic, and evolving, allowing for a step-by-step change process to be employed. See also Emergent Change.

Prescriptive Change: An approach to organizational change that focuses on results, action, and execution.

Process Consultant: A consultant (or coach) who helps the client define the process for accomplishing a certain goal or project. The consultant's expertise is used to organize people and processes in order to accomplish a change.

Profession: A type of job that requires special education, training, or skill and which is recognized by others as such.

Professional: A person who demonstrates the knowledge, skills, and abilities of a profession.

Professionally: A way of acting at a professional-level quality standard, whether or not the job is considered a profession.

Psychodynamic: The study and application (in therapy and coaching) of the interaction of various conscious and unconscious mental or emotional processes, especially as they influence personality, behavior, and attitudes.

Psychometrics: The theory and application of psychological measurement, which includes the measurement of knowledge, abilities, attitudes, personality traits, as well as educational measurements.

Reflection: Awareness of self within the moment; having a clear mind so as to be open to the possibility of that moment.

Reframing: To look at, present, or think of beliefs, ideas, or relationships in a new or different way; the skill of helping a coaching client reframe. Reframing may involve tools like metaphors, analogies, and roleplays.

Relationship: A situation in which two or more people's feelings, thoughts, and behaviors are mutually and causally interdependent.

Reliability: The extent to which a test or other instrument is consistent in its measures; a measure of predictability and consistency.

Reputation: An estimate, over time, of the consistency that an attribute (e.g., timeliness, quality) belongs to an individual or organization.

Return on Investment (ROI): A performance measure used to evaluate the efficiency of an investment. Calculated, the benefit (return) of an investment is divided by the cost of the investment; the result is expressed as a percentage or a ratio.

Sample: A subset of individuals selected from a larger population or database.

Scale: A group of items that have logical and empirical coherence.

Scope Creep: The phenomena of having the scope or boundaries of a task or project increase beyond the original focus—often without conscious attention to the expansion as it is occurring.

Six Sigma: A project-driven management approach to improve the organization's products, services, and processes by continually reducing defects in the organization.

Skill: The ability to do something.

Sponsor: The person or group responsible for initiating and sponsoring a change initiative.

Stakeholder: Any person, group, or organization whose interests will be affected positively or negatively by the change. Stakeholders can be internal or external to the organization.

Target: The person or group on whom a change initiative is focused; the individuals most directly impacted by the change and for whom change is expected.

Training: Organized activity focused on imparting information and/or instructions to improve a person's performance or to help the person attain a required level of knowledge or skill.

Trans-disciplinary: Two or more academic disciplines systematically coordinated among disciplines in order to study and develop theory and practice.

Transactional Analysis: A system of therapy developed by Eric Berne that can be applied to coaching and in which personal relationships and interactions are analyzed in terms of conflicting or complementary ego states that correspond to the roles of parent, child, and adult.

Transference: Feelings once felt by the client toward someone are projected onto the coach.

Trustworthy: An attribute describing a person or organization that has demonstrated to others that the person or organization will carry out an intention.

Use of Self: A person's consciousness of his own being or identity (the ego) and his striving to use self effectively and constructively in his interactions with others.

Validity: The extent to which an assessment instrument measures what it is supposed to measure; the appropriateness of the inferences made about scores from an assessment instrument.

Values: What is good and desirable.

Whole-Scale Change: A system that moves large groups rapidly in a focused direction to support an organizational change.

Index

Note: Page numbers in *italics* indicate figures or tables.